IRISH SOCCER MIGRANTS: A SOCIAL AND CULTURAL HISTORY

Irish Soccer Migrants: A Social and Cultural History

CONOR CURRAN

First published in 2017 by
Cork University Press
Youngline Industrial Estate
Pouladuff Road, Togher
Cork
T12 HT6V
Ireland

British Library Cataloguing in Publication Data
A CIP record for this book is available from the British Library.

ISBN: 978-1-78205-216-6

Printed by Gutenberg Press, Malta.
Print origination & design by Carrigboy Typesetting Services, www.carrigboy.com

www.corkuniversitypress.com

Contents

Acknowledgements

In February 1992, when the Republic of Ireland international soccer team were captivating the nation with a run that was unprecedented in the country's soccer history, I heard the news that every schoolboy footballer wants to hear. It was then that Denis McDaid, the manager of my schoolboy soccer club, Dunkineely Celtic under 15s, and a superb mentor, told myself and two other players, Conal Doherty and Mark Boyle, that he was going to try to get a cross-channel scout to look at us after some strong performances in the South Donegal League. Unfortunately for me, I suffered a stress fracture of a bone in my spine the following month and, having battled for six months with an arrogant local doctor who told me the injury was all in my head, I took up temporary residence with my brother John in Dublin where I eventually underwent an operation. This followed correct diagnosis from a leading surgeon in Crumlin Hospital, Dr Esmond E. Fogarty, who understood the ins and outs of the spine. I happily returned to play soccer for Dunkineely Celtic's youth team in the summer of 1994 as we won the South Donegal League, and later became a trainee with a then League of Ireland club, Home Farm, before eventually the lure of Gaelic football and my home town club, Ardara, proved greater than quiet Saturday nights in Dublin waiting for matches in the Leinster Senior League that were often rained off.

Undertaking this study has allowed me to temporarily glimpse a world which has always fascinated me. Academically, to be the first scholar to take on the study of Irish football migrants as the recipient of a FIFA Havelange Research Scholarship has been a privilege and I have enjoyed every moment of it. The research conducted for this book would not have been possible without the financial assistance of this award given to me by CIES (Centre International d'Étude du

Sport) and FIFA in 2013. That this award actually existed was brought to my attention initially by Professor Mike Cronin of Boston College, who suggested that I submit an application proposal based on the above research topic and even interrupted his holidays to advise me on the process required. I am also indebted to my other former PhD supervisor, Professor Matthew Taylor of De Montfort University, who also gave me much guidance throughout my PhD and has continued to do this through his assessment of my postdoctoral research and acted as supervisor for this project. I am also very grateful to Dr Tom Hunt and Dr Seamus Kelly for their friendship and advice on the migration of Irish footballers.

A large part of this project involved player interviews and I was able to contact a number of footballers with the help of those involved in the game. This part of the research essentially began for me with a meeting with Gerard Mooney of Belvedere FC in May 2013 and as well as giving me an insight into modern-day player recruitment, he was able to arrange a number of interviews which helped ease my passage into this method of research. Vincent Butler and Stephen McGuinness also took time to speak and discuss their views on the state of player migration from the Republic of Ireland to Britain. I am grateful too to former *Irish Independent* journalist, Seán Ryan, who invited me to his home and spent a full day discussing players. Dr Patrick McGovern also took time to discuss our similar research interests, although unfortunately we were unable to meet. Eoin Hand supplied me with a number of documents which otherwise I would not have been able to obtain and also showed a strong interest in my work.

In Northern Ireland, I was assisted initially in my search for interviewees by Professor David Hassan who put me in touch with Shane McCullough and I was able to contact a number of players based there after this. Northern Ireland football historian, John Duffy, also helped me in tracking down former footballers and was always available for conversation, while Andrew McCullough (Ards FC), Richard McKinney (Derry City FC), Trevor Clydesdale (Portadown FC), Laura Hillen (Newry City FC) and Andrew Conn of Linfield FC helped organise interviews which otherwise would not have been possible. Seamus Heath, formerly a professional footballer and now an IFA development officer, pointed me in the direction of a number of players who were available for interviews as well as looking after me on my visit to Downpatrick to discuss his career. On hearing of my scholarship, Robin Peake was quick to send me his master's thesis on earlier Irish football migration, which added to my understanding of the subject. I am also grateful to Bethany Sinclair and Lorraine Bourke for their help in gaining access to the archives of the Irish Football Association; they have always been very accommodating in dealing with my requests. Part of this book has been published in the academic journals, *Soccer & Society* and *Sport in Society*, and I am grateful to Taylor & Francis for granting me permission to publish part of the following articles which are available at www.tandfonline:

- 'The Migration of Irish-born footballers to England, 1945–2010' in *Soccer and Society* vol. 16, 2–3, Special Issue: 150 Years of Association Football (2015), pp. 360–76.
- 'The post-playing careers of Irish-born footballers in England, 1945–2010' in *Sport in Society*, Vol. 18, 10 (2015) pp. 1273–1286.
- 'Irish born players in Britain's football leagues, 1945–2010: A Geographical Assessment' in *Sport and Society*, vol. 19, 1, Special Issue: Sport in Ireland: Social and Historical Perspectives (2016), pp. 74–94.
- 'The Development of Schoolboy Coaching Structures for Association Football in Ireland, 1945–2010' in Conor Curran and David Toms (eds.) *Soccer and Society* (2016) 'Going beyond the "Garrison Game": New Perspectives on Association football in Irish history, http://dx.doi.org/10.1080/14660970.2016.1230340

Yves Brown of West Bromwich Albion took time to speak to me about the underage football system in England, while one of my former Gaelic football team mates, Gareth Concarr, gave me an interesting insight into his time as a trial player at Nottingham Forest although it was decided to include only the interviews of those who played league football in Britain. Dr Alex Jackson of the National Football Museum in Manchester was very helpful during my visits to the Football League Archives in Preston, while the staff of the British Library at Colindale also deserve praise for their assistance during the course of my research in London. The staff of the National Library of Ireland were, as always, courteous and accommodating during my visits there. Dr Kevin Tallec Marston took time to read a number of my interim reports to CIES and provided me with a number of suggestions. I am also grateful to Dr Matthew Stout, who drew the map which appears in this book, and to Laura Gleeson of Inpho Sports Photography for supplying me with most of the photographs. In addition, I am indebted to Alfie Hale, Seamus Heath, Andrew Conn and Declan Doherty (*Donegal News*) for kindly granting me permission to use a number of their photographs.

I would also like to thank Mike Collins and Maria O'Donovan of Cork University Press for agreeing to publish my work, and the two peer reviewers for their positive reviews and feedback.

Finally I would like to thank my girlfriend, Joanne O'Keeffe, and my family for their continuous support, and the thirty players who took time to meet or speak on the telephone and showed great patience and understanding in answering my questions, although unfortunately not all of their views have been published. I hope that my book has managed to share some of their playing experiences and views in a satisfactory manner and that it may be of benefit to those who contemplate a career in professional football, and that it will be of interest to historians and supporters of the game alike.

Illustrations

TABLES

MAP

PHOTOGRAPHS

INTRODUCTION

Irish-born Football Migrants and History

> I mean there's different levels of 'making it' as well. You can make it like I made it, you can make it like Roy Keane made it, you can make it like someone that drops out of the game at twenty-one who played professionally for three years. I played professionally for twelve years. I played for Ireland underage but I never played for Ireland seniors, I never won the Premier League, so there's different levels of 'making it' [in professional football].[1]
>
> Barry Prenderville, 12 July 2013

Irish-born footballers have been present in England's professional football leagues since the late 1880s. While Sky Sports continuously promotes the idea that English league football did not have a history before 1992 and 'the Premier League Years', many scholars and supporters of association football will be well aware that there is a much more extensive story to be told, not only in terms of 'who won what' but also with regard to the players' own experiences. Irish-born footballers' migration has generally been to England, where the English Football League was founded in 1888 with professionalism in England legalised by the Football Association three years before this.[2] Certainly, there were notable successes for Irish-born players in England in the pre-Second World War period. In particular, by the outbreak of the Second World War in 1939, Donegal-born Billy Gillespie had become the first Irishman to captain an FA Cup-winning team in 1925, while Dublin native Jimmy Dunne's record of scoring in twelve consecutive English league matches in the 1931–2 season remained unbeaten in 2017.[3] The presence of Irish-born football migrants in England, and of course in Scotland, was also reflected within the international game. Ireland's first outright victory in the British Home Championship was in 1914, when they captured the title after drawing with Scotland, having beaten England and Wales over a three-week period.[4] As Cormac Moore has noted, of the fifteen players used in the Irish squad in that campaign, ten were based at Scottish or English clubs, illustrating a change in selection policies since the late 1890s.[5]

A greater number of Irish-born players appeared in the English league in the 1945–2010 period, with 917 playing English league football as opposed to the 286 recorded as doing so in the pre-Second World War days, although of course the former period was a longer time span.[6] While the majority of pre-Second World War players were born in present-day Northern Ireland, 500 of the post-war footballers were born in the Republic of Ireland while 417 were born in Northern Ireland. Irish football migration to England in the post-war years reflected wider movement from Ireland to Britain, with Donald M. MacRaild stating that 'further waves of settlement in the post-1945 period renewed migrations' and 'became far larger, in absolute terms than ever they had been in the early Victorian years'.[7] It was in the post-war years that the idea of a move to England gained more acceptance among Irish footballers as relations between British and Irish football governing bodies, transport, communications networks and rates of pay gradually all improved.

During the second half of the twentieth century, Republic of Ireland and Northern Irish-born footballers played a significant part in the domestic and European success of a number of British clubs.[8] Success continued for Irish-born players in these years as Johnny Carey and Noel Cantwell captained Manchester United to FA Cup victory in 1948 and 1963 respectively, while Danny Blanchflower led Tottenham Hotspur to their only First Division league and FA Cup double in 1961.[9] Blanchflower had also played for a London selection in the final of the first Fairs Cup (later UEFA Cup) in 1958 along with Cantwell as they lost to Barcelona.[10] The formation of three major European club competitions by the early 1960s brought more glamour to the game and the availability of televised matches meant that viewers could, for example, see live footage of George Best and

Tony Dunne in Manchester United's 1968 European Cup victory over Benfica at Wembley Stadium.[11]

In the following decades, Liverpool went on to dominate European football, winning four European Cups between 1977 and 1984. Steve Heighway collected European Cup winners' medals in the first two of these victories, having also won UEFA Cup winners' medals in 1973 and 1976.[12] Ronnie Whelan was part of Liverpool's 1984 European Cup winning team in Rome while domestic success in winning the First Division and FA Cup was also shared by Jim Beglin and Steve Staunton at the same club. FA Cup success for a number of Irish-born Arsenal players in the late 1970s was also later experienced by Kevin Moran and Norman Whiteside at Manchester United in 1983 and 1985 while Frank Stapleton also added to his FA Cup winners' medals tally there.[13] Success also came at international level in qualification for major tournaments, with Whiteside becoming the youngest player to appear in the World Cup finals in 1982 when he was aged just seventeen years and forty-one days as he took to the field for Northern Ireland against Yugoslavia.[14]

Whiteside's now classic FA Cup final winning goal against treble-seekers Everton in 1985 was shown almost daily on BBC Northern Ireland's evening sports news round-up for a period in the 1980s, as part of the introduction to the programme. Although his career was ended prematurely through injury a few years later, his status within the game was permanently secured. Nostalgic Republic of Ireland supporters will remember fondly the Jack Charlton era between 1986 and 1995 as the team rose to a ranking of number six in the world in 1993 and qualified for two World Cups and a European Championship.[15] At the time, many of these players became household names in Ireland while Roy Keane's row with Mick McCarthy in 2002 on the eve of the World Cup left 'virtually the entire nation in thrall' according to Alan Bairner.[16]

Most footballers who were born in Ireland and migrated to Britain to take up a professional career in league football will not have their career highlights shown as the opening sequence of a peak viewing time sports programme or sit on a television panel critiquing big matches. Therefore, this book is not overly focused on chronicling the achievements, while important, of the above players or providing a 'who won what' account of Irish football migrants in the professional game. As Martin Roderick has stated, 'in professional football, enormous rewards are concentrated in the hands of a minority of players' while the majority of players do not gain as much attention or fame.[17] Less is publicly known about those who generally did not reach these heights of club and international success, but were able to make a living in English and Scottish professional football at various levels. Some others enjoyed the additional adventure of playing for clubs outside of the United Kingdom but have similarly received scarce recognition in the press or in other publications. A number of players took no part in England's or Scotland's leagues but did migrate to other clubs and were also able to take up their dream of playing professional football in a full-time capacity.

Non-academic studies of footballers' careers, as Roderick states, are centred mainly on the game's 'heroes' and frequently illustrate 'a nostalgic and sentimental attachment to past eras'.[18] The reality is that the majority of Irish-born players have not represented their countries or played at the highest level of English league football, and many ex-professional footballers who are now retired have had nothing to fall back on except their football experience and know-how when their careers came to an end. This book will examine the challenges many Irish football migrants have faced, both in Ireland prior to departure and on their return post-career, including difficulties in securing first-team places while abroad as well as general issues faced by all Irish migrants. It also illustrates some of the highs that a number of players have reached on their personal journeys, and the joy they have experienced in the game, as well as some of the lower moments. As MacRaild has noted, 'emigration, in fact, must be seen as an element of the life cycle: a survival strategy as well as a means of adapting and improving the lives people knew'.[19]

Graham Davis has argued that the Irish migrant experience in Britain has been a diverse one, despite the negative press Irish migrants have sometimes received.[20] For professional footballers, there are differing attitudes towards the concept of 'making it' in the game. As former Coventry City, Hibernian and Oldham Athletic player Barry Prenderville stated when interviewed for this study,

> I mean there's different levels of 'making it' as well. You can make it like I made it, you can make it like Roy Keane made it, you can make it like someone that drops out of the game at twenty-one who played professionally for three years. I played professionally for twelve years. I played for Ireland underage but I never played for Ireland seniors, I never won the Premier League, so there's different levels of 'making it' [in professional football].[21]

This book provides an assessment of the role and place of Irish-born footballers in British football leagues and further afield. It will focus primarily on those who have played English league football, but an assessment of the careers of Irish-born football migrants to Scotland, continental Europe and the United States of America will also be given. This publication has its origins in a FIFA Havelange Research Scholarship awarded to the author in 2013 to investigate the migration of Irish-born footballers to Britain in the period from 1945 until 2010. This research has been expanded to take into account the first Irish-born players who moved to England to play the game professionally and to set these football migrants' movements within the context of wider assessments of the Irish diaspora, and within the game in Britain and further afield.

IRISH-BORN FOOTBALL MIGRANTS AS A PART OF THE IRISH DIASPORA

Since the Act of Union in 1800, Ireland, comprising thirty-two counties, had been part of the United Kingdom. The War of Independence, which took place between the Irish Republican Army and the British forces from 1919 to 1921, led to the formation of the Irish Free State in December 1921.Under the Government of Ireland Act of 1920, Northern Ireland, comprising six Ulster counties, was formed, with Belfast as its capital, and they remained separate from the Free State. The Free State became known as Éire in 1937, and the country later became more commonly known as the Republic of Ireland.[22] Despite a departure from the Commonwealth in 1948, the British government's Ireland Act of 1949 allowed citizens of the Republic of Ireland to be treated on a par with those from other Commonwealth countries and saw that they would not be treated as 'aliens' in Britain, thereby continuing to facilitate migration of footballers there from Ireland.[23] Therefore, apart from the years of the Second World War (1939–45) and briefly afterwards, those born in independent Ireland were entitled to pursue 'the right of free entry into the United Kingdom' and could enjoy similar residential and voting rights to those held by British citizens.[24] Northern Ireland migrants were entitled to British citizenship, thereby also easing the migration of Northern Irish-born footballers to English and Scottish football clubs.

As Matthew Taylor has noted, 'football migration should not be isolated from general migratory trends and patterns'.[25] Therefore it is important to see this analysis of Irish football migrants as a part of the wider history of Irish emigration. According to Enda Delaney, 'from the early 1920s until the end of the twentieth century roughly 1.5 million people left independent Ireland and in excess of 500,000 people emigrated from Northern Ireland'.[26] In addition, he has noted that Britain was 'the principal destination for twentieth-century Irish emigrants' with greater accessibility available than to other places such as North America and Australia, the need for labour and strong, inexpensive transport networks all fundamental to this. Similarities in culture and a lack of entry restrictions were significant in making this decision.[27] Although Irish emigration to Britain was certainly not a new phenomenon in the post-partition years, 'what was new was that it now became the destination of the great majority'.[28] In the nineteenth century, North America had been the main destination for most Irish emigrants but its significance declined in this regard in the years between the First and Second World Wars.[29] As MacRaild and Malcolm Smith have shown, 'bitter sectarian cleavage prompted a steady flow of migration from Northern Ireland to Britain after 1922', although this type of movement as a result of religious discrimination was not unique to this area of the island of Ireland, with more than 100,000 Southern Protestants emigrating between 1911 and 1926.[30] As will be shown in this book, sectarianism has also been a problem for Irish football migrants in their new countries of residence, particularly in Scotland.

ASSOCIATION FOOTBALL IN IRELAND

The island of Ireland has had two separate governing bodies for association football since the early 1920s. The Irish Football Association was formed in Belfast on 18 November 1880 but after relations between a number of Dublin clubs and the IFA in Belfast deteriorated, the Football Association of Ireland was formed in Dublin on 2 September 1921. This was renamed the Football Association of the Irish Free State (FAIFS) in September 1923 but is today again known as the FAI.[31] After the split from the IFA in 1921, Irish-born players were eligible for both Irelands until 1950 when FIFA ruled against this dual representation. In 1954 FIFA decided that the twenty-six counties would be known as the Republic of Ireland and the remaining six would be named Northern Ireland for football purposes.[32] In 2009 then FIFA president, Sepp Blatter, announced that Northern Ireland-born players could play for the Republic.[33] This allows Roman Catholics born in Northern Ireland to play for a country some feel is more representative of their social and political backgrounds as a number of Catholics have suffered sectarian abuse from spectators while playing for Northern Ireland.[34] While this movement of Northern Irish-born players to the Republic of Ireland's international teams has led to tension between the IFA and the FAI, the former governing body now has a more adequate system in place to deal with religious discrimination within the game in line with laws for spectator behaviour at sporting events in Northern Ireland.[35]

It would be fair to say that the conditions and infrastructure for developing a career in professional football in Ireland have generally not been to the advantage of all aspiring players. As Neal Garnham has stated, 'large-scale professional football' in Ireland has failed to develop mainly because of 'the attraction of top Irish players to the British game, and the rivalry of Gaelic football'.[36] Domestic Irish soccer has also suffered as a result of the movement of Ireland's best young footballers to the English and Scottish leagues. As will be shown, the early migration of talent to Britain continues to be a problem for domestic soccer in Ireland, although many returning players have sought to take up part-time careers in the game on arriving home. However, it is also important to note, as D. H. Akenson has stated in relation to many Irish emigrants, emigration was 'part of a set of conscious decisions, which, in most cases, improved their life-chances'.[37] Therefore, the rewards for those who do make it to the highest levels of the game are immense. However, as will be shown, figures for Irish-born players who do break into top-flight English football and appear for their countries at senior international level have declined in the late twentieth century.

THE HISTORIOGRAPHY OF IRISH FOOTBALL MIGRATION

As Taylor has stated, 'football migration is nothing new, but has a long and complicated history'.[38] Despite this, academic studies of the history of pre- and post-Second World War Irish football migrants have been scarce. As Garnham has noted, Irish-born footballers have migrated to Britain since the late nineteenth century, with Belfast-based players being sought for recruitment by Scottish clubs since 1889.[39] Taylor has discussed relations between the Football League and Ireland's governing bodies for the game in his book, *The Leaguers: the making of professional football in England, 1900–1939* (2005), noting how the English Football League's difficulties in dealing with the movement of its players continued despite the formation of an Anglo-Irish Football League Board in 1914.[40] In his major work on football migration, *Moving with the Ball: the migration of professional footballers* (2001), written jointly with Pierre Lanfranchi, the movement of Irish players to Manchester, Liverpool and Glasgow is briefly discussed, while less is noted about who they actually were, with more attention paid to the movement of Mickey Hamill and Mick O'Brien to the American Soccer League (ASL) in the 1920s.[41] The work of Robin Peake has examined the migration of a number of Irish international footballers in the early twentieth century, although his unpublished MA thesis (2010) generally focuses on the career of Patrick O'Connell.[42] Despite these assessments, the period from the beginning of English league football in 1888 until the early twenty-first century still lacks a comprehensive overall analysis of the experiences of Irish-born players who appeared at that level.[43]

This lack of a general study of pre-war football migrants is part of a wider neglect of engagement with the history of Irish soccer on the part of academics undertaking studies of Ireland's broader history. In comparison with the volume of historical research undertaken on the growth of the Gaelic Athletic Association, academic studies of association football in Ireland have been limited to the work of a handful of historians. The early macro-developments affecting the growth of Irish soccer have been well addressed by Mike Cronin (1999) and Garnham (2004) and initial developments concerning its spread in more regional areas are beginning to be unearthed through new research undertaken by Tom Hunt on Westmeath, David Toms on Munster and my own work on west and south Ulster over the past decade.[44] Other key works specialising in the history of Irish soccer recently published include Cormac Moore's *The Irish Soccer Split* (2015) while in 2013 Mark Tynan completed his PhD on the game in Ireland during the inter-war years.[45] In 2016, a special edition of *Soccer & Society*, co-edited by this author and David Toms, became the first academic journal publication to focus solely on the history and development of soccer in Ireland, while this was followed by a one-day symposium, based on this publication's articles and supported by the British Society of Sports History, held at the Public Record Office of Northern Ireland in February 2017.[46]

Despite this progress, soccer still awaits a comprehensive general history assessing events throughout the twentieth and early twenty-first centuries, as Garnham's *Association Football and Society in Pre-partition Ireland* reaches its conclusion in the early 1920s. In addition, an academic book assessing Anglo-Irish football relationships still awaits publication. While Patrick McGovern's study of Irish players' migration to England (1999) is an important starting point for this research, his study of Irish players finishes in 1995 and gives no indication of factors such as place of birth by county, number of clubs and transfers, their post-playing career employment or country of settlement.[47] Sociologists Seamus Kelly (2011, 2014), Anne Bourke (2002, 2003) and Richard Elliott (2016), have also looked at the recruitment process and the factors which influence young Irish footballers' career choices.[48]

Specialised works on sports migration and the migration of professional footballers, in particular, have not examined Irish-born players' career trajectories or their experiences to any great extent. As noted above, Lanfranchi and Taylor's publication *Moving with the Ball: the migration of professional footballers* devotes little space to Irish football migrants, as does Paul Darby and David Hassan's edited 2008 work, *Emigrant Players: sport and the Irish diaspora.*[49] Joseph Maguire and John Bale's 1994 work, *The Global Sports Arena: athletic talent migration in an interdependent world* similarly gives scarce attention to Irish players' movements.[50] In addition, major publications on British football such as Tony Mason's *Association Football and English Society, 1863–1915* (1980) and David Russell's *Football and the English: a social history of association football in England* (1997) have focused less on football immigration than on the other aspects of the game's history in England.[51] Taylor's *The Association Game: a history of British football* (2008) briefly addresses the role of Irish players within Scottish and English clubs, but he focuses mainly on the game's identity within Northern Ireland in his analysis of Irish professional football.[52]

Global histories of the game have given scarce attention to the migration of Irish-born footballers, with FIFA's 2004 study of soccer's development, *100 Years of Football: the FIFA centennial book,* devoting little attention to these players, while David Goldblatt's *The Ball is Round* (2006) focuses largely on nationalist–unionist politics and its impact on the game's popularity.[53] Similarly, his 2014 publication, *The Game of Our Lives: the meaning and making of English football,* assesses the development of soccer in Ireland mainly through looking at its relationship with Northern Ireland politics and religious conflict.[54]

Government publications have given scarce attention to Irish footballers abroad. Published in Dublin in the mid-1950s, the *Commission on Emigration and other Population Problems 1948–54* noted the diversity of emigrants' motives for leaving Ireland, but stated that 'the fundamental causes of emigration are economic', with the need for 'social amenities' cited as of high significance. As well as consulting government departments, the report utilised the collective opinions of twenty-nine national, regional and local bodies ranging from the Irish Tourist Board to the Swinford Parish Council, but the majority of these were based in Ireland.[55] While acknowledging that 'a limited inquiry into the social and economic conditions of emigrants was carried out by the Commission in certain areas of Great Britain where large numbers of Irish were employed', those interviewed did include 'emigrants, clergy, welfare officers, employers, foremen and others whose activities brought them into close contact with Irish emigrants'. However, there is little indication from the report's contents that the views of any professional sportspeople were sought.[56]

Other major studies on Irish migration to Britain have similarly given Irish players scant consideration. The work of Patrick Sullivan (1992), Enda Delaney and Donald M. MacRaild (2007) has failed to consider football's role in the labour market or the social effects migration had on these players.[57] Tim Pat Coogan has touched on the success of a small number of Irish players in England in *Wherever Green is Worn: the story of the Irish diaspora* (2000) but without any in-depth analysis of their overall levels of achievement.[58] Diarmaid Ferriter (2012) has also noted the success of a number of Republic of Ireland international players, such as Liam Brady in England in the 1970s.[59]

In examining the geography of these players, this current study of Irish football migrants is significant not only for the focus on football migration but also for the more mainstream history of Irish migration, and for geographical studies of Irish history itself. In particular, the work of Ruth Dudley Edwards (2005) on the latter subject gives little attention to soccer players' migration from Ireland or the places of origin of Irish men entering the British workforce as professional footballers.[60]

In addition, the post-playing careers of Irish football migrants have received scant academic attention. Garnham has stated in regard to Ireland's early professional footballers that 'even the greatest achievements on the football field could count for little in later years'.[61] How much this has changed will be addressed here as the first comprehensive analysis of the post-playing careers of Irish-born football migrants is provided in this book, along with an assessment of the places of settlement of a number of players. Academic studies of the post-career employment of sportsmen in Britain and Ireland have been scarce, particularly those of an historical nature, with most studies of professional footballers' retirement utilising the views of more recent players. Rare exceptions to this would be Wray Vamplew's work on the insecure nature of the careers of sporting professionals in Britain in the late Victorian/Edwardian era and Mason's work on footballers in the same period.[62] Gavin Brown and Paul Potrac's assessment of four scholars at professional clubs has illustrated how elite youth-level players experience negative emotions following the end of their professional careers and have been shown to be critical of club support systems despite their attempts to construct new identities in other occupations.[63] The work of Jerome Berthoud and Raffaele Poli has shown how the club, cultural and social environment and the family in which the player grew up have all impacted upon the post-playing career options of South African footballers.[64] More recently, Luke Jones and Jim Denison noted that leaving professional football was 'simultaneously both a challenge and a relief for the majority of retiring players' featured in their study of twenty-five former professional footballers.[65]

OTHER DESTINATIONS

Mainstream academics have generally not concerned themselves with accounting for how the migration patterns of professional footballers, and other athletes, have fitted into the more general study of migration. An exception is Tony Judt, who, writing in *Post-War: a history of Europe since 1945* (2010) briefly assesses the impact of association football on European society, pointing out that 'what really united Europe was football'.[66] He also gives a short analysis of player movement in the late twentieth century, stating that a generation after England had been beaten on home soil by Hungary in 1953, major European football clubs 'had a cosmopolitan roster of players drawn from many different countries'.[67] John Merriman's *A History of Modern Europe: from the Renaissance to the present* (2010) contains a very brief assessment of the early development of professional football in England but fails to assess how the English game was affected by immigration.[68] Although Irish-born players' movement to European clubs has been patchy, a full-length analysis of this is given here.

The migration of Irish-born soccer players to North America has received scarce academic interest, with Paul Darby's major publication in 2009 examining the role of Irish migrants in the development of the GAA in the United States of America.[69] Patrick Redmond, in his more recent work *The Irish and the Making of American Sport, 1835–1920* (2014), notes how soccer was, while a 'minority' sport, 'a popular, if unlikely, center of Irish activity', with an American born of Irish parents, Thomas W. Cahill, a leading figure in the growth of soccer there.[70] However, a comprehensive account of Irish-born player movement to soccer leagues in the USA has not yet been offered. Therefore an analysis of Irish migration to the American Soccer League, which ran from 1921 to 1931 is given, while a discussion of player movement to the United States Association League of 1967 and the North American Soccer League (1968–84) is included. The movement of players to South Africa and Australia has also been assessed in this book, although it focuses mainly on Irish-born footballers in England as this has been the main overseas destination as football migrants.

METHODOLOGY

An important part of this project involved conducting player interviews. Their inclusion means that an oral primary source can be used to gain Irish football migrants' personal experiences and allows for a more comprehensive analysis of their movement patterns. The availability of recent player interviews also allows for a more first-hand assessment of Irish football migrants' experiences across the Irish Sea rather than relying on secondary sources. Despite studies of note by Martin Roderick, John Sugden, Jonathan Magee, David Stead and Joseph Maguire using this method of historical research, Irish-born English Football League and Premiership players have generally been neglected as a quantitative group.[71] An attempt was made to interview two players from both the Republic and Northern Ireland who migrated in each decade since 1945 until 2010, with an emphasis placed on their early development and the initial recruitment process, settling in at an English club, why players chose a particular club, the culture of the football club, the playing experience, relationships with managers, the use of sports psychology, post-career options and retirement from the game. In interviewing those who had participated in the differing levels of English professional football, a more balanced account of players' experiences was obtained than if interviews had been undertaken only with those with experience of, for example, the Premier League or former First Division.

A total of thirty players, from various areas in the Republic and Northern Ireland, were initially interviewed for the FIFA Havelange study, although they did not all wish to have their views published in this book. Those who reacted positively to the request included thirteen Republic of Ireland-born players. Five were full internationals (Mick Meagan, Alfie Hale, Paddy Mulligan, Damien Richardson and Richie Sadlier); five were former Second Division players (Brian Mooney, Martin Russell, Seamus Kelly, Michael McHugh and Barry Prenderville); two had played in League One (Dean Kelly and Denis Behan) and one footballer, Shane Supple, had appeared in the Championship. Of the eleven Northern Ireland-born players who consented to having their views published, four had represented their country at senior international level (Hubert Barr, Billy Humphries, John McClelland and Alan Blayney); one had also played in the First Division (Gerry Burrell), one had played in the Second Division (David Miskelly), one had appeared in League Two (Michael Carvill) and one was a former Third Division player (Seamus Heath). In addition, two had played in the Fourth Division (Raymond Campbell and Brendan Bradley) and one had played in the Scottish First Division (Andy Waterworth). Four players interviewed had experience of both English and Scottish league football. These were Gerry Burrell, John McClelland, Barry Prenderville and Shane Supple.

To supplement the interviews undertaken, it was decided to construct a number of databases to examine players' migration using the following categories: name; year and place of birth; youth club(s); source of migrational transfer; direct transfer or apprentice signing from Ireland; age when migrated; age when signed as a football league professional; senior clubs; number of football league clubs signed with; number of loans while in the Football League; length of Football League career; highest club level played at; senior international caps; post-career employment position(s) and country of settlement. Only players born in Ireland were included as the number of second-generation Irish living in Britain who played professionally at various levels would have been too great. Inclusion of those capped internationally, who were born outside Ireland but qualified under the parents and grandparents rule (e.g. Mick McCarthy, Tony Grealish), would have added greatly to the volume of players and it would also have led to extreme difficulty in tracing the 'nationality' of the parents/grandparents of players who were not capped internationally but regard themselves as Irish. More significantly, many of these players did not need to migrate as they were already living in England.[72] However, others such as Joe Kinnear, Steve Finnan, Paddy Hasty and Stephen Jones who were born in Ireland but moved to England with their parents at an early age have been included and the migration of players such as Steve Heighway (born in 1947 but moved to England aged ten as his father was looking for work) can be traced to more widespread migrational trends from Ireland to England, in this case in search of employment in the 1950s.[73]

The construction of these detailed databases helped the examination of the following key questions: From 1888 until 2010, how many Irish-born players have played professionally in Britain? What is the balance of Irish-born players who arrived in England on transfer from Irish clubs as opposed to those who were recruited young and developed their talent in English youth academies? At what level have Irish-born players played? What has been the career length of these players, and how frequently have they been transferred or had their contracts ended? After the ending of their careers, what happened to these Irish-born players? Ireland has been the longest-standing 'foreign' talent pool for British clubs, and was the dominant country of origin for non-British-born players until the 1980s. How did the recruitment of other European, South American and African players, from the 1980s, affect the opportunities afforded to the Irish-born player?

Michael Joyce's *Football League Players' Records 1888–1939* (2002) has been utilised to identify Irish-born footballers who played in the English Football League in the pre-Second World War era.[74] Barry J. Hugman's *The PFA Premier & Football League Players' Records 1946–2005* (2005), along with yearly volumes produced after this, similarly allows the researcher a basic introduction as they include 'a list of every footballer to have played in the Football League since the Second World War' and gives details such as place of birth, source of transfer to England, league clubs, date signed (professionally), seasons played, career appearances and goals scored along with international appearances.[75]

It was decided not to include trial players or apprentices who migrated to England but did not sign professionally as the volume of players would have been too great and there is no comprehensive record of each player on trial or apprentice who did not play league football in Britain. Irish internationals such as Paul McGrath and David O'Leary who were born in England but moved back to Ireland before migrating to England to play professionally were also left out. Along with an assessment of players who migrated to Scotland, those who migrated initially to Scotland then transferred to England have also been included in the categories of Irish-born players in England as they played in the English Football League. Although Wales is also part of Britain, players who migrated from Ireland to professional football clubs in Wales such as Swansea City and Cardiff City, which are part of the English Football League, have been included as part of this overall study and have been identified.

Hugman's breakdown of the type of migration – whether as a direct transfer, as trainee or signing professionally from a junior club or from school – allows for a categorisation of their moves to

England, although given that he only notes the date they signed professionally for a football league club and not the date players signed trainee forms, it is difficult to be totally precise about the age of migration for those who 'succeeded' as apprentices and gained a professional contract. This is not always the case and there is clear biographical data available in some cases to indicate dates of moves; for example, Liam Brady makes it clear in his 1980 publication *So Far So Good: a decade in football* that he joined Arsenal aged fifteen and served a two-year apprenticeship before being offered a contract, while Norman Whiteside did not have to serve this length of time although he was still signed as an apprentice.[76] However, a more accurate assessment can be made of when players actually signed professionally using Hugman's work. Therefore, dates used for the category 'age when signed as a football league professional' were given more significance as this is when they actually enter the British labour force, and these years were used for categorisation of players, for example those signed professionally in each year from 1976 to 1985 were grouped in that category, although some may have joined clubs as apprentices prior to 1976.

In addition, a number of other secondary sources such as players' autobiographies and internet sources were used to complete data categorised as part of this study but not included in Hugman's work. Matthew Taylor has shown how sports autobiographies can shed light on 'the relationships between performer and audience, the private and public sphere, and the self and society.'[77] They also provide crucial data on footballers' schoolboy clubs and their own experiences of migration.

Although McGovern indicates that the majority of players have been recruited from clubs in Belfast and Dublin, the inclusion of data pertaining to the geography of Irish players, through an assessment of their birthplaces, as well as club sources of players transferred, will add to the understanding of transfer and recruitment. In recording and assessing the highest level played at, an assessment of the 'success' levels of players can be made. While many post-war players were also involved in European club competitions (and international matches), it was decided to focus on the divisions of the English Football League. From the early 1920s until 1958, along with the First and Second Divisions, there were two Third Divisions, north and south, with one club from each gaining promotion. These were amalgamated into the Third Division in the latter year and a Fourth Division was put in place.[78] After the 1991–2 season, the First Division became known as the Premier League, with the new First Division being replaced by the Championship in the 2004–5 season. In addition, a study using the categories mentioned above allows for a more detailed examination of Irish-born players.

While Hugman's work does not state what players did when they retired or where they have settled, this additional information was gathered using player interviews and through discussion with those with 'insider information' such as schoolboy managers, journalists and other contacts within the game. Secondary sources including autobiographies and books such as Andy Pringle and Neil Fissler's *Where Are They Now?* series were assessed while newspapers and online sources were also used.[79] The term 'post-career employment position' was clarified as what employment positions were taken up after retiring, although, as will be shown, a number of players moved from job to job. 'Place of settlement' was defined as the country these players decided to reside in when retired from the game, using the most up to date sources and taking 2015 as the cut-off point for where they were living.

The migration of players to Scotland is also addressed here, although there is no published record for this as comprehensive as Barry J. Hugman's work on the English Premiership and Football League. Steve Emms and Richard Wells' *Scottish League Players' Records Division One 1890/91 to 1938/9*, Richard Beal and Steve Emms' *Scottish League Players' Records: Division One 1946/47 to 1974/75* and Derek Gray and Emms' *Scottish League Players' Records: Premier Division and Premier League 1975/76 to 1999/2000*, as their titles suggest, focus only on football in Scotland's top tier and fail to indicate whether players arrived as apprentices or direct transfers, and do not address those who played professionally in the lower Scottish leagues.[80] In addition, some details, such as birthdates and place of birth, are missing in the publications covering the earlier decades.

While the movement of Irish-born players to North America has paled into insignificance compared to migration to British clubs, data for this book was also collected for Irish-born players who took the opportunity to play in North America in the twentieth century and an analysis of this is included, although player data gathered for this was procured heavily from Colin Jose's *American Soccer League, 1921–1931: the golden years of American soccer* (1998) and *North American Soccer League Encyclopaedia* (2003).[81] Using internet sources and newspaper data as well as biographical material, it was also possible to compile a database of Irish-born players who have moved to European clubs in the period covered here.

The book is generally structured thematically. In Chapter 1, the birthplaces of Irish-born soccer migrants are explored in terms of the areas which have produced the most players, and the geography of Irish football migrants is assessed. Chapter 2 looks at the schools' and coaching infrastructures that have been in place in Ireland for the early development of Irish footballers throughout the late nineteenth, twentieth and early twenty-first centuries, and the challenges facing young players, particularly in more peripheral areas. Chapter 3 assesses the methods by which Irish-born players have been recruited to English clubs and how a number of post-war migrants have settled into their new environment. The various playing experiences of a number of pre-Second World War football migrants and post-war interviewees for this study are examined in Chapter 4. Chapter 5 discusses the movement of Irish-born players to Scotland, continental Europe and to the United States and again explores a number of these players' experiences. Chapter 6 examines the post-playing careers of Irish-born footballers, and the insufficient educational structures which have been in place within professional football clubs are outlined. Finally, Chapter 7 examines the decline of Irish-born footballers in top-flight English football and discusses some of the challenges facing future Irish football migrants.

CHAPTER 1

The Geography of Irish Soccer Migrants

> I was very lucky, when I was seven years of age, I saw my first game with Shamrock Rovers in Milltown … I remember being lifted over the turnstile by my brother … we made our way through the throng on the terrace and down to the front where the kids stood by the wall, and a whole new life opened up in front of my eyes. It was colour – Shamrock Rovers were playing Drumcondra, I'll never forget it … it's in my mind still vividly … the green and white of Shamrock Rovers, the gold and blue of Drumcondra, the pristine, brilliant green pitch. It was early season, about September, it was a Shield game … and the excitement of the crowd, and that took me into a different world. It was almost like a new birth to me … it opened [up] something.[1]
>
> Damien Richardson, 13 August 2013

INTRODUCTION

As Enda Delaney has noted of Irish migrants in the United Kingdom, 'any understanding of how the Irish interacted with each other and the wider society was as much shaped by experiences prior to leaving Ireland as by subsequent events in Britain'.[2] This chapter addresses a number of experiences of Irish-born football migrants prior to leaving home while identifying the areas which have produced the most Irish-born players who have gone on to play league football in England. Although more pre-Second World War players migrated from Belfast than from Dublin, by the late twentieth century figures for Dublin-born players had surpassed those from Belfast. While the majority of Ireland's footballers who migrated to England and played league football have been born in these two cities, as will be shown, there were a number of reasons why

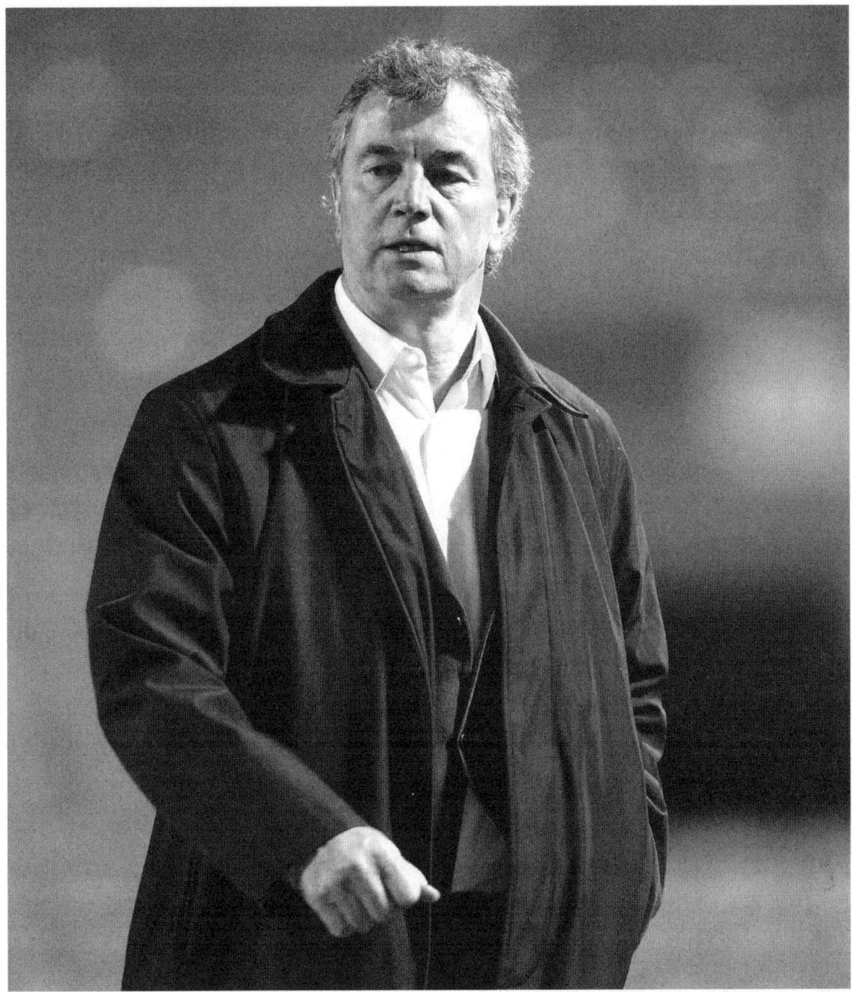

A relative latecomer to English league football with Gillingham, **Damien Richardson** has gone on to manage the club as well as a number of League of Ireland teams, including Cork City. Picture: © Inpho

rates of production were significantly lower in other areas. The recent emergence of more players from peripheral regions, both north and south of the border, will also be discussed. In addition, the trend of migration of young players from more peripheral counties to clubs on the east coast of Ireland in order to increase their chances of getting noticed by English and Scottish clubs will also be assessed. While there is less evidence that regional structures for youth football were weak in Northern Ireland, the game in Fermanagh was hampered by administrative difficulties. It will also be shown that schoolboy and adult leagues were absent or inconsistently organised in many areas in the Republic of Ireland. This chapter also illustrates how scouting networks outside Belfast and Dublin have been slow to develop while there is also strong evidence that regional players were ignored in the selection process for international schoolboy level for much of the twentieth century.

THE EARLY DEVELOPMENT OF THE GAME IN BELFAST AND DUBLIN

The historiography of soccer in Ireland still lacks the type of analysis carried out by John Bale in his 1986 article 'Sport and National Identity: a geographical view'.[3] Through his construction of 'images or mental maps of the regional geography of certain sports', Bale has highlighted areas within Britain which are perceived to be associated with cricket, rugby, golf and soccer and has looked at the media's role in the formation of 'sport-place images' as well as examining continental patterns.[4] In regard to association football he states that 'in England and Wales professional league clubs are, in a relative sense, concentrated in the north with relative deprivation in the south' and 'a similar pattern exists in player "production", counties in the north and midlands being relative over-producers, though since 1950 there had been a tendency for regional convergence in this respect'.[5] Joyce Woolridge's analysis of the geographical origins of a sample of professionals playing in English league football in the periods 1890–1939 and 1946–1985 has shown that the percentage of players born in the south-east of England was almost double in the latter period and had reached 17.5 per cent of 2000 players assessed, the highest of any region.[6] She states that by 1955, 'the majority of these new south-east professionals were playing for clubs in the south of England' and 'it appears that the main reason for this change was an economic and ideological climate which applauded the development of the home-grown player, and stimulated southern clubs to recruit more actively in their environs'.[7] More recently, coach and television analyst Gary Neville has noted a decline in the strength of England's top clubs in areas of Lancashire, Yorkshire and the north-east with a loss of atmosphere at some grounds, a lack of local player presence in clubs and 'a disconnect between the teams and the fans' at Newcastle and Sunderland.[8]

In Ireland, centres of industry have differed geographically from those in England with the leading industrial cities, and professional football clubs, located on the east coast. While Bale has linked the early strength of football to 'the English industrial heartland' with Scotland playing a significant yet lesser role, Ireland has lacked this type of concentrated industrial infrastructure.[9] Belfast and Dublin are the two cities most prominently associated with soccer in Ireland. By the beginning of the twentieth century, Belfast's population of 349,180 was almost equal to that of Dublin, which stood at 375,135 including suburban municipalities.[10] The industrialised Belfast area had more similarities with Manchester, Liverpool and Glasgow than with the rest of Ireland at this time.[11] Unsurprisingly, Belfast and Dublin were the early centres of professional football in Ireland, with the Irish Football Association legalising the payment of players in 1894, although professional football was not fully accepted in the Leinster Football Association's area until 1905.[12] Garnham has illustrated how social and economic conditions such as Factory and Workshop Acts impacted on soccer's popularity, and notes in particular the 1874 act as having a greater impact in Belfast than in other urban areas, such as Dublin.[13] He has also stated that 'the Belfast working population, more than any other in Ireland, therefore seems to have had the necessary leisure and financial resources to participate in some form of modern sporting pastime'.[14]

Belfast was the centre of industry in Ireland and as Kennedy and Ollerenshaw have stated, 'by 1900, despite the absence of coal and iron, the Belfast region had emerged as a significant industrial and commercial centre by UK and European standards'.[15] Garnham has also shown how, once the game had been formally introduced at the Ulster Cricket Ground through an exhibition match involving two Glasgow teams, Caledonians and Queen's Park, in 1878, the later growth of clubs in the city was assisted by 'pre-existing entities, notably the workplace' and 'the urban neighbourhood, and established social organisations including churches and church sponsored movements'.[16] These included Cliftonville, formed by members of a cricket club bearing the same name in 1879, while Distillery were established by employees of Dunville's distillery the same year and Linfield were formed by mill workers in 1885.[17]

There were four clubs playing regularly in east Ulster – Cliftonville and Knock of Belfast, Moyola (Castledawson) and Banbridge Academy (County Down) – by the middle of 1880.[18] The majority of winners in the IFA's Challenge Cup, first won in 1881 by Moyola Park, and the Irish Football League, initially won by Linfield in 1891, were based in Belfast in the pre-First World War period.[19] An assessment of finalists from the period when the IFA Junior Cup was initiated in 1888 until 1914 illustrates that the majority of winners came from the east of the province, illustrating the strength of the game in this area.[20] A similar situation existed with regard to the Irish Junior League which was operational by 1890.[21] By 1901 there were twenty-eight soccer clubs in Ulster that employed professionals, with fifteen located in Belfast, while 'eight were based in the town of Lisburn or in the Lagan valley area between the two urban centres, three in County Down, and one each was situated in Counties Armagh and Tyrone'.[22]

The majority of pre-Second World War players generally migrated from present-day Northern Ireland. This greater number migrating from northern clubs is indicative of the higher standard of the Belfast-based clubs for much of these years. As early as 1902, one local newspaper noted 'the undoubted superiority of Belfast over Dublin football', although this later evened out.[23] By May of 1921 the game in Dublin was said to be growing in strength after the split from the Irish League, with one reporter noting how 'the attachment to Belfast has always been viewed unfavourably by the bulk of the people, and the game in Dublin has never enjoyed their wholehearted support', while the IFA's ban on Sunday football was also said to have weakened interest.[24] Links between clubs in the northern city and those in Scotland and England were also early to be established. Cliftonville were beaten by Partick Thistle in an FA Cup qualifying match in 1886 while in 1888, Linfield had played Bolton Wanderers and Nottingham Forest in the same competition, with Irish clubs allowed to participate at that point, and in 1894 a Sheffield United selection had played Linfield in Belfast.[25]

By the late 1890s Belfast clubs were attracting the visits of a number of those in England and Scotland with Glentoran taking on Everton at the Oval at Easter 1896 while Sunderland also visited the city to play the Merseyside club in a friendly a few days later.[26] The following year Glasgow Celtic visited to play then Irish Cup holders Cliftonville, thereby strengthening links between Irish and cross-channel clubs.[27] The visit of Irish League clubs to England on tour was also noted at that time, with Cliftonville's trips 'across the channel' being 'looked forward to and heartily enjoyed by the players' at the turn of the century.[28] In 1906 one reporter mentioned how Liverpool had already been 'most intimately associated in a football sense with Belfast, and some of its clubs'.[29]

The game was initially slower to develop in Dublin; it was first played there in 1883 as opposed to 1878 in Belfast. The much-documented initial match involving the Dublin Association Football Club, viewed by only six people, consisted of twelve players including one of the goalkeepers who was 'considerably over thirty years of age, with thick-set beard, silver looking watch-guard, in ordinary clothes, minus his coat'.[30] Soccer in Dublin was later nurtured by a number of migrants to the capital from Ulster, including former Belfast school pupils such as Alexander Blaney, who had attended St Malachy's College and later became the first chairman of Bohemians FC, founded in 1890.[31] In addition, some clubs developed through industrial paternalism, such as Jacob's, a biscuit producer, and St James's Gate, which had its links with the alcohol company, Guinness.[32] Shelbourne were formed in a pub in Ringsend in 1895.[33] The Leinster FA was founded in 1892, while, further south, the Munster FA was established in 1901.[34]

The first Irish-born footballer to feature in English league football, Archie Goodall, played at the beginning of the 1888–89 season for initial double winners Preston North End, appearing in two games before moving to Aston Villa.[35] He was born in Belfast to a Scottish soldier in 1864, a year after his brother John, who had a slightly longer spell at Preston, was born in London. The younger Goodall brother began his early football career in Liverpool having evidently moved there without playing the game at a senior level in Ireland.[36] Later capped at international level, his style of play was described vividly in *Sport* in 1900:

> When in his togs on the field his every manner at once proclaims the master. He never seems to bustle or move about much, but he has the instinct which always prompts correct movements, and he is generally in the proximity of the ball and doing the right thing. He is equally good at attack or defence, and is a dangerous shot.[37]

Although Belfast-born John McVicker had moved to Accrington via Birmingham St George's in 1891 and both Bob Crone and Jack Taggart had joined West Bromwich Albion in 1892 via Middlesbrough, having left Distillery, it was not until 1893 that direct moves from Irish League clubs to those in the English league were beginning to become more common.[38] Tommy 'Ching' Morrison and Zeke Johnston both joined Burnley from Glentoran, said to be 'one of the most entertaining' clubs in Belfast at that time, while William Michael Purves also left the Belfast club to join Small Heath.[39] In addition, John Peden left Linfield to join Newton Heath (later to become Manchester United) that year, with money a significant motivating factor. Peden, described as 'the celebrated left winger of Linfield', was said to have 'at last succumbed to the blandishments of the English professional agent and taken a place in England, at £100 down and £3 a week afterwards' in March of that year.[40]

Direct moves from Dublin clubs to England were slower to develop, which suggests that scouting networks there were not as strong along with the reputation of the game there as opposed to Belfast. Val Harris appears to be the first player who moved from a Dublin club to England to play league football, joining Everton from Shelbourne in 1907, while, the following year, Billy Lacey also joined the Merseyside team from the same club.[41] Glentoran was found to have been the most prominent source club for the 1888–1939 period, with twenty-four players leaving from the east Belfast club, while Belfast Celtic followed closely, supplying twenty-two players. Linfield supplied sixteen, although figures for Dublin-based clubs were much lower, with only six leaving from Shamrock Rovers and three from Bohemians.

GEOGRAPHICAL DISCREPANCIES IN PLAYER MIGRATION, 1888–2010

Table 1.1 Places of birth of Irish-born football migrants by county, 1888–1939.

City/Town	Number	Percentage
Belfast	97	37%
Dublin	43	16%
Cork	5	2%
Galway	0	0%
Derry	8	3%
Waterford	1	0.38%
Enniskillen	2	0.76%
Newry	4	1.53%
Donegal	5	2%
Athlone	6	2.29%
Sligo	2	0.76%
Kilkenny	1	0.38%
Limerick	1	0.38%
Other areas	87	33.00%
Total Identified	**262**	**100%**

Source: Michael Joyce, *Football League Players' Records, 1888 to 1939* [3rd edn] (Nottingham: Tony Brown, 2012).

As shown in Table 1.1, a total of 262 players' birthplaces were positively identified out of the overall pre-Second World War total of 286, with ninety-seven players or 37 per cent of the total identified born in Belfast. Although, as noted earlier, Ireland was divided geographically and politically into the Irish Free State and Northern Ireland after the Anglo-Irish Treaty of 1921, areas in the new Northern Ireland state have been included in Table 1.1 as the figures run from 1888 to 1939. One might expect the Belfast figure to be higher but a number of birthplaces are recorded simply as 'Ireland', while this can also be explained partially by more outlying areas such as Whiteabbey and Ballymacarrett (near Belfast) being given as place of birth in the records. This illustrates the strength of clubs in Belfast in the pre-Second World War years, with forty-three or 16 per cent born in Dublin. Figures from other cities were low in comparison, with only eight or 3 per cent born in Derry. Cork-born players made up only five of the total identified or 2 per cent, while other major regional centres such as Waterford, Galway, Limerick and Kilkenny had similarly low numbers.[42] The development of the game throughout Ireland and the impact this had on player production will be discussed in more detail later. These overall patterns generally remained the same for much of the twentieth century, with regional areas struggling to challenge the two main centres of association football on the island of Ireland, although Belfast was replaced as the overall leading city of player production by Dublin in the post-Second World War period.

Enda Delaney, writing in his analysis of Irish emigration since 1921, has stated that 'no county, north or south, was left untouched by emigration, but its impact was greatest on those areas with a predominantly rural population, small farm holdings and an absence of industrial or manufacturing employment'.[43] While the majority of Irish counties supplied players who moved to England and played league football there, albeit at differing levels, the migration of Irish-born footballers to England contrasted greatly with this more general trend discussed by Delaney. As noted, players' movement generally took place from Dublin and Belfast, two east coast cities, while rates from more rural areas associated with agriculture rather than industry were generally much lower.

Table 1.2 and Figure 1.1 establish the birthplaces of the 500 Republic of Ireland-born footballers who played in the English Premier or football leagues between 1945 and 2010 on a county by county basis. While care must be taken in acknowledging that some players, such as Shane Long, may have been born in hospitals outside their own counties, this illustrates that the majority, just over 64 per cent, were born in the capital and Ireland's largest city, Dublin. In addition, it is difficult to accurately set these figures against county populations on a decade by decade basis or through the number of registered players

Table 1.2 Birthplaces of players who migrated from the Republic of Ireland to England, 1945–2010.

Republic of Ireland Players by County	Number	Percentage
Dublin	322	64.40%
Meath	1	0.20%
Wicklow	5	1%
Westmeath	5	1%
Kilkenny	3	0.60%
Carlow	1	0.20%
Offaly	3	0.60%
Laois	2	0.40%
Kildare	0	0%
Wexford	5	1%
Louth	23	4.60%
Longford	1	0.20%
Mayo	5	1%
Galway	8	1.60%
Roscommon	0	0%
Sligo	4	0.80%
Leitrim	0	0%
Donegal	9	1.80%
Monaghan	2	0.40%
Cavan	1	0.20%
Kerry	6	1.20%
Cork	54	10.80%
Waterford	16	3.20%
Tipperary	2	0.40%
Limerick	21	4.20%
Clare	1	0.20%
Total	**500**	**100%**

Source: Barry J. Hugman (ed.), *The PFA Premier & Football League Players' Records, 1946–2005* (Harpenden, 2005); *The PFA Footballers' Who's Who, 2005–6* (Harpenden, 2005); *The PFA Footballers' Who's Who, 2006–7* (Edinburgh, 2006); *The PFA Footballers' Who's Who, 2007–8* (Edinburgh, 2007); *The PFA Footballers' Who's Who, 2008–9* (Edinburgh, 2008); *The PFA Footballers' Who's Who, 2009–10* (Edinburgh, 2009); *The PFA Footballers' Who's Who, 2010–11* (Edinburgh, 2010).

Map 1.1 Birthplaces of Irish-born footballers who played in the English Premier or football leagues, 1945–2010, shown by each county's number of football migrants (ROI=500, NI=417).

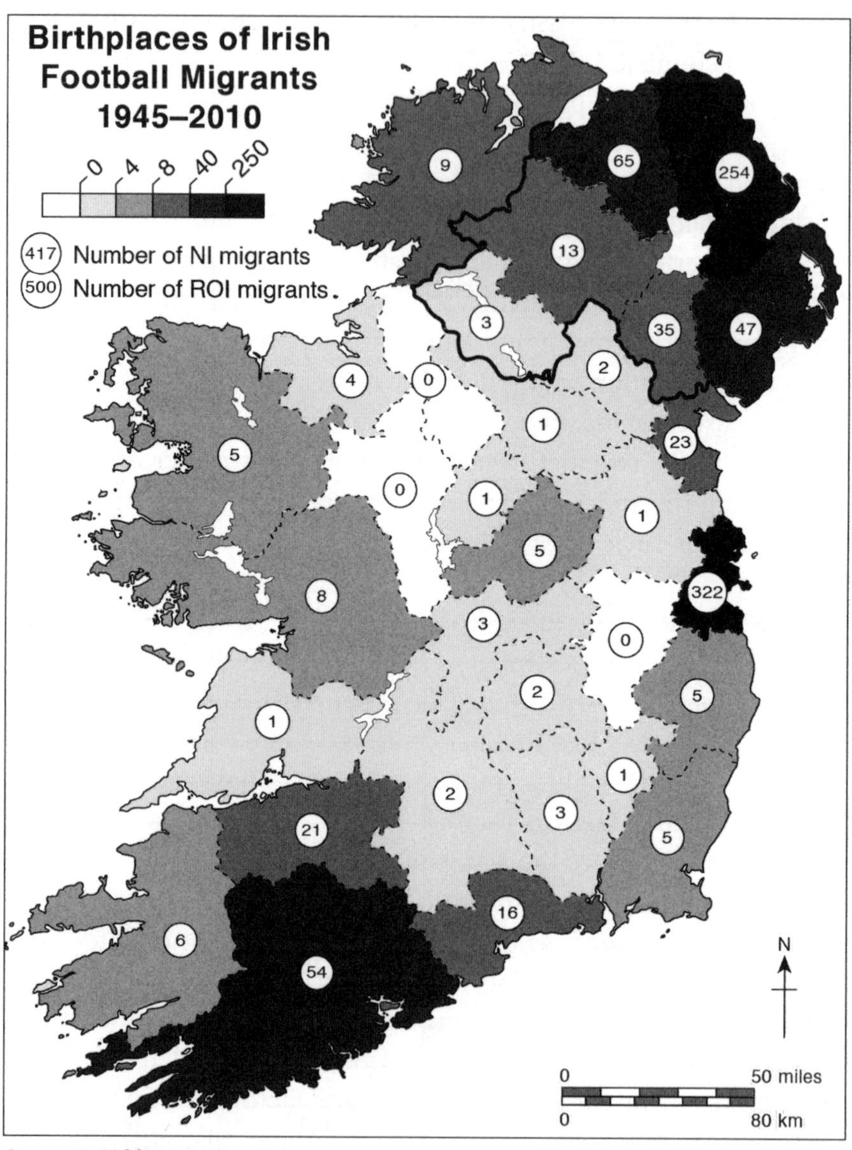

Source: As Table 1.2.

in each county per decade and therefore both Dublin and Belfast's figures must be seen in proportion to their overall populations as Ireland's biggest cities. Irish society certainly became more urbanised as the twentieth century progressed, but by 1961 only four Republic of Ireland counties – Dublin, Kildare, Meath and Louth – had higher populations than those recorded in 1926.[44] However, in 2007 it was reported by the Central Statistics Office that 'in common with many developed countries', the Republic had 'moved from having a largely rural population to a predominantly urban one'.[45]

Key areas of soccer migration in Ireland have been very densely populated and traditionally associated with cities. Players born in Cork city made up over one tenth of the total number while those born in Limerick (4.20 per cent), Waterford (3.20 per cent), Galway (1.60 per cent) and Kilkenny (0.60 per cent) did not feature as prominently. This highlights Dublin's position as the powerhouse of football migration in the Republic of Ireland and is unsurprising given its east coast location, with shipping links with British sea ports and, later in the twentieth century, air links between cross-channel cities easing transport difficulties and indeed strengthening support bases of clubs such as Manchester United, Liverpool and Glasgow Celtic.[46]

Player production rates from 'peripheral' Irish counties have been minimal. An assessment of counties along the west coast has indicated that along with Donegal (1.8 per cent), Kerry (1.2 per cent), Mayo (1 per cent), Sligo (0.8 per cent) and Clare (0.2 per cent) have failed to produce significant numbers of professional footballers appearing in the English football leagues. Donegal has produced only nine players since the war while only one Clare-born footballer has played English league football, with Willie Boland appearing for Coventry City in 1992. Midland counties have fared no better, with Westmeath (1 per cent), Offaly (0.6 per cent), Laois (0.4 per cent) and Longford (0.2 per cent) producing only eleven players in total. Three counties – Roscommon, Leitrim and Kildare – have failed to produce any players during the post-war period and factors behind these low rates will be addressed later. Delaney has stated that after 1921 'the areas that endured the highest rates of emigration over time were those along the western seaboard and north-western counties such as Leitrim and Roscommon'.[47] The migration of Republic of Ireland-born footballers was not reflective of this more general migratory trend, although, as Delaney has noted, by the 1980s, 'Dublin was an area of net emigration' and 'many emigrants in the 1980s and 1990s came from urban backgrounds, reflecting the changes in the overall distribution of the population'.[48]

THE BIRTHPLACES OF POST-WAR REPUBLIC OF IRELAND-BORN FOOTBALL MIGRANTS, DECADE BY DECADE

Table 1.3 illustrates the overall figures of player production per city in the Republic of Ireland and more rural areas in the post-war years as well as providing a breakdown of how these figures have changed on a decade by decade basis. While Dermot Keogh has noted that soccer has attracted much support in Belfast and Dublin as well as having 'a strong following in Cork, Limerick, Waterford, Sligo and Dundalk', player production outside the island's capital cities has been less significant.[49] As shown here, despite a small decrease in the 2006–10 period, there was no major change in Dublin's dominance as the leading birthplace of Republic of Ireland-born football migrants. Per decade, it was Dublin that consistently produced the most players who broke into English first-team league football.[50] The country's other cities have failed to challenge Dublin in terms of player production, with Cork's total of 17 per cent in the decade immediately following the war the highest total produced in any other city. Limerick has similarly consistently struggled to produce English league players on anywhere near the same scale as Dublin, while in some decades Waterford has not produced any, although the overall lack of players in the 1966–75 period may be at least partially explained by Waterford's domestic success in winning the League of Ireland six times in these years.[51] As Alfie Hale has stated, the impact of Frank Davis on the club was a significant factor in this success.[52]

In producing only three players, all in the 1996–2005 period, Kilkenny's general failure to contribute significantly to the overall total can be attributed to the county's strength in hurling, while Galway's rate of player production (1.6 per cent overall) can be linked to its west coast location, and the competition with hurling and Gaelic football. Despite claims by one journalist in 1946 that 'the entry of a CIE team and a team of the Army Medical Corps into competitive

Table 1.3 Birthplaces by decade of players who migrated from the Republic of Ireland to England, 1945–2010.

City	1945–55	1956–65	1966–75	1976–85	1986–95	1996–2005	2006–10	Total
Dublin	**58** (61%)	**31** (75%)	**29** (70.73%)	**24** (72.7%)	**55** (61.11%)	**94** (63.51%)	**31** (59.61%)	**322 (64.4%)**
Cork	**16** (16.90%)	**2** (4.87)	**2** (4.87%)	**2** (6.06%)	**9** (10%)	**16** (10.81%)	7 (13.46%)	**54 (10.8%)**
Limerick	**6** (6.31%)	**1** (2.43%)	**5** (12.19%)	**0**	**4** (4.44%)	**4** (2.70%)	**1** (1.92%)	**21 (4.20%)**
Waterford	**3** (3.15%)	**3** (7.31%)	**0**	**2** (6.06%)	**0**	**8** (5.40%)	**0**	**16 (3.2%)**
Galway	**0**	**0**	**1** (2.43%)	**1** (3.03%)	**4** (4.44%)	**0**	**2** (3.84%)	**8 (1.60%)**
Kilkenny	**0**	**0**	**0**	**0**	**0**	**3** (2.02%)	**0**	**3 (0.60%)**
Other	**12** (12.60%)	**4** (9.75%)	**4** (9.75%)	**4** (12.12%)	**18** (20%)	**23** (15.54%)	**11** (21.15%)	**76 (15.2%)**
Total	**95**	**41**	**41**	**33**	**90**	**148**	**52**	**100%**

Source: As Table 1.2.

football gave a considerable fillip to soccer' with 'about a dozen teams of various grades in the city', Galway has struggled to produce English league footballers as the game had to compete culturally with Gaelic football and hurling.[53] Apparently in Kilkenny city soccer had been 'disbanded because most of the members answered the country's call' during the Second World War, although scarce detail was given as to what they actually did at this time. The game in Kilkenny was revived with a club and then a Football Association being formed in the spring of 1948.[54] Like Galway, players produced in the city have not gone on to have a significant impact on rates of Irish-born players appearing in English league football, with the county's hurling team dominant in the All-Ireland senior hurling championship, which probably lessened interest in other codes.[55] The remainder of players not born in the Republic of Ireland's cities came from smaller urban areas – such as Dundalk, Drogheda, Sligo and Athlone – and were placed in the 'other' category along with those in other less urbanised areas, and made up just over 15 per cent of the overall total. Rates of player production from areas in this category have also been quite low but recently have risen to just over 21 per cent, reaching a peak in the 2006–10 period, and this will be addressed below.

REPUBLIC OF IRELAND SOURCE CLUBS: THE STRENGTH OF DUBLIN

As McGovern has noted in his study of Irish football migrants, the majority of players came from clubs located in or relatively near to Ireland's cities, with Shamrock Rovers, Shelbourne, Dundalk, Home Farm and Bohemians being identified as the top five Republic of Ireland selling clubs in the period from 1946 to 1995.[56] Shelbourne have now replaced Shamrock Rovers as the leading transferring club, although in terms of overall suppliers (i.e. taking into account source clubs as trainee and transfer suppliers), schoolboy clubs have supplied more players than these League of Ireland clubs. As shown in Table 1.4, Home Farm (7 per cent) has supplied the greatest number of players per club since the Second World War, while other Dublin clubs – Cherry Orchard (6.8 per cent) and Belvedere (6.2 per cent) –

Table 1.4 Top ten Republic of Ireland-born migrants' source clubs, 1945–2010.

Club	Number	Percentage of overall total (500)
Home Farm	35	7.00%
Cherry Orchard	34	6.80%
Belvedere	31	6.20%
Shelbourne	30	6.00%
Bohemians	21	4.20%
Shamrock Rovers	21	4.20%
Stella Maris	21	4.20%
Dundalk	17	3.40%
St Joseph's (Sallynoggin)	14	2.80%
Drumcondra	8	1.60%

Source: As Table 1.2.

follow behind. Only one non-Dublin club, Dundalk, of nearby County Louth (3.40 per cent), features in the top ten.

Home Farm was founded in 1928 'by a few schoolboys for the Altar Societies and Sodalities League' and by the middle of the 1950s was described by one national reporter as 'an institution, a soccer *alma mater* whose sons have gone to practically every senior club in the country – and to many an English club'.[57] These included post-war football migrants Dr Kevin O'Flanagan, Robin Lawler, Tommy Godwin, Liam Whelan and Joe Haverty. By 1956 the club was said to have eleven teams, including seven schoolboy selections, one minor team, two junior sides and a Leinster Senior League eleven. They acquired their Whitehall ground in 1935 and in 1954 completed the building of a £12,000 pavilion, and were also able to spend £600 on a floodlit training ground around that time.[58] As a 'strictly amateur club', they were said to depend on 'raffles, etc. and on their annual exhibition match' for funds.[59] By the end of the 1950s they were being described in the national press as 'a progressive soccer nursery that has produced more Irish football "greats" than any other club in the country' and were able to attract visits from German, Manchester United and Arsenal youth teams.[60]

Paddy Mulligan, who came through the Dublin club's underage system in the 1960s, having scored four goals and made two in a trial game there, felt that 'they just couldn't do enough for you. They educated you both on and off the pitch – in a football sense and how to behave yourself, look after yourself off the pitch'.[61] Damien Richardson remembered the club having two teams in the FAI Youth Cup final at one point during his time there, such was their footballing strength.[62] In 1971 they organised a mini-league for six- to eleven-year-olds as there were no competitions for this age group in the Dublin Schoolboys League, and thirty-four teams were involved in its initial year.[63] Other Dublin clubs also gained a reputation for producing promising players, with 'the famous Johnville soccer nursery' noted in 1953 for the development of Liam Munroe, while by 1968, Sallynoggin club St Joseph's was said to be 'a thriving soccer nursery', with the club in their tenth year of existence, having been founded by a priest, Fr McCabe.[64] In 1970, Cherry Orchard, a

Ballyfermot-based club which had been established in 1957, entered schoolboy football for the first time.[65] This is not to say that other prominent schoolboy clubs did not develop in Ireland's other cities, with David Toms noting St Joseph's FC, founded in 1924, as 'one of the most significant cradles of young footballing talent in Waterford city until the emergence of Villa FC in 1953'.[66] Alfie Hale was a product of the St Joseph's club, and, when interviewed, recalled being invited to join by Paddy Toms along with his good friend Greg Clooney as a ten-year-old in 1949.[67]

As Paul Rowan wrote in 2013, Dublin-based clubs have been guilty of poaching the best young schoolboy players and this has affected the development of clubs in external leagues, such as in Kildare and in the midlands.[68] In addition, aspiring players have travelled long distances to play for Dublin clubs on a weekly basis, such as Cork-born Alan Smith and Diarmuid O'Carroll of Kerry.[69] This recruitment has led to tension between the FAI and the Schoolboys Football Association of Ireland (SFAI) over player movement. As John Fallon has noted, the FAI passed a rule in 2013 which permitted players aged sixteen and under 'to sign for clubs based within 80km of their usual place of residence', despite the SFAI being eager to implement their own 50km rule.[70]

This 'poaching' is not a new phenomenon, with the *Irish Examiner* reporting in 1937 that city clubs in Cork were approaching talented minors at more rural clubs 'with the view of promoting them to higher ranks'.[71] In 1960, the Waterford and District Schoolboys' Association proposed to bring in a rule that 'would bind all schoolboys up to the age of sixteen to a particular club regardless of their own wishes', although it is unclear how strictly this was implemented.[72] Some Dublin-born players have also realised the value of moving to stronger schoolboy clubs in the city to get noticed, as illustrated in the case of Richie Sadlier, who moved from Belvedere to Millwall in 1996:

> I was playing for Leicester Celtic and the Belvedere manager approached me and asked me would I sign. I was probably only fifteen at this stage. I kind of knew then that if you wanted to go to England, which I did, you needed to play for a club that

> scouts watched. And Leicester Celtic were never going to be in the latter stages of the FAI [Youth] Cup, they were never going to win a league, so I needed to go to a club that would be in that category and Belvo was one of them so I signed for Belvedere in the start of the under 16 season. So I was only there for under 16s and 17s.[73]

Similarly, fellow Dublin-born player, Barry Prenderville, left his local club Hillcrest to sign for Cherry Orchard as an under fourteen player earlier in that decade.[74] This favouring of leading Dublin clubs by young players strengthens the idea that Dublin is considered the best location for Irish schoolboys wishing to migrate to English clubs, despite the recent transfers of Irish internationals and regionally born players – such as Kevin Doyle, Shane Long, Seamus Coleman and Noel Hunt (via Scotland) – without serving scholar terms in England or Scotland.[75] As well as being home to the Republic of Ireland's top schoolboy clubs and having a higher density of soccer clubs than many regional counties, Dublin is also where the strongest League of Ireland clubs have been based, with seven of the nineteen clubs that have won this championship located there.[76]

The presence of a professional football club in a regional county, however, does not necessarily mean that rates of player production will be that much higher there than in counties where there are no such clubs. While rates of production in Louth (4.6 per cent) have been boosted by its east coast location, the presence of two professional clubs (Dundalk and Drogheda), and the county's close proximity to Dublin, other counties with professional clubs such as Donegal (Finn Harps), Sligo (Sligo Rovers), Longford (Longford United) and Westmeath (Athlone Town) could hardly be said to be high producers of players who break into English league football. This further illustrates the strength of Dublin soccer, with its concentration of League of Ireland clubs. Regional Irish professional clubs have struggled to create a type of identity similar to the county identity fostered by the GAA in many Irish counties.[77] The role of these clubs within their counties has differed significantly from industrialised parts of England, where Gavin Mellor has illustrated how they were significant in fostering local and regional identities in Lancashire in the post-war period, while the work of Alan Metcalfe on east Northumberland has shown how the presence of Newcastle United helped strengthen the identity of miners in this area in the early twentieth century.[78]

INITIATION INTO THE GAME

While, as will be seen later, the availability of soccer clubs for young players varied from area to area in both the Republic and Northern Ireland, the presence of nearby professional clubs was a help to a number of players in initially gaining interest in the game in some of Ireland's cities. While televised English matches may have led to increased interest in soccer in rural Ireland, domestic professional football in the Republic of Ireland was hindered by live coverage of English soccer on television in the latter decades of the twentieth century. This was particularly the case when matches were staged on Sunday afternoons, with a decline of 60 per cent in League of Ireland attendances over four years noted in 1973.[79] Although the status of domestic football in Ireland has suffered since the 1970s, some players' earliest memories of soccer came through supporting League of Ireland and Irish League clubs and informal playing networks, while street football was also an important part of growing up. An early part of childhood initiation into the game and the formation of positive memories associated with it involved a trip to a local match. When interviewed, former Irish international Damien Richardson spoke of his childhood love for the game growing up in Dublin in the 1950s, and how it stayed with him throughout his professional career:

> I was very lucky, when I was seven years of age, I saw my first game with Shamrock Rovers in Milltown … I remember being lifted over the turnstile by my brother … we made our way through the throng on the terrace and down to the front where the kids stood by the wall, and a whole new life opened up in front of my eyes. It was colour – Shamrock Rovers were playing Drumcondra, I'll never forget it – it's in my mind still vividly, the green and

> white of Shamrock Rovers, the gold and blue of Drumcondra, the pristine, brilliant green pitch … it was early season, about September, it was a Shield game … and the excitement of the crowd, and that took me into a different world. It was almost like a new birth to me … it opened [up] something.[80]

The presence of a local club can certainly be said to have a strong influence on the childhood memories of a number of players and in strengthening their desire to emulate their childhood heroes. Paddy Mulligan, who shared his childhood between Dublin and Tuam, recalled attending the 'magnificent' 1956 FAI Cup final between Shamrock Rovers and Cork Athletic as an eleven-year-old along with 35,000 other supporters and being 'just overwhelmed by the whole thing'.[81]

The availability of a strong club nearby to watch has also impacted on players in Northern Ireland. Belfast-born Billy Humphries, who joined Leeds United in 1958 and later played for Coventry City and Swansea City as well as Northern Ireland, 'grew up in the shadow of Windsor Park'. Although a Linfield supporter, he stated that there was 'a triangle of clubs in the local area … Linfield, Distillery and Belfast Celtic, and you could have found me at any of those grounds at any time'.[82] Similarly, Brendan Bradley felt that, growing up in the 1960s in Derry City, 'all the Derry City team then were like football heroes to me'.[83] Other players benefited from exposure to professional footballers, with Dublin-born Mick Meagan, who attended school opposite Shamrock Rovers' Milltown, joking that 'during the war years, they had a few full-time players, and we spent more time watching Rovers train than we did at school, so that would have been the main influence [in wanting to play soccer]'.[84] The visit of English teams to Dublin during the summer months to play exhibition and benefit matches was also a help, and Meagan recalled watching England legends such as Sir Stanley Matthews, Sir Tom Finney, Tommy Lawton and Nat Lofthouse at Dalymount Park, and thinking, 'God, I'd love to be part of that'.[85] Much later, former Southampton, Doncaster Rovers, Oldham Athletic and Northern Ireland goalkeeper, Alan Blayney was, as a teenager in the 1990s, able to visit the nearby

Crusaders' training sessions to watch his Scottish goalkeeping hero Kevin McKeown train, which left him 'mesmerised'.[86]

Despite this, being able to attend a nearby professional football club's ground was, of course, not sufficient to help a young player develop the skills of the game. Meagan also states that 'the big lads on the road' who 'were only about two or three years older' than himself and his childhood friends were also a big influence in that they brought them to watch Shamrock Rovers train and passed on football information to the younger boys.[87]

Growing up in a neutral Free State Ireland during the Emergency was obviously a lot less severe than in countries where war was raging, but as Diarmaid Ferriter has stated, with the decline in the availability of coal, 'the production of turf was essential to keep Ireland self-sufficient in fuel'.[88] By the early 1940s over 26,000 people were engaged in work on 803 bogs, 'many of them having been diverted from local-authority road and construction employment' and 'it invoked a sense of camaraderie and a spirit of co-operation'.[89] This work had some benefits for young footballers, as Meagan explains:

> Well it was a funny thing, in those days, during the war years with the fuel crisis – there was no coal, so it was all turf fires. Now the council had lads up in the mountains, the 'burbs, cutting turf, and we'd go up during the holidays, and we'd be sort of spreading out the turf, footing it, up in the mountains to dry. And you got a pound a week for that, so the minute you got your pound, there was a shop in Camden Street that had boots, all hanging up outside, nineteen shillings and eleven pence. So once you got your pound, you were into Camden Street, bought yourself a pair of boots, and that was the finish of your work. Once you got your boots. That was all during the war years and as I say, they were hard days, but they were great days. The fun factor was tremendous.[90]

Other players, such as former Republic of Ireland international Alfie Hale and former Northern Ireland captain John McClelland, also felt that playing with older boys as children was helpful to their football development, while Limerick-born Johnny Gavin began to play soccer as a twelve-year-old in an under 16 team.[91] Paddy Mulligan felt that his participation in a Dublin street league organised by a local man was an important part of his progress, as playing against older boys toughened him up.[92] Family involvement could also be a help in getting a young player interested in football. David Miskelly, who grew up in Comber, County Down, in the 1980s, first became interested in the game through his uncle, who played at an amateur level.[93] Finglas native, Dean Kelly, got involved through his older brother Jay, who was managing Tolka Rovers in the late 1990s.[94]

A number of players interviewed for this study have stated that street football was crucial to their development, and conditions in cities meant that street football was more prominent and this undoubtedly helped players' development. Paddy Mulligan has remarked that 'from the very moment I could understand football, whatever it was – three, four or five years of age – I just wanted to have a ball with me at all times'.[95] Mick Meagan's skills were developed in the 1940s playing a game known locally as 'combo' with older players, where under informal rules, players were prohibited from letting the ball touch the ground.[96] Damien Richardson has noted the impact of street football in his local area in Dublin on his early development in the 1950s as he played 'day in, day out, mostly all day long' and felt that 'it was great to grow up in the inner city like that'.[97] In particular, Billy Humphries noted that the streets were where he learned his 'technique and control of the ball' and felt that 'without actually being coached I was actually coaching myself'.[98] Street football was, however, more commonly associated with cities. While there is evidence to suggest that this informal way of playing 'gradually gave way to matches on waste ground or public parks' in the inter-war period in England, it appears to have survived slightly longer in Ireland.[99]

NORTHERN IRELAND-BORN PLAYERS' BIRTHPLACES BY COUNTY

Of the 417 players born in Northern Ireland who migrated between 1945 and 2010, 197 players (47.24 per cent) were born in Belfast while

Table 1.5 Birthplaces of players who migrated from Northern Ireland to England, 1945–2010.

Northern Ireland Players by County	Number	Percentage
Antrim	254	60.9%
Derry	65	15.58%
Down	47	11.27%
Armagh	35	8.39%
Tyrone	13	3.11%
Fermanagh	3	0.71%
Total	**417**	**100%**

Source: As Table 1.2.

forty-seven (11.27 per cent) were born in Derry City, again illustrating the advantages of growing up in a large urbanised area for those aspiring to become professional footballers. A number of players have linked this to environmental conditions within these cities which may have helped their development as teenage footballers. Seamus Heath, formerly of Luton Town, Lincoln City, Wrexham and Tranmere Rovers, has stated that growing up in Belfast in the 1970s gave him a toughness which helped him in his later playing career, and as a youth player facing regional selections from country areas he felt that Belfast teams had a certain hardness which 'country' teams lacked.[100]

Brendan Bradley stated that soccer was generally the most popular game in his native Derry city, with the county's Gaelic football selection mainly drawing their support from areas outside the city for its home matches.[101] In 1973, former Derry City player Dougie Wood, a Scot, was of the opinion that 'if you want to get a footballer, Derry is the place to go'. He also claimed that it was clubs such as 'Oxford United, St Eugene's Boys' Club, St Mary's and many others who field ten or twelve teams for lads from ten to seventeen every week that makes Derry such a fabulous supply line of footballers'.[102] The first Derry Football Association had been founded in 1886 and, as Desmond Murphy has noted, encouraged by the clergy of the Catholic Church, the game had become the most popular sport there by the middle of the 1890s, while the GAA struggled to become established within the city at this time.[103]

While overall, as shown in Table 1.5, a total of 254 footballers (60.9 per cent) were born in Belfast and County Antrim and sixty-five players (15.58 per cent) were born inside the city and county of Derry, other western counties in Ulster have produced fewer players, with only thirteen players born in County Tyrone (3.11 per cent) and three born in Fermanagh (0.71 per cent). This highlights the footballing benefits of growing up in east Ulster for aspiring Northern Ireland footballers. It again contrasts with more general Irish migration after 1921, with Delaney noting that 'in Northern Ireland, many emigrants came from rural areas of Armagh, Fermanagh and Tyrone, although all counties experienced out-migration, in part to other areas' within the country.[104] He has also stated that 'the depopulation of rural areas that had characterised the late nineteenth century was from 1921 onwards more or less confined to remote rural districts', although between 1926 and 1971, counties Fermanagh and Tyrone both underwent 'significant population decline'.[105]

Fermanagh's three players who went on to play in the English football leagues in the 1945–2010 period earned professional contracts over a period of forty-four years, with Pat Corr turning professional at Burnley in 1951 and Roy Carroll successfully completing his trainee period and signing for Hull City in 1995. This was followed by Kyle Lafferty who joined Burnley in 2005, and all three players were born in the county's principal town, Enniskillen. Similarly, Tyrone's first football migrant to play English league football in the 1945–2010 period did not break through at this level until 1962, when Cookstown-born Bert McGonigal appeared for Brighton & Hove Albion in the English Third Division. The 1996–2005 period saw the number of Tyrone-born players making their debuts in English league football peak at just five, while previously there had also been sporadic breakthroughs by Billy Johnston (1966), Allan Hunter (1967), Patrick Sharkey (1973), Noel Ward (1976), Stephen Devine (1982) and Rodney McAree (1991). In particular, Sharkey's transfer to Ipswich Town from Portadown in 1973 came only after much groundwork was done by Omagh man Eamon McGale in attempting to get the player noticed, while the work of Portadown coach Gibby MacKenzie, said to be 'the best manager in the Irish game to take a young player under his wing' at that time, was also fundamental to the move.[106]

As will be discussed in more detail later, scouting networks have been stronger along the east coast of Ireland, although competition from rugby union and Gaelic football, to some degree, must again be considered. Gaelic football has not just been more prominent in some schools, but throughout certain areas. In particular, a number of players interviewed felt that the game was more prominent than soccer in Fermanagh and Tyrone.[107] While Neal Garnham has identified former Irish international goalkeeper Matt 'Gunner' Reilly as having had some experience of Gaelic football while growing up in Dublin in the late nineteenth century, it is doubtful that he achieved the same level of competence in both codes as Derry-born Gerry McElhinney, who won an All-Star for his Gaelic football performances in 1975 before moving to play for Bolton Wanderers in 1980.[108] Current Irish League goalkeeper David Miskelly, who had a spell with Oldham Athletic before returning home with a career-threatening injury to play in the Irish League, felt that 'a lot of good football players in our league can also play Gaelic' and switching between codes is relatively easy for skilled players, although serious commitment to both is difficult.[109] A recent example of a dual player is Eoin Bradley, who has appeared for a number of Irish League clubs and Derry Gaelic football team.[110]

Forty-seven players, 11.27 per cent of the overall 1945–2010 total, were born in County Down while thirty-five Armagh-born players or 8.39 per cent experienced English league football in the period covered here. In addition, Seamus Heath stated that with regard to the geographical distribution of player production:

> In our day, a lot of the main programmes happened around the big cities. So unless somebody's proactive out in the sticks, and a prime example in Northern Ireland is Fermanagh – it's such an untapped [county] and there's children there I know for a fact are missing out, they just are not getting the opportunity and it could be to do [with distance from Belfast] – in my era [the 1970s], they struggled because the drive to Belfast would have been a three-day camel ride.[111]

Fermanagh and Tyrone remained on the periphery of more centralised developments in soccer in the east of the province for much of the twentieth century. In 1955, the Fermanagh and Western FA wrote to the IFA Youth International Committee asking for the following year's fixture versus England to be held in Enniskillen, as they felt it would boost the game there. The request was refused by the committee, with the financial considerations of hosting the match outside Belfast seemingly a key factor in the decision.[112] The IFA did, however, give a grant of £100 to the Fermanagh and Western FA three years later to help develop the game after the regional body stated that 'they had been working at a loss during the past number of seasons'.[113] Difficulties remained, however, and in 1963 an IFA sub-committee met with the league's council to discuss the state of soccer in the area after complaints from one ex-council member that competitions were not being run properly and 'youth football in the area was not being encouraged'.[114] In the mid-1970s a number of underage competitions in the area were postponed, seemingly reflecting organisational difficulties at adult level in the Fermanagh and Western League, which included clubs from Tyrone as well and had a backlog of eighty-six league games in 1973, with both poor weather and late arrivals by teams factors in this.[115] By the 1980s problems remained, with the Fermanagh and Western Youth Committee stripping the winners of the Enda Love trophy for under 14s, Barrowfield Albion, of their title in 1986 because they fielded eight overage players in the final. Plans to send a selection to the Milk Cup in Coleraine that year were said to be dependent on raising funds, with £2,000 needed to cover travel and accommodation costs.[116] Later that year, four underage competitions were revived, with the Fermanagh and Western League's committee said to be determined to stamp out the fielding of overage players, although one suspects this was a common problem elsewhere at underage level.[117]

Fermanagh and Tyrone are not the only counties where soccer struggles to compete with Gaelic games. County Down native, Raymond Campbell, who had spells at Nottingham Forest and Hereford United in the late 1980s before becoming a physical education teacher, felt that with the strength of hurling in Portaferry and Gaelic football in Downpatrick, a culture of Gaelic games meant that there was not much soccer being played there. In relation to the GAA's prominence in Downpatrick, he felt that 'they're brought up with that and the parents have played it so their sons and daughters are expected to play it as well … if there hadn't been Gaelic football there would have been a hell of a lot more soccer players come out of this town.'[118] Seamus Heath, who is now an IFA Development Officer, has also stated that a lack of soccer teams in 'GAA areas' was still a problem for young players.[119]

Belfast's strength in producing players has been helped by its greater concentration of schools football, leagues and clubs and the opportunities that players in this area have. Campbell felt that in regard to getting noticed, young players would 'probably have to travel into Belfast, as you've got a lot more opportunities, you've got a lot more clubs there and a lot more coaches, it's the centre of the universe for football [in Northern Ireland]. Probably a lot of the academies are based there as well.'[120] Glentoran's Academy was founded in 2008 and caters for players from six to nineteen years of age, while Linfield and Cliftonville also have similar structures in place.[121]

Advancement in soccer at the highest levels of the game in Northern Ireland appears to have favoured those located near the capital. Along with the movement of young players to teams of a higher standard in many areas, there is also some evidence of a wider internal migration to the strongest underage clubs in Northern Ireland.[122] David Miskelly felt that 'it's well known that the highest quality leagues are always in Belfast, really.'[123] A former youth club team mate of his travelled over eighty miles from Tyrone to play with a more successful team than was available locally and was recruited by 'word of mouth'; 'all the best players played in the one league as such … usually it was the Lisburn Youth League and South Belfast League that were the best leagues' as aspiring players 'knew that was where they had to be playing.'[124] As a result of this Lisburn/Belfast concentration, he feels that the best players were produced in these areas, and cites the example of Northern Ireland's Aaron Hughes who was born in Cookstown, County Tyrone but played his youth football with Antrim club Lisburn Youth, a team for whom David Healy,

Jonny Evans, Gareth McAuley, Marc Wilson and Sammy Clingan also starred before migrating to England.[125] Internal migration to Belfast has been a common feature of life in Ulster since the late eighteenth century with the development of the textile industry there.[126] Delaney has noted how 'up to the 1970s internal migration was more common in Northern Ireland' than in the Republic, although it is difficult to establish the exact extent of this internal migration for professional football purposes.[127]

Scouts have traditionally been more interested in players in Belfast than other parts of Northern Ireland. Matthew Taylor has noted that international and inter-league matches were initially seen by top British clubs as a way of spotting talent, while scouts at Linfield and Glentoran matches in the 1920s included those from Aston Villa, Burnley, Liverpool and Everton. In addition, 'the sporting press likewise kept its readers acquainted with the scouting activities of Football League clubs in the Irish Free State, a number of whom had dedicated Dublin-based representatives'.[128] *Sport*'s northern football correspondent noted with glee in 1921 that one Cliftonville player was being watched by Swansea Town, Preston North End and Dundee having been brought to attention through his reporting.[129] Inter-league matches against the Scottish league can be traced back to 1893 while the following year, the first fixture between Irish and English league selections took place.[130] *Football Sports Weekly* noted how four Irish players had received offers 'running into four figures' from 'representatives of big cross-channel clubs' following the Irish and Welsh leagues' fixture at Swansea in November 1925.[131] In addition, by 1921 – players at lesser-known clubs in the Belfast area – such as Dunmurry and Forth River – were attracting the attention of scouts from Everton, Woolwich Arsenal and Bradford City.[132]

Interest in players in more regional areas was slower to spread. Raymond Campbell felt that, growing up in the 1980s, he would not have been spotted only for doing well in a tournament in Mallusk in the Greater Belfast area:

> We played a lot of our football in Downpatrick and I mean there wasn't too many scouts that came to this town to watch football

> matches and when they did come down, I mean the whole town knew about it, so it must have been a big thing for them scouts to come down and watch our games … They didn't really venture too far out of the Greater Belfast area, when I was growing up anyway.[133]

Similarly, Saintfield-native Michael Carvill, who had spells at Charlton Athletic and Wrexham in the opening decade of the twenty-first century, felt that it was difficult for rural players to get spotted by scouts:

> I think if we didn't have that reach of the Belfast League – 'cause that's where all the scouts went – every scout was watching the Lisburn League, or any matches in around Belfast, the main city, if you're anywhere outside it, you were lucky you got on the county team. The counties went into the county draw and you played against each other … but I think in terms of finding the best players, it's always going to be very difficult, because Belfast is the main place, or Derry.[134]

He also admitted that distance and transport to clubs was probably a problem for young players in more outlying counties.[135] John McClelland also felt that scouts were more likely to stick to areas with a higher density of quality players rather than attend matches in more regional areas where there was less talent on show.[136] He also noted factors such as clubs' networks and the cost-effectiveness of sending scouts to look for players in more rural areas, and the actual cost of English clubs recruiting Irish-born players when local talent may be more accessible.[137] According to the Northern Ireland football historian, John Duffy, clubs such as Linfield and Portadown have also looked to recruit schoolboy footballers from Fermanagh and Tyrone to their youth teams, while smaller clubs would have struggled to pay these players' travel allowances and this would also have affected their chances of attracting them.[138]

Some smaller clubs have acted as nursery clubs for Irish League clubs, with Pitt Street Mission from Belfast acting as a feeder club for Glentoran, according to Billy Humphries, who played for these

Michael Carvill celebrating a goal for Linfield against Glasgow Rangers at Windsor Park in a pre-season friendly in 2011. Links between these clubs date back to the late Victorian era. Picture: © Inpho

clubs in the early 1950s.[139] As early as 1899, Linfield and Glentoran were said to be subsidising junior clubs in line with what a number of English and Scottish clubs were already doing in Britain.[140] In addition, transnational links between some Northern Irish clubs and those across the Irish Sea have been strong. The religious and cultural links between Glasgow Rangers and Linfield, as shown in the latter's Academy teams' trip to Murray Park, the Scottish club's training ground, in July 2015, have fostered the 'special relationship between the two clubs'.[141] By the early 1900s, Rangers had visited both Linfield and Glentoran for friendly matches.[142] The *Belfast Telegraph* noted how Sunderland had offered 'unbounded hospitality and generosity' to two Cliftonville officials who visited for a match in 1902, illustrating how relations between clubs could be developed.[143]

THE TROUBLES

The work of Lanfranchi and Taylor has shown how economic causes have greatly outweighed political reasons in terms of football migration, despite noting that 'the Spanish Civil War [1936–39] and the Budapest uprising of 1956 precipitated the dispersal of the best Spanish and Hungarian players of the day'.[144] As will be shown in Chapter 3, the tense Irish political situation did influence player movement from clubs in Belfast in the early 1920s. Given the relative financial weakness of the Irish League in economic terms in comparison with English professional football, it would be incorrect to view those who moved from Northern Ireland in that decade or during the Troubles of 1968 to 1998 as political refugees. However, local conditions for the development of young players were certainly not ideal, with over 3,000 people killed in the Troubles as a result of the violent conflict between the provisional Irish Republican Army, the British security forces and loyalist paramilitaries, with the majority of deaths occurring in Belfast.[145] While debates over the identity of clubs and players in Northern Ireland have received much attention over the past two decades, less has been written on the impact of this conflict on player movement within Northern Ireland itself and to England.[146] In the summer of 1972, the IFA decided that Northern

Ireland teams would take no part in European club competition. The Senior Clubs' Committee were of the opinion that they could not risk bringing teams there because of the Troubles, with the poor attendance at Distillery's European Cup Winners' Cup match against Barcelona the previous season noted.[147] As Mike Cronin has shown, Derry City's withdrawal from the Irish League in October of that year was illustrative of the difficulties in sustaining a football club's identity in a conflict zone.[148] In addition, the 1981 British Home Championship was not completed as England and Wales refused to travel to Belfast to play, while in the period from 1972 until May 1975 Northern Ireland played no home matches in this competition.[149]

Although Thomas Bartlett has noted that the annual death toll was at its peak in the mid-1970s, Ferriter has stated that there were 2,100 people in jail by the end of 1977 and most inmates came from republican and loyalist ghettos.[150] Most players interviewed for this study felt that the Troubles did not have a major impact on player production, although Seamus Heath has noted that 'if there hadn't have been the Troubles, there would have been more opportunities and you would've ventured further afield together'.[151] It is difficult, therefore, to quantify how many aspiring players may have missed out in their early development because of the social dislocation at the time. Heath felt that he had consciously decided to stay away from anything that would have affected his football:

> The Troubles were on my doorstep. Most of my friends that I grew up with are now either in jail or dead. I was fortunate – I know people say, 'oh, you were lucky, you got away' [but] I knew what I wanted to do. I didn't get caught up with my other close friends at that seventeen age – [they] made their choices.[152]

John McClelland recalled having to get a team-run minibus for training from Belfast City Hall to Portadown on a regular basis in the early 1970s as transport was disrupted with public buses being burned out, but he didn't think this impeded his development as a player.[153] Although he later experienced problems playing for his country at senior level (which led to his early retirement from international football), Neil Lennon's early development was not affected by the conflict. The former Manchester City, Crewe Alexandra, Leicester City and Celtic player stated in his book that he was 'welcomed with open arms' and 'nary a cross word was spoken about the religious and political problems' in Northern Ireland when he joined Hillsborough, a schoolboy club with a strong Protestant tradition, from Lurgan Celtic along with fellow Catholic, Gerry Taggart.[154] Despite the repercussions for Derry City FC noted above, the movement of players within the city was similarly not affected, according to Brendan Bradley:

> I can't say that there was any great upheaval, you know. With Finn Harps, we would travel over the border all the time and there were only a few times that it would sort of get scary, you know? Maybe if you were crossing over and maybe a patrol of UDR would step out in front of you, you would say to yourself, you know, 'is this really a UDR patrol ... or ones dressed up', you know. That's what happened to the Miami Showband [in 1975] ... we just battered on, and made the most of it, [you] played your football.[155]

Like the League of Ireland with its heavy concentration of clubs around Dublin, the strength of the Irish League lies in and around its capital city, with its most successful clubs located in the north-east of Ireland. Glentoran (6.71 per cent), Linfield (6.23 per cent) and Coleraine (5.27 per cent) were found to have supplied the most players transferred to England in the post-war period until 2010. Of the twelve clubs that have won the championship, the majority have been from Belfast, with teams from Lurgan, Portadown and Newtownards also enjoying success and only two clubs from outside this region – Coleraine and Derry City – having won titles.[156] Although former junior clubs such as Dungannon Swifts (Tyrone) and Ballinamallard United (Fermanagh) now appear in the Danske Bank Premier League, these clubs have only recently been affiliated to this competition.[157] Similarly, teams from east Ulster have been dominant in the Harry Cavan Youth Cup, Northern Ireland's leading competition for youth teams.[158]

THE DEVELOPMENT OF REGIONAL STRUCTURES FOR SOCCER IN THE REPUBLIC OF IRELAND

While opportunities for players in Northern Ireland to gain the attention of scouts have been shown to still favour Belfast and Derry clubs rather than those based more rurally, developments of league structures at schoolboy and adult level throughout the Republic of Ireland have increased young players' chances to get noticed, although progress has been slow and Dublin-based players still have greater opportunities to shine. In 1970, Arsenal scout Gordon Clark estimated that he had already watched 'close on 1,000 schoolboy games' and assessed 'over 22,000 would-be stars'. He felt that only around six of these would 'make the grade' but he also stated that 'only three would become First Division players'.[159] Clark would probably have raised the odds if he had come to rural Ireland to look at young players, although the club did have a strong reputation for fielding Irish players in the late 1970s, with Irish internationals Liam Brady, Frank Stapleton, David O'Leary, Sammy Nelson, Pat Rice and Pat Jennings featuring heavily in their 1979 FA Cup winning team, managed by former Northern Ireland international, Terry Neill. The inclusion of John Devine took the figure to seven Irish squad players for the Cup final against West Ham the following year.[160] But these players were, with the exception of Jennings, brought-up in Dublin or Belfast. The recruitment of players from regional Irish counties has been hampered by a failure of scouts to branch out into these areas, although this improved over the past number of decades as soccer's popularity grew with the success of the Republic of Ireland's national team in the late twentieth century.

British clubs have also been slow to pay attention to players in other more rural counties in the Republic of Ireland, with Roscommon apparently not being visited by scouts until 1995, although it had not produced any players in the 1945–2010 period.[161] Since 1993, the Gaelic football stronghold of Kerry, traditionally known as the bedrock of Gaelic football with a record number of All-Ireland championship wins in this code, has produced six players who migrated and played in the English football leagues, which would suggest a widening in scouting networks and an improvement in local structures for association football.[162] *Irish Independent* journalist, Seán Ryan, was able to state early in 1971 that 'English soccer is getting a grip on rural areas which have for long been considered strongholds of Gaelic games'.[163]

Despite the common perception that the 1966 World Cup was the turning point in soccer's popularity in the Irish countryside, there is some evidence that this development was underway in some areas before that, with one provincial newspaper reporter stating in December 1965 after a Cavan selection had entered the FAI Youth Challenge Cup for the first time, that 'the advent of televised soccer has undoubtedly glamorised soccer for the youth and one can only be amazed at the depth to which it has penetrated into rural areas. It has been given quite a fillip in parts of the country where it had never been known before.'[164] The writer also felt that the GAA in Cavan town was to blame for soccer's growth there at that time as they had not provided enough facilities for local youths to play 'the native games', and in particular he noted how Breffni Park was being kept 'under lock and key' while Gaelic football there was 'near its lowest ever ebb'.[165] Other reporters expressed concern that Gaelic football was in decline in the latter part of the decade, with one writer of the opinion in 1967 that a crowd of just 28,370, the lowest attendance at an All-Ireland Gaelic football semi-final since the war, was evidence that 'something is radically wrong in the playing or displaying of our national games'.[166] While acknowledging the advent of televised matches, he felt that there was not enough 'skilled, open, attacking football' being displayed and that cynical tactics were also creeping in at minor and colleges level.[167] In comparison, by the opening of the 1966–67 season, Irish viewers in some eastern and border areas could look forward to fifty minutes of 'a top soccer league match' on BBC's *Match of the Day* on Saturday nights while highlights of international fixtures – such as Northern Ireland versus England in October 1966 – could be found on UTV.[168]

Despite Kerry's continued success in Gaelic football's All-Ireland championship, by the early 1970s a change in interest levels in sport was noted to some degree. One local reporter felt that:

> Here in Tralee, the GAA is on the very brink of a precipice. Games have been postponed because of the English Cup Final on T.V. Boys can name the full panel for most English First Division soccer teams, but get bogged down fairly soon even in naming the all-conquering Kerry team. This malaise is not confined to urban districts alone. A rural club, once noted for the high-fielding 'aeroplane-type' footballer it gave to the Kerry team, recently refused to play a visiting team in [Gaelic] football, but was quite willing to take them on in soccer.[169]

While the 'glamour and appeal' of English soccer was said to be a threat, the lack of investment by the GAA in grassroots Gaelic football, and hurling, was said to be a problem.[170] Although an inter-firms competition was in operation in 1971, Kerry did not get its first junior soccer league until 1972, with the removal of the GAA's ban on 'foreign' games the previous year.[171] Apparently Tralee Dynamos, said to have been founded in the late 1950s, 'were keeping the flag flying on their own in the sixties'.[172] Some of Kerry's top Gaelic football players during the 'golden years' from 1975 to 1986 had honed their skills playing soccer, with Paídí Ó Sé playing the game in the schoolyard as a student and Mikey Sheehy – famous among GAA supporters throughout Ireland for his soccer-style goal in the 1978 All-Ireland final when he chipped Dublin goalkeeper Paddy Cullen from a free-kick – participating in The Park FC team which won the 1974–75 Kerry District League and Shield.[173] By May 1975, Kerry had eighteen soccer clubs and 456 registered players.[174]

In general, league structures for soccer in rural Ireland have been slow to gain permanency, although this does not mean that leagues and cups did not exist, with many sporadic junior competitions taking place throughout Ulster in the 1890s, although gaining permanency remained problematic in some counties (such as Donegal and Monaghan) for much of the twentieth century.[175] Initially, soccer in the Irish Free State was organised on a regional rather than county basis. By early 1922 there were approximately 200 clubs affiliated to the FAI with regional associations for Leinster, Belfast and District, Athlone and District and Munster.[176] One reporter felt in 1928 that 'soccer football is taking root in County Mayo, almost every town having a club', but county-based leagues were difficult to establish on a permanent basis.[177] In September of that year the Connacht FA was founded, with clubs in Donegal, Sligo, Roscommon, Galway, Mayo, Longford and Westmeath affiliating.[178] Despite this development, by 1948 Connacht was still said to be 'the "baby province" as far as soccer is concerned'.[179]

Although a league was founded in Mayo in 1953, it was slow to develop, while Donegal and Roscommon did not get their first sustained structures for junior soccer until 1971, perhaps illustrating an increase in organisational freedom and movement coming with the removal of 'the Ban' that year.[180] In a number of areas, including Clones – said to be 'the home of soccer' in County Monaghan – by 1935, localised leagues and cups were in place with the Duncan Cup, an inter-town competition, attracting entries from teams in Cavan, Fermanagh, Tyrone and Monaghan in 1958, illustrating how the border between north and south was at times ignored at a local level of competition.[181] County and district leagues were operational in Cavan by September 1966 and in Longford by 1973, but some more eastern counties were slower to develop their own leagues, with the Meath and District League not founded until 1980, highlighting their sporadic growth throughout Ireland.[182] This can be partly explained by Meath clubs' involvement in Leinster FA-run leagues.[183] Not every county managed to organise their own league and clubs continued to play in leagues outside their own counties, particularly in Kildare.[184] The Kildare and District Football League was not founded until the summer of 1994 when the USA World Cup saw interest in soccer in Ireland grow further as the Republic of Ireland defeated Italy, with league founder Michael Casey then noting that 'Gaelic football is the primary game [in Kildare] and soccer is currently the underdog'.[185] While progress has been made in Roscommon and Kildare in terms of league infrastructure, there are only six soccer clubs in Leitrim and no soccer league in this county, with teams still involved in external leagues.[186] In addition, population rates in this county have consistently been among the lowest in Ireland in the period covered here.[187]

SCHOOLBOY LEAGUES

Club structures for schoolboys were similarly slow to spread around the Republic of Ireland. Although the Schoolboys Football Association of Ireland was founded in 1943, some regional developments did not get underway until much later, with the Clare Schoolboys and Girls Soccer League not formed until 1985, the Meath and District schoolboy section first organised in 1986, the South Donegal Schoolboys League founded in 1988 and the Midlands Schoolboys/Girls League formed only in 1996.[188] This differed significantly from more urban areas with a schoolboys' league being initiated in Limerick city by 1933, minor and juvenile leagues in existence in Galway city by 1935, while an under 15 league competition was in operation in Waterford city by the late 1940s.[189]

Understandably, Dublin was the early centre of schoolboy football in the Republic of Ireland prior to the war. As Mick Meagan notes: 'It was all Dublin in those days, now there were schoolboy teams around the country – Waterford, Cork and these places – but Dublin was the main place.'[190] In Dublin, an under 14 schoolboys league was organised by the Leinster Junior FA in 1933, while by 1937 the Dublin Schoolboys Cup competition attracted sixteen teams in the first-round draw.[191] By 1957 there were 123 schoolboys clubs in Dublin out of a nationwide total of approximately 200.[192] Similarly, minor and schoolboy competitions were also operational in Cork by 1937, while the Cork Schoolboys League was inaugurated in 1948.[193] A minor league was also established along with a junior one in Kilkenny city in 1948.[194] Outside these cities, there were sporadic attempts to run leagues and cups in some urban areas. A league for minors was established in Mullingar, County Westmeath, by 1946 and in Carrickmacross, County Monaghan, an under 14 street league was operational in 1959, while a league for juveniles was in place in Clones in 1963, but these respective competitions do not appear to have spread throughout these counties until much later.[195] A league for juveniles had been established in Longford town by the summer of 1948.[196] Despite this progress, one reporter lamented the weak state of junior soccer in the west and north-west of Ireland in 1951, claiming that the game had reached 'an alarmingly low standard' in Sligo, with the lack of suitable competitions for boys who had completed their school years said to be the problem. It was felt that 'after leaving school at fifteen or sixteen boys are too young and light to join any of the cup teams, and for two or three years have to be content with the role of spectator until they mature'.[197]

The Kennedy Cup, traditionally the Republic's top under 14 soccer competition, was not held until 1976 and has been won by schoolboy selections representing Dublin and its districts, Cork, Limerick and Waterford only, again illustrating the strength of soccer in these areas.[198] After a Donegal selection was easily defeated by Dublin in 1976 in the quarter final of the O'Kennedy Cup, a competition for older boys, one reporter felt that the Donegal League 'must realise it is pointless for Donegal teams to take on city teams at this level. Invariably the opposition is always bigger, stronger and much more mature.'[199] Despite efforts to organise competitions, Mick Meagan felt that it would have been difficult for anyone trying to establish soccer leagues in rural Ireland in the 1940s and 1950s as the support would not have been there and it would not have been welcome generally within Irish society at the time as 'you'd step in on the GAA's territory' while soccer was consistently portrayed as a 'foreign game', particularly in the provincial press.[200]

There is strong evidence from throughout the twentieth century to back up the view that soccer was not wanted in some areas. In 1929, the pavilion at the Sligo Agricultural Society's Showgrounds was said to have been deliberately damaged with some indication given in the press that this was done as a result of soccer being played there.[201] In Donegal, the playing of soccer was continuously attacked in the local press in the opening decades of the twentieth century.[202] In turn, some junior soccer clubs, such as the West Donegal Gweedore Celtic club in 1976 and 1977, had their property vandalised, such was the opposition to the playing of soccer from some sections of society.[203] Social pressure was also exerted to prevent the development of soccer grounds, with the award of £150 to Mayo club Westport FC by the local urban district council for work to be undertaken on a playing field they were developing bringing protest

One of the few players from a peripheral Irish county who managed to break into English league football in the late twentieth century, **Michael McHugh** was spotted playing in the Ulster Senior League for Swilly Rovers. Picture: *Donegal News*

from the local GAA club in the winter of 1948.[204] The grant was later withdrawn by the Department of Local Government who ruled that 'the park was not dedicated to the public and the site did not belong to the Council'.[205]

Like those in Kerry, Donegal's soccer players struggled to get noticed until the 1990s, despite one provincial reporter noting the player potential there in 1953.[206] Alfie Hale felt that schoolboy players in more peripheral areas would have struggled to gain the attention of scouts while he was growing up.[207] For those playing schoolboy football in the north-west of Ireland in the 1980s there were few scouts attending matches or connected to local clubs, according to Michael McHugh, who migrated from Donegal club Swilly Rovers to join Bradford City in 1989.[208] He recalled that he was spotted while playing in the Ulster Senior League against Culdaff through Derry-based scout Eddie Davis, whose son was managing Culdaff at that time.[209] McHugh also felt that there were many youth players in Donegal who were better than some of those he saw in professional football in England.[210] Other more inland counties have also struggled to produce top-flight players. The first Cavan-born player to feature in the English football leagues during the post-war years, Cillian Sheridan, did not sign professionally with Plymouth Argyle until 2009 (on loan), and he had initially come to Dublin club Belvedere FC for trials.[211] In 2009, there were forty-seven legitimate scouts based in Ireland working for thirty-five clubs outside the FAI's jurisdiction, while by 2013 the number of registered FAI scouts had risen to fifty-two according to their website.[212]

INTERNATIONAL SCHOOLBOY SELECTION

Although IFA-backed schoolboy internationals had been taking place since 1927, from the early 1950s at least, they seem to have been keen to acknowledge the presence of possible youth international players from outside the Belfast area.[213] At an IFA meeting in November 1951, Harry Cavan raised the issue of 'the many promising players in the Co. Down area who did not appear to come under the notice of selectors'. It was subsequently arranged that a trial for those in the Bangor and Newtownards districts would be held.[214] IFA youth team trials were also taking place in Enniskillen by December 1959, with a Fermanagh and Western FA selection taking on a County Antrim FA representative side with 'talent scouts from senior clubs in Belfast' said to be in attendance; as noted, rates of English league football player production from Fermanagh have been low.[215] By the late 1970s, there was still a tendency to stick to players from 'trusted' areas, such as Belfast and to some extent Derry; the Northern Ireland under 18 team that won the 1979 European Schools Championship was made up of players based mainly in Antrim, Armagh and Down, with only one Derry-based player identified. This squad, which contained Norman Whiteside and Alan McDonald, does not appear to have included any players from Tyrone or Fermanagh schools.[216] In a recent publication focusing on the life of Strabane-born footballer, Adrian Doherty, a number of those based in the Derry area expressed the view that Catholic players were overlooked for underage international selection as a result of religious discrimination, but these were refuted by IFA coach Bob Nesbitt in Oliver Kay's book.[217]

Developments to incorporate more peripherally located players into international underage squads appear to also have been slow south of the border. Some players, such as Roy Keane, have previously complained of a Dublin bias in the selection of Republic of Ireland schoolboy squads, although this was not unique to Ireland; Steven Gerrard claimed that international selection for England was difficult at underage level for those not part of the Lilleshall set-up.[218] An FAI Schoolboys team, which faced their IFA counterparts at Larne in March 1947, was made up of Dublin-only players.[219] One reason for this lack of a more regional spread may have been funding problems in organising trials, with the FAI Junior and Minor selection committee stating in 1954 that plans 'to arrange special trials embracing Connacht and Midland players' had been hindered by the costs involved, and it was noted that 'the most promising of them' would be included in a Dublin trial, with selectors also hoping to attend regional FAI Junior Cup matches instead.[220] By the late 1950s, players from Meath, Cork and Waterford clubs were also being selected for the national schoolboys XI.[221] In 1964, it was reported that the FAI selection committee were 'spreading a wider net than usual in an effort to rope in all the talent available', with two national youth team trials being held in Dublin and 'a series of trials held in the provinces'.[222] These were to be followed by matches between regional selections representing Connacht, Waterford and Limerick, with a final trial involving a provincial XI taking on their Dublin counterparts.[223] It is unclear if players from the Ulster counties of Donegal, Cavan and Monaghan were to be involved or similarly those in more peripheral counties such as Kerry. By 1971, the annual fixture between Dublin and Belfast Schoolboys was said to be 'a trial for full internationals', thereby isolating players from outside the Republic's capital.[224] This appears to have been a problem for more rurally based players at various levels.

By 1973, plans had been made for the Republic of Ireland under 15 team to take on non-British opposition for the first time, but selection events for this squad mainly involved players from Dublin, Limerick, Waterford and Cork.[225] By the middle part of this decade inter-provincial trials for youth selections were taking place, with

Donegal players representing Ulster in 1975, while it appears Cavan and Monaghan had no representatives at this point.[226] Later that same year, an Irish youth team, said to be made up 'mostly of Home Farm and Stella Maris players', hammered a Connacht selection by six goals to nil at Terryland Park, illustrating the definite gulf in technique between Dublin players and their regional counterparts in this province. The international team did, however, also include Donegal players McGowan and Kelly, highlighting a breakthrough of sorts for these peripherally based players.[227] One reporter's comments that 'Connacht lost heavily because their teamwork was not good … they had not the ability of their opponents, but also their passing was not good' are also illustrative of a general lack of combination and coaching among the westerners.[228]

Although players such as Declan Boyle and Paddy McDaid were also involved in Irish underage teams by the beginning of the 1990s, involvement of Donegal-born footballers in these teams was subject to slower development than that of Dublin-based players, but was probably helped to some extent by Alex Harkin's role as Irish Schoolboys' Under 18 manager, with four from Donegal in the international squad in 1992.[229] In 1991, John Gorey Curran was elected to the Executive Council of the FAI Youth Council, the first Donegal representative to achieve this. He stated that his 'immediate aim' was 'to push for inter-provincial youth trials to give younger players from this part of the country an opportunity to impress national selectors'.[230] It appears the trial system mentioned earlier was not as consistently implemented as planned. Curran claimed that despite the fact the Letterkenny Rovers' youth team had only been beaten 1-0 by Home Farm in the semi-final of the FAI Youth Cup that year, none of their players had received a national trial, while the Dublin club had six players on the international team.[231]

Michael McHugh has stated that the FAI only became aware of his presence in England as a professional footballer and international team candidate in the early 1990s after Billy Bingham, then Northern Ireland manager, enquired if he was eligible for Northern Ireland.[232] Indeed, one Donegal-born player, Alan Oliver, an apprentice at Peterborough around the same time, elected to join the Northern

Ireland Youth squad in 1992 after he felt he had received no interest from Republic of Ireland selectors, with one reporter claiming that 'they haven't even bothered to turn up to London Road and even have a look at the player'.[233]

Damien Richardson has stated that a lack of experience of consistent quality opposition for those living outside Dublin has probably impeded their development as players, as many provincial schoolboy clubs lack the quality found in such a concentrated area among clubs in the capital.[234] As noted elsewhere, leading Republic of Ireland clubs have also acted as nurseries for English clubs in recent times, while some Dublin-based clubs such as St Kevin's Boys and Home Farm, also host international tournaments.[235] In addition, English schoolboy teams have taken part in friendly matches against Dublin opposition for much longer than regional counties, with the visit in 1946 of a Liverpool team from a local Catholic Schools League said to be 'the first cross-channel schoolboys' representative team to play in Dublin'.[236] A Dublin Schoolboys team had played in Liverpool against a Merseyside Catholic Schools XI in April 1935.[237]

This type of interaction undoubtedly increased chances for Dublin players to get noticed, and by the mid-1950s annual matches against Liverpool selections seemed to have been a fairly well-established part of the FAI international underage scene.[238] This is not to say that more peripherally based teams did not take on English opposition in friendlies in the latter part of the twentieth century, but again their development appears to have been a lot slower. A Birmingham under 14 team travelled to Ireland to play their Westport United counterparts in 1967 and by the early 1970s, teams such as Summerhill College of Sligo were visiting Liverpool, with Paul McGee, who later joined a number of English clubs, scoring five goals in a match versus a local secondary school.[239] By the early 1990s, regional schoolboy selections were travelling abroad to take part in international tournaments with, for example, Donegal under 14s and under 16s travelling annually to the Ian Rush International Soccer Tournament in Aberystwyth in Wales.[240]

As shown elsewhere by this author, the game in Donegal had been popular since the 1880s, with strong links to Derry city and Tyrone in the north-east and seasonal migration to Scotland from west Donegal helping to give the game an early start.[241] Shay Given provides an interesting case study of someone from Donegal who managed to make the breakthrough into the English Premier League, although he was not the first Donegal-born footballer to feature in English football's top flight. Given was brought up in Lifford where he appeared for his local club, Lifford Celtic, in the 1991–92 FAI Junior Cup as a fifteen-year-old.[242] The son of a former goalkeeper and a noted local athlete, he has remarked that he got his athletic spring from his mother.[243] He first attracted the attention of Packie Bonner at the Glasgow Celtic star's goalkeeping course in Letterkenny in 1991 and he was also a pivotal figure in his secondary school team, St Columba's College Stranorlar, as they reached consecutive All-Ireland senior finals in the early 1990s.[244] He also represented Donegal Schoolboys at the Ian Rush International Soccer Tournament and was later capped by the Republic of Ireland at schoolboy level.[245] While clearly an exceptional talent, Given's pathway highlights some environmental factors – particularly his school's enthusiasm for soccer and the presence of a strong local club that competed on a national level – which probably helped his development. Finally, on moving from Ireland to Glasgow Celtic as a teenager in 1992, he initially stayed with relatives in the city. While he still had a hell of a long way to go at that stage – he was released by Celtic but snapped up by Blackburn Rovers in 1994 – Given's schoolboy development offers an interesting case study of someone from a fairly rural part of Ireland who became a massive success in English football.

CONCLUSION

It can clearly be stated that Dublin is the powerhouse of football migration in the Republic of Ireland, with, in Northern Ireland, Belfast supplying the greatest number of players who have migrated to play in the English Premier and Football Leagues. Affiliation with a city-based Irish club has been shown to be a major help to Irish youngsters aspiring to play in England at a professional level, and despite improvements in structures in many rural counties, schoolboy players are still eager to move to Dublin-based clubs. In Northern Ireland, there is certainly some evidence that the movement of regional schoolboy players to more successful clubs in the east of Ulster exists. While this book does not by any means attempt to offer a blueprint for what it takes to make a career in English football, it would appear that a number of environmental factors have been shown to help in players' early development. A number of players interviewed clearly felt that playing in leagues in Dublin or Belfast is fundamental to getting spotted by scouts. The role of other Irish cities has not been as significant, with Cork and Derry providing lesser numbers of those who have played in English league football.

A 2002 study undertaken by Anne Bourke on the recruitment of ninety Irish-born players who had professional contracts in England, has shown that the presence of a local soccer club in Ireland played a more significant part in these players' development than association football at school, as 'many attended schools where soccer was not an option'. However, it must be noted that structures for junior and schoolboy soccer were slow to be developed in many parts of Ireland and her study mainly uses players from the larger urban settlements of Dublin, Cork, Galway and Limerick, and also County Louth (which, as noted above, has two professional clubs), with only eleven players from outside these areas assessed.[246] Chapter 2 examines the sporadic development of coaching in Ireland and the growth of schools' soccer and how this has also impacted on opportunities for aspiring football migrants to learn the skills of the game.

CHAPTER 2

Schools' Soccer and Coaching in Ireland

> The lack of training and coaching has been responsible for more failures than what may appear to the man about town. Without it, no man can hope to succeed. That is one of the reasons why the cross-channel clubs usually hold us in subjection.[1]
>
> Charlie O'Hagan, *Football Sports Weekly*, 26 June 1926

INTRODUCTION

Although Irish professional clubs have used trainers since the late nineteenth century, opportunities for young players to receive coaching at schoolboy level appear to have taken longer to develop.[2] As will be demonstrated, competitive schools soccer was slow to take hold throughout Ireland and its growth was sporadic. Former Manchester United and Manchester City star, Mickey Hamill, once stated that he had learned the game informally in Belfast at his Christian Brothers school, St Mary's of Divis Street, in the late 1890s, before progressing to competitive soccer at the Trades Preparatory School in Harding Street.[3] Despite his early introduction to soccer, some other pre-Second World War players were less complimentary about infrastructures for young players in Ireland. Fellow Irish international Charlie O'Hagan claimed in 1926 that 'the lack of training and coaching has been responsible for more failures than what may appear to the man about town. Without it, no man can hope to succeed. That is one of the reasons why the cross-channel clubs usually hold us in subjection.'[4] Peter Doherty, who managed Northern Ireland at the 1958 World Cup finals in Sweden, stated in

1946 that 'Ireland is not like England where there are coaches for the schools and colleges, the period when a young footballer is made'.[5] As Matthew Taylor has noted, the English Football Association had focused mainly on coaching schoolboys in the 1930s but after 1945 began to extend its courses to managers and professional footballers.[6] However, English attitudes towards coaching courses for managers and coaches were slow to evolve in comparison with those in continental Europe.[7] Developments in Ireland were slower than in England and both the IFA and FAI at times relied on the FA for assistance. Developing structures was not a straightforward process with the level of finance needed, and the difficulties in getting educational authorities on board. This chapter examines attempts to promote soccer in Irish schools and offers a comparison between strategies for developing coaching structures for the game in Northern Ireland and the Republic of Ireland. The difficulties facing soccer organisers in attempting to initiate soccer within respective educational systems are discussed and the role of the Boys' Brigade in assisting young players' development is examined. It will be shown that in Northern Ireland, the Belfast-based IFA's implementation of coaching courses was at a more advanced level in the decades immediately following the Second World War, with the Dublin-based FAI hindered by a lack of facilities and funds for most of the twentieth century. Finally, the state of developmental programmes for young Irish footballers in the early twenty-first century will be discussed.

SCHOOLS' SOCCER IN NORTHERN IRELAND

Mickey Hamill's experience of competitive soccer while at secondary school in the early 1900s appears to have been a localised affair. Along with a scarcity of kit in his youth – he apparently had to play using football boots which were too big for him, wearing extra socks and inserting soles – there was a general lack of schoolboy soccer competitions in Ireland at that time.[8] Despite the IFA's implementation of a schools cup in 1884, four years later the competition had been disbanded. Neal Garnham has stated in his analysis of the early development of the game in Ireland that association football struggled to gain a foothold in many of Ireland's schools and colleges, with rugby particularly popular in those in Ulster.[9] This poor start for soccer in schools was slow to be rectified in many areas in the newly formed Northern Ireland state in the pre-Second World War era. In examining developments within Irish football in the inter-war years, Garnham has also noted that while the IFA did organise a schools' cup and occasionally subsidised and encouraged other competitions, their efforts were somewhat limited in promoting schools' soccer in this period.[10] While proposals for underage leagues to be started in the Belfast area in the mid-1890s were circulated in the local press, with a shield competition, said to be 'one of the first, as well as the finest, of its class, ever offered to juveniles, to whom a rare opportunity is offered', progress appears to have been slow at schools level.[11] Malcolm Brodie has noted the efforts of Cliftonville to organise schools' soccer in the 1912–15 period with a 'successful competition' being run at this time, although he offers little detail on the teams involved.[12] It would appear that the First World War put paid to this attempt. Early developments for schoolboy players within Northern Ireland therefore appear to have been focused mainly in soccer's heartland in the north-east of Ulster with Cliftonville also encouraging visits from cross-Channel schools associations in Sheffield and Birmingham.[13]

Despite this, there were sporadic attempts to play the game in some schools, although a difficulty remains in establishing whether it was soccer or rugby in which they were actually engaged. There is some evidence of how Charlie O'Hagan may have learned to play soccer. Both he and his nephew Billy had played the game (or at least some form of football) at St Columb's College in Derry before later joining English and Scottish clubs.[14] Another player noted as having played schools' football was Bessbrook-born Jimmy Mulligan, who joined Manchester City in 1921 from Belfast Celtic, and was said to have gained some experience of it while at St Patrick's College in Armagh.[15] Billy Crooks, who had spells at Manchester United and New Brighton in the 1920s, apparently started his career at a club called University FC before moving to Glentoran.[16] Belfast-born John McKenna, who played a handful of games for Barrow and New

Brighton in the same decade, had started playing soccer while at St Malachy's College in Belfast.[17] A number of Irish League players were also said to have learned the game at the Mercantile Academy School. Thomas Scott, who joined Scottish club Partick Thistle from Cliftonville in 1898, was a former student there.[18]

By the early 1920s schools' soccer in Northern Ireland was beginning to take on a more competitive structure. *Sport* reported in 1924 that a schools' cup competition, under the auspices of the IFA's Junior Association, was set up with R. S. Holland, who had experience as chairman of the Junior Committee of the IFA, said to be the driving force behind it.[19] Twenty-one schools were said to have entered for the under 14 and under 17 competitions. These mainly appear to have been based in the Belfast area which suggests it generally catered for schools there, although some in more outlying areas such as Portadown also registered.[20] By the middle of the decade, the 'North of Ireland Schools Association' was operating in conjunction with the IFA, who donated two cups while they also supplied a trophy and assisted in the setting up of the North-West FA's Schools Association in 1929.[21] They also agreed to donate a cup to the Regional Education Committee in 1928 for day technical schools, and in 1934 the Mid-Ulster Association were given a cup for their schools' competition.[22] In 1935 the Kilrea Schools FA, based in Derry, also wrote to the IFA requesting a cup but in general, initial district associations were mainly centred in the east of the province.[23] In 1959 a cup was presented by Kesh (Fermanagh) school principal, A.W. McKee, for competition between secondary schools in Fermanagh and Tyrone.[24] By the early 1960s, Tyrone schools were also participating in competitions run by the Derry Schools FA, while the Magee Cup, a competition for schools in Tyrone and Fermanagh, was underway by 1965.[25]

Among the initial schools football associations founded in Northern Ireland were the Belfast SFA in 1924, mentioned above, and the Coleraine (Derry) SFA and the Northern Ireland Day Tech. SSA, the East Antrim SFA, the Mid-Ulster SFA and the Lisburn (Antrim) SFA, which were all operational by the mid-1930s.[26] By 2015 there were nineteen district schoolboy associations registered with the Northern Ireland Schools Football Association, and while the

Northern Ireland Boys Football Association was not founded until 1976, by 2012 it catered for 1,070 teams within 240 clubs.[27]

Two prominent competitions, in particular, have helped give young Irish footballers the opportunity to illustrate their talents on an international stage. The Super Cup Northern Ireland, formerly known as the Milk Cup, was founded in 1983 and is held annually in Derry and Antrim.[28] While, as noted in the previous chapter, funding to enter has been a problem for some regional associations, it is now a renowned international competition which attracts clubs such as Manchester United and Glasgow Rangers, as well as the interest of football scouts.[29] The Foyle Cup, first held in 1992 and organised by the Derry and District Youth FA, provides competition for under 10s to under 19s and in 2011 had a record 144 entries, and the development of these international competitions means that young players can showcase their skills and gain the attention of English clubs.[30] Along with participation in the Milk and Foyle Cups, some Northern Ireland football migrants, including Norman Whiteside, have also benefited from their involvement in Boys' Brigade football clubs, which Garnham has noted as being significant in the early spread of football in Belfast and Dublin.[31]

By the late 1890s the fixture between Dublin and Belfast Boys' Brigades selections was said to be an annual one.[32] Some earlier football migrants were part of this organisation. Johnnie 'Toby' Mercer played for both the 81st North Lancashire Regiment and the 8th Belfast Boys' Brigade prior to appearing for both Leicester Fosse and Derby County in the period from 1899 until 1904.[33] Liverpool and Ireland goalkeeper Elisha Scott was also a member of the Boys' Brigade before joining Linfield.[34] One reporter felt in 1925 that 'it was in the Boys' Brigade that many of Ireland's best [footballers] were found' with players in the Free State competing for the McCrae and Duckett cups.[35] However, there is more evidence of Northern Ireland-born players being involved in the Boys' Brigade than their Republic of Ireland counterparts in the period covered here although this is probably due to the higher proportion of Protestants in Belfast than in Dublin and admittedly, a number of youth clubs of Republic of Ireland-born players from the 1945–55 period could not be traced.

Although Dublin had the fourth largest battalion in the United Kingdom and Ireland in 1900, the Belfast battalion is now the largest overall.[36] A number of Scots also played for Boys' Brigade teams including Edward McLachlan, who played for the Glasgow selection before joining a number of Scottish and English league clubs in the 1920s.[37]

In Northern Ireland, along with Whiteside, post-war migrants Danny Blanchflower, Hubert Barr, Ray Gough, Steve McKee, Alan Blayney and David Miskelly were all noted as having had experience of the Boys' Brigade, although again there were probably others involved who could not be traced. In particular, Miskelly recalled while interviewed that, along with going to watch his uncle play, the club had helped him get involved in football as an eight-year-old, while Blayney had been chosen for North Abbey, 'a BB select', as a result of being one of the best local young Boys' Brigade players.[38]

EARLY POST-SECOND WORLD WAR COACHING

In Northern Ireland, links between soccer organisers and governing bodies for physical recreation were stronger, and the IFA had begun to develop a coherent structure for the qualification of coaches by the early 1950s. Similarly they had begun to put coaching structures in place for schoolboy players at that time, while youth internationals were also offered the chance to learn the game from formally qualified men. This contrasted with the structures put in place by the FAI, with the implementation of the position of national coach by the Dublin organisation lasting only briefly in the 1950s. It was not until a national commission into the state of association football in the Republic was launched in the early 1970s that a new national coach was appointed, but work was hindered by funding problems. With the success of the Jack Charlton era (1986–1995), the FAI were finally able to put in place a nationwide system for the development of the game at grassroots and schoolboy level as interest in the game and sponsorship opportunities increased.

The development of young Irish players has been affected by the levels of coaching available to them and the attitudes of educational and government authorities in both the Republic and Northern Ireland. The IFA, although rejecting a proposal by Peter Doherty in 1945 for a coaching scheme to be set up throughout Northern Ireland because of the expense involved, enjoyed greater co-operation than the FAI with their national governmental and educational authorities in the decades immediately following the Second World War. Doherty had hoped to set up soccer centres run and funded by the IFA and Irish League clubs with players also having time to undertake their education and gain 'a sound basic trade' before turning professional.[39] Despite this rejection, the IFA had their own structured plan in place by the early 1950s for the training of adults to become coaches and for the coaching of young players, having clarified their position on the coaching of underage players in 1948. Their Youth International Committee, at a meeting in July of that year, was of the view that a coaching scheme was 'essential' for players aged from fourteen to eighteen years old.[40] They advertised for former players to take up coaching positions and asked Stanley Rous of the FA to choose an appropriate lecturer for their coaching courses. It appears he picked Walter Winterbottom, who conducted a course at Grosvenor Park, the home of Distillery FC, that year.[41]

This meant that prior to the establishment of an IFA coaching committee in 1950, coaching classes had been held under their Youth International committee in a number of areas, with potential coaches and international youth team players receiving instruction from Winterbottom and R.P. Fulton respectively.[42] Fulton appears to have been the only locally based FA-qualified coach the IFA had available at this point and was 'highly recommended' by Winterbottom, who was England manager from 1946 until 1962 and also the FA's Director of Coaching.[43] A few senior clubs, such as Linfield and Derry City, had also held coaching classes for youths.[44] By June 1949 a plan for developing the IFA's coaching structure had been drawn up by E.T.F. Spence, the Technical Representative of the Central Council for Physical Recreation (CCPR), a body whose aim was 'to improve the physical and mental health of the community through physical recreation'. This organisation had been set up in 1936 under the patronage of the King and Queen of England and was extended to

Northern Ireland in May 1949.[45] In particular, Spence recommended that a panel consisting of coaches be established to give instruction in the basic skills of the game. There were five steps which he felt would benefit overall development, with the appointment of local coaching sub-committees to oversee events in their respective districts recommended. He also encouraged 'propaganda events' to be organised with films and demonstrations deemed necessary, while the recruiting of potential coaches, through these local sub-committees in conjunction with the CCPR, was also advised. The IFA was also instructed to put in place a coaching award which would be gained through an examination in local and central venues. Finally it was felt that the work of the coaches would have to be carefully organised, with the CCPR to act as agents and advisors for the national governing body.[46] The IFA seem to have stuck closely to Spence's plan.

Fulton continued his coaching work under the IFA's new coaching committee, with an IFA coaching course taking place over eight weeks from April to June 1950; the fifteen participants received 'the routine training of every first class coach' with the help of the Distillery and Cliftonville clubs.[47] Gradually coaching spread to more outlying areas. In October of that year, a coaching course for boys was started in Portadown with the help of the County Armagh Education Committee, the Portadown Technical School Management Committee and the Central Council of Physical Education. Grading of coaches was categorised into two awards by the beginning of 1951 while by April, coaching for boys had taken place in Ballymena and Lurgan as well as Portadown and training classes for potential coaches had also been held in Belfast.[48]

Later that year, the IFA added prestige to the qualification by agreeing that a certificate and badge would be given to those who had passed the required exams. Over 100 schoolboys took part in outdoor coaching in Belfast in the summer of 1951 at three venues, while by the spring of the following year a coaching course for youth leaders had been organised by the Federation of Boys' Clubs in the capital.[49] At this point the majority of coaching courses appear to have been held in the east of the province, with CCPR-backed courses also taking place in Portrush during the summer months in the early 1950s, although by 1953 international youth trial players from the north-west were also said to be receiving IFA coaching.[50]

THE DIFFICULTY IN IMPLEMENTING ASSOCIATION FOOTBALL IN SCHOOLS

Those initially organising coaching in Northern Ireland had a number of advantages over their counterparts in the Republic in that they could attract support from government-sponsored bodies. But difficulties were evident within schools. The IFA's coaching committee were 'co-operating with various local education authorities' by October of 1950, something which, as will be seen, their rival soccer body down south could not claim at this point.[51] A lack of schools' soccer has probably impeded the development of young players in some areas of Ireland. Twenty-one players or 5 per cent of the Northern Ireland total of 417 footballers who played league football in England in the post-war period were born in the east Ulster town of Lurgan, County Armagh, with former Northern Ireland goalkeeper, Norman Uprichard, claiming in his autobiography that it has produced more international footballers than any other in Ireland. Although he was unsure why, he stated that 'there were some very good footballers around' when he was at school, which would indicate the value of schools' football in a young player's development.[52]

This may sound obvious, but some players have expressed a need to attend a school which provided soccer for them, the most famous case being George Best, who switched schools partially because of this, while Terry Neill also changed to a soccer-playing technical college after getting into trouble with the headmaster for not playing rugby at grammar school.[53] Best's brief attendance at a rugby-playing institution came at Belfast's Grosvenor High School in the late 1950s, although the lack of soccer there had not gone unnoticed by the IFA prior to this. By the latter years of the 1940s they were expressing serious concerns about the football policies of grammar schools and resolved to contact the Northern Ireland Director of Education, Dr Stuart Hawnt, about the favouring of rugby in grammar schools in

December 1947.[54] Having contacted the headmaster of Grosvenor High School, Hawnt replied to say that the headmaster felt that soccer was not played in any of the grammar schools in Northern Ireland and if the school were to attempt to play it they would be unable to organise fixtures against other schools.[55]

Prior to the Second World War, there were almost 14,000 students attending sixty-six grammar schools in Northern Ireland, and by 1956 nearly 200,000 additional pupils were enrolled in 'the new tripartite network of intermediate schools'.[56] Under the 1947 Education Act, compulsory free education was to be provided for all students up to fifteen years old.[57] Despite this, as Jonathan Bardon states, 'educational reform had a modernising effect in Northern Ireland only within the limits of a strictly segregated system' as 'the full social and political impact of educational advance was not felt until the mid-1960s' and 'the traditional grammar schools successfully resisted direct control and preserved their identity largely intact'.[58] Gaining recognition for soccer in grammar schools was difficult in Northern Ireland. After meeting an IFA deputation in March 1954, then Minister for Education, Harry Midgley, issued a circular to the headmasters of forty-four grammar schools to ascertain if they would consider bringing soccer into their schools. The nineteen replies received revealed that there was much resistance to the idea.[59] Four schools were said to have agreed that 'association football should be allowed the same freedom as the other traditional games', although they did not all play soccer. 'About an equal number' expressed sympathy for the idea but felt that they could not provide the facilities needed for the game. Several of the remainder were said to be 'directly opposed to the suggestion' while others were 'unable or unwilling to consider the introduction of the game'. These schools put forward a number of 'chief difficulties' they felt they had in implementing it, including the view that they could not run two games at the same time and that neither would succeed if both were played. Playing fields were also said to be lacking, while a scarcity of masters who were able to referee and coach soccer was noted. It was also felt that these men had enough to do without having to take on more work, particularly in smaller grammar schools.[60]

Additionally, some schools felt that with their strong rugby ethos, change would be opposed by 'parents and old boys brought up in that tradition'. Views were also expressed that rugby was a better game for schoolmasters as 'it gives opportunities for star performers' and 'depends much more on the spirit of the team as a whole'. The point about it being easier to arrange fixtures against schools of the same type was also reiterated while some schools were opposed to 'soccer's commercialisation and professionalism'. In some cases it was felt that there were not enough boys in the sixteen to eighteen age group interested in games to justify playing another code. Travelling costs were also said to be a consideration, while a number of correspondents felt aggrieved about IFA comments in the press about grammar schools and headmasters.[61] A lack of assistance in developing the game was mentioned by the principal of Down High School. He expressed the view that 'the [Irish] Rugby [Football] Union fostered the game with financial assistance and expenses' while the IFA had not done this 'in the formative days'.[62] There is some evidence to back up this view, with one reporter stating in 1924 that the IFA had done little to promote the game in the public schools after the failure of the Schools Cup in the 1880s, while he also wrote that 'north and south, the rugby authorities have fostered that very desirable connection. As a result many of the best men of the carrying code have had their elementary knowledge imparted in their school days.'[63] It was also noted that the Schools' Cup and inter-provincial matches had done much to keep rugby alive.[64]

Others disliked the ethos of soccer with its professional clubs. The headmaster at Belfast's Grosvenor High School felt that the professionalism attached to soccer was 'a real stumbling block' and stated that 'two of our boys have already terminated inglorious careers as trainees of English clubs', although he did not give any further details of this.[65] A clear exception was the principal of St Malachy's school in Belfast, who noted that they were 'the only grammar school to play [soccer] unashamedly under its own name', while stating that some of their past pupils had gone on to represent Northern Ireland at international level. The school also participated in the aforementioned league and cup run by Cliftonville FC and had a tradition of success in competitive soccer dating back to the 1880s.[66] While a few schools which were asked to foster soccer, such as Portadown College, played intra-school association football matches, rugby was clearly the main choice of sport.[67]

Despite this opposition from rugby-favouring teachers, some football migrants obviously were able to benefit from favourable soccer conditions in their schools, illustrating the mixed nature of organised football at this level. Willie Irvine, who joined Burnley in 1960, was grateful to his former sports master, described as 'a tremendous football fan', for his early input, as noted in a magazine interview.[68] Opportunities varied, as Hubert Barr played no schools' soccer and instead played rugby for Ballymena Academy's first XV.[69] Billy Humphries played soccer at elementary school on the Donegall Road and also for his local church, St Simon's.[70]

Garnham has stated that the decision of Belfast's elite schools to stick to rugby over soccer 'probably reflected a certain sporting snobbery'.[71] As Sugden and Bairner have stated, from the early 1870s onwards, 'schools rugby has been an important feature of Ulster's social as well as sporting life'.[72] This attitude can be seen in a number of the principals' replies. Grosvenor High's principal felt that aligning soccer with rugby 'smacks of the comprehensive school' and wrote that maintaining rugby's status was also down to the view that 'our prestige, to put the matter in a nutshell, demands it'.[73] This was written in view of the rivalry the school had with other rugby-playing educational establishments such as INST, Methodist College (Methody), Campbell, Coleraine and Dungannon.[74] As Liam O'Callaghan has stated in his major study of Munster rugby, 'though developing the moral character of boys no doubt underpinned the promotion of the game within schools to a certain extent, the prestige of winning competitions was a far more palpable motivation'.[75] There was clearly a lack of progress in some Northern Irish schools in catering for young soccer players, despite a strong desire on the part of some students to play the game. In particular, one Ballymena principal, who stated that 'many pupils would prefer it to rugby football', was of the view that caution should be taken in allowing the curriculum to be guided by students' wishes.[76]

In 1950, having met an IFA deputation, the Board of Governors at INST promised the soccer body that the inclusion of the game in their sports curriculum would be discussed 'in due course'.[77] Four years later the school principal's reply to Midgley was that 'our existing programme of games affords an ample outlet for the energies of our pupils and I do not consider that any addition is at present likely'.[78] As can be seen above, practical issues such as organisation were apparent but the perceived need to preserve the ethos of the grammar schools was a major factor in the lack of encouragement of soccer in many Northern Ireland grammar schools. In addition, there was no major pressure put on these schools by the Minister of Education to change or implement a broader sporting curriculum at this time.

FURTHER COACHING DEVELOPMENTS

Despite these difficulties in schools, the IFA remained steadfast in their efforts to promote soccer among schoolboys and to develop coaching structures. By 1954 the annual summer school, again held in conjunction with the CCPR, took place in Stranmillis Training College, Belfast, illustrating a shift away from Portrush and a move into a more centrally located educational institution.[79] A schoolboys course was organised during the Easter holidays with fifty selected players participating in the three-day event, which was the first run in conjunction with the Irish Schools FA, although the schools' football body did not gain affiliation to the IFA until 1980.[80] In 1955 there was increased involvement with local schools' associations with courses held in Derry, Larne and Carrickfergus, while coaching for schoolboys in Coleraine was also provided in 1956, along with that for a selection of boys from the minor league.[81] Some individual schools, such as Whiteabbey Primary School in 1958, also contacted the IFA about organising coaching courses, and they generally appear to have facilitated these requests. In December of that year, Gibby MacKenzie, a Grade I IFA coach, was appointed by the Minister of Education and the Belfast Education Committee to assist teachers in various Belfast schools with their coaching.[82]

In 1957 the IFA began to use films and lectures more frequently under the guidance of their Coaching Committee chairman, Harry Cavan. These were held in Belfast, Newry, Ballyclare, Downpatrick, Derry and Armagh, with over 1,000 boys in attendance. These events were also held in Rathfriland, Newtownards, Enniskillen and Ballymena the following year as they branched out further into the province.[83] A residential course, in conjunction with the Belfast Education Authority, was organised for 'possible' schoolboy international players at Orangefield Boys Secondary School in Belfast in August 1959. The IFA began to take stronger steps to have soccer played in schools through the organisation of coaching classes for school teachers and training college students with a summer course held in Stranmillis that year. A school leavers' course was also organised with the assistance of the CCPR.[84]

Other youth groups also benefited. By 1963 a summer coaching course had been set up for Boys' Brigade senior boys at that organisation's training and conference centre in Larne, while the following year members of the Belfast battalion of the Boys' Brigade also received coaching.[85] By the early 1960s the IFA were able to offer a subsidy of £200 to assist the Belfast Education Authority with the above course at Orangefield. This appears to have been the norm for this event throughout this decade, illustrating their interest in investing in coaching at this time, and the finance they had available to do this.[86] The Northern Ireland Coaches' Association was established in 1966 with Ted Smyth as chairman, while IFA coach Eric Trevorrow took up the role of secretary.[87]

Coaching was also beginning to gain more attention in the west of the province by the end of the decade, although its development was much slower than in the east. Fifty-four secondary school and technical college students took part in a course overseen by Cliftonville coach Jackie Cummings and physical training teacher Roy Downing at Omagh, County Tyrone, in 1967. This was organised by the county youth officer with the Tyrone Education Committee, in conjunction with the IFA, with other schoolboy courses being held in Belfast, Derry and Portadown at that time.[88] Some teachers took it upon themselves to organise courses in areas that were receiving less attention. A coaching course for fifteen-year-olds, held over four days, took place in Lisnaskea, County Fermanagh in August 1969 and was organised by Tom McFarlane, a PT instructor at the local secondary school, who stated that 'there just wasn't enough being done to help young people to learn the skills of soccer' in the area.[89]

In 1967, the IFA began to examine the possibility of appointing a national coach and the further development of a national coaching scheme. Concrete steps were taken towards this, although they do not appear to have immediately appointed anybody in that role.[90] In 1971, 'realising the necessity and demand for coaching facilities at all levels throughout Northern Ireland', a coaching scheme was implemented by the IFA to cater for 2,000 schoolboys at fifty centres in Northern Ireland.[91] A total of fifty-one courses for schoolboys, grammar schoolboys, potential youth internationals, regular coaches and Irish League club managers and staff coaches were held. The IFA's part-time coaching advisor, Brian Halliday, supervised the scheme while FIFA technical adviser/coach Detmar Cramer provided instruction for the Irish League managers and staff.[92]

Despite this, problems remained in the west of the country. Speaking in May 1971, one Tyrone-based coaching organiser felt that 'people in the north-west have always said that everything is kept in Belfast'.[93] In July of that year, fourteen schoolboys attended the first course for these players in Strabane, County Tyrone, with Halliday, who conducted the training along with Liam Kennedy, of the opinion that 'there is a tremendous amount of untapped footballing talent in the area' while one reporter felt that 'it was a breakthrough in this part of the world'.[94] However, the course was called off the following year after only six people applied to participate, with a minimum of twelve necessary.[95] Similarly, coaching structures for those in Enniskillen, County Fermanagh appear to have been slow to develop. Despite the hosting of a 'soccer teach-in' at the High School Playing Fields in the town in November 1976 with plans to later take the forty-seven boys present to Belfast for a national coaching session, it appears this had less impact than was intended. One writer expressed hopes that a course held in Enniskillen for under 15s during the 1986 Christmas holidays would be 'only the first of many courses of this nature in the area', illustrating the slow implementation of coaching structures for young players there.[96]

In April 1975, Roy Millar was appointed as the IFA's full-time coaching development officer on a three-year contract, after the Northern Ireland Sports Council had approved their move.[97] Millar began to give increased attention to university and teacher training colleges and the IFA introduced a new teacher coaching certificate and a teachers' referee course. There was said to be 1,483 participants in the 1975–76 season, with eight preparatory coaching courses, six teacher coaching certificate courses, thirteen schoolboy courses, three youth courses, three grade two coaching courses, one grade one coaching course and six referees' courses taking place.[98]

By the late twentieth century, soccer schools conducted by Irish internationals were being organised for the summer holidays in more regional areas in both the Republic and Northern Ireland. The Packie Bonner Goalkeeping School was staged initially in west Donegal in 1986, while the Gerry Armstrong Soccer School, a three-day event, was first held in Omagh in 1991.[99] By 1993 the Armstrong coaching event was said to be 'the most popular soccer school in Northern Ireland' with 'top IFA qualified coaches in attendance', along with George Best.[100] In 1994 it was estimated that 400 children would attend, 'making the event the biggest of its kind in Northern Ireland'.[101] IFA soccer schools were also operational in more outlying areas of Fermanagh such as Lisnaskea in the early part of this decade, illustrating how these structures had become a lot more firmly implemented by the eve of the twenty-first century.[102]

THE NATIONALIST ETHOS, SCHOOLS' SOCCER AND COACHING IN THE REPUBLIC OF IRELAND

Coaching structures within schools in the Republic have been slow to become established, particularly in more rural areas which have been strongholds of the GAA and, like in Northern Ireland's grammar schools, instruction in soccer techniques suffered as a result of this in the post-war years. This lack of interest on the part of the Department of Education can be seen as part of a wider attempt by the new Free

State government 'to establish an Irish Catholic nationalist ethos in terms of cultural production, education and general intellectual atmosphere'.[103] Mike Cronin has noted how soccer in the Free State received little support from the government or the Catholic Church after 1922 as it was seen as a 'foreign' game.[104] As David Goldblatt has stated, 'there was no official enthusiasm and less money available to the game in de Valera's Irish Free State' after Fianna Fáil gained power in 1932.[105] In addition, the FAI had noted difficulties in implementing the game in schools and colleges in 1938 and it was decided to attempt to meet with the Minister for Education about this, but there is little evidence of any great change as they again sought to meet in 1943 to secure his assistance in gaining acceptance for the game within schools.[106] In 1945 'the difficulties confronting these [schoolboy] leagues, in view of official school prejudices' was acknowledged in an FAI annual report, which does not suggest much progress.[107]

Opportunities for aspiring soccer players in both Northern Ireland and the Republic were hindered by the presence of the Gaelic Athletic Association's 'Ban' on 'foreign' games, enforced until 1971. While the image of association football within Irish society was not helped by some of those running educational establishments, social pressure was also exerted on GAA players to stay away from soccer, with vigilance committees in operation throughout Ireland.[108] Under the 'Ban', permanently established by the GAA in the early 1900s and not removed until 1971, GAA players who participated in rugby, soccer, hockey and cricket could be suspended from Gaelic games, although this rule was often ignored by GAA clubs in some counties.[109] Admittedly, the inconsistency of monitoring by these vigilance committees, set up in the 1920s to assess players' non-GAA-playing movements, was often a key factor in its failure to be rigidly enforced in some areas such as Donegal, but there were many areas throughout Ireland where it was more respected.[110]

Gaining interest in coaching in schools was difficult in many areas as priority was given to other codes, and teachers with an interest in soccer were not always to be found. Growing up in Dublin in the 1940s, Mick Meagan has noted how most teachers in his Christian

Brothers school were from the countryside and were more interested in promoting Gaelic football; children were encouraged to pick up the ball rather than dribble it, with some members of the Catholic clergy resorting to physical abuse to ensure soccer was not played during Gaelic football matches.[111] He felt that a lack of choice of codes had impacted on the development of players in regional areas:

> It's a shame to think that, if you look at Waterford, the players that they had in Cork and all these other areas … Longford, Athlone … if you had been encouraged, given the opportunity [they could have progressed]. Now if you want to play Gaelic, good, that's great. But give them the opportunity if they want to play soccer. So that was the sad thing, so we had a lot to put up with.[112]

Like in Northern Ireland, a lack of variety in sporting codes has been problematic for many young players. Johnny Gavin, Noel Cantwell, Johnny Giles, Joe Carolan, Terry Conroy and Liam Brady have all alluded to this while Damien Richardson also stated when interviewed that there was no soccer allowed in his school.[113] Additionally, pressure was put on young players to play Gaelic football for their school selections.[114] In the 'Ban' years, many GAA players covertly participated in soccer both as spectators and players, but there was a reluctance to publicise this and this may have hindered some players' chances of a career in England, particularly those from more rural areas.[115] Admittedly, some pre-1971 GAA players who played soccer, including 1960s' Down All-Ireland winner Paddy Doherty who had experience of the game with Ballyclare Comrades, were keener than others to pursue a career in the game. He had trials at Lincoln City before focusing more fully on Gaelic football and then went back to soccer again after a suspension following an incident in a county championship semi-final in 1966.[116] By 1968 he was back in Down's last All-Ireland-winning team of that decade, illustrating the complexities in the rule, whereby players who were caught playing 'foreign' games generally received a temporary suspension, while others' indiscretions were often ignored.[117]

Some Catholic schools in Northern Ireland also operated a strict policy of playing Gaelic games only and this has been slow to change. Peter McParland has written that during his time at the Christian Brothers school in Newry in the 1940s, 'you played Gaelic football whether you liked it or not and soccer was a forbidden word' although he admits that this lack of sporting choice was not unique to Irish-born schoolboys, with rugby-only schools common in England.[118] Raymond Campbell noted that while the primary school he attended in Downpatrick in the 1980s had a strong soccer team, at his secondary school there was none, and Gaelic football was the only football code available.[119]

Many schools catering primarily for Catholic pupils had no time for association football given its British links. Soccer had initially been played in St Patrick's of Armagh but apparently 'following the national revival it became a bastion for Gaelic games' while some other schools in the same county also had a GAA-only policy.[120] Neil Lennon has written in his autobiography of how he faced the threat of expulsion from his Lurgan grammar school, St Michael's, in the 1980s, for daring to play for Lurgan United rather than the school Gaelic football team on a Saturday morning, until a compromise was reached between his father and the nun who ran the school.[121] However, Campbell feels that there is now a broader physical education curriculum in place which means that young students experience a wider range of sports.[122] There is also some evidence that schools' soccer fixtures in Northern Ireland have been hindered by religious tension during the Troubles, with St Colman's of Strabane refusing to travel to Belfast for the 1974 Irish Schools Cup final, with the result that their opponents, Ashfield, received the trophy.[123] The Strabane school had apparently been the first non-Belfast school to reach the final and asked the Schools Council if the game could be played in Coleraine or Ballymena, as Ashfield would otherwise have had more or less a home venue, but this was refused.[124]

Occasionally, students in the Republic of Ireland have attempted to do something about the restrictions placed upon them by their schools. While David Toms has noted how soccer was being played in some Waterford schools – such as Lismore College, Waterpark

College, De La Salle and in Tramore – in the opening decades of the twentieth century, a strong culture of the game did not continue to develop in the post-Independence years.[125] In 1970, pupils in Mount Sion Christian Brothers school in Waterford held a protest outside the building after the Superior, Reverend Brother Collins, declined to allow their soccer team to use the school's name in the national secondary school competition, which resulted in them being disqualified at the semi-final stage.[126] A teacher in the school later claimed he was dismissed for supporting the 'unofficial soccer team' and the students' protest, although it appears he did not have a permanent contract.[127] Despite the lifting of the 'Ban', many schools in the Republic of Ireland were also still slow to set up association football teams. Seamus Kelly, who migrated from the midlands of Ireland in the late 1990s to play for Cardiff City, has also stated that the game was not played at his secondary school, and he did not appear in a soccer match until he was seventeen due to the lack of soccer clubs nearby during his youth.[128] However, Kelly was an exceptional case among in his area at that time in terms of his later progress, and therefore while those in more urbanised areas have been able to play for their local soccer clubs, player production in many places has probably suffered through having neither school nor club teams to turn out for, especially in rural areas.

With the lack of general guidance from those in authority in schools in running soccer teams, boys initially had to take it upon themselves to organise schoolboy sides in the post-war years in many areas. One national reporter stated in December 1952 that despite the monopoly enjoyed by rugby and Gaelic football in the Republic of Ireland's schools, there were 200 schoolboy soccer teams in operation throughout the country. However, he also felt that 'the majority of these are run by a couple of senior enthusiasts, or often by the boys themselves'.[129] Relationships between soccer organisers and educational bodies have been slow to evolve in the Republic of Ireland. One journalist contrasted these with developments in West Germany in 1959 when he stated that 'all their football is integrated from the schools upwards. The [West] German FA as distinct from our own, get 100 per cent co-operation from their education authority.'[130]

Seamus Kelly in action for Longford Town in 2007. Now Director of Sports Studies at University College Dublin, he was one of only a few players from the midlands of Ireland who experienced English league football in the twentieth-century. Picture: © Inpho

Early structures for schools' football south of the border were centred mainly in Dublin, with Bohemians involved in an attempt to set up a schools' league and cup-competition there in 1925.[131] This was said to have been influenced by the English FA's efforts to attract the public schools to the game, while the prominence of rugby within Irish schools was also noted.[132] Progress was slow, but the Leinster Schools Easter Vacation League was in operation by the middle of the 1950s. Teams were joined in competition for the Irish Schools' Senior Cup by the winners of the Connacht Schools Cup in 1966 and the Football Association of Irish Schools was formed in 1970.[133] Despite this, by the spring of 1969 soccer was still said to be 'the poor relation in school sports life up to now', with the continuous emphasis on Gaelic football and rugby ensuring that 'soccer was mainly a game played by the few, and then played in a haphazard way'.[134] Teams participating in the Easter Vacation League had not even used their own school names and although under 13, 15 and 18 leagues were established, these were not to be played until the third term to avoid clashing with these other codes.[135]

THE FAI AND COACHING

The FAI's attempts to develop coaching structures seem to have increased around the same time as those of the IFA in the post-war years. In 1948, one journalist felt that League of Ireland clubs should look to younger players and 'devise ways and means of providing them with proper coaching and training.'[136] It was also felt by another reporter that year that the FAI had only begun to look at using international coaches to help with coaching. In bringing English international, George Hardwick of Middlesbrough to Dublin to instruct local coaches, they were making progress in that regard, but the journalist felt that 'this coaching scheme must be speeded up and enlarged upon and extended to the provincial areas.'[137] The following year saw Republic of Ireland and Manchester United star, Jackie Carey, conduct a three-day coaching clinic organised by the Galway FA, while in the summer of 1950 the FAI organised a coaching course in Dublin with Scottish international Ken Chisholm conducting matters.[138] Coaching films and lectures on developing soccer skills were also initiated around this time.[139] One reporter hoped that the visit of Jimmy Hogan, 'one of the best coaches in the world', to Castlebar, County Mayo, in 1951 for a fortnight's coaching would 'prove a great boon to soccer in the district.'[140] This general interest in the value of coaching culminated in the FAI appointing Scotsman, Dougald Livingstone, as national coach that year.[141]

Livingstone identified 'three great needs' that he saw soccer in Ireland as having: improved playing pitches, a higher quality of training facilities with heated dressing rooms, and a better standard of coaching.[142] His efforts did not go unnoticed by the president of the GAA, M.V. O'Donoghue, who claimed at the Association's annual congress in 1953 that Livingstone was, in fact, 'the chief of the new Saxon recruiting campaign' and had been 'busy enticing young

Irish boys by various inducements to become happy little English children, and heirs to the joy of a soccer paradise'.[143] This 'campaign', which included giving lectures and instruction in areas as peripheral as Westport in County Mayo, appears to have lasted only briefly at this time but these comments are indicative of the anti-soccer feeling among some sections of Irish society.[144] By July 1953, Livingstone had left his job in Ireland, having been appointed as coach to the Belgian FA for a salary of £3,000, and was replaced by former Everton and Ireland inside-right, Alex Stevenson.[145] Not all League of Ireland clubs were in favour of the appointment of a national coach as they would have to help 'foot the bill', and this is illustrative of the difficulties in financing this position.[146] The following year, Stevenson resigned the £600 a year FAI coaching position in order to take up a vacancy as player-coach with League of Ireland club St Patrick's Athletic, citing the lack of daytime activity as national coach as a factor in this decision; the FAI did not reappoint a national coach until the early 1970s.[147]

Despite these setbacks, by the middle of the 1950s, coaching of young players was gaining a lot more support at club level, with current and ex-players keen to get involved. In 1956 leading Irish schoolboy club, Home Farm, had eleven teams, each with their own coach; it was also reported that 'these volunteer enthusiasts, former club players, have attended summer courses given by international player Noel Kelly, holder of an FA coaching certificate'.[148] Coaching courses were also organised by the Dublin-based United Churches League, with examinations taking place for the English FA's Coaching Certificate.[149] These catered for 'club coaches, games masters, youth leaders and players', while schoolboy sessions were also organised.[150] By the end of the decade, funding for coaching was still a problem for the FAI with sponsorship from 'private bodies' necessary in the organisation of coaching courses.[151]

In 1960 there was said to be 'between twenty and thirty preliminary certificate coaches in [the Republic of] Ireland and most of these gained the award at courses organised by the United Churches League'.[152] It was also the first year that a full FA coaching award was available in the Republic of Ireland. Despite this progress, by the beginning of 1963 structured coaching throughout the Republic was still in its infancy, with Professional Footballers' Association of Ireland secretary, Alan Glynn, expressing hopes that 'a proper coaching scheme' would be established as he felt that 'there are not enough good coaches in this country'.[153] This came at a time when the recruitment of coaches by League of Ireland clubs was becoming more firmly established. Glynn hoped that the English FA would be of assistance in this attempt to improve the standard of football at senior and junior level.[154] In addition, a lack of coaching facilities was also said to be still a problem at this time, with Shamrock Rovers sending their coaches to English sports schools 'for specialised training' by the middle of the 1960s.[155]

By the summer of 1967 it was reported that facilities for sport in vocational schools were improving, but difficulties remained in many counties, with the Meath Vocational Education Committee rejecting an application from local club, Parkvilla, to have soccer coaching implemented in a technical school in Navan that year.[156] The following year, a five-day coaching course 'for games masters', under the guidance of Bohemians manager Sean Thomas and organised by the Irish Universities and Colleges Football Union, was held at Belfield, having gained recognition from the FAI and was said to be 'the latest stage in the proposed development of soccer in Irish Secondary Schools'.[157] By the middle of 1969 the course had been recognised by the Department of Education, who sent a lecturer to talk about 'educational aspects of soccer and sport in general', with a medical doctor also present to speak about injuries. Applications were received from 'schoolmasters as far apart as Donegal and Cork', with written and oral exams part of the week's activities.[158] Writing in 1969, one reporter felt that in the Republic of Ireland, 'PE has been almost totally absent from most primary schools due to two factors – lack of trained teachers and an over-constricted curriculum'.[159]

Despite the Department of Defence's attempts to introduce the Sokol system of physical education into 1930s' Free State schools, a general lack of emphasis on the subject at primary and secondary school level had been evident up until the late 1960s, with funding noted as being a problem.[160] Thomas O'Donoghue has highlighted the appointment of an inspector for physical education in 1965 as being a key development in its later growth.[161] A new syllabus was introduced in 1971 and specialised instruction for trainee teachers was given at the National College of Physical Education in Limerick, which was operational by 1973.[162] Previously, physical training had been implemented in some schools by drill instructors focusing on fitness, but this was to become a thing of the past with PE said to be 'almost the direct opposite' of this style of learning.[163] This new era in secondary education – free education for secondary school students up to intermediate level was to be implemented in 1969 having been announced by the Minister for Education, Donogh O'Malley in 1967 – also saw funding applications for schools' sports facilities being encouraged by Brian Lenihan, who took up this ministerial role in 1968. Community and comprehensive schools were also established towards the end of the decade.[164] O'Malley appears to have been more in favour of encouraging soccer than most other government ministers and had been president of the FAI for a period in the 1960s, although he died suddenly in 1968.[165]

In January 1967, O'Malley made what journalist Peter Byrne has described as 'a policy-defining statement on education and sport' in which he challenged a member of the Cork GAA county board, Jim Barry, about the notion that children playing soccer were unpatriotic, and stated that equality of education should also mean that a choice of sports should be available.[166] While Byrne suggests that this public criticism of the GAA's policy 'empowered other organisations to adopt a more militant stance in the manner in which they interacted with schools in protecting the interests of all sports', loosening the GAA's grip on sport was a slow process in many schools.[167] Progress was slow in the implementation of physical education in any case, with Mike Sleap writing in 1978 that there was still 'a low percentage of vocational and secondary boys' schools which employ physical education teachers' while 'it was also found that there was an uneven distribution of physical education teachers between different areas of the country'.[168] Areas which had institutions for physical education, Ling and Sion Hill (formerly operational in Dublin) and the then newly developed Thomond College in Limerick, were noted as having 'the highest proportion of schools with physical education teachers', which Sleap states was a result of their proximity and possible awareness of physical education's value along with the impact of student teachers visiting on teaching practice.[169] A scarcity of facilities and employment quotas also meant that many schools were not devoting the recommended amount of time to this subject.[170]

This earlier general lack of physical education may also have impacted on young Irish players' development to some extent. Mick Meagan felt that the lack of physical education during his schooldays had repercussions in terms of his physical development in comparison with players from England:

> There were always niggles … hamstrings, achilles tendons … I used to suffer with my back. Now I blame a lot of that on that we never did PT at school when we were younger. There was never any PT at school, whereas the English lads, that was all part of their school programme – physical training. When you'd go in the gym on a bad morning … we couldn't even do a forward roll, they'd be hopping over, we wouldn't be allowed do it, 'cause we'd kill ourselves, 'cause we were never used to doing it. We were never taught how to do it.[171]

By 1970, the FAI did have a coaching committee in operation, although one sportswriter felt that the finance simply was not there to develop a national coaching course.[172] However, a 'countrywide coaching scheme' for secondary school students, teachers and other adults involved in schools soccer was set up by the FAI with the aid of a FIFA development grant, with one reporter feeling that this aspect of young players' development had been 'too long neglected'.[173] Initial sessions, with the help of former Manchester United goalkeeper Ray Wood, an FA coach, were organised for Cork and Dublin and other provincial centres.[174] Despite this progress, one reporter wrote in November of that year that there were 'very few talented players coming up through the ranks', with a failure in the system highlighted. He noted that a national coaching scheme needed to be implemented, but it was again stressed that the FAI did not have sufficient funds for this, and that 'soccer is not taught in the majority of schools, while in youth clubs there is no one to coach the boys with the real skills of the game'.[175] Facilities such as playing fields continued to be a problem, with Limerick manager Ewan Fenton of the view the following year that the Republic of Ireland was twenty years behind Britain when it came to coaching.[176]

A NEW NATIONAL DIRECTOR OF COACHING: JOHN JARMAN

On 27 August 1973 'the biggest coaching scheme ever attempted in Ireland' at that point was launched. The scheme was organised by the National Commission for Amateur Football, which had been set up in 1972 through government involvement, to investigate the state of soccer in the Republic of Ireland.[177] The report was published in May 1973, with chairman David Andrews, TD, noting in his introduction that 'any changes necessary must have the support of the majority of legislators if they are to be implemented'.[178] He prioritised the organisation of 'teams in every factory, school and college and playing facilities for these teams', an all-Ireland league and international team and the creation of a number of Irish teams of a significant standard to compete in Europe. The Commission also hoped to see former professional players and referees acting on a council and youth teams for League of Ireland clubs. They also advocated the formation of regional leagues and a Second Division to be run along with the 'B' division connected to the League of Ireland. It was proposed that the Republic of Ireland apply for admission to the Home International Championship and that a full-time manager be appointed for the national team, 'with no nationality qualifications', and that League of Ireland clubs should have full-time professional coaches.[179]

Funding for the new coaching scheme was to be provided via a grant from COSAC, the National Council for Sport and Recreation. The course lasted for five days with a number of League of Ireland clubs participating, and was developed around the plans of the English FA's Amateur Midland Regional Coach, John Jarman, who had overseen a 'pilot scheme' in Dublin the previous year.[180] Jarman was appointed FAI national coach later that year and took up the post in 1974.[181] In November 1973, the FAI announced the organisation of a private sweep, known as the FAI Development Fund Members Draw, with the profits to go towards providing facilities and coaching.[182]

While Jarman had been the first national coach the FAI had appointed since Alex Stevenson, the same problems experienced by Dougald Livingstone were obvious early in the new coach's tenure. Despite trips to regional areas throughout Ireland such as Athenry, Sligo and Letterkenny in 1974, and a proposal drawn up by Jarman to be viewed by government officials in the hope of gaining more concrete support in the form of funds, facilities and finance remained problematic for the development of the game at grassroots and schoolboy level.[183] In November of that year, Jarman called on the FAI to establish an £11,000 a year scheme for a permanent coaching structure. A year and a half into his contract, he felt that unless the scheme could be implemented, his work in Ireland was more or less finished, with the development of soccer being impeded by the lack of a regional administrative structure.[184] He felt that this was not something new, it being 'one of the principal recommendations' of the Football Commission in 1973. This lack of finance was said to have been a common problem within Irish soccer at this point, with one reporter noting its 'poverty-stricken state' in October 1975.[185] Jarman wanted to see the setting up of more regional centres for coaching, as although seven had been established, they did not have the proper facilities. He also felt that 'the schoolboys and youths of Ireland are crying out to be helped' while one reporter was of the view that the Welshman had 'virtually revolutionised the Irish soccer set-up at grass-roots level' with improvements shown in the fortunes of the Republic of Ireland's schoolboy and youth teams. In addition, 250 teacher-coaches had passed exams in coaching.[186] Jarman had also established a scheme for 280 boys in St Anne's Park in Dublin that summer, while eighteen former Irish internationals passed preliminary exams and eighteen Bohemians players received teacher awards. College students, including those of the National College of Physical Education in Limerick, had also passed exams along with army men, while an inter-provincial youth tournament had been held in Limerick.[187]

Jarman's efforts were at times hindered by poor attendances in some counties, while what he termed 'parochial attitudes' were said to be evident in Sligo, where he felt that 'everybody wants to develop his own corner but nobody is interested in co-operation with the result that all suffer'.[188] He added that 'nothing could develop properly in those circumstances', although he felt that there was 'a slight foundation' there already but it was 'not very solid'.[189] Jarman was also critical of the Irish government minister 'responsible for sport', John Bruton, in 1976, and called for clarification on his policy towards sport and facilities. He also felt that Department of Education grants were 'totally inadequate' in helping to keep people interested in the game.[190] The country, he suggested, was 'at least 15 years behind' Wales, Belgium and Holland 'in acquiring adequate facilities for sport'. In July 1977 he resigned from the role, citing family commitments as being key to this, despite reports highlighting tensions in his relationship with international manager, John Giles, and the FAI during his three and a half years as National Director of Coaching.[191] For all Jarman's hard work, in January 1977 one reporter felt that progress in 'successfully organising a coaching policy throughout the country' was hindered by 'the lack of playing and coaching facilities, the lack of freedom of choice for boys who would like to play soccer at school, and the lack of trained personnel to continue where he himself has engendered enthusiasm into hitherto untapped areas'.[192]

Earlier that month it was noted that less than half of the fourteen major recommendations of the 1973 Commission had been implemented, with Shamrock Rovers director Louis Kilcoyne noting that the FAI was in 'a serious financial debt' and that the money needed to develop soccer had to come from the game itself. Plans to bring in a levy with each player in the country contributing £1 had not materialised and the move did not have the support of the junior clubs, with whom the majority of the players were registered. Suggestions to improve facilities were also said to have been largely ignored, while Kilcoyne felt that 'there are a lot of people with vested interests who want to cling to power'. The FAI chairman at the time of the report, Donie O'Halloran, believed that not enough progress had been made in setting up divisional rather than provincial structures.[193]

THE IMPACT OF INTERNATIONAL SUCCESS ON SCHOOLS' AND COACHING INFRASTRUCTURES

By the middle of the 1980s soccer organisers in the Republic were still struggling to cement a coherent nationwide infrastructure, with one Cork-based correspondent to a national soccer magazine stating that the game was 'going through a very bad period'. He made a number of observations, with a lack of facilities again highlighted. He also recommended the building of a national stadium, the promotion of soccer in schools, the implementation of more coaching courses and the provision of a lottery by the FAI to help grassroots clubs reach a decent standard.[194] This situation was to change with the Republic of Ireland's qualification for Euro '88 following the appointment of Jack Charlton as international manager in 1986. Dave Hannigan has highlighted the impact of the Jack Charlton era and satellite transmissions of live English matches on the popularisation of association football throughout the country in the 1990s.[195]

According to sports sociologist, Richard Giulianotti, in Ireland, 'the post-modernization of national identity has been a key facilitator of [association] football's new appeal'.[196] As noted by Mike Cronin, a lack of success at international level and the poor state of the game here meant that Irish people could not properly embrace soccer.[197] The Republic of Ireland team's performance in Euro '88 – beating England, drawing with the USSR and being narrowly defeated by the Netherlands – meant that interest in soccer grew along with the confidence to set up competitions, particularly in some areas where soccer had struggled to gain a foothold at schoolboy level. (The South Donegal Schoolboys' League was founded in September of that year.[198]) This progress at international level also had a strong effect on the development of coaching. In the winter of 1989, FAI Director of Coaching, Noel King, noted:

> The level of interest nationwide has been enormous and more counties and people have become involved than ever before. Courses have taken place in Mayo, Clare, Limerick, Cork, Meath, Galway, Sligo, Donegal and, of course, north and south Dublin. Throw in the teachers' association, the VEC and you begin to feel the growth that we are experiencing … Undoubtedly, this is largely due to the success of the national team, but regardless of the reason, the facts are that we are in the process of creating a coaching structure that can mean something and have a genuine effect on the future of many children, now and well into the future … with every region now forming coaching associations, it may be possible to effect, not only potential coaches, but more importantly, potential players with the introduction of schools of excellence, FÁS courses and so on.[199]

International success meant greater sponsorship opportunities and more finance. One journalist was of the opinion that year that 'the first signs of benefits from the national team's success on the field of play showed themselves when the FAI announced a number of grants and interest-free loans to various soccer bodies throughout the country'.[200] The Avonmore Ireland Cup, sponsored by a milk company, was said to be 'the first schoolboy international tournament to be held in [the Republic of] Ireland', with 'in excess of 1,200 boys at under 12, under 14, under 16 and under 18 years of age' taking part in this competition in April 1988 in Dublin.[201] In February 1990, in the build up to the World Cup, a joint venture between the confectionery manufacturer Mars and the Football Association of Ireland Schools (FAIS) saw soccer skills competitions set up, with three age groups – under 9, under 11 and over 11 – put into place. Some 106 schools in Dublin, Donegal, Limerick, Mayo and Waterford were to take part, with regional winners going through to the finals at Lansdowne Road, scheduled to be held before an international match. This system was devised by Noel King, with over 2,000 children participating in the 1990 programme.[202] In 1995 there were 133 new school entries, bringing the overall total of schools involved to 500, within eighteen regions.[203] The dissemination of soccer in Irish primary schools was also helped by the publication of a book on the game by the Football Association of Ireland, said to include lesson plans, and sent to every school in the country. Written by three primary school teachers, it was launched by the Minister for Education, Liam Aylward, in April 1994.[204] In 1992, Coca-Cola became involved in FAI coaching clinics, providing £150,000 to the Association over three years, although this was not the first time they had been involved in sponsorship for soccer coaching in Ireland.[205] This appears to be part of a broader Coca-Cola policy to involve itself in football generally, and youth football specifically, at a global level.[206]

Denis Behan is an example of a player who benefited from the new structures put in place for the development of young talent in the late twentieth century, and from having a school teacher with a strong interest in soccer to encourage him. He participated in the Mars/FAIS Soccer Skills under 9 national final in 1993, representing his primary school, Abbeyfeale NS, in west Limerick.[207] He had a teacher at primary school, Frank Nelligan, who was particularly encouraging of the playing of soccer. Behan, who, when interviewed, described his local area as 'a predominantly GAA stronghold', felt that his selection for Irish underage squads in the period after 1999 was largely due to the help of Tralee-based Regional Development Officer, Brian McCarthy, 'because it was predominantly Cork and Dublin [players selected] at that time, the scouts or the managers really didn't go outside those areas … anybody who was good were probably going to play in those leagues'.[208] He added:

> You can understand then why clubs from England go to Dublin and Cork, because it's an easy flight over, they have the pick of ten to fifteen really well-run clubs, with huge numbers … as a scout, you kind of look for the easiest way out, get one or two players and then that's your job done, you know, whereas to the FAI, to be fair to them, they did put out the development officers which helped us get on the ladder to things.[209]

However, the organisation of these officers by the FAI did not take place until late in the twentieth century, thereby hindering the chances of peripherally based players to get noticed for long periods in the years covered in this book.

The development of schoolboys' soccer in Ireland was also helped by a shift in attitudes towards the game in some educational institutions. Some traditional GAA-playing schools began to accommodate the game in the late twentieth century, with students at St Kieran's in Kilkenny, an institute said to be 'devoid of any kind of a tradition in the game of billions', benefiting from the input of Tipperary-born teacher, Jim Carew, to win the Leinster Schools Senior Cup for the first time in 1993. The game had first been included as part of their sporting calendar during the 1975–76 season.[210] A similar development occurred at St Macartan's College in Monaghan in the 1980s where 'maths teacher and enthusiastic football fan', Aidan McCabe, was behind the development of soccer in what was traditionally a Gaelic football college.[211] It is important to note that in both of these second-level institutions, these teachers were helped by the co-operation of their principals, who were both clergymen, illustrating a change in attitudes towards soccer from the previous stance of many members of the clergy which had been evident for much of the twentieth century, particularly in many Christian Brothers schools. In addition, there is some indication that schools traditionally known for their rugby-playing prowess in the Republic are becoming more open to playing soccer at a serious schools level, with Blackrock College, who hold the record number of Leinster Schools Senior Cup titles in rugby, winning the All-Ireland Senior Schools soccer competition for the first time in 2003.[212] Their opponents in the final in 2003 were a school with a strong GAA tradition, St Patrick's of Cavan. North of the border, there has also been progress made in establishing soccer's place within Northern Ireland's schools. In 2015, INST won their first soccer trophy, the Belfast under 18 league title.[213] This development was said to be the result of structures put in place by teacher, Paul McKinstry, in the late 1970s, while traditional rugby-playing educational institutions Methodist College and Campbell College, also now have soccer teams.[214]

Despite recent improvements, progress has not always been smooth, and some problems remain, particularly in more peripheral areas. Prior to the FAI's Emerging Talent Scheme being initiated in 2006, it was reported in one provincial newspaper that there was 'no consistent, integrated and structured coaching and development programme for the most talented Irish players'. A 'representative squad structure' had existed, but this was 'more advanced in some parts of the country than in others'. Additionally, it was stated that 'the quality and quantity of the training sessions for these squads' was varied.[215] However, it must be noted that much progress has been made since the opening decade of the twenty-first century through the new scheme, with twelve Emerging Talent centres now in operation.[216] There is still room for improvement, according to League of Ireland manager Martin Russell:

> I think the idea's right in terms of getting the best players playing with the best players but it needs to be broader in terms of just being once a week, so probably in an environment where it's done daily, in terms of they go to school together, they train more often together, and it's done more full-time and I think that will happen, but we need to do more for our elite young players in terms of their development in making them more at a standard that the international competition is.[217]

In Northern Ireland, centres of excellence have also been put in place, although the financial considerations of the attendance fee and transport may hinder some families from sending their children.[218] In addition, the 'Small-Sided Games' strategy has been implemented as a model for primary school children participating in football, with fifteen centres for this development established by 2012.[219] Thirty specialist coaches are now employed as part of the IFA's Curriculum Sports Programme within 270 Northern Ireland schools.[220] The IFA implemented their new strategy, 'Let Them Play', in 2015, with a view to improving participation of young players in soccer. This is supported by UEFA and includes a plan to develop a pathway for young players to progress further in the game.[221]

CONCLUSION

As Seamus Heath has stated, some school principals will point to the fact that students know their sporting policies before enrolling, and he has noted the loss of talented soccer players in his local area in Downpatrick as a result of this lack of choice.[222] Although the education systems in Northern Ireland and the Republic are obviously different, a lack of schools' soccer has probably hindered levels of player production in both countries in the period covered here. As shown above, those attempting to implement coaching structures for young players in Ireland have faced many challenges at local, regional and national level. Northern Ireland, in contrast to the Republic of Ireland, received some of the benefits of the post-war consensus in Britain that saw, and encouraged, the state as a benign and beneficent facilitator in people's lives and this impacted on the implementation and organisation of coaching. While the IFA had a smaller area to work with than the FAI, they too had to face competition from other sports and indifference from those running educational institutions.

However, it appears that financially, the former body were initially able to cope a lot better in organising coaching structures than its counterpart in Dublin, and support from government and educational bodies came a lot quicker in the decades immediately following the war. Admittedly, some players – such as Pat Jennings, Seamus Heath and Raymond Campbell – have stated that they were never coached as schoolboy players, but it is clear here that the slow progress and lack of implementation of coaching structures and school teams has been a factor in the low rates of player production in many peripheral Irish towns and villages, particularly where soccer clubs were unwelcome.[223]

While developments in the Republic of Ireland were hindered by the game's lack of a national identity in many areas, it would be interesting to know if qualification for a major international tournament prior to the late 1980s would have boosted interest in developing soccer, not only through player participation but also in the attitudes of those in government, educational establishments and businesses. It is difficult to establish the impact of qualification for Sweden '58, Spain '82 and Mexico '86 on soccer in Northern Ireland at these times, although the game there has also faced difficulties with the Troubles and the identity associated with the national team. Whether or not Euro 2016 will lead to a boost in developments in the game's coaching structures at schoolboy level in both countries remains to be seen, while more research needs to be undertaken on the impact of international tournaments on other less successful footballing nations at grassroots level so that a more international comparison can be made.

Chapter 3 examines how players have been recruited and some of their experiences of the process of moving to England to sign for a professional club.

CHAPTER 3

The Movement Process

> If it's not the thing you most want to do, and if it's not the thing you love doing more than anything else, and if you don't have a passion for [it], or just an indescribable obsession, you're not going to make it. All the luck, the lack of injuries, the manager that likes you, the timing of a good performance in front of a scout, it'll all catch up in the end if it's not something you love doing. I genuinely believe this.[1]
>
> Richie Sadlier, 23 July 2013

INTRODUCTION

This chapter begins by providing an assessment of pre-Second World War Irish football migration to England along with an analysis of some of the factors that affected rates of movement in this period. The social backgrounds of a number of early Irish football migrants are assessed, and the way players have generally been recruited is discussed. The views of a number of footballers interviewed for this study are given on the role and place of agents in the modern game. The various types of migration undertaken by Irish-born players in the post-war years until 2010 are identified. These moves have mainly been through transfer, trainee systems or as juniors, and an analysis of the reasons why the rates of movement associated with these categories changed over time is offered. It determines which English clubs were initially favoured by these players and assesses why some clubs have attracted more Irish players than others. It examines how Irish-born footballers have adapted to life as footballers in England and attempts to set this within the context of wider migration there from Ireland. The role of local communities and organisations in the lives of Irish footballers is assessed and players' off-the-field activities are discussed. The importance of assistance from other Irish players in adapting to a new environment is of particular significance along with the obvious benefits of a welcoming atmosphere in accommodation and the need to maintain links with families at home in Ireland. The lack of support systems for young players within professional clubs is discussed, although this is an aspect of the game that has improved since the twentieth century. Finally, an assessment of some of the qualities required to become a professional footballer, through the views of some of those who have played league football in England, are discussed.

PRE-SECOND WORLD WAR FOOTBALL MIGRATION FROM IRELAND

As noted earlier, in the period from 1888 to 1939, 286 Irish-born footballers played league football in England.[2] The movement of players between Ireland and England led to frosty relations between the respective football governing bodies for much of the pre-Second World War period. The transfer of Harry Buckle from Cliftonville to Sunderland in 1902 drew concern from the *Belfast Telegraph*'s football columnist 'Ralph the Rover':

> I must say that I am distinctly opposed to this promiscuous signing on by Irish players for English clubs. The English clubs, I am convinced, have two ends in view when they approach an Irish player of ability. The first is the possibility of his playing for them, and the second the possibility of a substantial fee being obtained should such a player sign a professional form for another club. It has been stated that Sunderland has signed on Harry Buckle of Cliftonville. If this be correct, Buckle cannot now play for another team in the English league competition until he has been transferred by Sunderland, who will probably ask a substantial sum for doing so. Who is the gainer in this case?[3]

By the early 1900s, the IFA were also raising concerns with the International Football League Board, an Anglo-Scot organisation founded in 1897, about English clubs' poaching of Irish players with the Board agreeing in June 1904 that during the month of May, the traditional end-of-season time, forty-eight hours' notice had to be given to Scottish and Irish clubs before their players could be approached about relocating.[4] This did not resolve the issue, however, as in 1908, Distillery FC reported Glasgow Rangers to the IFA for approaching McCracken, their right full back, in his place of employment before seven o'clock in the morning, 'without either asking or receiving permission to do so'.[5] They also offered him work in the Fairfield Shipyard, prompting the Belfast club to ask the IFA if they would 'take such steps as would prevent the Rangers or any other club from tampering with their players in the future'.[6] The IFA committee agreed to send a letter to the Scottish FA as the chairman said that it was the first time 'such a thing had cropped up, so far as the Scottish Football Association was concerned, with a club in Ireland'.[7] This seems unlikely. By 1902 one Belfast reporter estimated that a total of twenty-one Irish players had migrated to play for cross-channel clubs while in August 1904, it was stated in the same newspaper that 'the migration of Irish players has set in'.[8]

As Garnham has stated, by the early 1900s the system of 'retain and transfer' was operational for over a decade and meant that clubs could, at the end of the season, retain those players they needed for the next campaign.[9] A player not re-signed could only move to a different club if a transfer fee was paid, while those not wanted by any club had no choice but to retire from the professional game. The system differed in Ireland, with players only signed on a season-by-season basis, but in 1914 the English method was introduced.[10] Despite agreements between league governing bodies to respect contracts, problems continued.

An Anglo-Irish Football League Board was set up in 1914, mainly to prevent English-based players moving to Ireland, and this body aimed to meet on the eve of Inter-League matches 'or as occasion may require'. The Board claimed to have 'power to deal with offenders' who 'improperly' approached players, but as Taylor states, 'the major threat to the Football League's control over its labour force continued to come from Ireland'.[11] The following year, the Scottish and Irish Football League Board was established, with four representatives selected from the Scottish league while the Irish League was to have three delegates.[12]

Table 3.1 Breakdown of Irish-born footballers' migration to English league football, 1888–1939. The exact places of birth could not be identified in a number of cases and therefore have been placed as 'Unidentified place of birth recorded only as "Ireland"'.

Years	Present day Northern Ireland	Present day Republic of Ireland	Unidentified place of birth recorded only as 'Ireland'	Overall Number
1888–99	12	10	3	25
1900–09	15	13	7	35
1910–19	15	16	5	36
1920–29	79	26	1	106
1930–39	46	30	8	84
Overall Total	**167**	**95**	**24**	**286**

Source: Joyce, *Football League Players' Records.*

Figures for Irish football migrants in the late nineteenth century were not reflective of wider migration trends, with David Fitzpatrick noting that 'around 1890 only three-fifths of those born in Ireland were still at home, with three million living overseas'.[13] At the beginning of the twentieth century there were more than 600,000 Irish-born people living in Britain.[14] Initially, Irish footballers were slow to move to England. Overall figures per decade illustrate a rise from twenty-five between 1888 and 1899 to, in the opening decade of the twentieth century, thirty-five. The only slightly marginal increase to thirty-six between 1910 and 1919 can be explained by the outbreak of the First World War. As Taylor states, 'top-level football survived the war by modifying its rules and truncating its competitions' with league championship, FA Cup and international matches suspended, although regional 'skeletal competitions continued throughout the war'.[15] The years 1915, 1916, 1917 and 1918 saw no Irish-born players recorded as migrating to England, although a number of pre- and post-war Irish football migrants to England – including Bert Smith, Bernard Donaghey, Jack Doran, Jack Wright, Jack McCandless,

Joe Enright, Harry Hampton, Johnny Houston, Billy O'Hagan and Charlie O'Hagan – served. Bernard Donaghey was killed on the first day of the Battle of the Somme in 1916.[16] The work of Dónal McAnallen has illustrated how recruitment from GAA clubs was greater than has been recognised, with Donaghey also playing Gaelic football for Derry Celtic prior to the war after the club had switched from soccer.[17] While research on soccer players in Ireland who fought is still in its infancy, there is strong evidence that the country's clubs also provided players. Andrew Toland has stated that Belfast Celtic and Glenavon's squads were both 'severely depleted by enlistment' in the war.[18] In addition, Dublin club Bendigo became 'very much disorganised at the outbreak of the European war, as at that time about seventy-five percent of the members were in the British Army Reserve, all of whom were called to the front'.[19] Forty Bohemians players were also said to have joined the military by the end of 1914.[20] At a more localised level, preliminary research indicates that players from clubs in Omagh, Strabane and Enniskillen were involved in the war effort.[21]

In England, a footballers' battalion was established at the end of 1914 but by the following spring only 122 out of 1,800 professional players had volunteered to participate, with some indications that this was no more than a propaganda move to silence criticism in the press of the game's continuance.[22] Garnham has written that in Ireland, in the early days of the war, '[association] football was maintained at such a level that it could divert men from less savoury pastimes, but would not prove an impediment to the war effort'. Leagues in Belfast and Dublin became more regionalised and finance was badly affected, with a reduction in manpower affecting the levels of players and spectators involved, although by 1917 the numbers enlisting had 'slowed considerably'.[23] As Taylor has stated, 'this north–south split was to have profound consequences in the immediate post-war years. By 1915, the basic partition that was to define Irish football for the rest of the century had been effected.'[24]

Some Irish-born players clearly gained the attention of cross-channel clubs having learned the game while serving as soldiers throughout the pre-Second World War period. Early professional players in Ireland were at times drawn from the military.[25] Given the British military's presence throughout Ireland before the initiation of the Irish Free State in 1922, and the level of football available to soldiers, it is notable that some of these Irish football migrants had military links along with the aforementioned Archie Goodall. In 1901, there were 21,000 soldiers and officers in Ireland, while there were also almost 4,000 militiamen and yeomanry and more than 2,000 Royal Marines and members of the Royal Navy, although most were British, with under 30 per cent of each group noted as Catholics.[26] A few players were born in the Curragh camp, including Henry Whitworth Garden in 1869. He played once for Derby County in 1892 and probably was the son of an army man who moved back to England after completing his service at the camp.[27] Bill Toms, who joined Manchester United from Eccles Borough in 1919, was also born there in 1896 and does not appear to have played in the Irish League.[28] The Curragh camp, lying in County Kildare, had been established during the Crimean War 'to serve the military in the nearby garrison towns of Kildare and Newbridge' and 'expanded rapidly and the Curragh became one of the first examples of a complete military town'.[29] As T. Ryle Dwyer also states, it was taken over by the Irish army after 1921 and 'being a military camp it had the advantage of having some of the country's most advanced sporting facilities'.[30] On the eve of the inaugural English Football League championship, in the latter months of 1887, the 71st Highlanders based in the camp were said to have had 'a busy time of it with the popular winter game', illustrating how it had become a well-liked pastime there with matches watched 'with an intense interest by a large concourse of spectators'.[31] Although there is less direct evidence that the players mentioned above experienced the game there, Joe Connor, born in 1877 in what was then known as King's County (Offaly), moved to Scotland as a fifteen-year-old with his father, a soldier, and played for the Gordon Highlanders before going on to feature for West Bromwich Albion, Walsall, Bristol City and Woolwich Arsenal, as well as Ireland.[32]

A few other Irish-born footballers who played English league football took up the game while in the military. Bert Smith was born in Cavan in 1890 and is said to have fought in the Indian

Army during the First World War. He apparently learned to play association football in the army before being signed by Cardiff City in 1920.[33] J.D. Hanna, an Irish international who joined Nottingham Forest from Linfield in 1911 and made ninety-seven English league appearances, had previously played association football while in the Royal Artillery, where he was a sergeant based in Portsmouth.[34] Downpatrick-born Sam Russell, who played for Newcastle United from 1920 until 1924, learned 'the rudiments of the game during military service'.[35] Apparently, however, he 'never took seriously to the sport 'till he returned to civil life, where he began with a Belfast junior club called Oldpark'.[36]

Difficult relations between the Football League and the Irish League had been evident during the First World War with some English players joining Irish clubs and using false names, while the IFA were in turn unhappy with some English clubs for signing players registered with Belfast clubs and temporarily insisted on sanctioning all transfers of Irish players to England in the years before the foundation of the FAI in 1921.[37] In particular, a dispute over Crystal Palace's signing of Robert McCracken from Distillery in 1920 led to the Football League threatening to scrap the agreement between the Irish and English football leagues when the former body had asked for the president of the Scottish league to intervene to give a final decision, although this was later resolved and an £800 transfer fee was agreed upon.[38] Crystal Palace, as a Third Division club, were, in the view of the Football League, 'an associate rather than a full member' and therefore had not been a Football League member when they pursued McCracken. As Taylor also states, 'contact between the two bodies was resumed when the Irish League eventually accepted the position of the Football League's new associate members'.[39]

It was in the 1920s that the greatest figures for Irish football migrants in the pre-Second World War period appeared, with a total of 106 recorded. Conditions in Ireland in the early 1920s saw an increase in Irish-born players' movement to England as a result of political strife, particularly within the game's main centres. Garnham has stated that soccer in Ireland 'was under considerable pressures' in the post-First World War years with the effects of the War of Independence, which lasted from January 1919 until July 1921, impacting on the game in Belfast and Dublin. In 1920, the income of Belfast clubs was said to have been reduced significantly by 'the levels of unemployment in the city and the imposition of martial law'.[40] By March 1922 it was reported that a combination of political unrest and the poor state of the game in Belfast (the latter exacerbated by the loss of Dublin clubs Shelbourne and Bohemians following their decision to leave the IFA's competitions in 1921 and join the newly formed Football Association of Ireland's league), had led to a situation whereby players who had a chance to leave Belfast were said to be 'embracing the opportunity'.[41] Later that month Glentoran were said to have been in the process of losing their four best players, Billy Emerson, Billy Crooks, Davy Lyner and Hugh Davey, to English clubs, the latter of whom, seemingly of a nationalist background, was 'not at home at the Oval under present conditions'.[42] It was also reported that the IFA's balance had dropped significantly from 'about £2000 in hand' in 1920 to 'only £340'.[43] By the end of the 1921–22 season the game was said to be 'dying a natural death', with 'gates, never great at any period' being described as 'meagre', and the reporter felt that 'there won't be any change until [Belfast] Celtic and the two Dublin clubs return'.[44]

The political conflict was a concern for supporters, and clubs suffered economically. As Jonathan Bardon has stated, 'as the Anglo-Irish War edged into Ulster it triggered off a sectarian conflict there more vicious and lethal than all the northern riots of the previous century put together'.[45] More than 100 people were killed in Belfast in 1921 while the following year this total had risen to almost 300.[46] With the onset of the Irish Civil War in June 1922, which lasted until the following May, it was reported that in Belfast, 'outdoor sport which attracts the crowds has been at a standstill practically every weekend of the summer. True, cricket and boxing flourishes, but it only interests those playing', while 'at all events those [football] players who can escape by the open door to clubs not connected with the leagues, or by transfer, are tricking it'.[47]

By October, many Irish League clubs were unable to pay players' wages. One reporter felt that 'gates are so poor and expenses have to be met, so no sooner is a player in the limelight than a cheque is taken for his transfer. Since May last over 30 good players left Belfast for England and Scotland, and they are still going.'[48] Dublin clubs were also said to be affected, and 'Shelbourne went practically en bloc'. This did little to help these clubs, with teams weakened while the public stayed away, which had 'a double damaging effect'.[49] By November 1922 Distillery were said to have released all their professional players, while some players such as Bert Mehaffey, who had a trial period with Tottenham Hotspur, chose to sign for junior clubs on returning to Ireland, with the failure of Irish League clubs to pay 'big wages' said to have been the reason he decided to join Carrickfergus junior club Woodburn.[50] The following year, Mehaffey signed for New Brighton after his season in junior football.[51]

Belfast Celtic's return to Irish League football in 1924 was a help in improving the standard of competitive football, but 'very few' of their 1920 team were available because they were 'in the service of cross-channel clubs', with the 'chief members of the big team of 1921', Hamill, Barrett and Mehaffey, having taken up positions at English clubs.[52] The loss of top players was said to have had a detrimental effect on public interest, despite the funds these transfers could raise for clubs. In 1924, it was reported that 'in three seasons, a sum of practically £12,000 in English and Scottish gold' had 'found its way into the coffers of Irish clubs'.[53] The success of a club could certainly mean the loss of its best players, with Queen's Island losing their 'mainstay' – Morton and McCleery – to Blackburn Rovers and Gowdy to Falkirk following their Irish League and Cup double in the 1923–24 season.[54] According to Jonathan Bardon, 'at the close of 1920 the post-war boom shuddered to a halt. For the next two decades a deep slump settled on Belfast and around one quarter of insured workers were unemployed until the renewal of international conflict.'[55]

As Aaron Ó Maonaigh has stated, 'militant Irish nationalists who played non-Gaelic games have tended to dwell upon the fringes of the historiography of the [Revolutionary] period until quite recently'.[56] Overall figures for Irish revolutionaries who moved to England as football migrants are unclear, although Ó Maonaigh has noted how a number of players from St James's Gate, Strandville and Distillery were imprisoned during the Revolutionary period (1913–23) for their nationalist activities, while 1923 FAIFS Cup winners Alton United featured a number of IRA members.[57] As David Toms has written, stories of 1927 Cardiff City FA Cup-winning goalkeeper Tom Farquharson's apparent movement to Wales as a result of his father's embarrassment for his support of the Irish Republican Army are unproven.[58] While there is some suggestion that Jimmy Dunne was a member of the 1st Battalion, 'D' Company, Dublin Brigade of the IRA, Tom Feeney has stated that he was arrested in 1922 in a case of mistaken identity, and it was his brother who was actually wanted by Free State forces for republican activity during the Civil War.[59]

The overall figure for Irish footballers' migration to England in the 1920s (106) dropped in the 1930s to eighty-four players migrating and playing first-team football. As David Toms has stated, football migration between Ireland and England in the pre-Second World War years was mainly a one-way phenomenon with the exception of a brief spell during the economic recession of the 1930s, 'when the Irish Free State became a haven for disgruntled players from the Football League', which may partly explain the reduction in the number of Irish players migrating in this decade.[60] As Taylor has noted, Free State clubs also ran into trouble with the Football League for signing their players during the Depression, when the wages and playing conditions in England declined, with the result that 'the Football League remained hostile to League of Ireland clubs, refusing to recognise player registrations or even to organise representative fixtures until after the Second World War'.[61] In addition, some Irish football migrants, such as Andrew McCluggage, returned to Ireland in the early 1930s due to the adverse playing terms available.[62] Admittedly, some talented Irish players, such as Jack Simpson, turned down moves to cross-channel clubs for business reasons, illustrating how the wages English clubs were willing to pay players were still relatively low before the 1960s, and this may have affected levels of player recruitment.[63] These factors help partially explain why the figures for Irish football migrants to England were much lower than in the 1945–2010 period.

Throughout the nineteenth and early twentieth centuries, improvements in literacy and the spread of shipping information and the sending of letters home, particularly from the USA, helped increase migrants' awareness of work opportunities abroad.[64] Along with the growing presence of British scouts in Belfast and Dublin, which was referred to earlier in this book, Irish-born players' cross-channel opportunities increased in a number of other ways in the early 1900s. As well as learning about the game in Britain from newspapers such as *Sport* and *Ulster's Saturday Night* and having their local achievements publicised in the sporting press, players could also gain the notice of English clubs through word of mouth, with Billy McCracken recommending Bert Mehaffey and Sam Russell to Tottenham Hotspur and Newcastle United respectively.[65] At times, close family ties could lead to a move, with Elisha Scott joining Liverpool in 1912 a few years after his brother Billy, then Everton goalkeeper, had recommended him to his own club, who apparently rejected him as a seventeen-year-old on account of his youthful age.[66]

McCracken's own move to Newcastle United in 1904 was said to have come after 'a scouting expedition of another great all-time player, Andrew McCombie', a Scottish international who was at Newcastle United from 1903 to 1909, playing 113 times.[67] In this regard, Irish-born players were no different from British players in gaining the attention of Football League clubs. While some players undoubtedly gained recognition from English clubs through international appearances, McCracken, who later fell out with the IFA over international appearance payment, had never been capped by Ireland prior to moving to Newcastle. *Sport*'s reporter felt in 1922 that 'in those days Irish internationals were not considered of much account'.[68]

The average age of migration for those whose age could be positively identified in the 1888–1939 period was 22.65, while the average age of turning professional and making a first team debut was found to be 22.96. Some 159 or 55.59 per cent of the 286 were capped at international level by Ireland, while Newry-born Willie Maley was exceptional among Irish-born players in that he won two caps for Scotland.[69] Some players' moves came at a younger age, such as Jimmy Dunne, who was twenty years old when he moved to New Brighton in 1925.[70] Dunne's progress to top-flight football began with Shamrock Rovers B team, and at the start of his second season of competitive football in Ireland he was given a month's trial at New Brighton. Having signed for them, he joined Sheffield United after only two months for £700.[71] Movement of Irish players to Football League clubs from the lesser ranks of English football was not uncommon throughout the period covered here. Centre-half Pat Nelis made his way to Nottingham Forest from Accrington Stanley in 1922 having joined the latter the previous year. *Sport* noted the migratory route he undertook to reach that point:

> This chap is a Derry product, and up to two seasons ago he played for Derry Distillery. He went to a small Lancashire club, later to Accrington Stanley, and last week to the Forest. With Accrington he scored 14 goals in 11 games.[72]

Others moved through less structured contacts. Mickey Hamill claimed that he received a trial from Manchester United in the 1909–10 season having been recommended to the club by Harry Politt, an English referee who was a regular visitor to Belfast with other officials, and was quickly signed up.[73] A few others were spotted by Irish League clubs playing for work teams before later moving to England. Belfast-born Jackie Brown, who moved to Wolves in 1934 from Belfast Celtic, had been noticed by the Irish League club playing for linen manufacturers William Ewart and Son.[74] Less common was the case of Dr Tom Waddell, captain of Cliftonville from 1904 to 1906, who moved to Glossop from Ireland in 1906 to work there as a medical practitioner and signed for the local Second Division club.[75] While Fitzpatrick has written of more general Irish migrants in the pre-Independence years that 'most of those who left were virtually unencumbered by training, expertise or accomplishment', along with his football skills, Waddell was a clear exception.[76]

THE SOCIAL BACKGROUND OF PRE-SECOND WORLD WAR IRISH-BORN ASSOCIATION FOOTBALLERS

An analysis of early Irish football migrants undertaken for this book demonstrates that a number of players came from what could be described as an industrial background in socio-economic terms. As noted earlier, by the opening years of the twentieth century, Belfast was the centre of industry in Ireland and a number of players' jobs before migrating to England reflect the work opportunities in the north-east of Ireland at that time. Along with the aforementioned linen worker Jackie Brown, English McConnell, who moved to Sunderland from Glentoran in 1905, was employed as an apprentice engineer in the early 1900s; Alfie Harland, who joined Everton from Linfield in 1922, was initially a spinning mill tenter while Davy Lyner, who migrated from Glentoran to Manchester United the same year, had trained as an apprentice shipwright.[77] Fred McKee, who moved from Cliftonville to Sunderland in 1907, was formerly a general labourer; Dave Rollo, who left Linfield for Blackburn Rovers in 1919, was a boilermaker, while Joe Toner, who joined Arsenal from Belfast United in 1919, had been a labourer in a mineral water factory.[78] Naturally, some Dublin-born players were also involved in industrial work. Val Harris was a gas worker before signing for Everton from Shelbourne in 1907, while Patrick O'Connell, later to join Sheffield Wednesday in 1908, was initially employed as a glass fitter, and Jack C. Slemin, who joined Bradford from Bohemians in 1909, was an unspecified fitter.[79] Not every player, like Dr Tom Waddell noted above, went down the industrial employment route. William Emerson from Enniskillen, who joined Burnley from Glentoran in 1921, had been a rural postman while Buncrana-born Billy O'Hagan was a general clerk in the office of his father, who was a solicitor based in Derry city.[80]

It was not possible to construct a significant database of players' pre-migration employment for the 1888–1939 period due to a general lack of clarity in the Irish census returns, particularly where young players were not yet in employment in 1901 or 1911, or where in the majority of cases, their census details simply could not be traced. However, using data gathered, it was possible to compile a list of the occupations of players' parents to establish family backgrounds. A total of fifty players' parents' occupations were identified, with the main employment of each parent used to establish the class of social background. In most cases, it was the father who was listed as employed as most of the mothers had no occupation listed or were registered as housewives.[81] In only two players' details out of the fifty identified were both parents recorded as being employed. These were Fred McKee (his father was a general labourer and his mother was an embroiderer) and Joe Toner (his father was a general labourer and his mother was a dressmaker).[82] This data was compiled using the same categories classified by Garnham in his analysis of fifty-five early professional footballers in Ireland. These were described as labourers and unskilled; artisans; skilled; and lastly, white collar.[83] An additional category, classified as belonging to the military, was also included here.

Table 3.2 Categories of primary employment of pre-Second World War Irish-born football migrants' parents, 1888–1939.

Category	Number	Percentage
Labourers and unskilled	24	48%
White collar	10	20%
Skilled	10	20%
Artisan	4	8%
Military	2	4%
Total	**50**	**100%**

Source: Joyce, *Football League Players' Records* and Census of Ireland Returns 1901 and 1911, http://www.census.nationalarchives.ie/search [accessed 24 March 2017].

As shown in Table 3.2, twenty-four or 48 per cent of the fifty pre-Second World War football migrants identified for this book had a parent who was classified as employed in the labourers and unskilled category. Ten or 20 per cent were categorised as white collar while an additional ten (20 per cent) were noted as skilled. Only four (8 per cent) were identified as artisans while an additional two (4 per cent) were military men. This is reflective of other trends noted within professional football in Britain and Ireland at that time. As Dixon and Garnham have stated, 'the majority of early professional players in both England and Ireland came from the working classes'.[84] In particular, Garnham's study, noted above, illustrated that over 36 per cent of his fifty-five players were categorised as labourers and unskilled, while skilled workers made up 38 per cent. Almost 13 per cent were described as artisans while a similar number were white collar employees.[85] Mason's study of fifty-one professionals with 'elite clubs' in England between 1884 and 1900 illustrates that just over half of these players could be defined as 'skilled manual workers' while he has also established that of 114 professionals identified between 1907 and 1910, 'the skilled trades appear to dominate'.[86] Therefore he concludes that 'the first generation of professional footballers was largely drawn from the ranks of the skilled manual workers'.[87]

A recent study of 215 early grassroots soccer players in Fermanagh, Tyrone, Monaghan and Cavan who participated in matches for clubs in these counties between 1887 and 1915 has revealed similar patterns to the fifty Irish football migrants' data, although differing categories were utilised.[88] The greatest number of these players were employed in the industrial sector (36 per cent), while those involved in agriculture made up 27 per cent of the overall total. There was less involvement of those from the commercial class (15 per cent) and the indefinite and non-productive class (9 per cent), while those described as professional class made up just 8 per cent. The lowest percentage of players came from the domestic sector (4 per cent). The dominance of the industrial category as soccer players, as opposed to the agricultural category as GAA players, is reflective of trends in other counties. For example, an analysis of players in Donegal who participated between 1881 and 1915 illustrated that the majority (44 per cent) of 286 footballers were classified as being involved in the industrial sector, with the majority of the county's early GAA players involved in agricultural work.[89] Tom Hunt's assessment of seventy-five Westmeath soccer players who were involved locally between 1900 and 1904 has shown that 67 per cent were skilled workers,[90] while only 18.6 per cent of the 215 Ulster soccer players were classified as skilled employees. This may be reflective of the wider variety of rural teams used as opposed to Hunt's focus on clubs in Athlone and Mullingar.

Of the fifty players identified above who migrated, twenty-four or 48 per cent were Roman Catholic while eleven or 22 per cent were Presbyterian and an additional 22 per cent were identified as Church of Ireland. The remainder were Congregationalist (2 per cent), Methodist (2 per cent), Protestant Episcopalian (2 per cent) and unknown (2 per cent). Players were drawn from counties Antrim, Armagh, Cork, Derry, Donegal, Down, Fermanagh, King's County (Offaly) and Waterford. This contrasted with Garnham's assessment of professional footballers, based in Belfast, which has illustrated that the majority (43.6 per cent) were Presbyterian. Episcopalian Protestants made up 18.2 per cent while 25.5 per cent were found to be Roman Catholics. Methodists consisted of 7.2 per cent of the overall total in addition to other unnamed denominations (3.6 per cent).[91]

However, as Garnham has stated, 'the religious balance of players is comparable with the religious complexion of the city as a whole', although he has noted that Church of Ireland members were 'the most under-represented group'.[92] While a more feasible examination of Belfast-born football migrants would probably have revealed a closer comparison with Garnham's players, this is still indicative of wider trends among association football in Ireland at that time. Like those in Donegal (85 per cent) and Westmeath (100 per cent), the majority of players in the south and west Ulster area were identified as being Roman Catholic (60 per cent), with Church of Ireland members making up 34 per cent of the religious total of players examined in Cavan, Fermanagh, Monaghan and Tyrone while the involvement of Presbyterians (4 per cent), Methodists and Episcopalians (less than 1 per cent per group) was not as significant.[93]

FOOTBALL IN ENGLAND IN THE POST-SECOND WORLD WAR PERIOD AND IRISH PLAYER RECRUITMENT

Soccer in England did not cease during the Second World War, which broke out in 1939 and lasted until 1945, with Taylor noting that 'as in the First World War, football continued in a modified form, involving a mixture of home internationals, representative fixtures, inter-service games and a limited league and cup programme'.[94]

Regional groupings were established in Wales and England, with eighty-two of the Football League's eighty-eight teams involved, with special cup competitions being initiated. In 1942 it was decided to introduce north and south divisions although London clubs took the decision to break away and set up their own War League.[95] Needless to say, the game was affected by restrictions such as disruption from air raids, which led to matches being abandoned at times, although after 1942 there was a rise in attendances with a lessening of bombing during the day and the introduction of a spotter system at many grounds. Despite this, travel disruptions remained a problem, with professional clubs not allowed to travel any further than fifty miles by road. However, as Taylor states, 'as a national sport, it [soccer] benefited more than most from the position of tolerance that came to characterise government policy towards civilian sport'.[96] Many professional footballers struggled to make ends meet although by the spring of 1940 154 players had become physical training instructors in the army.[97] Plans were also made during the war for the strengthening of the game afterwards, and although not all elements of FA secretary Stanley Rous' 1943 memorandum for 'Post-War Development' were accepted, structures for coaching benefited. In 1946, English league football once again took on the same structure and fixtures present in 1939, although changes were implemented within Scotland to take pre-war records and 'wartime commitment' into account in the formation of A and B leagues.[98]

In Ireland, football also continued to be played during the Emergency, as it was known in the Free State, and Peter Byrne has noted that wartime conditions necessitated Irish football authorities coming closer together, with the inter-city club competitions at the end of the domestic season proving to be 'an instant success', while inter-league matches held twice a year at Dalymount Park and Windsor Park were 'the biggest attractions in those times of undisguised penury'.[99] Some Irish-born players inevitably served in the British Army, with Johnny Carey stationed in Italy and the Middle East, while he also appeared as a guest for a number of English clubs, and Shamrock Rovers, before returning to English league football after the war.[100]

While, as Taylor states, 'not everything returned to the way it had been before the war' within the English game, but continuity rather than change generally characterised the immediate post-war years.[101] There is little evidence to suggest any major change in the way Irish players were recruited, which generally resulted from being spotted playing for League of Ireland and Irish League clubs or junior or schoolboy teams of a decent standard. As noted earlier, some clubs had acted as feeder teams to specific clubs and developed strong links; although it is unclear when this practice began, it was certainly in existence in the 1950s as Billy Humphries has stated. There were a variety of other ways in which players were recruited in the period covered in this study, although the early twentieth century practice of prospective Football League players attending a meeting of agents in Liverpool every May Day is long gone.[102]

Irish footballers with connections and status within English league football continued to have an influence in the recruitment of others after the war, with Everton goalkeeper Jimmy O'Neill recommending George Cummins to the club in 1950, while Jimmy Magill joined his former full-back partner at Portadown, Billy McCullough, at Arsenal in 1959.[103] Alfie Hale was recommended to Aston Villa manager, Joe Mercer, in 1960 by Alex Stevenson, having scored two hat-tricks in ten days for the Irish amateur team and the League of Ireland eleven against Dutch and German selections respectively.[104] Similarly, in 1972, Damien Richardson was recommended to Gillingham manager, Andy Nelson, by his Shamrock Rovers teammate Pat Dunne, who had experience of English football at Manchester United and Plymouth Argyle.[105] Brendan Bradley came to Lincoln City's attention the same year having been mentioned to the club by Jimmy McGeough, who had joined the English club that year. McGeough then wrote a letter to Bradley asking him if he would be interesting in signing.[106] As Roderick has noted, 'friendship networks' are 'highly significant in relation to labour mobility', although he also notes that 'players will eventually lose direct contact with most teammates'.[107]

Some earlier Irish football migrants, such as Tommy Eglington and Peter Farrell, who joined Everton from Shamrock Rovers in 1946, and Norman Lockhart and Sam McCrory, who were both recruited

Dean Kelly celebrates scoring for Bohemians in 2015. He was spotted by Oldham Athletic while playing for the Republic of Ireland amateur team. Picture: © Inpho

by Swansea Town from Linfield the same year, appear to have been signed together.[108] Most players interviewed here were simply spotted while playing for their clubs, although *Shoot!* reported that Willie Irvine was spotted by Burnley playing for Northern Ireland in a schoolboy international in 1961 and joined the club as a junior straight from school.[109] Much later, Crumlin United player, Dean Kelly, was spotted by Oldham Athletic having played for the Republic of Ireland's amateur international team in 2010.[110]

With the widening of scouting networks in the late twentieth century and the growth in the development of underage teams, particularly in urban areas, players' chances of getting spotted increased while playing for their schoolboy clubs. For some other players who moved as teenagers in the 1990s, getting spotted was a fairly straightforward process, as noted by Richie Sadlier:

> The Millwall scout who at the time happened to be running the Millwall under 14 team, Gerry Smullen, started watching us a few times and then the head of the youth development, the head of the Academy at Millwall, came over a couple of times to watch me play. I don't think I did particularly well while he watched me play but on the back of that, I was invited over on trial and then asked back a couple of times and eventually signed. So it's very straightforward – someone watches you play, invites you over, you play in a trial and sign.[111]

Similarly, Alan Blayney was asked to go on trial, having been approached by Southampton as a fourteen-year-old in 1995:

> I was actually playing for North Abbey – we used to play in the South Belfast Boys League and the scout then, a boy called Denis Weir, just came and watched a few of our games. And then that was it basically – he came and watched me, I think, about five or six times, and then approached me and wanted to come and ask my mum and dad if they'd be happy for me to go on a trial.[112]

In addition, stronger clubs could also attract more scouts, with David Miskelly receiving 'two or three offers off the one game' having played a blinder as a makeshift goalkeeper for Dungoyne Youths against Lisburn Youths, 'the best side in the country at the time' at that level in the same decade.[113] Some players, such as Barry Prenderville and Brian Mooney, had been attracting the attention of leading English clubs since the age of fourteen, with Mooney going on trial at Liverpool, Manchester United, Arsenal and Everton in the early 1980s.[114]

Clubs could at times take advantage of young players' eagerness to get a move. Seamus Heath felt, in hindsight, he was a bit naïve in considering his options in terms of moving to England. He was signed by Luton Town in 1978 as a seventeen-year-old having, he initially thought, been sent there by his club, Cromac Albion, 'the top amateur team in Northern Ireland', to keep an older player who was going on trial there company. Having played well in a trial game, he was approached by manager David Pleat and, although he was delighted to sign, he now admits that 'it was all on their terms' as he quickly signed without considering other opportunities which may have arisen elsewhere.[115]

The re-emergence of agents within English football in the late twentieth century has seen their use by Irish League and League of Ireland players become more common in more recent years prior to moving to England. As Seamus Kelly has written, 'players employ agents to alleviate any potential pressure and intimidation during contract negotiations, while managers employ agents for the level of knowledge that agents possess'.[116] Their role includes contract negotiations, scouting, managing image rights of players and managers and the provision of financial advice and other support.[117] According to John Harding, in England, 'agents were quite influential for a period in the late nineteenth century, until clubs established their own scouting networks and, later still, developed youth policies and even football "nursery" clubs'.[118] For more immediate post-war players, scouts could serve as a mediator in getting a player a move. Billy Humphries felt that anything that would now be regarded as an agent's duty was then the responsibility of the player.[119] Brian Mooney was accompanied by his father, who had experience of the game, when negotiating his early contracts in the 1980s.[120] Similarly Barry Prenderville's first contract at Coventry City in the following decade was negotiated by his father.[121] The late twentieth century saw the re-introduction of professional player representatives, such as Mel Stein, into English football and, as Harding states, 'since the introduction of the Premiership … agents have proliferated and their remit in terms of services to players has expanded too'.[122]

Some twenty-first-century schoolboy recruits, such as Shane Supple, have taken on agents as they are about to sign their first professional contract.[123] As a player becomes more valuable, agents will invest more in them initially and give footballers presentations of what they can expect if they sign up.[124] Players' experiences of the use of agents in order to get them moves can vary, as Seamus Kelly illustrated when interviewed:

> I'd two agents, one was Mickey Walsh, he was bang on, but we weren't talking about big money, I mean it wasn't anything mad. He was fine, he was one of the better ones because some of them – a lot of my mates have agents – they get you a deal, they get 10 per cent, they get the signing-on fee, they get the bonus, you don't hear from them, and then, when your contract is nearly up, they'll either negotiate it or they'll orchestrate a move to get more money … I've been stitched up by another agent once, the contract wasn't what I looked for or agreed, by him or the club. I'd to pay him like nearly sixteen grand, it was four four-grand instalments, and it was a footnote in the contract, font size was six, at the bottom, and it was a performance-related statement or payment that I was due to pay every four months, so … I've tonnes of friends who've had that, I mean, you've got to look after yourself.[125]

Kelly also felt that 'agent wise, that whole industry is frightening, but an agent can get you a move, he can get you the money, so that's why players want them.'[126] Similarly, Dean Kelly was of the view that his agent was important:

> He negotiated everything for my contract. Anything like that he was good … because there's a lot of young lads that really haven't got a clue what they're talking about, so they sort out wages and bonuses and anything like that. You really have to have someone that knows what they're doing.[127]

While Alan Blayney and David Miskelly also felt that any agents they had were fine, Seamus Heath reckoned that 'you don't even need an agent, the best agent for you can be the Professional Footballers' Association. The PFA will advise you.' He also stated that 'what's happened now, young lads want to say to their friends, "I've got an agent." Agents work for themselves, and I've yet to meet an agent who's out there for the player.'[128] Michael McHugh negotiated his own contracts having declined to take up the offer of being represented by a well-known company who were charging an 'extortionate' fee, which was a flat payment rather than a percentage of what he earned.[129] Martin Russell was of the opinion that 'there's pros and cons to them – like they can open doors but then again they can scupper things as well.'[130] Negotiating contracts can certainly be difficult for players, however. Richie Sadlier illustrated how two of his contracts were settled:

> One of them was … the manager rang me, gave me the figures. I said 'yes', and he called around and I signed the contract by leaning on the boot of his car, outside my front door. Another one, Billy Bonds, sat me down in an office and said, 'Son, this is what we're offering you, there's a phone, if you want to ring the PFA, ring them, you're in front of me now, do you have an agent?' And I didn't [so he said], 'Do you want to ring your dad?' and my dad knows … as little as I do, [about negotiating football contracts], [so I declined and Billy Bonds said], 'Well then sign it.'[131]

Sadlier was therefore of the opinion that it was more beneficial for the player to use an agent in negotiations:

> The easiest way to do it is you get someone else to negotiate on your behalf. I've never met an eighteen-year-old who's as good a negotiator as a middle-aged businessman – he's been doing it for years. So that's generally how it is – you get the initial approach either from an agent or from the club. But people start talking then and after that it's down to the negotiating skills of the people involved. I always preferred when I wasn't involved, but it often didn't work out that way.[132]

POST-WAR CATEGORIES OF MIGRATION: REPUBLIC OF IRELAND

As Harding has noted, prior to 1960, young players could not be signed as full-time professional footballers until they were seventeen years old. However, in the inter-war years, the 'ground-staff option' was developed whereby a teenager could join a club to work in an office or with the groundsman, having left school at fifteen. The young player could train with the club twice a week and sign amateur forms and 'in effect, it gave the club that had first spotted the boy some quasi-legal hold over him'.[133] In addition, there was no formal apprentice structure for footballers in England until 1960.[134] Under the English trainee system, teenage players who joined as trainees were known as 'apprentices' until 1986 when the British government began to sponsor these players under their 'Youth Training Scheme'. Trainees became known as 'scholars' in 1999–2000 under a new scholarship scheme and these terms will be used here.[135] Players who signed professionally from school or college without serving an apprenticeship period have been identified as 'juniors' in Hugman's publication and this categorisation has also been used in this book.

A total of 500 players born in the Republic of Ireland who went on to play in the English Premiership or Football League migrated to England between 1945 and 2010 (see Table 3.3). Some 258 (51.6 per cent) of these were transfers while 207 (41.4 per cent) were trainees and ten players (2 per cent) were signed from 'juniors'. The nature of seventeen migrations (3.4 per cent) has not been clearly established while eight players (1.6 per cent) were involved in non-football-related migrations.

Table 3.3 Republic of Ireland born players' migration to England, 1945–2010: categories of migration.

Years	Transfer	Trainee	Juniors	Unknown	N/A	Number
1945–55	83	0	2	9	1	95
1956–65	25	7	2	4	3	41
1966–75	24	14	0	2	1	41
1976–85	17	15	1	0	0	33
1986–95	45	39	4	1	1	90
1996–2005	41	103	1	1	2	148
2006–10	23	29	0	0	0	52
Total	**258**	**207**	**10**	**17**	**8**	**500**

Source: As Table 1.2.

During the first period examined, 1945–55, the vast majority of migration was through direct transfers. A total of ninety-five players migrated in this period and eighty-three of these were direct, football-related transfers. The Irish source clubs of an additional nine players could not be traced and one player was involved in non-football-related migration: Charlie Hurley migrated to England as a baby. McGovern suggests this high level of recruitment was because players were needed to replace those lost or injured in the Second World War.[136] Only forty-one football league players migrated in the period 1956–65. Twenty-five of these were direct while seven apprentices who went on to play in the English Football League were signed. An additional two were signed as 'juniors'. There is some indication that a number of earlier League of Ireland footballers, such as Paddy Coad, were still of the pre-war mindset that it was more financially beneficial for them to stay at home and work part-time as, up until 1961, players couldn't earn more than £20 a week in England.[137] In 1959, for example, players could earn £17 per week during the close season while £4 was additionally given for a win and £2 for a draw as a bonus.[138] However, with these changes, by the late 1960s, George Best was said to be earning at least £125 a week which gave him £6,500 per annum plus bonuses while in contrast, Sir Stanley Matthews, who retired in 1965, had apparently only earned £12,500 in his whole career, which stretched back to 1932.[139]

There is no evidence of a significant influx of Republic of Ireland-born players in the 1960s, however. The overall figure from 1966 to 1975 was the same (forty-one) although the number of apprentices had grown to fourteen as opposed to twenty-four transfers. Only thirty-three Irish-born footballers broke into English league football in the period 1976–85, with seventeen registered as transfers and fifteen as apprentices, while one signed as a 'junior'. Delaney has noted how Irish emigration 'reached its peak in the 1950s and 1980s', although the figures compiled for this study do not indicate that this was the case in terms of football migration and entering the workplace as professionals.[140] This is unsurprising, however, given the differing nature of professional football as opposed to other occupations within the labour market.

There was a vast increase in the number of players who moved in the period 1986–95. A total of ninety players were noted and forty-five players transferred, with thirty-nine trainees signing as professionals during this period of time. Between 1996 and 2005 the number of migrants signing professionally continued to grow and the number of trainees began to vastly outnumber those signed as transfers. There were a total of 103 trainees registered for this period (sixty-nine under the Youth Training Scheme and thirty-four under the new scholarship system) while only forty-one transfers were noted. This increase in figures can probably be attributed to the success of the Jack Charlton era, although English football's general popularity and the money available within clubs had improved since the 1970s and 1980s.[141] In addition, the success of Irish players at Liverpool, Arsenal and Manchester United in the 1980s probably increased the reputations of aspiring Irish-born players. Data for the period 2006–10 shows that a total of fifty-two players signed professionally and went on to play league football, with twenty-three transfers and twenty-nine scholars noted.

NORTHERN IRELAND

As can be seen in Table 3.4, there were 417 players born in Northern Ireland who migrated between 1945 and 2010 and went on to play in the English Premiership or Football League. Some 250 of these players (59.95 per cent) migrated as transfers while an additional 127 players

Table 3.4 Northern Irish-born players' migration to England, 1945–2010: categories of migration.

Years	Transfer	Trainee	Juniors	Unknown	N/A	Number
1945–55	92	0	4	5	1	**102**
1956–65	52	1	12	1	1	**67**
1966–75	42	12	6	1	0	**61**
1976–85	29	16	3	1	0	**49**
1986–95	13	27	0	0	1	**41**
1996–2005	18	60	2	2	0	**82**
2006–10	4	11	0	0	0	**15**
Total	**250**	**127**	**27**	**10**	**3**	**417**

Source: As Table 1.2.

(30.45 per cent) were identified as trainees. Twenty-seven were noted as being signed from 'juniors' (6.47 per cent) while there were only three (0.71 per cent) earlier migrations as non-footballers. It has not been possible to identify the migration sources of ten players (2.39 per cent).

This table also illustrates that the figure of 102 in the 1946–55 period was the highest recorded and after this there was a gradual reduction until the 1996–2005 period when figures rose again (eighty-two). Unlike in the Republic of Ireland, it was in the 1986–95 period that the recruitment of players as trainees (twenty-seven) became more prominent than transfers (thirteen) and McGovern has identified this period as 'a watershed in buyer–supplier relations between the Irish and English leagues' and feels this was due to a change in clubs' youth policies.[142] It was also in this period that rates of player migration from the Republic of Ireland overtook those from Northern Ireland for the first time since the 1910–19 period (although Ireland was still united at that stage). After the 1986 World Cup, Northern Ireland failed to qualify for another tournament until Euro 2016, while the Republic of Ireland qualified for three major tournaments in the 1986–95 period, although admittedly, many of the players utilised were not born in Ireland.

INITIAL RECRUITING CLUBS

As Fitzpatrick has written of the pre-Independence period, 'the distribution of Irish settlers was also stable over time' and 'marked regional clusters developed by comparison with other migrant groups, the characteristically "Irish" regions being south-west Scotland and England north of the Mersey'.[143] Irish football migrants to England in the pre-Second World War period differed to some extent in where they initially settled, although, like non-football migrants they also showed geographical mobility, with players averaging two English league clubs. Manchester United initially recruited and gave first-team football to the most Irish-born players in the pre-Second World War period, with 3.25 per cent of the overall total of 286 noted, followed by Leeds City (3.15 per cent), Liverpool (2.8 per cent),

Burnley (2.45 per cent) and Arsenal (1.75 per cent).[144] Peake's study of early Irish football migrants has illustrated that 'while many of these footballers were following an established migration route, it was not necessarily due to the appeal of congregating in areas where first and second generation Irish lived'.[145]

A similar pattern was noted in the 1945–2010 period. It is also possible to establish the English cities which were most prominent among Irish-born players who played English league football during these years and again, Manchester United was the club which placed most value on signing and giving first-team football to Irish football migrants. An examination of initial recruiting clubs indicates a correlation with Taylor and Lanfranchi's assessment that Irish footballers 'seem to have been drawn to cities or regions with high migrant populations'.[146] Manchester United (5.2 per cent), Arsenal (3.2 per cent) and Millwall of London (3.2 per cent) have emerged as the top three recruiting clubs for players born in the Republic of Ireland.[147]

These post-war players do, on paper, appear to have favoured cities with an Irish emigrant population as places of settlement, with ninety-one players or 18.2 per cent opting to initially play their English league football in London and thirty-eight players or 7.6 per cent initially joining Manchester clubs City and United. Merseyside clubs Everton, Tranmere Rovers and Liverpool made up 6.2 per cent of this total with thirty-one players initially being recruited in this area. Admittedly, there is a greater range of London-based clubs but this still partially reflects the English capital's strength as an Irish emigrant base as well as its other advantages. Fitzpatrick has identified 'the great "Irish" cities abroad' as being New York, Philadelphia, Boston and Chicago in the USA and in Britain, Liverpool, Glasgow, Manchester and London.[148] Despite these cultural links, it would be incorrect to assume that Irish-born players consciously decide to settle in a particular city with strong Irish links.

A number of players interviewed felt that most players usually go to the club that offers them a contract and the chance of first-team football rather than considering geographical locations. Seamus Kelly has stated that 'you don't go to a club because it's in a nice area,

Like Damien Richardson, **Paddy Mulligan** moved to England after proving himself in the League of Ireland with Shamrock Rovers. He won fifty caps for the Republic of Ireland along with the European Cup Winners' Cup at Chelsea in 1971. Picture: © Inpho

like say Southampton, you go because the manager wants you and he's going to pay enough'.[149] Paddy Mulligan, who had initially joined Chelsea from Shamrock Rovers in 1969, felt that the opportunity for first-team football was paramount:

> If the club wants you, you go, that's the way I'd been. West Brom wanted me [in 1975]. I took a drop in wages to go to West Brom, because they couldn't pay me what I was on at Crystal Palace, so that was it. It didn't matter whether it was Birmingham or Timbuktu, you just wanted to play and resurrect your career and get sorted, that was all.[150]

First-team football is clearly a major factor, with Barry Prenderville admitting he chose Coventry City over Manchester United in 1994 because he felt he would have a better chance of playing for the first team.[151] Shane Supple chose Ipswich Town in 2003 as they had a reputation for bringing young players through:

> Financially the club wasn't that well off, so there were opportunities for players to break through, which was another reason I went there in the first place. When I went over first, there was probably the two first-team 'keepers, and two youth team 'keepers, and then myself, so there was competition there obviously, but not to the extent you would have at top Premier League clubs where they might have seven, eight 'keepers, or two from every age group, so I was quite lucky in that respect.[152]

While there is therefore some indication that Irish schoolboy clubs now recommend young players to join less prominent clubs in order to have a better chance of breaking into first-team football, Alfie Hale and David Miskelly both stated that a player who started playing with a top club like Manchester United would have a better chance of making a career for himself later on, if released, as he would have a better reputation as a result of playing for or being linked with a team of that calibre.[153] There is also some evidence from Hunter Davies' study of Tottenham Hotspur in the 1971–72 season to strengthen this argument. A number of apprentices at the club felt that 'having once got to Spurs, you could always go somewhere else' but 'if you started at a lower club and failed, that was it'.[154]

In 2015 Gary Neville stated in his newspaper column that 'what is becoming most important to today's player is not the culture or history of a club, but the location, for the family, and the distance back to where they want to live', while he also notes the wages available as being 'a huge factor'.[155] This geographical consideration would appear to be a choice available only to the most high-profile players such as David Beckham, however, as most lower league players would be thinking mainly of where they can get a game and earn a living. As Seamus Heath has stated, 'The millionaire player, who's played in Manchester and suddenly wants a high life in London would maybe do that, but 99 per cent of footballers are going to a place for the football reason, without even knowing what's in the city or town.'[156]

Similarly, Manchester United was found to be the top recruiting club of Northern Ireland-born players (6.71 per cent), with Arsenal (3.59 per cent) and Newcastle United (3.59 per cent) following behind. Sixty players or 14.38 per cent initially joined London clubs while thirty-nine players or 9.35 per cent opted to first settle in Manchester at City or United. Therefore it is more a case of big cities in England having the biggest clubs and having Irish emigrant populations rather than players choosing to move to cities associated with Irish migration.

The above data can also be partially explained by managers' attitudes. As Seamus Kelly has written, 'English soccer clubs have a long history of recruiting young Irish players which constitutes a form of "demonstration effect" in which the success (or failure) of previous Irish migrant players influences future recruitment decisions.'[157] Some Irish managers in England, such as Damien Richardson, Roddy Collins and Mick McCarthy, have shown a tendency to sign Irish players.[158] When interviewed about his role in this while managing Gillingham from 1989–92, Richardson stated:

> We'd a good little nucleus of Irish players; there were other Irish players who didn't come through. And I found the lesson I'd

> learned of being an Irishman and understanding the problems Irish players had, I took those onto the lads from other parts of the country as well, because almost all of a sudden, Gillingham, instead of taking lads local to the county of Kent, started taking lads from Scotland and different parts. As their reputation grew as regards player development, more and more people wanted to come to them around the country, so it then became an international set-up.[159]

During his time as manager of Gillingham, Richardson had five Irish internationals (at differing levels) at the club.[160] He added:

> [If] somebody speaks about an Irish player going over, I always say, go to a club that has an understanding of Irish players, because Irish players are different – there is no denying that – the same way Scottish players are different. We all have our indigenous qualities and if you can go to a club that is used to the Irish personality and the Irish ways then you're far better off, you've got a far better chance of coming through the system; if there are other Irish lads there, that's even better. If there's an Irish connection in the hierarchy of the coaching system, that's even better [for the player's chances of making the breakthrough] again.[161]

As Seamus Kelly has stated, 'Managers pick players to fit the system, but also to fit the culture of the team that they want ... [they] pick players that they trust to do the job, and trust that they're not going to be bad eggs.'[162] Some players, such as Timothy Dalton, clearly availed of Irish connections and more than once moved to English clubs where Irish managers were in charge.[163] This is not unique to Irish-born players, however, with a number of players showing a tendency to move to clubs where they are familiar with the manager and his methods. Ralph Coates stated after he joined Tottenham Hotspur in 1971 that his earlier impressions of manager Bill Nicholson, formed while a member of the England under-23 manager's squad, were a 'major factor' in choosing the London club.[164] Additionally, there is some evidence that prior to the internationalisation of the Premier League, in the early 1970s Tottenham Hotspur had shown a tendency to build squads from the London area, with Coates the only Newcastle-born player at the club, while in contrast, Burnley were noted as recruiting heavily from Newcastle.[165] The presence of an Irish manager could improve the chances of an Irish-born player signing for a club (although breaking into the first team was still difficult), with Millwall earning a reputation as an Irish player-friendly club in some sections of the media in the early 1990s, although this was not always reflected on the terraces.[166]

Table 3.5 Leading initial recruiting clubs by decade of Republic of Ireland and Northern Ireland-born football migrants, 1945–2010 (with number of players per decade in brackets).

Period	1945–55	1956–65	1966–75	1976–85	1986–95	1996–2005	2006–10
Rep. of Ireland-born players	Everton (9)	Man. Utd (5)	Man. Utd (6)	Arsenal (4), Liverpool (4), Man. Utd (4), Wolves (4)	Brighton & Hove Albion (7)	Wolves (10)	Nottm For. (4)
Northern Ireland-born players	Burnley (6)	Sunderland (10)	Oldham Athletic (7)	Man. Utd (5)	Man. Utd, Man. City (4)	Blackburn Rovs (4)	Everton (2), Man. Utd (2)

Source: As Table 1.2.

As shown in Table 3.5, Manchester United have been replaced as the leading recruitment club of Republic of Ireland-born Premier and Football League players who have signed professionally per decade since the 1980s, while Arsenal have similarly declined in signing and giving first-team opportunities to these migrants. In the 1996–2005 period, Wolves (ten players) have been more willing to give these footballers a chance in their first teams, illustrating the elite clubs' interest in signing foreign players and a switch in their recruitment policies since the 1980s. Similarly, Manchester United have not always been the club which initially recruited the highest number of Northern Ireland-born players per decade, although they have consistently higher figures than any other Premiership or Football League club. Initially, Burnley, Sunderland and Oldham have shown a strong interest in offering professional terms and first-team appearances to these players, with Manchester United becoming the leading recruiting club per decade only in the 1976–85 period. Burnley's prominence in this regard in the 1945–55 period can be explained by the presence of a club scout, Tommy Coulter, in the Belfast area. Since the late 1980s and early 1990s (per decade), Manchester City, Blackburn Rovers and Everton have also been more willing than others to give Northern Irish-born players a chance, although not in the same numbers as Manchester United over the sixty-five-year period covered here.

EARLY RECRUITMENT: A WELCOMING CLUB?

Along with the obvious need for financial security, many players have expressed the desire to be part of a club that made them feel welcome. Lanfranchi and Taylor have highlighted the problems faced by international and British footballing migrants in adapting to new cultures with homesickness a particular problem for Brazilian footballers in Italian football in the early 1930s.[167] Difficulties in embracing the local way of life were also a problem for British players in France, Columbia and Italy.[168] While English traditions and culture have many similarities to those in Ireland, Irish footballers have, like many foreign players, struggled to adapt to life in England and Scotland, with young trainees and adults frequently citing homesickness as a problem.[169] Leaving home initially, returning to England after holidays in Ireland, and changes in accommodation were all identified in a 2003 FAI/PFA study as problematic to recruits.[170] It was also stated that players' failure to discuss homesickness could lead to the development of negative feelings about their experiences in England and Woods, Buckley and Kirrane recommended that Irish players be placed together in accommodation and that increased formal communications with club officials be encouraged.[171]

A report by FAI welfare officer, Terry Conroy, produced in 2011, established that 'many of the young Irish players experience problems such as homesickness, bullying, rejection and disciplinary issues'.[172] In addition, it was stated that '85 per cent of those who sign professional contracts with a club at the age of sixteen will no longer be there three years later'.[173] Conroy had been appointed to give support to young Irish players resident in Britain in 2008 with funding for the position coming from the FAI and the Irish Department of Foreign Affairs.[174] As Harding stated in 2003, 'in previous decades … apprentice schemes were often little more than a means to providing cheap labour for clubs and the young men involved were rarely encouraged to feel that they were part of the first or even second team "pool"' and 'being an apprentice or scholar can, therefore, be a potentially heartbreaking business'.[175]

The twenty-first-century appointment of Conroy appears to have been one of the first moves on the part of the Irish government to cater for young Irish footballers abroad, but this delay can be seen as part of a wider trend of neglect on the government's behalf in looking after the welfare of Irish emigrants. One of the recommendations of the *Commission on Emigration* in the 1950s was that 'some type of social bureau should be established in Great Britain to look after the welfare of its [Irish] emigrants there' with Irish state funds to be used in consultation with the government, illustrating the slowness in establishing an agency for their welfare.[176] As Mary Daly has stated, the Irish Free State had from its early days 'trod a slippery line on emigration' and initially, 'the standard rhetoric of successive governments, irrespective of party allegiance, was that the Irish state did not promote emigration – it was determined to create conditions that would make emigration unnecessary'.[177] Given the lack of interest invested in soccer by state bodies for much of the twentieth century (noted previously in this book), it is perhaps unsurprising that the wellbeing of Irish football migrants received scant government attention until the early twenty-first century. In Northern Ireland, one recent report found that 87 per cent of young players leaving the country to join English and Scottish clubs returned home within two years 'for various reasons' and there is also scant evidence of government involvement in catering for those who moved across the Irish sea for professional football purposes.[178]

This problem of homesickness is also reflective of wider trends within the Irish diaspora, with a 2015 study of the views of around 500 Irish emigrants undertaken by an organisation catering for those in Irish society affected by migration issues, Crosscare, revealing that 71 per cent experienced homesickness on a regular basis while 64 per cent said that they felt that migration was harder than they had anticipated.[179] There are numerous references in contemporary newspapers and magazines to Irish footballers suffering from homesickness, while most biographies of these players unsurprisingly illustrate their battles with it, particularly when moving as teenagers. George Best famously returned home the day after joining Manchester United in 1961 and while he changed his mind about staying in England shortly afterwards, his companion on the trip, Eric McMordie, did not go back until he was older and claimed in 1969 that he was only at Middlesbrough because the wages in Ireland were so low.[180] Pat Jennings felt that two things stopped him from returning home after joining Watford in 1963 – his affection for football and the kindness of his host family.[181] Arsenal's Liam Brady wrote of the trauma of leaving home in 1971 and felt that 'it is very important for a boy to move into friendly, homely digs', and the fact that he was treated 'tremendously' well and lived in close proximity to the club's ground also helped him settle in London.[182]

Similarly, Richie Sadlier found the settling-in process in the 1990s very tough:

> I was really, really close to my family, had a big circle of mates that I was really close with in Dublin, and had to go from a kind of fairly active social life in Dublin to little or no social life in England, because that's the restrictions of the job. Obviously I didn't know anyone, I was an outsider, all that. It was really difficult, like I was bawling crying in the airport the day I left in August '96. And probably for the next two or three trips back which would have been in September, November and at Christmas, I was in tears leaving Dublin each time getting the

> flight back. I found it really hard going on because I was playing on a Saturday morning in the youth team, so [it was with] a team, like the same experience as playing with Belvedere, during the week [and] then you'd be cleaning players' boots and you were cleaning the toilets and cleaning up after players and all this kind of stuff. I don't think the lads do that now, but we were doing that, and it didn't seem like what I thought it would be.[183]

A change in the weekly playing routine could therefore impact on a player's lifestyle. Paddy Mulligan became homesick only on Sundays, when he felt there was nothing to do as matches in England were played on Saturdays or midweek as opposed to mainly being played on Sundays in the League of Ireland.[184] He stated that:

> There was no such thing as a hurling match or a Gaelic football match or a soccer match that you could just drift off to. But that was your recovery day anyway, because, what I would have done, I would have gone out on a Saturday night, after the game, and gone out until maybe two or three in the morning – go to a disco, whatever it was, get back, and just recover then. I never drank [and] I didn't want to lose out on too much sleep.[185]

The difference between an Irish and an English Sunday was also problematic for Eamon Dunphy, who wrote that 'the English Sunday took some getting used to. Nothing happened', while 'in Ireland, Sunday was the big day for sport'.[186]

It is no surprise then that some migrating Irish players have looked to join English clubs which they feel will help them settle and where they feel welcome. As Enda Delaney has noted in his study of Irish emigrants in post-war Britain, 'networks lessened the obvious dislocation of emigration' and 'for many who left, a sense of home, in the concrete form of kin and friends, was a defining feature of their adaption to life in Britain'.[187] As well as a welcoming atmosphere, Irish players have, down through the years, expressed a desire for the company of those from their native land while relocating to England. Having joined Aston Villa in 1952, Peter McParland experienced some trouble settling in his digs before moving in with Con Martin, which proved 'a big help' in adapting to life in Birmingham.[188] Conditions varied, with John Giles noting the poor quality of his digs at Manchester United in the late 1950s.[189] Much later, Pat Rice benefited from living with his family in London in the 1970s in his teenage years while Norman Whiteside wrote of the importance of the company of other Irish players during his early years at Manchester United in the early 1980s, where his first accommodation as a professional was 'something of an Irish enclave'.[190] His landlady, Beth Fannon, spoke with affection in 1985 about the Irish footballers she had accommodated: 'We treated them like our own, they had the full run of the place, they hadn't got to isolate themselves away in their rooms.'[191] A caring landlady could certainly be a significant factor in helping players settle in, with Seamus Heath and a team mate sufficiently affected by his landlady's kindness while in digs at Luton Town in the late 1970s to attend her funeral over thirty years later.[192] As he recalled, 'In those days, you didn't have Skype, if you could afford to phone home maybe once a week, going to the phone box with your 10ps, it was a big thing.'[193]

Shane Supple also stated that he signed for Ipswich Town as they made him feel 'most at home' and had a 'family-orientated' set-up, despite trials with a number of Premier League clubs and another Championship team.[194] He recalled that, unlike his Drogheda-born room mate who left after a week, he did not suffer from homesickness in the beginning:

> It was something I really wanted to do and I wanted to have a career as a professional footballer so I prepared myself mentally for it. I was really enjoying the training – full-time training, getting up in the morning and doing something you love.[195]

Similarly, Michael McHugh stated that on moving to Bradford City in 1989, he 'was not homesick at all … it was all excitement … there was always about three or four of us in the digs which was great like, there was always something to do'.[196]

David Miskelly, who initially left Northern Ireland in 1995, also felt that Oldham Athletic were more impressive in creating a 'family' type setting than the other clubs he had trials with, placing young players in digs with others, while he was left in an hotel room on his own at another club while on trial.[197] While one would expect advances to have been made in accommodating a wider range of international football migrants by the early 2000s, difficulties remained. Former League Two player, Michael Carvill, felt that it was hard to settle as a scholar at Charlton Athletic in 2004 with the system of keeping young players in the same house together, and stated that he 'lived in a house with six fellas which was so tough. Around that time, there was obviously a lot of testosterone floating around the house and things like that there, boys were injured, boys were huffing – and I think it got unhealthy.'[198] He would have preferred to live with a family as in the house-share there was no respite from football after training. In addition, resentment from other non-Irish scholars about his professional contract, which was an exceptional status among his group, led to an uneasy situation.[199]

While there is therefore some suggestion that team mates become an extension of a player's family, the absence of those from a similar background could be difficult, particularly for younger players. With no Irish team mates, he did however benefit from the assistance of an Irish education officer who, he states, 'was very helpful – he would have taken me out for the weekend or took me around to his house, and they (Charlton Athletic) were very supportive in that way'.[200] After successfully finishing his scholarship, he moved into a family home and things improved. Therefore, experiences have varied depending on the club and the level of seniority and age of the player. Damien Richardson's move to Gillingham in the early 1970s was helped by the club's system for housing players:

> At that time, clubhouses were the regular, and around the area we moved into there were probably six or seven clubhouses – so you were meeting people on a regular basis, [some] were moving from the north of England, from Scotland, in my instance from Ireland. And the club was well versed in the art of bringing players together. And obviously that meant bringing families together. So my wife had similar-minded people around her.

> We had a lad called Dave Peach who played in the cup final for Southampton, lived across the road, he and his wife, and other players were in the immediate vicinity.[201]

IRISH-BORN FOOTBALLERS AS PART OF IRISH EMIGRANT COMMUNITIES

The *Commission on Emigration* noted that 'tradition and example have also been very powerful influences' in the decision to leave Ireland, with the emigration of family members cited as being 'part of the established custom of the people in certain areas'.[202] In 1950s' Ireland, 'the great majority' of emigrants were said to be unskilled although the movement of skilled Irish workers to Britain was said to have increased during the Second World War.[203] Delaney has shown how 'in the mid-twentieth century thinking about emigrating was deeply embedded in the psychology of young Irish people'.[204] In addition, 'the departure of complete whole families became more common' with significant rises in emigration, although it must be stated that Irish-born footballers generally did not migrate in this way when moving to English clubs given the singular nature of football recruitment, while most players also moved as unmarried teenagers.[205] Some players, such as Liam Brady, had brothers who had also played there, and he has written that 'I think it is natural for a boy to want to copy his big brothers in a lot of ways'.[206] Carrickfergus native, Bobby Irvine, followed his brother Willie, who was a year younger, into English football in the early 1960s.[207] At least one Irish-born player was noted as following in his father's footsteps into the English game. Ray Ferris, a centre-half at Crewe Alexandra and Birmingham City between 1945 and 1953, was the son of Jimmy Ferris, an inside-forward with Chelsea and Preston North End in the 1920s.[208] Similarly, John Giles' cousin, Christy, had a spell at Doncaster Rovers in the 1950s.[209]

The report also highlighted the difficulties for families, such as separation of children from parents and fathers being away from their wives and families, although the presence of family members in Britain could be of some benefit.[210] This problem continues to this day. Brian Mooney's decision to join Liverpool in 1983 was influenced by the tradition of the club and a family presence in the city, along with the fact that his former schoolboy team mate, Ken DeMange, had also signed for them.[211] Mooney also felt that the north of England was a friendlier place than London, having also had trials there,[212] while Michael Carvill stated that he 'would have preferred to have been more up north in England' as he felt 'it's a wee bit more like home'.[213]

Unsurprisingly many of those who migrated were keen to find similarities with home life. In a 2002 newspaper interview, Liam Tuohy, who spent three seasons at Newcastle in the early 1960s, was of the opinion that he 'found the Newcastle people to be more like the Irish than any other part of England' and still had friends there at that time.[214] After joining Newcastle United in the winter of 1988, Liam O'Brien stated that 'it wasn't difficult to settle down in the north of England. Newcastle is very much like Dublin in the sense that the people are very friendly and it is like one big community'.[215]

Mick Meagan, who joined Everton in 1952, settled in well and he feels that Liverpudlians and Dubliners share the same sense of humour, while Everton club director, Dick Cyril, had connections within Dublin and nine Irish players were recruited in the period from 1945 to 1955.[216] Meagan himself had been asked to attend a trial by Harold Pickering, the club's scout in Dublin, and felt that:

> In those days, England seemed so far away, you thought, 'God almighty, where are you going to?' and I went over for a month's trial and lucky enough, they liked me, and then they signed me. So I came home then for a week after the month's trial and went back. But you loved football and you wanted to play football, so that sort of helped you to settle down.[217]

Similarly, Liam Whelan stated in a 1957 magazine interview that leaving his family and friends and 'sailing cross-channel' to join Manchester United in 1953 was 'quite an experience'.[218] Coming from an Irish society ravaged by emigration, Meagan was well aware that in joining a football club, he was still better off than those forced to emigrate in search of work:

> Now I used to feel very sad when I'd be going over on the boat, in those days, and to see all the young boys and girls setting off for England, and they didn't know when the boat docked which way to move – and I always felt so sorry for them. At least I was going to nice digs, and being looked after, and I thought it was very sad to see all these younger boys and girls, just standing there, with a look that said, 'Which way will I go?' 'Where will I go?'[219]

Liverpool was beginning to lose its prominence as a destination for Irish migrants by the mid-twentieth century and Delaney noted that 'many of the new arrivals in the 1940s and 1950s went south'.[220] By the latter half of the twentieth century, 'only London of the four nineteenth-century cities of Irish settlement (Glasgow, Manchester, Liverpool and London) retained its importance as a destination'.[221] He has also noted that 'reports of young Irish migrants arriving in London's train stations with little information or even a place to stay were common in the late 1950s', although he also illustrates how welfare officers were present at ports while volunteers from organisations such as the Catholic Women's League and the Legion of Mary, also gave advice to arriving migrants.[222] As Mary Daly has noted, 'the key goal for most emigrants was to survive and improve their economic and social status in their new homes'. Assistance came mainly from 'family, neighbours, the Catholic Church – commonly staffed by Irish priests and nuns – and Irish voluntary associations'.[223] The *Commission on Emigration* had, in particular, noted 'a real danger' in the 'abrupt change to a new environment' without the guidance of parents and expressed concerns that migrants 'may succumb to the temptations of city life', although admittedly this was written in what would now be seen as a hugely repressive era in Irish society, overshadowed by the dominance of the Catholic Church, particularly in the Republic of Ireland.[224]

As MacRaild has stated, 'the ethnicity of the Irish may have mutated or adapted, but it continued to be sustained by features of religion, politics and daily life which were inherently Irish'.[225] Meagan himself felt that many Irish migrants to Liverpool that he encountered, particularly those from the countryside, were too shy to move outside their own circles, and had a tendency to focus mainly on socialising in Irish clubs.[226] In the period immediately after the Second World War until the middle of the 1960s, more than 400,000 Irish people moved to Britain but, as Daly states, 'no consideration was given to opening consular offices to cater for their needs'.[227] For Meagan, life at Everton in the 1950s and early 1960s meant being part of two communities the club – and the area where he resided:

> We were lucky that the lads were great – after training, we used to play head-tennis, you know, like volleyball only you use your head. And we used to spend the afternoon playing head-tennis – it was great fun, it wasn't really training as such, it was just great fun. And after that, you were happy to go home, have your tea, and nearly [be ready to] go to bed. And you spent a lot of time going to the cinemas. Things like that … there might be other shows on that you'd go to … you'd go to the boxing. Boxing was very popular then in Liverpool … you had 'Pop' McAteer and Hogan 'Kid Bassey', so there were a lot of things like that you'd go to. Everton were a great club. The people of Liverpool now were great, whether they were Liverpool supporters or Everton supporters. Now I was lucky, I was living in a parish known as St Theresa's. And they had a billiard hall and used to have little dances and things like that. So I'd spend a lot of the time there, playing snooker or going to discos.[228]

In addition, in the early 1960s Liverpool began to take off as a cultural centre; Liverpool FC gained promotion to the First Division in 1962 and the Beatles' first hit 'Love Me Do' was released, while Meagan was part of the Everton team that won the First Division in 1963. There was also the attraction of New Brighton, a ferry ride across the Mersey, while Southport was also located nearby, so, as Meagan recalls, 'there was plenty of things to do'.[229] In the 1960s, access to top-flight players was a lot more open for supporters, and Meagan feels that nowadays, top-level players are under intense scrutiny from the media, unlike when he was playing:

> I think we were playing in a great era, where there's no television or pressman hounding you, you could go out after the match and have a bit of fun – have a drink and that – and you might knock over a drink or something, but there was never anything in the paper. Now if a man knocks over a drink, it's headlines, and that's the sad thing about it. Sunday morning, you'd go down to mass if you won – you'd go to ten mass or something, and all the neighbours would say 'well done'. Now when you had a bad one, you got up and you'd go to eight o'clock mass, but they'd be all there: 'If you think we're going to pay to watch that rubbish …' Oh yeh, even your best neighbours, they weren't afraid to have a go at you, and you would accept it because they were right.[230]

As Taylor states, 'professional footballers at the turn of the century were paradoxically among the most celebrated and most derided of public figures'.[231] In particular, he believes that 'continually compared to the working-class heroes of the maximum wage era and the more glamorous but moderately paid stars of the 1960s and 1970s, the "pampered" celebrities of the noughties, with their £1 million-plus annual salaries, had few supporters'. In addition, 'excessive earnings were increasingly regarded as not just inequitable but morally indefensible'.[232] By the opening years of the twenty-first century, top Premier League players could earn as much as £100,000 a week, although wages were much lower further down the divisions.[233] As Seamus Kelly notes, top-flight players have had to adapt their off-the-field activities in the modern era:

> They have the post-match cool-downs and swims and stuff like that but sometimes you go out for a pint though those days are kind of gone now … with social media now, the game has changed, completely changed. You can't be seen anywhere, I mean if lads in the Premiership want to go for a jar, they tend to have two or three pubs they know, or bars they know, with private functions and entrances out the back, or they book a place. Some players still need to unwind, there's a huge problem in sport at the moment with gambling and drinking and drugs. I think it's getting worse to be honest with you.[234]

In 1960 more than 70,000 Irish migrants arrived in Britain.[235] Some Irish-born players simply couldn't adapt to living in England, with Alfie Hale, who joined Aston Villa that year, stating it was too hard to leave his close family and friends behind, while his love of the showbands and his local club, Waterford, meant that he returned home after six seasons in 1966, having played for Aston Villa, Doncaster Rovers and Newport County, scoring sixty-four league goals in 158 matches. He had been unsure about the move to Birmingham, but having been advised by his father that it was 'a very good opportunity', with the Waterford team going into decline and the lack of jobs available, he decided to leave Ireland:

> So it was agreed that I would sign for Aston Villa at the cup final of 1960, Blackburn Rovers versus Wolverhampton Wanderers. And I was to meet him [Joe Mercer] after – they left tickets for us there with the secretary of the football club – at the ground, at Wembley Stadium and meet him afterwards and sign for Aston Villa. And I remember being at the match and I recall being there, and it was Wembley Stadium, 100,000, something you read in the comics years ago and you'd always love to be there. And I never enjoyed a minute of it. I watched Blackburn and Dave Whelan broke his leg, and as you know, he went into the sports business, which I followed him into, later, and he became a multi-millionaire. And the only things I took out of the match was that I saw one or two Wolves players, brilliant players, a lad called Peter Broadbent, fantastic player. I enjoyed watching, but I didn't want to be there, I wanted to be with my pals and everything else, and I just felt alone in a huge stadium and I think I was only sitting fifty yards away from the Queen, who was presenting the cup afterwards. Immediately afterwards I met Joe Mercer and signed on the dotted line and I had to sign the professional contract for Waterford first before I could sign a professional contract for Aston Villa so that was the start. Then I was told to report – that was the cup final which was May, I think – to report the first week of June … so that was then [for me] the start of Aston Villa.[236]

During his first season in England, the divide between young, up-and-coming players and established, hardened professionals in his club's first team determined to look after their livelihood, did little to encourage him to stay. In particular, two first-team players refused to speak to him.[237] Given his superb talent despite his relative youth – he was just twenty when he joined Aston Villa – Hale found himself in the first-team dressing room when he had more in common with younger players known as the 'Mercer Minors', 'a copy of the Busby Babes', who were slightly younger than him, and feels that he could have achieved more at the club if it had been better organised.[238] Similarly, Liam Tuohy, who moved to England the same year, once stated that in terms of full-time professional football, 'it's very much a cut-throat business, even among your own club's players, who are all battling with each other for a living'.[239]

Delaney has noted how 'in the post-war period, British society was transformed as traditional sources of moral authority declined and well-established norms concerning sexuality, gender roles, the role of youth, individual rights, and freedoms were effectively undermined, most obviously in the 1960s as the "permissive" society slowly came into being'.[240] Hale felt that there were some aspects of English society that were at odds with what he was used to in Waterford, where he enjoyed the local music and craic in pubs and the social occasion of going to mass:

> I loved the social life of coming home … I was very big into American politics and JFK and Martin Luther King and all that stuff when I was there in England and I didn't understand English politics and I didn't understand their culture. They used to play dominos in the pubs and we used to play 60s, 30s … and then they go and they play pitch and putt! Aw God! And if they weren't playing pitch and putt they were playing bowls – and it was all foreign to me! You know, I could never get to grips with it … Basically I love the Beatles' music now, but I didn't socialise. It was different [to home] … I don't know … I saw too many marriages breaking up.[241]

In 1966, then Republic of Ireland Minister for Health, Donogh O'Malley, urged a crowd at a St Patrick's Day celebration at London's National University of Ireland Club to take on a fuller role in political and social life in Britain but, as shown above, this was easier said than done.[242] Without having his family nearby to watch him play, it was hard for Alfie Hale to maintain morale, despite his talent and ability to play at the highest level:

> I always felt I was good enough, but I never wanted it, and that's not a cop out in any sense because when I joined the Villa, I immediately went into the team and I played my first-[team] debut game against Leicester City and Gordon Banks was the best goalkeeper in England at the time and I scored on my debut, on a one-to-one against him, and I went into the FA Cup … [against Huddersfield Town], and I scored against Ray Wood – former Manchester United and England goalkeeper – and I'd no problem with it. The problem that I had is that it didn't mean anything to me – there was nobody to talk to the next day about it, there was no family there. I always wanted to play football for my father to let him see me play, and my brothers and everything else, and I got no kick out of it at all. I played against the Spurs double-winning team – Danny Blanchflower and Dave MacKay. Dave MacKay marked me, and I was in awe of Danny Blanchflower for years from listening to my brothers and my uncles talking about them. We drew with them at Villa Park, and I think there was over 60,000 there on a floodlit night, and this, long before the all-seating came in and was a fantastic game, but it passed me by.[243]

Hale felt he may not have been deserving of a place in the then First Division given that he could not commit fully as he constantly wanted to get home. He also believed that most Aston Villa first-team players living outside the city of Birmingham was a factor in the lack of team spirit during his time there, and while his digs were fine, most of the younger English players went home at the weekend. Living in a family-run accommodation in Sutton Coalfield outside the city, there was no real Irish community nearby to assimilate into.[244] As late-1960s Chelsea recruit, Paddy Mulligan, noted, team bonding was seen as an important part of fitting in, and in gaining acceptance at some clubs:

> Most of the time a few of us would stay back for maybe an hour after training and do an extra bit – you might practise crossing, your first touch, heading, timing of jumps, time your run. Just do these basics – kick the ball up in the air, take it on your chest, take it on your head, take it on your thigh, take it on your instep. Just stuff like that, even for an hour, because it was a long day, and if you were finished at half twelve, there was no such thing as going to a canteen at the club, or the restaurant at the club … you just had to fend for yourself and your diet wouldn't be anything near what the lads' diets are today. But you'd always find something to do. Now some lads liked the bookies, very few of them would go drinking in the afternoons, they'd leave that for the night. At Chelsea especially, you'd loads of lads who'd love to have a drink and they probably went overboard on occasions as well … they most certainly did go overboard on occasions. But that was what they chose … I just never bothered to drink 'cause I just couldn't be bothered. I'd go out with some of the lads, have a Sprite or 7 Up or a Coke in those days, and get out of it.[245]

Despite the fact that Aston Villa moved Alfie Hale's wife, Ciss, over and they received great assistance from Joe Mercer and his wife, Nora, it was hard to settle, and he constantly longed for a move back to his native Waterford.[246] Taylor has noted how 'post-war managers tended to present themselves less as distant autocrats and more as caring father figures' and cites the example of Matt Busby as someone who tried to become involved in the personal lives of players in order to improve the club's performances on the pitch, although he could also be ruthless.[247] Mercer too appears to have taken on a paternal role, although Hale believes that he was not present at the club enough, with the result that the senior players tended to dictate the atmosphere in the first-team dressing room.[248] In addition, each of the

Billy Humphries in action in the early 1960s prior to a return to English football with Coventry City. Picture: *Newtownards Chronicle*

club's four professional teams had coaches who were only interested in their own squads, which led to a lack of harmony within the club, Hale believes.[249]

While the young couple did visit a Dublin family living in Birmingham every Sunday for tea, family and social life in Ireland could not be replicated.[250] In contrast to the atmosphere at Aston Villa, Billy Humphries has stated that at Coventry City in the same decade, 'a lot of players lived in the same area so that was socially binding' and 'they had a great team spirit'.[251] However, he too had struggled to settle into First Division football during an earlier spell with Leeds United in the 1958–59 season, stating that 'the club wasn't very well run at that particular time' with star player, John Charles, having just left for Juventus, which 'was a big downer' for the Yorkshire team.[252] Hale himself felt that he had no problem in terms of the mental strength necessary on the pitch, but life off the pitch could be too quiet, with players disappearing quickly after a match. A trip to the shop to buy a newspaper was usually met with indifference from the shopkeeper, unlike at home in Waterford where a friendlier welcome was given.[253]

Some others were more eager to move on from their memories of Irish society. Eamon Dunphy has written in his book, *The Rocky Road*, that he 'had almost forgotten about Ireland' a few weeks after joining Manchester United in 1962.[254] Moving from a different occupation into professional football could certainly have an impact on a player's off-the-field pastimes. Hubert Barr, a teacher who played for Great Britain in the 1960 Olympic Games in Rome and scored fifty-one goals for Linfield in helping them to win seven trophies in the 1961–62 season, recalled in relation to his move to Coventry City from the Windsor Park club in 1962, that although most of his new team mates went to the bookies after training, he had no interest in this.[255] Instead, he often went shopping with his wife after returning home from a day at the club.

MAINTAINING LINKS WITH HOME

As Stead and Maguire have noted, Scandinavian/Nordic footballing migrants have expressed a strong desire to be near their friends and family and have 'placed overwhelming emphasis on maintaining relationships with people back home'.[256] Barry Prenderville felt that leaving those at home behind could also be difficult as 'your friends start moving on … that's a tough thing as well because then you realise "well they're not as much there for me when I go home" … but I used to really look forward to going home'.[257] After joining Cardiff City from Portadown as a seventeen-year-old in 1972, John McClelland was keen to keep in touch with the football scene in Northern Ireland:

> I wasn't in gangs or anything like that, I just sort of kept myself to myself, so I don't know if that helped me, but when I went over it was just … you don't really think about being homesick and that, but when you are over, if things aren't going right, or just living away from home, it's difficult, you know. I had the

> local papers sent there – *Ireland's Saturday Night* – so I could see all the players I knew, but over time, they all disappear.[258]

As Delaney has shown, the reading of Irish provincial newspapers and tuning in to Irish radio was common in 'thousands of Irish households across Britain' in the post-war years.[259] Irish-born players have at times been honoured by those representing Irish emigrant communities in England, with the tenth annual awards ceremony organised by the *Irish Post* to honour 'Irish Sports Stars of the Year in Britain', held at the Portman Hotel in London, attended by Irish internationals Pat Jennings, Tony Grealish, Martin O'Neill, Frank Stapleton, David O'Leary, Gerry Ryan, John Devine, Gerry Peyton and Mick Kearns in March 1979.[260] Other organisations with Irish links have also been keen to include high-profile footballers in their celebrations, with Frank Stapleton attending the Cavan Association's dinner at the Irish Centre in Camden in November of that year.[261] While acknowledging that the Irish did not face 'the obstacles of mastering a new language or getting to grips with a completely alien culture', Delaney has noted that there were other complexities which came with adjusting to life in Britain, with religion, pubs, dance halls and traditional music all used in strengthening links with home.[262] In addition, 'there was no one all-encompassing Irish identity in post-war Britain. How people saw themselves and how they wished to be perceived by others varied considerably between individuals.'[263]

As MacRaild has stated, 'the Irish were not a homogenous group'.[264] Despite the apparent harmony at Manchester United, Alan Bairner has noted the social dislocation George Best experienced on joining the club in terms of his 'social class, his place of origin and his Ulster Protestantism' and the club's strong 'Catholic tradition' during his years there.[265] This illustrates the complexities in making straightforward links between Irish-born footballers and the movement process to English clubs in terms of their differing religious and social backgrounds. Therefore more work needs to be undertaken on this aspect of the culture of football clubs and how recruits fit into their new environment in this respect.

Hubert Barr (*fourth from right, holding cup*) with members of Linfield's 1961–2 'seven trophy team', for whom he scored fifty-one goals that season. Picture: Linfield FC.

Good morale appears to be fundamental to progressing in professional football away from home. Delaney has noted the importance of holidays taken in Ireland for some post-war migrants, and professional footballers were no exception.[266] Damien Richardson would return home during the summer months with his wife and young family after he joined Gillingham in 1972:

> In those days, you'd get about ten, eleven weeks off, the season finished in April, you were off all May, June, so I'd come home, and they'd send the wages home, which was a lovely way of living at the time. I came home – then, when the kids started getting bigger, I stopped coming home in the summer. I came home regularly, maybe two or three times a year, for family occasions, but most of the family came over to me [instead].[267]

Structures for players to pass the time off the field have been slow to evolve, and what would be deemed as everyday celebrations for most people have had to be curtailed due to the commitment levels of the professional game. As well as the almost constant physical alienation from families back in Ireland, the lack of participation in celebrations such as birthdays and Christmas could be tough for those away from home. Richie Sadlier recalled spending his eighteenth birthday like any other weekday, while for Seamus Kelly, the lack of a break at Christmas was hard, and this was different to the mental toughness required on the playing field: 'Physically, you get battered as a 'keeper, you get on, you deal with it … fans hurl racist abuse at you, throw stuff at you. I mean, I soaked that stuff up, but the other, the softer stuff is probably the toughest thing.'[268] Although the availability of cheaper flights and more regional airports in both the United Kingdom and Ireland have increased opportunities for migrants' trips home, the necessity for players to be present on the training ground has hindered this movement. As Kelly recalls:

> If you don't train, you don't play, so I think over a season you'd probably get home maybe three, maybe four times. I mean I think the first year, you'd probably go home five or six times, and I was looking at training schedules to see … I was looking for every chance I could to get back. It took me a while to settle there. But then you got the whole summer off, it's fine, you know. Nowadays, with the number [of flights] … like Cardiff was awkward, but if you're in Birmingham or London, you can get a flight Saturday night after a match, and come back Monday morning for training, and you can probably do that twice a month, but back then, because of where you were living, it was difficult.[269]

A number of players interviewed, including Richie Sadlier and Martin Russell, have noted the importance of trips home for international matches in terms of boosting players' morale.[270] While modern-day players have flights home built into their contracts, Paddy Mulligan recalled the informal nature of getting time off during the season in the 1970s at Chelsea, with manager Dave Sexton giving permission to him to go back to Ireland on a Saturday evening if he had given the team the Monday off:

> They were the days you just arrived at the airport, with your cheque book or with your cash, fly to Dublin return … because you were invariably getting the last flight at eleven o'clock at night, and invariably I would get the last flight back in again – to spend as much time with my dad as possible and arrive back late on the Monday night.[271]

Some players thought that too much returning back to Ireland could be detrimental to a young player's progress, with Seamus Heath stating that 'you can get a wee bit comfortable, you don't want to go back, whereas when you make your decision to go to England, you've got to work every day and that's how competitive it is'.[272] Similarly Barry Prenderville felt that going home to Ireland too often was not good in terms of a player settling in at his English club.[273]

Assistance from clubs off the field has often been inadequate for migrants. Both Michael McHugh and Brian Mooney felt that they were very much left to their own devices in their accommodation having moved to England.[274] And Richie Sadlier outlined the lack of personal support for players at Millwall:

> When I hear a phrase like 'support system' I think, is there like a formal set up, is there a person employed as a counsellor, or psychologist or a player welfare officer or something? None of those existed at Millwall at the time – this was '96. I would have been told, if I've a problem, [they'd say] 'Jesus, come to us, let us know', but the reality is if you have a problem as a footballer, and my problems at the time would be 'I'm really missing my parents, I'm really missing my mates, I'm not really enjoying it, this is really hard for me' – that's not information I wanted my coach to know, because I was on a one year deal and I knew that out of sixteen or eighteen of us in the youth squad, maximum four of us would be given contracts. So I wasn't going to hand an

> advantage to everyone else in that process, or hamper my own chances by saying, 'Look at me, I can't cope.'[275]

While choosing to live with his sister in Ealing and having to work in a pub as his YTS payment of £400 a month was spent on rent, Brentford trainee Denis Behan admitted that this additional job had affected his performances on the field, although he felt there was nobody to share this problem with.[276]

Some other interviewees, however, felt that their recruiting clubs did everything they could to help them settle, with Alan Blayney describing Southampton as 'actually fantastic in regards that kind of thing, you know, they had counsellors and different things like that for all the young boys, and any problems you had, they had a whole group of people there you were able to go and speak to'. He still struggled to settle in, however, and states that he always had difficulties with living away from home, and returned to Belfast for eight months during his trainee spell with Southampton, which began in 2001.[277]

Homesickness has certainly been, and remains, a problem for Irish footballing migrants, but these problems can also be experienced by English players who have moved away from their own part of the country, as well as those from other parts of Britain who have moved to England.[278] Graeme Souness, for example, left Tottenham Hotspur to return to Edinburgh as a young apprentice in the late 1960s.[279] In addition, migration to clubs within Ireland can also be tough. Derry-born Eddie Crossan, who joined Blackburn Rovers in 1947, noted in a magazine interview that, having joined Glentoran as an eighteen-year-old, he returned home after only four games. It would appear that he had matured sufficiently to join the English club as a twenty-two-year-old, and stayed in English league football for eleven seasons before returning home.[280]

Despite these challenges, as Barry Prenderville noted, professional football clubs are 'very macho … it's a male-dominated world' where 'you didn't try to show anybody' you were homesick.[281] As Richie Sadlier admits, 'the culture of a club is, the unspoken culture is, you don't whinge, you don't show what would be perceived as a weakness, so I said nothing [about being homesick], which made the process more difficult'.[282] The commitment levels required at a professional club also meant that 'normal' teenage life quickly disappeared, and instead he relied heavily on visits from his family and friends in order to cope with homesickness:

> What was it like as a teenager? It's different, because when I think of 'teenager', I think of going out all the time, you're going to college, you're meeting girls, there was not really a lot of that the first year of me being there [at Millwall]. You're generally told to stick to people within the club, and all the people in the club my age went home to their families at weekends. There wasn't a lot happening at the weekend. So … you'd be fairly isolated, fairly lonely, but you're kind of told, you know, this is the tough early years, if you want to make it you've to suffer the tough early years, so you always have that in the back of your head as well. But … I used to have a lot of mates coming over, my family coming over, and I would be counting down the days to each trip home. There was never really more than two or three weeks where I didn't have contact with someone who was at home.[283]

As noted above, the weekend could be a very quiet time for a young player but clubs expect players to deal with this themselves as a part of fulfilling their contract. As Barry Prenderville states of his early years in Coventry City's Halls of Residence, 'there was no major, special effort made for us, you know, it was like, "You're a man now, you've made your decision to come over to England, you're getting paid for it, so get on with it"'.[284] Similarly, Michael Carvill felt that young players had little in the way of a social life. Despite living outside London, he rarely saw its attractions while a scholar at Charlton:

> We'd a curfew in our digs, we'd to be back in our digs for something like 9.30pm, and ten o'clock at the weekend, so in the digs there was nothing … and it's a completely different setup to over here [Belfast]. Like you can't go out with your friends, you don't have your friends to go out with so you can't really

> do much, you know – it was kind of just sitting in the house watching football, we just lazed about. And in terms of going into London, you don't do it by yourself, you need to go out with a group … getting the tube and all in and things like that there. As I got older, I went in more to London on the tube with a few older players, it was easier, but during the first two years I can't even remember a time when you really thought [about it]. And looking back now – and obviously now it would have been great 'cause it's London and all – but you weren't getting paid a massive amount of money, you had to be kind of careful as well with your money, 'cause you were only … I think we were on £90 a week for the first year, so it's £360 [a month] … obviously a lot back then, you think it's great, you're earning for playing football, but it didn't stretch far at the end of the day, so you had to be very careful with your money. So in terms of going out in London like, you didn't really do it at that age, and I wasn't really a touristy person, the attractions didn't really do anything for me or anything like that there [then].[285]

THE QUALITIES NEEDED TO BE A PROFESSIONAL FOOTBALLER

In a newspaper article published in 1945, then Derby County player Peter Doherty, who had migrated from Glentoran to join Blackpool in 1933, gave a breakdown of what he felt was necessary to have a career at the highest level of English football. He felt that 'keenness', regular practice and 'fighting spirit' were fundamental to succeeding as a professional footballer.[286] Similar sentiments were expressed by a number of scouts in a 1971 *Shoot!* magazine article. In particular, Arsenal chief scout, Gordon Clark, felt that 'ability, dedication, character, self-discipline and the ambition to do well' were key, while Manchester United's Jimmy Murphy was of the opinion that balance, kicking [technique] and reading of situations were critical. Jimmy Thompson, a freelance scout in Brighton said to have discovered Jimmy Greaves and Terry Venables, felt that ability was the defining factor.[287]

Seamus Heath believes that:

> Well, you've got to have the football ability, that's number one. That'll get you to the highest level, if you add in the other bits, and the other bits are obviously the dedication, you need the skill, and then it's all other bits – maybe the environment, where you're playing, who's coaching you, who's managing you, other players around you.[288]

David Miskelly stated that 'you have to have a high level of talent, dedication, and luck, to be honest, luck is probably the major thing, there's such a fine line between making it and not making it'.[289] Most players interviewed for this book believed that a positive mental attitude was paramount to making a career in professional football. Brian Mooney felt that 'you've got to be mentally strong and you've got to be happy in yourself living over there. If you're not happy, you won't perform as well and I think mental strength or happiness within yourself is crucially important to making it over there.'[290] Martin Russell also believed luck was important:

> I think most players will be honest and say, you know, I got a little bit of luck along the way, managers liked them a little bit or whatever, being able to establish [yourself] … because, to be honest with you, there's a hell of a lot of good players out there that don't get the rewards of some of the stars.[291]

Andy Waterworth stated that as well as luck and ability, 'there's small margins between success at a lower level and success at a higher level. I think you need that dedication, and the capacity to be mature and to learn, take things on in the process.'[292] Michael Carvill felt that 'once you've got yourself to a decent level, it then comes down to margins, and that margin could be based on a manager's preference, a manager's like, a manager's dislike, or maybe a coach'.[293] Similarly, Denis Behan was of the view that:

> Football is really about opinions, you know from one club to the other, one manager would love you and the other manager

> then might hate your guts, you know … if you're not a likeable character, or if you're not the player that they want … I've come across players who, I knew, at a young age, that wouldn't lace other players' boots but because they worked hard and hard and hard and did the right things and they found a part of the game that suits them and they know they can do it well and they've honed that skill so well [they succeeded].[294]

Damien Richardson felt that a player had to be able to come to terms with and overcome any weaknesses he might have:

> The stepping stone is talent, obviously, but a lot of people have made it without the natural talent, but football is a life within a life. It's a life and a life's lessons in a short period of time, and the one thing you have to face up to as a pro footballer is your own inadequacies as much as you have to face up to your talent. Your talent brings a responsibility – you've got to fulfil that talent, you've got to maximise it – but alongside that, and in many respects, more important than that, is how you face up to your own inadequacies. And how you stand up to your own fears. Because if you go out in front of a crowd with 60 or 6,000, doesn't matter – when you come back into the dressing room if you've let everybody down – and you know in your heart and soul you've let yourself down – that's a mind-numbing feeling, a desolate feeling. And so, it's facing up to your own inadequacies, most important of all, and being able to overcome those inadequacies, and accepting the responsibility, the challenge.[295]

The ability to never give up and ignore doubters is a key factor, according to Richie Sadlier:

> You need to be a persistent devil; I mean the physical ability and the talent is just the first bit – it's a given that you have to have that – but that in itself will get you nowhere near a career, it really won't. See in my scenario, I suppose you've to deal with the homesickness, and all that kind of stuff, the injuries, the mad

> days, the supporters' abuse, and that was just my experience. Someone else will talk to you about all the other reasons why it was really difficult for them. You kind of have to put up with the fact that everyone has an opinion about you, you're constantly going to get feedback – most of it is unwanted, a lot of it will be negative, some of it will be positive – and you have to just be able to put up with that.[296]

Mick Meagan felt that 'you must love the game of football' as well as having the desire to work hard, and in addition, Sadlier also was of the view that if a player wasn't 100 per cent committed to the game then he could forget about breaking into English league football:

> If it's not the thing you most want to do, and if it's not the thing you love doing more than anything else, and if you don't have a passion for [it], or just an indescribable obsession, you're not going to make it. All the luck, the lack of injuries, the manager that likes you, the timing of a good performance in front of a scout, it'll all catch up in the end if it's not something you love doing. I genuinely believe this.[297]

Along with obvious hard work and the determination to practice for long hours, another consideration in the development of players is natural talent. In particular, Brendan Bradley, the League of Ireland's all-time leading goalscorer, was at a loss to explain how he was able to find the net so frequently:

> It seems like a gift because I mean, I never sort of tried to improve with shooting or anything. I didn't try to improve my game so it proves that the natural instinct to scoring goals is always there, you know. Like I never stayed out on the pitch shooting or anything like that to try and improve, I just played my football, and played my matches in the League of Ireland – the goals came.[298]

A number of players interviewed alluded to their fathers' careers in football, with some, such as Alfie Hale, coming from a particularly strong football stock, his father and uncles having played in the League of Ireland.[299] John McClelland's father played for Cliftonville while Brian Mooney's father had been capped at schoolboy international level and had played League of Ireland football.[300] While there is obviously no substitute for hard work, a family background in the game may also have an effect on a young player's development, not just from the point of view of natural talent but through the player growing up with the game.

Arthur Hopcraft, in his classic study *The Football Man*, noted how some players such as Sir Bobby Charlton have had a strong football pedigree and their chances of breaking into football have been boosted by parental encouragement of their sons' talent. The former England World Cup winner's mother was a cousin of ex-Newcastle United and England star, Jackie Milburn, and Hopcraft noted the push given to Charlton by his mother towards making a career in the game, particularly through assistance in his individual training.[301] While much has been made of negative parental involvement in schools' football, this positive help provided is also something worth further research, with Dave Hannigan noting the involvement of Shay Given's father in promoting his son's aim of a place in English football in the goalkeeper's early career.[302]

CONCLUSION

This chapter has shown that the number of Irish-born players appearing in English league football in the pre-Second World War era was considerably lower than in the post-war period, with restrictions on player registration and scouting networks having a strong impact. Ireland's first professional and amateur association footballers were generally found to be involved in industrial work. How players have been recruited was examined and it was shown that it was in the 1996–2005 period that the greatest number of players from either the Republic or Northern Ireland moved and broke into first-team league football. While this movement was greatest from the Republic of Ireland in that decade, Northern Ireland figures never again reached the level of the first decade after the Second World War, although of course the former has a greater population. While Irish football migrants have differed from many more general migrants in the nature of their work and the conditions enjoyed in their workplace, settling into English society and professional football clubs has been problematic, and the need for a friendly environment where players can maintain ties with their families back home on a regular basis has been stressed. Although modern-day professionals have less social contact with supporters than in the immediate post-war period, the value of local communities in helping players settling in has been occasionally noteworthy, particularly in the case of Mick Meagan. However, the club itself plays the greatest role, although support systems for young players have been slow to develop and competition for places means that players are generally reluctant to discuss with their clubs anything that would make them appear of a fragile state of mind and therefore less able for first-team football.

While huge advances have been made in transport links between Ireland and Britain since the late twentieth century in terms of a greater availability of regional flights, and the increased development of communications has enabled players to have round-the-clock access to families in Ireland via social media, it appears there is no substitute for a stable family environment and the comfort of friends despite the perks available to top-flight players in the modern game. Any teenager hoping to break into English football will probably have to give up 'normal' family celebrations such as birthdays and Christmas, with mental strength being identified by a number of players as critical to having a career in professional football.

Players' opinions on agents were mixed, but it has been shown that many footballers favour them despite their poor reputation at times and despite the fact that the PFA is also on hand to offer advice on negotiating contracts. As Harding states, 'with hundreds of new agents entering the business each year … and with the complexities of sponsorship deals, "Bosman" style contracts, "image rights", etc., the influence of agents seems likely to expand even further'.[303] Statistically, Irish players have favoured moves to English cities with large Irish emigrant bases, while some players are keen to migrate to a club with an Irish presence, but the opportunity of first-team football is more significant than location. Some Irish managers have accommodated this by signing Irish players in greater numbers, although the option of joining a preferred club is not available to all players. How some of those who have managed to break into English league football have viewed the game at that level will be addressed in the next chapter.

CHAPTER 4

Playing Experiences

> When you go into a dressing room [initially], most lads will welcome you: 'Well done, the best of luck to you', but they'd take your head off two weeks later. It took me a while to suss out the ruthlessness of the dressing room. One of the coaches [Billy Ayre] said to me, after about three months, 'You know, you're actually taking some of these guys' jobs, the sooner you get that, the better.' And I went, 'OK, thanks' … that's the nature of the industry.[1]
>
> Seamus Kelly, 23 August 2013

INTRODUCTION

This chapter discusses some of the experiences of a number of Irish-born footballers within professional football in England, focusing mainly on the views of the players interviewed for this study. It examines the level of training and commitment necessary to play in English league football and the competitive nature of the professional game is outlined. Life in the first team and the pressures of being a professional footballer are assessed and what it actually feels like to play at this level is examined. The lack of structured psychological support for players for most of the period covered here is outlined, although admittedly this has come informally from managers and coaches. How players view 'banter' within the club is assessed and it will be shown that what could be termed anti-Irish abuse is tolerated within football clubs and is part of the 'banter'. What would be seen as bullying in other occupations is also commonplace within the culture of football. The experiences of a number of Irish players in England during the Troubles are also assessed. The threat of injury and the loss of form and positions in the first team are discussed, while player–manager relationships and the difficulties of relocating as a footballer are also examined. Finally, this chapter offers an analysis of the experience of international football through the views of a number of those who have represented the Republic or Northern Ireland at international level.

EARLY IRISH FOOTBALL MIGRANTS' VIEWS ON PROFESSIONAL FOOTBALL IN BRITAIN

As Tony Mason has shown, figures for professional footballers in England increased from the four registered with the Nottingham FA in 1885 to 448 Football League players in 1891, with the majority of these said to be 'almost certainly part or full-time professionals'.[2] By 1910 there were 6,800 players registered with the FA.[3] Specialised training for cup matches had been under way by 1883 and although early reports are patchy, by the early twentieth century players were regularly required to be at the club by 10.00 a.m. before participating in a variety of training including sprinting, walking, ball practice, weight training, skipping and ball-punching throughout the morning.[4]

In his column in *Football Sports Weekly* in 1926, Charlie O'Hagan, who had spells at Everton, Tottenham Hotspur, Middlesbrough, Aberdeen and Greenock Morton from 1902 until 1913, noted how a professional footballer in England needed to train at least three days a week and recommended 'a few short sprints on the Friday morning – an exercise known to the cross-channel professionals as "muscle-looseners"'. In addition, hot baths after training and matches were, he felt, necessary to remove any aches or stiffness while massages were said to be 'the most important injunction of all' in aiding recovery.[5] A Turkish bath every fortnight was also said to be a necessary part of a player's routine. O'Hagan had his own regime to stay in top shape, although he offered scarce information on team training or ball-work routines.[6] There is strong evidence to suggest that ball practice was often neglected by some clubs in the early twentieth century, with Aston Villa's directors agreeing in 1904 that more of this was needed.[7] On awakening in the morning, O'Hagan would open his bedroom window and breathe in fresh air for five minutes. He would then engage in a number of stretching exercises with what he described as 'all the energy' he could muster. This was followed by a routine of shadow-boxing and skipping and the taking of a cold bath. He also recommended a brisk walk before bedtime while warm milk was taken to help aid rest.[8] Players should, he felt, get ten to twelve hours' sleep before a big game and on the day of a match, food was to be restricted to just one meal, taken around noon or no later than 12.30 p.m. when kick-off was at 3 o'clock.[9]

As Dixon and Garnham have stated, 'for players, victories needed to be celebrated, the tensions of defeat needed to be eased and injuries required to be salved' although they also note that drink-related problems for most early professionals only developed after their playing careers had finished.[10] Mason has shown how some early players like Tom Brandon of England and Blackburn Rovers overindulged while some of Aston Villa's poor performances in the 1892–93 season were said to be the result of a drinking culture among their players at that time.[11] The good professional, O'Hagan felt, should 'shun the public house as he would typhus fever'. Although not teetotal himself, he reckoned that he would 'certainly draw the line at the "hard tack" (whisky)' as he felt that 'that unholy concoction is neither necessary or desirable'.[12] Poor playing conditions did, however, provide the opportunity for a swift drink at times. O'Hagan noted that 'on a heavy, wet day, when rain-sodden grounds take the last ounce out of a man no matter what the level, a drop of brandy and water at half-time is about the best medicine the trainer could administer. But then, and only then.'[13] He also went to lengths to advise aspiring players to 'cut tobacco supply to a minimum' while he recommended a laxative known as Sedlitz Powder to clear the digestive system before a match.[14] While players who complained of injuries were to be banished to the club doctor, burnout could, he felt, be avoided by taking a break of up to two weeks from the training ground after every six weeks of intense training.[15]

In 1927, John Joe Flood, who had spells at Leeds United and Crystal Palace in that decade, noted that he was being well treated at the London club and how the game in England was much faster than he was used to in the Free State League.[16] The following year, *Football Sports Weekly*'s columnist 'Nomad' was of the opinion that 'the visits of such clubs as Glasgow Celtic, Everton and Aberdeen help us realise how much behind the best cross-channel football is the standard shown here'.[17] He also felt that the game in Britain was 'a business' while 'the regular system of training and the efforts made by the numerous team-builders to get men to suit their style of play bring about a machine-like effort'. This 'collective effort' was, he stated, the 'big difference' between Irish and British clubs.[18] In illustrating the training undertaken by part-time players, he also highlighted how this differed to the system in Britain, where the players were 'employees' and were part of a more regimented system:

> He must attend every morning at headquarters and carry out the day's programme according to the trainer's chart. Ball practice, massaging and violet ray treatment, varied by such a pleasant diversion as a round of golf, are but a few of the items in his curriculum. His chief obligation to the club is to keep himself fit and always play his best.[19]

BECOMING A FULL-TIME PROFESSIONAL FOOTBALLER, 1945–2010

Throughout the rest of the twentieth century, Irish-born players knew that they generally had to seek a career in England or Scotland rather than their native soil in order to fulfil their dreams of playing professional football every day. As Damien Richardson states, 'there is an ethos about full-time football ... and it changed me immediately – it does induce in you a level of confidence that [makes you feel that] your talent is indeed worth investing in'.[20] Given the part-time nature of the game in Ireland, others have also alluded to being enticed by the prospect of concentrating full-time on professional football, with Roddy Collins stating in 1986 after joining Mansfield Town from Dundalk the previous year that 'it's so different because you're thinking football all the time'.[21] Moving from part-time jobs to full-time professional football could pose some work-related difficulties for those migrating in their twenties who were already in employment, with both Paddy Mulligan and Seamus Kelly experiencing conflict within the workplace due to football commitments.[22] For Kelly, who was working in a bank at the time of his transfer from UCD to Cardiff in 1998, the move happened very quickly:

> I went over there and it was pretty much whirlwind stuff. I went for the week's trial and they told me on the last day, 'Yeh, we'll take you.' I went, 'Grand.' Later I rang Mickey [Walsh (agent)] and said, 'What's the craic?' and he said, 'Well, you're training Monday.' I went, 'I've still got a job', so I had to go back, hand in my notice, they went ballistic. I packed my stuff, just for the next two weeks, so I was over and back maybe once a month, then I just said to the manager [Frank Burrows], 'Listen, I need three, four days on the spin here, just to sort out stuff, can I go back?' He went, 'Grand, yeh, no bother', he was fine.[23]

As noted earlier, coaching in England was beginning to gain more credibility in the post-war years. Despite this, not everybody noticed a huge difference in training having moved. For Mick Meagan, training in England and Ireland in the 1950s was initially much the same:

> There wasn't an awful lot of difference now. In the old days with the pre-season now, I used to do, in the [Dublin] mountains up here, three or four weeks when I'd be home, running around, just to get yourself [in shape]. Now you'd do a week's roadwork in the old days, running around the streets of Liverpool, and some of the lads, the older lads, they'd be behind you and you'd look up and there'd be a tram going by you, and they're on top of the tram waving at you! But, as it became then later on, with the Lilleshall thing [set up in 1984] – you know the coaching thing – it became a little bit more [creative], nice little darts here and darts there.[24]

However, making the switch to full-time professional football could be tough for players, and a number of those interviewed have highlighted how the fitness levels required are vastly different, such as Hubert Barr, who moved to Coventry City in 1962 from Linfield:

> Training was much tougher, but the thing that helped me was that I was a PE teacher, and I had been keeping myself fit all the time through various exercises in the gym and running with the boys and playing games with the boys, you know, I was always doing something with the pupils and that kept me pretty fit. But … I thought I was really fit when we were there and I still managed to lose over a stone in weight. No, it [part-time football in Ireland] just doesn't compare with professional training.[25]

In June of that year, Hungarian Janos Gerdov, who had been a professor of physical education at Vienna University, was recruited by manager Jimmy Hill as coach, which was 'rather unique' in English football in those days, and Barr felt that his toughest time as a professional came during the pre-season training.[26] Similarly, Billy Humphries felt that Hill was a highly innovative manager, with non-playing members of the team being requested to take notes on team mates during matches.[27]

As Hunter Davies stated in 1972, 'for any professional club, the four weeks of full-time pre-season training are four of the most vital of the year'.[28] Eamon Dunphy has written of pre-season training that, despite its tough nature, 'it is a marvellous spiritual feeling. You have worked hard, and are cleansed … there is nothing more exhilarating than coming home feeling tired, and sitting down and feeling pure in a way that you never do in the season.'[29] After moving from Finn Harps to Lincoln City in July 1972, Brendan Bradley was struck by its intensity:

> It was far different. The first couple of days at Lincoln we went up to this golf course, it was this hill and you had to carry a boy on your back up a hill. And then when you got up there you jogged down and you were just steady at it, about … I don't know how many times we done it. And this was the summer time, it was pretty warm. But the training was … it was just a completely different world. The training was far more professional and flat out. The training in the League of Ireland would have been just basic, basic sprints, and things like that.[30]

Physically and mentally a player could be transformed, as Damien Richardson recalled:

> Training at [Shamrock] Rovers was always with the ball anyway, essentially, so we were only at it two nights a week. I went to Gillingham and I was 11 stone 7 – within six weeks at Gillingham I was 12 stone 7, just by training properly, eating properly, resting properly, my body responded, my body became stronger. We weren't doing weights in those days, it was completely and utterly natural … the training every day, the consciousness, changed dramatically, I became a professional footballer – this became everything, all my life revolved around it. This was my living, and my total awareness was focused in and around the game. So the training was like becoming a kid again, I had no worries whatsoever, I was doing the job that I wanted to do, as I was good at it, I was getting well paid for it, and I was getting a lot of public attention for it, so it was a wonderful period and a big part of that was the training, day in, day out.[31]

Michael McHugh also described the difference in fitness levels after moving from Ulster Senior League club, Swilly Rovers, to Bradford in 1989:

> It was a lot different [laughs]. I remember being told before I left, to make sure you do plenty of long runs, before you go, and I thought I was doing long runs, but I got there, and I started training with the apprentices before the first team came back … the first couple of days we went for a long run up into the woods, I just couldn't keep up. I was looking lost, and a guy says to me, 'Just hang on there, we'll be back', and I didn't realise I wasn't fit for it. I found then the more training we did, the better I got and then the sharper I got and then once I got fit over there, it was unbelievable. I kept telling people … like you'd play a game of football, ninety minutes, and you wouldn't even be sweating afterwards and you'd feel that fresh that you'd go and play another – that's the way I felt. I know I was nineteen,

> twenty, whatever, you felt you could play another game straight after, that's how fresh you'd be and how fit I felt.[32]

Martin Russell noted a vast difference in the frequency of training and the intensity of it in England compared to Ireland during his professional career in the late twentieth century.[33] David Miskelly felt that in Ireland, 'the fitness level wouldn't be as high and then the quality gets let down by, you know, everybody not being able to train together more often'.[34] Similarly, Shane Supple also felt that professional football and training would take a player to the next level:

> [It's] completely different, obviously you're training every day, sometimes twice, three times a day, so it takes a little bit of time for your body to get used to that obviously, but when you do, it's fantastic, and that was one side of it I really enjoyed, the training, the intensity of it. Take you to the next level really, which is something that's hard to do probably back here [in Ireland], with lads in school and whatever else so that was something I really enjoyed – the intensity of the training and the quality as well.[35]

Richie Sadlier also noted an obvious difference in the level of professionalism and expertise available after he joined Millwall:

> Physically, it was much faster … lads were much fitter, and I know that now because the lads in a Millwall academy would be used to training four nights a week from the age of twelve, four maybe five days a week. They're active in Dublin one or two nights, at most. So they were physically bigger, they were faster, they were stronger. Had to kind of catch up on that one. But it's a professional environment, like you're a professional, so every day there's thought going into what the coaching session's gonna be, all this equipment, there's a gym there, there's a canteen giving you food to back up the training you're doing, so totally different. And you're dealing with lads who have a career in professional football behind them, the way your coach is, most

> would probably have coaching badges, all this kinda stuff. Again, in Dublin, it's the parents of one of the players that run the team, with the exception of Belvedere, because they were superb.[36]

For others who moved as schoolboys, one obvious difference was in tactics, as Barry Prenderville notes:

> [At] a schoolboy club you're having a match, doing some doggies, you're not doing any shape, you're not doing any tactical work at all, you know that way. So, when I played for representative teams here we'd touch on tactical stuff, like I played for Ireland under 15s, 16s, 18s … working on a bit of that but when you were going back to your club at Cherry Orchard there was very little of that going on. I mean everybody meant well, you were surrounded by good players, but … at the same time, there wasn't a lot of tactical stuff going on.[37]

Not everybody interviewed thought the English system was superior to what was available in Ireland by the early twenty-first century. Denis Behan believed the coaching that was available at Cork City was 'as good, if not a better standard' than what he had received in England, while 'the tempo of training was actually less' at Hartlepool United.[38]

COMPETITION FOR PLACES

The work of Roderick has illustrated how 'professional football as a career is short-term and the labour market for players is highly competitive'.[39] As Martin Russell has noted, in professional football 'you're judged on your performances and at the end of the day if it's not good enough they look at somebody who is delivering'.[40] Mick Meagan has noted how first teams rarely changed during the 1950s with no rotation and smaller first-team squads, having waited five years to cement a first-team place at Everton:

> In those days there was no kind of panels or anything like that, the first team was there, and it was there for four or five years. It was very hard to get into it. And you were playing in the second team or the third team and then you'd move up. But, as I say, it's amazing now, I could name the Bolton Wanderers team, the Wolves team ... they were the same team week in ... year in and year out ... [It was] hard to make the breakthrough then.[41]

Pre-season photos at Everton at that time could feature up to sixty players and according to Meagan, 'even to get in the third team, you'd feel quite good about it'.[42] Breaking into first-team football has been a daunting challenge for many players, with those signed as apprentices competing for maybe one solitary professional contract. Alfie Hale was told by one Aston Villa coach in 1960 that he should have felt 'privileged to be there' given the fact that the club had taken on only one of its 400 young trialists that summer.[43] By the late twentieth century the rates of success of those on trial at English clubs appear to have changed little. Michael McHugh similarly highlighted the low rate of success of trial players during five years at Bradford in the late 1980s/early 1990s when he stated: 'I would say I saw maybe two or three trials a week, like, I could have seen about four or five hundred trialists in that time, and not one of them were taken on, not one of them.'[44] As a player, he didn't think about this too much: 'If you sit back and think about it, it is quite ruthless, but when you're in the middle of it and you're playing away ... you don't think too much about it.'[45] As Barry Prenderville states: 'There's only about ... in and around 3,000 professional footballers in England at any one time, so it's not a lot of people, so there's a lot of people coming in, and a lot of people dropping out, so it's hugely competitive.'[46]

These estimates are backed up by PFA statistics. John Harding has stated that 'in the 1990s, fifty per cent of trainees taken on by league clubs at sixteen years of age were released at the end of the two-year stint and only twenty-five per cent remained after three years'.[47] David Miskelly highlighted that 'as a member of thirteen YTSs when I joined, I think there was two of us, possibly three of us, that made it a professional life. You know, there's a fine line, two or three, there's ten that's gone.'[48] For Richie Sadlier, gaining a professional contract with the first team gave trainees a heightened sense of competition, and this increased as he moved up the ladder:

> I suppose there's varying levels of competition. When I went over first, I always knew if I was fit I would get my game for the under 18 team. I never spent a week training thinking, 'God, I hope to get picked this weekend.' After that then I was kind of thinking, you always have it in the back of your head, will I get a call up for the reserves or how far am I away from the first team. But the main thing is, will I get another contract? So daily, you have this thing that you're trying to prove yourself.[49]

The nature of the challenge could also be picked up informally from those who had managed to progress at the club, as he recalls:

> How ruthless is it? I mean, you always … you know from listening to lads through previous years. Like, when I was seventeen, I was talking to a twenty-one-year-old at the club, and he was telling me that he was the only one of his youth team squad that's still playing professionally and he might just anecdotally tell you that over lunch – and that's not a lecture, that's not a 'buck up your ideas, son' speech, that's just a reality. So you'd go away home thinking, 'This is ruthless, one out of twenty is left, within four years of being in the youth team', so that's how ruthless it is. I don't even know if ruthless is the right word, it's just there's a limited place and there's a huge supply of footballers that can take those places. And in order to make sure you're the one that gets it, maybe you yourself have to be a little bit ruthless. And, like I said … [you] put up with the early years, put up with the slagging and verbal abuse, put up with the bullying if that's what you need to do, put up with the homesickness.[50]

Michael Carvill felt that the transition from being a scholar to breaking into the first team was tough, and could be harder than winning the professional contract. It was at times dictated by factors which affected a club's survival at a high level:

> From sixteen to eighteen everyone's fighting for that pro contract. Once you become professional, it was worse, because Charlton were a team that were trying to stay in the Premier League, and they needed to do anything they could to stay in it. So you had twenty first-team players who'd all played Football League or Premier League, and they'd experience of all playing together, so they're never going to change, whereas when you're a young player, you weren't really thought of, because at the end of the day you're not going to do anything unless you're in the first team. So the priority was the first team on Saturday – the boys that didn't play had training on the Sunday or came in on Monday and did a wee bit of running, played a reserve match, but that was it. So it was very, very difficult to come to a club that'd just been promoted, because all they care about [is survival]. So much money, and pressure on that manager's job, to keep that team in the Premier League, they can't constantly care that much about young players.[51]

Andy Waterworth felt that in regard to levels of competition in full-time professional football, 'it's not even [just for] places … boot deals, popularity with the fans, popularity with the manager, everything's a competition'.[52] Breaking into the first team was a clear signal a player was on the right track, and as Mick Meagan notes on joining Everton, 'when we went over, the first team were in the home dressing room, and the rest of us were in the away dressing room. And then, you'd be brought into the home dressing room, and that was kind of a big thing … you'd be thinking, 'God, I'm on my way' or 'I must be doing something right'.[53]

THE FIRST TEAM AND RELATED PRESSURE

As Roderick has written, 'Ultimately, a player may possess a fantastic "attitude" to training, levels of fitness, diet and pre-match preparation, but all that really concerns club staff are levels of performance and results in games.'[54] A number of those interviewed, including Barry Prenderville, Richie Sadlier and Michael McHugh, felt that they would have benefited from the assistance of a sports psychologist in dealing with homesickness and performance on the field, but none were available at their clubs at the time.[55] Seamus Kelly felt that the use of sports psychologists is still frowned upon today within professional football, while former England goalkeeper, David James, stated in his newspaper column in 2013 that during his time at Liverpool he was left to sort out his loss of form by himself and that psychological support off the pitch 'is so appallingly neglected'.[56] In addition, former Northern Ireland international Paul McVeigh, now a motivational speaker, has written that 'in fact, there has always been a stigma attached to those who seek help with their thinking, and experts in psychology are seen as men in white coats who talk gobbledegook. All complete rubbish of course, yet very few players work on their mental skills.'[57] He also felt that while visualisation is now used regularly by Olympians, Formula One drivers and golfers, 'I would guess that only one professional footballer in a thousand does this'.[58] As noted in the previous chapter, the majority of Irish-born players interviewed felt that mental attitude was a key factor in making it as a professional footballer. However, attitudes towards the use of psychology have been slow to evolve within clubs, as Richie Sadlier states of his time at Millwall:

> It started being mentioned around '99–2000 when Mark McGhee came in [as manager]. There was no talk before that and I remember a phrase the first time it was mentioned – real old school attitudes in the club and it was kind of typified by this comment – one of the lads turned around and said, 'Listen, there was no psychologists in 1966 and we didn't do badly then' and you're going, 'Really … is that how insightful you're gonna be?' But I think they're everywhere now, and I think if … it astonishes me why people wouldn't use them … well, I know why, I just don't agree with anyone not availing of expertise like that. At the time there wasn't [one at Millwall] … a couple of the lads did see them off their own bat like in the evenings but there was no formally appointed club psychologist that was in there at the time.[59]

Andy Waterworth felt that as a full-time professional, when things weren't going right it was difficult as 'everything's football', whereas with part-time football there was a job in the daytime and the game was more of a release.[60] Alan Blayney felt that the mental aspect of the game was now receiving more attention:

> It's starting to get a bit better now, where people are understanding that footballers aren't robots … there's things that go on in their minds and they aren't constantly thinking about football, 24/7. They have lives away from football and sometimes things don't go well for you and sometimes, your head's not right. It's in any walk of life and people just think because these players, they're getting paid thousands of pounds, whatever it is, they should just constantly be just 100 per cent focused on playing football and they should be just these happy-go-lucky guys. It's not as easy as that, there's a lot of pressure with being a footballer.[61]

Similarly, David Miskelly was of the view that many people felt that footballers 'have an easy life, with the money they're earning, whereas they don't really'.[62] The early twenty-first century has certainly seen an improvement in the mental side of the game, with clubs such as Liverpool employing sports psychiatrists in line with other sports such as cycling, although it is unclear if these services are available to lower-league players.[63] Hunter Davies has written that professional footballers are 'continually under pressure, both physical and mental'.[64] Denis Behan felt that there was a lot of responsibility being a professional footballer:

> The pressure is really [high] … at that level, because if you do not perform, you are cast aside, you are a bit of meat. When I was at Cork, I got a phone call to say that Hartlepool were looking to come in for me, which was great for myself, but I got that followed by another phone call from the chairman at the time saying, 'Well, if you don't go, nobody gets paid this month.' So you are literally a piece of meat within the game, there's no human nature to it, when it comes down to it, you're being traded off as much as possible as you can get for it, but then

> again, we go in looking for the best contract we can get as well … but there is that, there is a huge element of, I suppose, trading, as you need to know where you're going from one year to the other. Like, I spent, what, ten, twelve years as a pro now on two-year contracts, … I've never signed any more than that, so I can't guarantee anyone where I'll be in any given time. And it's for my wife as well, you know what I mean, that insecurity isn't great, but yeh, the two things, the pressure and the insecurity … you know you have to be on your best behaviour when you're out and about, representing the club but also you have to be on your best performance when you're playing, 'cause otherwise, one or two [bad] performances like that and you're gone.[65]

Not every player interviewed was worried about the lack of psychologists available, with Miskelly stating that while there were players who needed reassurance, he didn't think it would have benefited him and he could cope well with pressure. He did, however, have some experience of team-building exercises at Oldham Athletic.[66] As a goalkeeper, concentration was paramount, and he felt that this could be done through talking to his defence on the pitch.[67] Seamus Kelly learned how to break the game into quarters through the help of his former goalkeeping coach, George Wood. He also used his family as a motivation while at Cardiff City:

> You just have to focus – discipline's the key thing. They're all looking at breathing and imagery and stuff like that [now], [but] I used to think of my family as well. [I'd think] 'don't mess up, don't have them reading the paper the next day about you messin' up' … and that really used to get me. Or like, I was born and reared in a pub, down the country, I think the second game was against Swansea, live on Sky Sports, 12 o'clock on Sunday morning, the pub was packed and I'm thinking, 'You're not gonna make a mistake here today, because they're all gonna be in the pub, watching it, me mum' n' dad, brothers and sisters … nah, it's not gonna happen.'[68]

Shane Supple has stated that he was 'always decent at concentrating' although he didn't use any specific techniques, and he enjoyed the adrenaline rush of match day:

> Match days are a buzz, you know, you can't beat going in and preparing for games and the crowds being there … it is very exciting, I say that never changed, it never changed for me. I always loved training, every day I went out, I didn't dread it, the buzz was always there for me. Obviously you have your ups and downs, and that can affect you, but the buzz was there. Obviously, later on, it dried up a little bit, because of people's attitudes more so than my own, really.[69]

Alfie Hale remembered being taken into the corner of the dressing room with fellow inside-forward, Jimmy McMorran, by manager Joe Mercer as kick-off approached before a First Division game against Tottenham Hotspur in February 1962. Both players were told that they would have to focus on stopping the threat of Spurs' wing-backs, Danny Blanchflower and Dave McKay, with Hale told to stick tight to McKay to nullify him because of his reputation.[70]

Richie Sadlier recalled that the build-up to a game was something he missed after retiring:

> I used to love it, even before a game, when we used to get certain preparation or research that'd be done on the opposition, and I'd get [my direct opponent]. [The manager would say,] 'Right Richie, you're on number 6, so for all corners and free kicks, you're marking number 6.' I used to love standing in the tunnel looking up and down, you'd know who he is, but you'd look at him and go, 'Right, next hour and a half, it's just me and him', and that little battle goin' on in my head, I used to love it. 'Cause I used to focus on, like, I'm gonna get the better of this fella today, and that's my little target. I used to love the little battles like that.

As Mick Meagan noted, the pre-match build-up could be a nerve-wracking experience and the match itself could be a bitter-sweet experience:

> It's a great feeling, but I can't say now you enjoyed it. You'd be standing in the tunnel, and you could hear the buzz … the buzz … and you'd be [thinking], 'Bloody hell'. You'd be worried about 'can this fella run?' The first ball coming at you, are you going to fall over it … all these things, negative thoughts, would come into your head. As I say, it was great but it was scary, you'd get a fella running at you, and the bloody crowd, you know, it wasn't that nice! It wasn't that nice … but it was great.[71]

Similarly, for Michael McHugh, match day brought a range of mixed emotions:

> I hated the morning before a match. Aye, whether it was nervous tension, whatever, I just wanted to get out and get on the pitch, once I was on the pitch I was grand, but I hated the build-up, I really hated it. And you relax when you were playing, you'd relax afterwards, but the build-up before it – there's loads of them now, I think, sports psychologists, that would have been a big, big plus back then … I would have benefited, definitely benefited from it … just get your state of mind, I don't know how they work, I've never seen one or heard one of them, but that would have been a very big benefit to me, especially, later on, when I just needed to take that extra step [to recover from injuries], and you just need to get your head right, you know, it just never … you know, I kind of slipped away and I know like a few players as well … would definitely have helped them as well.[72]

However, he felt that the buzz of scoring in league football was …

> Amazing, amazing, you wouldn't swap that for anything. I scored five goals at Bradford and I remember every one of them, just the buzz you got from it and that feeling didn't leave you for days, you kept going over and over it in your head … [it was] amazing![73]

Alfie Hale felt that once the match began, it was 'a frenzy' where he did not notice the crowd. Opposition defenders would often try to leave their mark early on, with Dave McKay's late challenge on him early in the aforementioned league match at Villa Park in 1962 being followed up with another kick while he was on the ground, when it appeared the Scot was about to help him get up – although he was able to laugh it off, knowing it was part of the game.[74] Similarly, what is now commonly known in sport as 'sledging' was never a problem for the Waterford-born player as he had experienced this in the League of Ireland before moving to England, but it is a common part of professional football.[75]

Despite a general decline in figures attending matches in the 1960s after a boom in the late 1940s, which, as Taylor states, came with changes in the ways that people spent their leisure time, Everton's average attendance was at record levels for the club during their First Division title-winning season of 1962–63.[76] There was also a distinct difference between the noise levels of the crowd while playing in the first team or second team, as Meagan recalls:

> It's funny … you're kind of shut [out] … even … it's like a wall. Now, playing in the second team, you'd hear it more, you'd hear a few groups, but in the first team, it was just like a wall, that they're not people … a wall, a wall, a wall. And that was it. It sort of never bothered you, but in the second team, when there'd be only a few thousand, you'd hear it more.[77]

While Taylor states that after the mid-1950s, 'consistent levels of support throughout the top British leagues were never to be approached again', the adrenaline rush of playing before a large attendance remained a strong memory for most players interviewed for this book long after retirement from English football.[78] Playing in front of large attendances could have its pros and cons, as Denis Behan notes:

> When you're playing well you want loads there, when you're playing poor you want as small a crowd as possible, because they will let you know in no uncertain terms they're paying their money to come in, to watch you play, and if you don't produce,

A First Division championship winner with Everton in 1963, **Mick Meagan** was one of hundreds of thousands of Irish migrants who moved to England in the 1950s. Picture: ©Inpho

> they'll let you have it, but when you're playing in front of a crowd like that, that not many people in their lifetime will experience, … you're playing there, in front of people who want to be out there …[79]

Billy Humphries remembered fondly …

> The cup run with Coventry [in 1963], we played Portsmouth in the fourth round and they had a few internationals in their side that time. We won those games, big crowds, you're talking about 40,000 and then drawing Sunderland in the fifth round and they'd fellas like Charlie Hurley and John Crossan playing for them, and we defeated them before 50,000 at Highfield Road, Coventry. And then we played another big game with United – Manchester United – in the quarter finals but unfortunately we lost 3-1, that particular match was before a huge crowd again.[80]

A first-team debut could be an enthralling experience, as Alan Blayney recalls of his first match in the Premier League for Southampton against Newcastle United in May 2004 at St Mary's, in which he produced the Sky Sports 'Save of the Season' to deny Alan Shearer in a 3-3 draw:

> I'll always remember it … it was absolutely fantastic, but you know I didn't know anything about it until I actually got to the ground, the goalkeeper was lying sick. Obviously … young kid, I was twenty-two I think it was or something, absolutely nerve-wracking … but once I was out there I was 100 per cent fine and turned out that I had a really good game, got man of the match and stuff, it was absolutely fantastic. It was just one of them games, it was like, afterwards, it seemed like a dream, one of them ones … it was really good, now, I enjoyed it, it was a really good night.[81]

While, as noted, Mick Meagan felt that playing in the first eleven wasn't that enjoyable with the pressure it brought, particularly when

Everton were going for the league title in 1963, he also stated that he would do 'the same thing over and over' if given the chance again.[82] Enjoyment during the match itself could certainly be difficult, as Seamus Kelly notes:

> Actually you don't really enjoy it at the time … because if you're in the zone, if you're focused and concentrating, you don't actually see the crowd. If you were to start looking at the crowd, you might get a glimpse every now and again, or in goals, if the ball went out behind you, you might have a little look, and hear lads shouting at you, but it's … but then if you let it get to you you're kind of screwed as well, but … at the end of the game, when you win … that's one of the feelings I miss, you'll never get that in any other experience in your life. Maybe, I don't know … people have said to me, having a kid 'n' stuff is close, but even people who've had kids … you know … scoring a header, or winning 1-0 or saving a penalty, and winning 1-0, and that … there's nothing to beat that. That is … if you could bottle that … it's raw, it's great. [It] makes all the pain worthwhile.[83]

Afterwards, sleep could be difficult, as Shane Supple has stated, while he felt that 'obviously fluid and diet' were fundamental to a professional footballer's recovery, and while some players participated in ice baths after training and matches, he was more in favour of stretching and yoga.[84] Denis Behan also felt that sleeping after a match could be hard, and at times a few drinks would help with this. He usually spent the day after a match playing snooker and watching television and trying to forget about football for a while.[85] In addition, David Miskelly noted how recovery from matches could get harder as a player aged, particularly after playing on all-weather pitches.[86] Richie Sadlier illustrated how much post-match recovery had advanced by the early twenty-first century:

> You look after your diet, you get plenty of water, there was recovery drinks, there's food supplements, there's all sorts of things that make it as easy as possible for you to prepare and to

> recover from matches and training. Players are educated in all that, there's backroom staff – it's full of people who are employed specifically to help you through that. When I first played, like away trips … in 1996–97, an away match would be, someone would be sent into the players' bar of the away ground, couple of … few crates of beer, everyone could drink on the way home, and then get in their car and drink drive from the stadium back to the houses. The options of your post-match meal would be fish and chips, burger 'n' chips or chicken 'n' chips, like we'd stop at the local takeaway in the vicinity of the away ground so by the time I retired (so no thought of diet or dehydration or recovery), by 2003 it was the opposite – you played, you had a recovery drink, a drink at half time specifically for replenishing whatever you'd lost in the first half, so you'd be getting a real education in terms of diet and stuff so there was much more emphasis put on the importance of what you do between games and how you recover from games. There was a nutritionist employed by the club for the first time.[87]

Most players interviewed expressed a huge passion for the game, and the adrenaline rush and competitive feeling it brought. The game in England could provide a player with fantastic memories and the opportunity to challenge oneself against other footballers of the highest level, as Alfie Hale recalls of a match for Aston Villa versus Manchester City in April 1961:

> One of my best games was against a man who died in 2013 – Bert Trautmann, the famous goalkeeper, who broke his neck in the 1956 FA Cup final – and he was the only goalkeeper I ever remember in my career, over fifty years in the game, that I ever saw send an outfield player the wrong way. Of the few shots I got at goal I remember running through on one through ball and Trautmann came out to me, I saw this big 6 foot 4 inches guy, huge guy, and I threw him a dummy, and I went one way and went to hit it with my right and I decided to hit it with my left, and he went just as I was going to hit it … and I saw him

> going the wrong way and I switched sides and I smacked it in the other corner, up in the top corner – buried. And as he went one way, he turned back, and he made the save – top drawer. He deliberately moved one way, to make me go the other way, and he did it, and I was the sucker, and it was fantastic … Bert Trautmann. They were great memories.[88]

Seamus Kelly felt that it was the professionalism of the game, and the buzz of making saves, which appealed to him:

> I just loved the excitement of actually making a save or tipping it over the bar and then you get up off the ground and the guy is cursing at you and you give him a wink and he's effin 'n' blinding you and you're kind of … but the other side of goalkeeping is like two minutes later you let one between your legs and you've a couple of thousand lads screaming at you.[89]

This was a similar view to that expressed by Shane Supple, who won the FA Youth Cup with Ipswich Town in 2005 and made his league debut later that year. He was attracted to the professional lifestyle and the discipline this brought:

> I just loved being a professional, I loved the training, preparing for games, doing the right things, eating the right foods, all that kind of stuff, that was the reason I went over. [It] was to be the best I could be really, hopefully get to the Premier League, that was the main aim.[90]

Players' commitment levels can vary even at the highest levels. As Seamus Heath has stated, dedication to the game is fundamental, although he jokingly noted that players could go too far sometimes:

> Our normal day would have been just training, home, maybe a sleep in the afternoon, or a game of snooker, dinner, watch a bit of TV and [then] bed. In fact, I was actually pulled in a few times at Luton, because they said, what was it … 'All work and no play makes Jack a dull boy'. They thought I was just the total pro …

> and you've got to let your hair down sometime, but me coming from Ireland, football was just everything to me and I thought you had to live that way to be a footballer.[91]

Supple, however, felt there was a downside to getting paid to play the game, and it was other players' attitudes which left him disillusioned with football, as he explains:

> I suppose when I got older and into the first team I disliked the attitudes of the senior professionals and their mindset really. They didn't care, a lot of them, whether they won or lost on a Saturday, it was the same difference really for them. When they got opportunities to make the play-offs and stuff like that they were worrying about their holidays being cut into, and obviously, the older lads, not getting contracts if we could make it to the Premier League … and just really attitudes towards the game, everybody's probably out for themselves, and trying to look out for themselves, so it's hard to create a team spirit.[92]

As Roderick has stated, 'conflictual situations may arise in the context of the professional game between players who strive for economic success (or stability) and those who seek personal fulfilment'.[93] Like every job, as employees, players' attitudes to the game can vary, as Richie Sadlier admits:

> I remember once … we played [names club], and [names former Premier League player] was marking me, he was my number six that day, right, it's you against [player]. And he had been at [names club] so I knew of him. I knew at the time he was on something like eighteen or twenty grand a week, and he couldn't have given less of a …, if he tried, during the game. He more or less stopped. He was kind of having a bit of craic with me on the pitch and we beat them [easily], we ran them ragged … and when you come up against lads whose attitudes are stinking, some of them were in our dressing room, we'd lose and within ten minutes of the final whistle you're talking about going out that night, or 'we're still getting paid', or 'we didn't get our win

> bonus'. Now all the things … and that kind of grates on you after a while, I assume that's in every job, you're going to get that in every job … if you sit in an office, you're going to sit next to people who don't have the same attitude as you … and that's more and more of an issue now than it was ten years ago.[94]

Although, as Roderick notes, footballers' attitudes to the game can vary depending on the circumstances, 'a player who possesses a good attitude is someone who always works hard, both for himself in terms of personal development and for the team'.[95] Along with having to keep motivated throughout the season, professional footballers also live with the constant threat of injury, as former West German goalkeeper Harald 'Toni' Schumacher has shown in his book, *Blowing the Whistle*.[96] Some Irish football migrants have even begun their league careers in England while already less than 100 per cent fit through earlier injuries they have received, or simply through wear and tear as young players. In 1967, having returned from playing in the USA, Paddy Mulligan was given just two years to play football by a surgeon after a knee operation in Dublin. In those days, rehabilitation was less developed, and he was surprised how he was able to play in English football for so long after joining Chelsea in 1969:

> [I] built up the muscle, walked up to the Hellfire Club [an eighteenth-century ruin in the Dublin Mountains] every day, I wasn't working … every day up to the Hellfire Club, up and back, up and back, up and back. Build up all the muscle, get the quad strong, so it takes all the pressure off the knee … so I did all of that, got back playing, and when I went for the medical at Chelsea, I was sure I was going to fail it. I was absolutely convinced, because that was only two years later, and I said to myself, 'My knee must have gone a little bit wobbly now at this stage. I'm not so sure that I'm going to pass this medical.' I didn't speak to anybody about it … I actually couldn't believe that I passed the medical, to be perfectly honest with you. I'm not a medical expert, but if he tells me, [the surgeon], that I've got

> two years to play, well I'm looking at it – well, maybe I might get three or four out of it. I might. And then all of a sudden, I get a clearance from the medical at Chelsea – and the medical in those days wasn't anything like they are today. So I'm sure if I had the same problem today, I mightn't be as lucky as to overcome it.[97]

Norman Whiteside stated in his autobiography that a knee cartilage operation he had in 1981 as a fifteen-year-old was 'the day the countdown to my retirement from football began'.[98] Whiteside felt that more modern techniques would have extended his career, but at that stage, removal of part of the cartilage was the regular procedure.[99] Diagnosis and treatment of injuries can also be problematic, even with full-time professional services available to clubs, with Brian Mooney stating that while at Sunderland in the early 1990s, he missed almost a season with an injury that would have cleared up in less than a month had it been properly diagnosed.[100]

Players are also under continuous pressure to make themselves available to play, despite injuries and illnesses. As Roderick has noted, 'in a culture which emphasises *playing* and which normalises playing with pain and taking risks, those who do not *play* are denied, or deny themselves, the means necessary to sustain a meaningful life and a valued sense of self-identity'.[101] The Workman's Compensation Act of 1906 had allowed for injured footballers to continually receive pay and medical expenses, while compensation was to be given in the form of a lump sum in the case of retirement through injury.[102] The foundation of 'a joint FA-Union accident insurance scheme' in 1956, which supplemented the Provident Fund established in 1949, gave players in the immediate post-war era 'a degree of financial protection', as Taylor states. However, 'the increasing demand for results meant that physical wellbeing of players was not always the foremost consideration of employers'.[103] Roderick's work has illustrated the tough working environment of the football club and how players who frequently suffer from injury run the risk of gaining a soft reputation.[104] For Mick Meagan, niggly injuries were worse than really bad ones, as players in his era were often forced to play through them, with the result they would be 'found out' and eventually dropped:

> It would take you months to get back into the team. The old saying was 'run it off'. You know you'd be lying down dying, [and the club would say] 'get up and run it off!' So that was the worst thing about football, the injuries. And not the bad injuries, the niggles, because they'd say, 'There's nothing wrong with him, that's all right.'[105]

Similarly, Alfie Hale stated that playing with injuries and the 'flu was commonplace within professional football.[106] Playing while injured could also damage a player's future chances, with Hubert Barr feeling that he shouldn't have played for Northern Ireland in their 3-1 defeat to England at Wembley in 1962. Despite scoring his team's only goal, he was unable to add to his tally of four caps after this appearance.[107]

A broken ankle saw Gerry Burrell lose his place at Huddersfield Town and he decided to move to Chesterfield in 1956.[108] Similarly, a medial ligament knee injury for Michael McHugh in the early 1990s saw him fall out of favour with first-team manager, Frank Stapleton, and lose his position in the Bradford City team, as his recovery took longer than he expected.[109] By the early 2000s, the pressure to play while less than 100 per cent fit to sustain one's position in the team remained within the culture of football clubs. Denis Behan felt that once a player declared himself fit, there were no excuses from the point of view of the manager for performing poorly as he couldn't recover his form quickly enough. He feels he tried to come back too quickly from an ankle injury:

> The minute I said, 'Look, I'm OK' that was it, they took it that I was OK, there was no such thing as 'are you sure, are you sure?' … I was out for six to eight weeks, and I went from somebody who was starting and one of their go-to players to somebody that was out, maybe it was a case of – 'you're not fit enough anymore', all this kind of stuff, so it's cut-throat.[110]

In addition, a failure to recover full fitness quickly enough could spell the end of first-team football, as he explains:

> At Cork before that I'd been very lucky you know that I had a manager that liked me, not only that but Chris Turner at Hartlepool, he was really on my side, but then, it just wasn't working out. When you get two or three or four bad performances and the crowd are on your back, you couldn't play at the level you were at beforehand, you have to make a decision – the decision was to leave me out and put somebody else in.[111]

As Roderick states, 'A football club is a positive, self-enhancing workplace for a player who is performing well; by contrast, a club environment for one who has lost form can be unsupportive and marginalizing.'[112] He also notes that being forced to play through injury can depend on the situation and varies from division to division and 'can be dependent upon factors such as the degree to which the player has "established" himself, the stage of the season and the significance of the match, the number of "fit" players available to the manager, and the extent of internal competition for places'.[113] Playing with an injury had serious career repercussions for Alan Blayney, and this was his toughest time in football, with a lack of support from his club evident, as he explains:

> [I] think I was [aged] twenty-three/twenty-four, Southampton actually sold me to Doncaster, then I went there, it was just hell on earth, basically, it was … first few months, went grand, everything was great, and then, I just got a bad injury on my elbow and kept playing … it was just an absolute nightmare, I was out for nearly a whole year with this dodgy elbow that I had and was living on me own … and to be honest, I was out drinking a lot as well, it was just, [a] really tough time. And I think that … it was a bad mistake for me to actually leave Southampton, it was my decision if I wanted to go or not and I went there and it was the wrong people managing the club, different things like that, they didn't understand that I was living on my own and it

Denis Behan seen here after scoring for Cork City in 2013. He had returned to League of Ireland football having lost his place at Hartlepool United through injury. Picture: © Inpho

> was a tough time. It was basically just, 'well, you're not effing delivering here, you know, we don't care what's going on in your head, or you're living on your own, or this, that and the other', it was basically just, 'you're not delivering on the pitch, we don't care about anything else, so we're going to have to let you go', and that was basically it, so that's definitely the worst time, I think, when I was a professional.[114]

Paddy Mulligan felt that a bad achilles injury near the end of his career was brought on by what he thought was inappropriate training scheduled at his club, West Bromwich Albion, by the manager at the time, Ron Atkinson.[115] The worst-case scenario for a professional player in this regard is to have to retire from the game through injury. As Roderick has noted, 'for many players, football is the only thing they have ever done and the only thing they know how to do' and 'a professional footballer's identity is rooted in his body'.[116] One estimate is that around fifty professional footballers in England are forced to retire through injury each year.[117] For Richie Sadlier, who was forced to retire with a damaged hip relatively early in his career, dealing with a long-term injury was difficult, and he illustrated how non-professionals and supporters fail to appreciate how frustrating it is for players:

> Days when you're injured, when you're sitting on a bench with an ice pack on your hip and you can't do anything, you're told not to do anything, that's crap. I remember I used to think when I'd be out long-term injured, lads would ask me, 'You still get paid, don't you? Well, why is being injured hard? You get paid and you're just sitting down.' You know, you're not getting it, the buzz is removed. There's no highs or lows, there's no looking forward to Saturday, there's no looking back on Saturday or regretting Saturday, it's just the same – you're in at nine and you're home at three, making no progress, that's crap.[118]

This is not a new trend, with Norman Uprichard revealing in 1955 that a bad injury had left him 'fighting worry and depression', while a loss of form can also affect players' mental states, with Con Martin revealing the same year that his 'food was tasteless' as he struggled to regain his form in the 1954–55 season.[119] Barry Prenderville illustrated the roller-coaster nature of professional football: 'To be honest, I think, unless you're really lucky, a lot of it is tough … because you have periods when you're playing in the first team and you're flying and they're highs, but you've got injuries and you're out for a long time.'[120]

Seamus Kelly was particularly aware of the up and down nature of the game:

> I think if you speak to anyone who's played for maybe ten years or more, they actually take the highs and the lows with a pinch of salt, because it's the nature of the game. I mean, I've won leagues, and it's great, and you milk it, and then I've been relegated as

> well with teams, and you get on with it, and you deal with it. And that's the nature of it because, whether you're a goalkeeper or not, a change of a manager, you can be out. You break a leg, you're out. You've a great game, you're back in, you've a bad game, you're out. And it's that insecure, it's week to week.[121]

Similarly Paddy Mulligan felt that that players need to be practical and not get over-anxious about poor performances:

> You never really got too high and you never [get too low] – I never got too low about stuff. You don't like to play badly, nobody likes to play badly, but you have to deal with it, and say, 'right I'll get in training on Monday', get back … 'what happened there' … and you would try and – without overdoing it – you would try and dissect, where did you go wrong that particular day, what was wrong.[122]

ANTI-IRISH SENTIMENT WITHIN THE GAME

As MacRaild has stated, 'wherever in the world they settled, Irish migrants were often the victims of antipathy and violence', while 'religion, perceived Irish criminality, workplace tension and organised sectarianism' had been factors in anti-Irish sentiment in Victorian Britain.[123] In addition, he notes these feelings could rise during times of economic recession, 'or when Irish politics brought ancient enmities to the fore, as was certainly true during the IRA campaigns of the early 1920s, the late 1930s and during the 1970s and 1980s'.[124] Writing in 1995, Mary J. Hickman stated that there has been a general assumption throughout the historiography of racism that 'because the Irish are white, because anti-Catholicism has faded, and because of cultural similarities, the Irish are able with great ease to assimilate to the "British way of life"'.[125] The emphasis placed on colour in debates about racism, particularly in those originating in America, has meant that the treatment of Irish people has usually been excluded from discussions of the topic.[126] This also appears to be the case within the literature on racism in football, and the prevention of targeting of Irish players has not featured heavily in anti-racism campaigns within the English game.[127]

A number of players interviewed for this study admitted that being called 'Paddy' and 'Irish' was commonplace in their clubs, and part of the banter, but there was nothing malicious about it and claimed they were able to give as good as they got.[128] Paddy Mulligan was called an 'Irish bastard' by one former Liverpool player after a late tackle but stated that he saw no harm in it as it was part of the game. Irish and other footballers have been targeted by supporters and other players due to defining physical characteristics and ethnic backgrounds, as Brian Mooney states: 'You were a "Paddy", you were a "Mick" … if you were black you were black, if you'd big ears, you'd big ears, it was part of the banter like, so you had to take it.'[129] As Seamus Kelly has written, the majority of Irish players are not offended unless the comment comes from a player they dislike.[130] When interviewed on the subject, he felt that this type of conversation was due to 'sometimes maybe a bit of lack of education on their part or … sometimes just because they didn't know how to converse with anyone unless it was banter. But it was nothing, never taken personally, it was … I mean, you'd give it back.'[131] As Richie Sadlier remarked, 'It's good-natured, maybe, it's just banter, it's just the way people in the dressing room communicate … you're not talking lofty considered views being exchanged, that's not how dressing rooms … that's not how football clubs operate.'[132] Although admitting that certain types of behaviour would get people sacked in a normal work environment, he also questioned whether it is really 'bullying' which goes on at football clubs:

> It's just the culture of football clubs is that, the thinking is, a few slags and comments … if you can't take comments in the dressing room internally, you're not going to survive a minute in front of 20,000 on Saturday. So there's a method to it as well. Yeh, 'bullying' is rife, but it's not bullying, it's just what happens.[133]

This view was backed up by Kelly, who stated that being part of the banter was part and parcel of being accepted in the team:

> You see they don't term it as bullying. It's banter, but in the football industry, it's accepted because it's the norm. I went through college and worked, for a bank, and then a marketing company, in sales, if you did that in that industry, you'd get jail. In football, if you didn't conform to it, you weren't one of the lads, and the key thing in the dressing room is, you've got to be one of the lads ... I wouldn't say it's bullying but it's a kind of a strict style of management, it comes from the coach and the manager, but also within the group. I've seen homophobia, I've seen racism, within the group, it does go on. I don't think it's changed either – people say it's not – with the YTS system gone, it's always going to be in an industry where there's such competition for places, so you know, I would say you've got to deal with it.[134]

In addition, Alan Blayney felt that 'bullying' takes place 'in any walk of life, things like that happen, I don't think it can just be pinpointed to football, I think no matter ... even if there's a young boy going into a factory to work, there could be a case there where they're being picked on, so I don't think it can be pinpointed to football'.[135] He also felt that:

> If you go into any dressing room ... footballers are brutally honest with each other, [if] they don't like the way your hair is, or what you're wearing ... I don't think it's anything personal a lot of the time, it's just banter to try and instil a bit of fun and things like that, sometimes some people are more sensitive than others. I think sometimes you just have to work that out, who's more sensitive than others and watch what you say.[136]

Occasionally, this tension could boil over, as Paddy Mulligan recalls:

> Things will go on in the dressing room that if they happened in a bank, in an insurance company, wherever, you'd be sacked. But it's accepted in the dressing room. And rightly or wrongly [it happens]. Now, I don't ever recall anything getting really out

> of hand, just once, in Athens, before the replay of the European Cup Winners' Cup final against Real Madrid in 1971. Ossie [Peter Osgood] and Ronnie Harris had a bust-up at the dinner table. Now, a [proper] bust-up. Twenty-four hours before we replayed against Real Madrid, so there's no logic in football – we got up and beat them in the match, however. And this was a serious bust-up, because there was alcohol partaken, certainly by Ossie, I'm not so sure that Ronnie had taken too much that day but certainly Ossie had taken a lot on board that day, and it just got totally out of hand. Just criticising each other and just … I couldn't believe it, just crazy stuff altogether. But however, that was about the only [time] … I could easily say it's a miracle that the stuff that goes on in the dressing room, every dressing room I've been in, doesn't get out of hand to the degree that you would think it would, because it could be just horrendous.[137]

Norman Whiteside candidly admits in his book that bullying was a problem for younger players at Manchester United and while he was 'welcomed wholeheartedly' by fellow countrymen Sammy McIlroy, Jimmy Nicholl and Dave McCreery, it was more difficult to win the respect of some other senior players, which suggests a pecking order among footballers. Richie Sadlier also felt this exists within football clubs.[138]

As a participant in Oldham Athletic's traditional club activities for young players, David Miskelly had to get up to sing a Christmas song and 'run the gauntlet' as a YTS recruit. However, he notes that there has been a shift in attitudes shown by clubs towards young recruits since the 1990s, with cleaning duties no longer part and parcel of their responsibilities, although he felt that this had the effect of making them less disciplined.[139] Damien Richardson also felt that the system was there for a reason, and that it helped build character, but at times it could go too far and sometimes as a player he had to step in when it got out of hand:

> I saw how excited the kids were, how wide-eyed they'd come in at sixteen, seventeen and how some of them handled it in a

> natural manner, how some of them had to work very hard to handle it, and how some indeed actually never came to terms with it, because you're leaving school at sixteen years of age, and you're being thrown into a man's world, and you're looking after men and you're looking after professional footballers. Now most, the vast majority of professional footballers were good people, they appreciated their boots being cleaned, every pro had his own apprentice who looked after him. [The apprentice had] every two or three players, and [although] 99 per cent respected that, you always got the one who didn't, who wanted to try and belittle the kid. There was always banter, sometimes the banter verged on bullying.[140]

In a 2016 television interview, former England captain, John Terry, stated that there was less interaction between young players and first-team players as a result of the change in recruits' responsibilities.[141] Terry began his career at West Ham United in the early 1990s before moving to Chelsea as a fourteen-year-old and was part of a system where youth players were expected to look after senior players' needs around the training ground, and were generally in receipt of a low payment, with the exception of occasional bonuses from senior professionals.

In 1988, James Power, a seventeen-year-old from Kilmacthomas, County Waterford, who was on the Youth Training Scheme at Chelsea, could expect to earn £28.50 a week along with having his digs and travelling expenses paid for. Duties included tidying up the dressing room, laying out kits and cleaning boots. A £2 voucher was given daily for players to be used in a kebab restaurant beside Stamford Bridge after training at Harlington.[142] Youth players were also subjected to initiation and bonding rituals which sometimes went too far. The recent court case of a Northern Ireland-born trainee who claimed to have been abused by senior players at Stoke City in the 1980s has highlighted the hierarchical set-up which has traditionally been in place at many clubs, although the case was dismissed.[143]

As Mick Meagan has stated, Irish footballers were not the only ones who got stick, and it was almost a rite of passage as to when a younger player would eventually have enough of a reputation to be the one dishing out the slagging:

> I remember poor young fellas coming down from Wigan to Everton, and they used to get some terrible stick, that they had a different kind of a lingo, kind of a Lancashire accent – so everyone got it! And then, as you grew up, your turn came for to be handing it out. Now it was all fun, everything was all kind of fun, no insult, and don't you know, it was all part and parcel of growing up.[144]

Denis Behan felt that because of his size he was better able to cope with 'the banter', being over six feet tall.[145] However, as Seamus Kelly has noted, 'implicit in dressing-room banter is an underlying theme of competitiveness and ruthlessness'.[146] Along with the desire to be the best, the amount of money to be made in the first team could also be a factor in this. Paddy Mulligan has also stated that the game was a ruthless business:

> It's vicious. It's winner take all. Be under no illusions. And certainly in my day, because there weren't big squads – we had a squad of about sixteen or seventeen at Chelsea, which was unusual, Liverpool had fourteen or fifteen maybe – but it was dog eat dog and that was it, that was the way that it was. If you weren't in the team you were useless, and that's how you felt. And you were nearly made to feel like that.[147]

According to Damien Richardson, 'in professional football, the most difficult place to survive is the dressing room', while Richie Sadlier felt that 'it's an odd kind of atmosphere: it can be friendly and welcoming, but so ruthless as well'.[148] The realisation that this was in fact a highly competitive employment position came as a shock to some players, with Seamus Kelly recalling:

> When you go into a dressing room [initially], most lads will welcome you: 'Well done, the best of luck to you', but they'd take your head off two weeks later. It took me a while to suss out the

> ruthlessness of the dressing room … one of the coaches [Billy Ayre] said to me, after about three months, 'You know, you're actually taking some of these guys' jobs, the sooner you get that, the better.' And I went, 'OK, thanks' … that's the nature of the industry.[149]

As Hunter Davies has written in relation to new signings at a club, the arrival of a new player could raise questions within the existing group.[150] Similarly, Paddy Mulligan felt that the forming of initial impressions was pivotal to what would follow in terms of gaining respect:

> The camaraderie wouldn't have been there, because you're new, and players are sizing you up as well. They're looking to see 'what's he like' both on a personal level, and what's he like as a footballer – is he brave, is he a coward, what is he? They're sizing you up. I mean 'Chopper' Harris went over the top on me – tried to go over the top on me – in my first training session [at Chelsea]. I eyeballed him. I said, 'Ron, you don't do stuff like that to me. Don't ever do that to me again.' And we understood each other from there on in, there was no problem after that. Whether he thought he'd get away with it – but he could have no complaints about going over the top irrespective of whether you're a team mate or not – it didn't matter.[151]

In Mulligan's case, he moved from a top League of Ireland club, Shamrock Rovers, where, as noted in the press, he had been outstanding, to Chelsea of the First Division, where he felt that he had to play at 'about 400 per cent' for manager, Dave Sexton, to be happy with his performance.[152] As Roderick has stated, 'In cases where a player moves to a club of a higher status – in terms of league or league position, or even economic situation – he must learn to deal with the status transformation which such a move may bestow upon him.'[153] In addition, Mulligan noted that players will look for a flaw in the new addition to the team straight from the beginning:

> They're looking at you every which way. They're looking for any fault that they can find. Any weakness that they can find, and they will hound you. And they will turn around and if they find it, you're a goner. So you have to be very, very strong, and stand up to these people, because if you don't stand up to them, your life is a misery. When you go messing on somebody, if they bite, you keep doing it and doing it and doing it. It's the same [in professional football], that's it.[154]

IRISH FOOTBALL MIGRANTS IN ENGLAND AND THE TROUBLES

By 1971, Britain had 'the largest number of people born in Ireland who lived overseas, at just under one million people'.[155] Irish footballers were not immune to tensions within English society caused by the Irish Republican Army's bombing campaign in Britain during the latter decades of the twentieth century, although experiences differed. Under the Prevention of Terrorism Act, implemented after these attacks, nearly 7,000 people were detained 'but of these, only three or four persons on average "received a significant custodial sentence"'.[156] As Delaney has noted, Luton was an 'expanding industrial area' after the Second World War and 'roughly a third of the Irish-born population in England and Wales in the mid-twentieth century lived in Greater London'. Along with Dagenham and Slough, Luton was home to 'significant numbers of Irish'.[157] Despite this, Seamus Heath remembered moving to England as being the first time he was conscious of his accent, stating that 'it was sad because of the atrocities that happened, but to label a young person, just because he's from Ireland with an accent, [that] was hard, so yes, that was a difficult time'.[158] Paddy Mulligan noted that 'in London, I was very, very careful not to speak too much, which is a major miracle for me. Because if you did, you always had somebody turn around to look at you.'[159] It was during a match at Millwall where Mulligan experienced the most abuse from opposition supporters, although he had no real problems from team mates or opponents about his Irish background.[160] Damien Richardson was called 'a car bomber' by one opponent, but admitted that he knew it was part and parcel of the game that he would receive psychological abuse during a match and was able to deal with it.[161]

Some players feared for their families back in Ireland, with Sammy McIlroy and Tommy Cassidy moving their parents from Belfast to Manchester and Newcastle respectively.[162] In addition, a few, including George Best and Pat Jennings, received death threats.[163] Sometimes the 'banter' could be a bit insensitive, and memories of home would return instinctively, as John McClelland recalls:

> It's funny what you do remember – I remember once about to board the reserve bus at Cardiff, and one of the players said, 'There's a phone call from Belfast, for you, it's your family' and you automatically think something happened. And I wasn't very happy when I came back and he was only joking! I wasn't very happy at that, because obviously … at that time … your heart … Jesus, if something happened … and they just wanted you to miss the bus or something: 'Oh yeh, there's a call for you from your family.' You're about to leave, and you rush to the office, and there's no call for ya, it's funny that little thing sort of stuck in my head. I remember at night outside sometimes when I heard a car backfiring, you sort of went into the bushes! Or when you're walking down the street, you sort of stay out of the cars, just move out of the way, out of the shadows, you don't realise that it's probably what you did, the way it was happening in Northern Ireland, you know what I mean? At one in the morning [in Northern Ireland at that time], you wouldn't want to be running down the street and a car just [appears] …[164]

Richie Sadlier stated that he received abuse in London because of his Irish background while the IRA's campaign was still active and 'it was a different experience being in London in the mid-'90s compared to now.'[165] David Miskelly was also subjected to some abuse away from his club after the Manchester bombing in 1996 and felt it was because 'people were on edge' at the time and 'it was probably tongue in cheek but … you don't take anything from it.'[166] Both Damien Richardson and Brian Mooney felt that English players simply weren't educated about life in Ireland, with Mooney stating that during his time in England in the 1980s and 1990s, 'I felt that a lot of the English players, or nearly all of them, weren't educated about the Irish system, or about what was going on up in Northern Ireland, and they didn't really know why the conflict was going on.'[167] Similarly, Alan Blayney stated:

> You get the odd boy asking you questions like 'are there boys just walking up and down the street with guns?' and this, that and the other, that don't have a clue what it's like, they just think that Northern Ireland is just like a war zone and things like that. It's true, you do get called 'Paddy' … but it's nothing, its nothing terrible or anything, it's just one of them things … there was me and Chris Baird, me and him actually lived together at Southampton, Steven Gray as well, he was from Dublin, played for Derry, and we never got any abuse from anybody, I didn't really see that when I was there.[168]

Players in the Irish League, such as Raymond Campbell while at east Belfast club Glentoran (1989–93), have been targeted by supporters, although he felt things had changed a lot since then.[169] In particular, the work of Daniel Brown has noted how Linfield's recruitment policy towards the signing of Catholics changed in the early 1990s.[170] The majority of players interviewed for this book felt that they had not suffered any anti-Irish abuse in England.

PLAYER–MANAGER RELATIONSHIPS AND TRANSFERRAL TO OTHER CLUBS

As Harding states, 'To be a professional footballer can thus mean being part of a world of uncertainty and manipulation.'[171] Player–manager relationships, as Roderick has noted, 'are strained by the constant demands of managers for performance returns on player investments'.[172] These could frequently determine a player's future at a club and some, such as former 1980s Liverpool reserve Ken DeMange, who stated in a magazine interview that there was 'a poisonous atmosphere' at Hull City during his time there, felt they were deliberately frozen out by managers. As well as not being allowed to train with the first team, DeMange was no longer on speaking terms with manager, Terry Dolan, by the time he left in 1990 and claimed he was only given one match a month in the reserves as this was the minimal required by the PFA.[173] After apparently being pressurised into playing by manager, Tommy Docherty, while recovering from a knee operation in the late 1980s, Wolves' Martin Bayly was forced to train alone when he refused to comply after the injury worsened and he eventually needed another operation. Refusing an order to leave the club without payment, he put in his own transfer request and later moved to Coventry City for a short period before returning to Ireland.[174]

John McClelland's career in the game, which lasted for over twenty years and saw him play in the World Cup finals twice, brought a number of difficult struggles when he stood up to what he felt was unfair management, having realised early that professional clubs were often exploitative of players in their contract negotiations. He recalled the lack of choice available as a teenager on joining Cardiff in 1972 when he explained that 'they just tell you, "You're worth £25 a week", from what I remember. You don't really negotiate, … you're so naïve, you just go over [and it's] "OK, there you are"'.[175] He was poorly treated by Mansfield later in the 1970s, particularly after an informal agreement with the manager that he would be put in a hotel with his wife went unfulfilled and he was left to foot the bill for his lodgings, with the club refusing to pay his landlady.[176] As Roderick has stated, despite progress in players' rights in the early 1960s, in the years prior to the Bosman Ruling in 1995, 'players were not unconditionally free to negotiate a contact with a different club unless they were given a "free transfer" by their employing club'.[177] McClelland was later frozen out at Glasgow Rangers by new manager, Jock Wallace in 1984, despite being the club captain and a regular international at the time, and feels that this turmoil 'was probably the start of my first marriage disappearing'.[178] This club–player struggle developed after his request for a pay rise was refused, and he was later sold to Watford, despite interest from Tottenham Hotspur, illustrating a side of the game which supporters are rarely made aware of:

> I walked in after playing against Inter Milan [in the 1984–85 UEFA Cup] and he [Wallace] said, 'I've just sold you to Watford.' I said, 'Well, Tottenham want me.' He said, 'You're not going there.' So they could even force you to a smaller club. But now the tide's turned with the Bosman, now the player can say, 'Well, I'm going here, arrange the deal.' So it's gone from one bad system which bullied the players, to another bad system [in] which the players have all the power. You know what I mean, so yeh that was probably the worst time in my career, when you're doing things right … injuries happen, loss of form happens, but when you're on top of your form, and you're being slaughtered [in the press] and being accused of, everything, it's not a nice thing. I know it still bothers me today! But you see players trying to leave clubs, and I was trying to stay at Rangers … I said, 'I just want to stay' … good club, and the fans like me, that's all I want, I wanted my reward and they don't give you it … and when I left they made out I wasn't that good because only Watford wanted me. But they'd stopped me going to a bigger club than Watford.[179]

The club had also refused to allow him to use a player representative during negotiations, despite Wallace being allowed to use agent Bill McMurdo to negotiate, and he feels they also used the press to portray him in a poor light when he had initially tried to negotiate the pay rise:

> The media said, 'John, you've got to talk to us' and I said, 'Listen, it's private, you know.' [They said], 'Well, John, it's not private, you're keeping it private, but they're phoning us and they're stitching you up, left, right and centre, and you're a sitting duck, and you're sitting there not saying a word.' And I said, 'Well, that's my morals' and then, he [Wallace] brought me in one day and said he'd put me out of football forever if I don't sign the contract. So he dropped me and wouldn't play me. So you're doing your job right, that's the demoralising thing, emotionally it's very difficult.[180]

Denis Behan also suffered personally when his club, Hartlepool United, refused to assist with his insurance following the offer of a move from Hamilton Academical in 2010 after, as mentioned, he had lost his place in the first team through, failing to recover quickly enough from injury:

> I was supposed to be going to Hamilton, in Scotland, and Hartlepool wouldn't pay for my insurance. Basically they said if I was going that it would be at my own risk if anything happened up there and they couldn't pay any follow-up, so I think the insurance was going to cost a couple of hundred quid and they weren't going to pay for that because obviously they wanted me off the books ... so I said, 'No, I'll stay where I am', and I spent the bones, of, before and after Christmas, about six months basically training with the reserves or with the youth team on a Friday.[181]

At times, family bereavements could be coldly dealt with by clubs. Alfie Hale, having joined Doncaster Rovers from Aston Villa in 1962, was forced to play for the former club in a match against Brighton & Hove Albion when he and his family were in mourning over the death of his nephew.[182] He was told by manager Oscar Holt that if he missed the game he would be suspended from the club indefinitely as it was in his contract that he played every game.[183] As Harding states of managers' ways of dealing with players, 'sometimes the methods employed are so remarkably crude, they border on the manic'.[184] Raymond Campbell said that Brian Clough's treatment of him, particularly after he had returned to Nottingham from his mother's funeral in the late 1980s, was hard to take:

> He gave me a pretty hard time, I suppose, if I'm being honest. He was ... he gave me a lot of grief in training ... Irish such and such and Paddy this and Paddy that ... and then when, I'll never forget, when my mother died, when I was seventeen and I was over there at the time, and I came back ... she died and the week after the funeral, my first day back in training actually in England, he brought me out in front of the squad and said, 'This

> is a guy here, he's been back at home but he hasn't trained, what do yiz think of that, that's a disgrace.' You know he said this to the whole club … I couldn't believe … I'm like … I remember Stuart Pearce bringing me in, he said, 'Don't listen to him.' I was only a young boy at the time, I'd just lost my mother, and I just couldn't believe it then, but that's the kind of thing he did. Whether it was meant to gee me up or … I think it had the adverse effect.[185]

A life in the reserves could also damage a player's morale, but for many players, dropping down a few divisions was a necessity to secure first-team matches. As Roderick has stated, 'players are only able to sustain their sense of self by playing in the first team' and 'they can only maintain their identities either by continuing to play or by continuing, in their terms, to make progress towards their career goals'.[186] The prospect of transferring to a club at a different level can also be problematic, with some adaption required, and perhaps a drop in standards, as Seamus Heath recalls on his move from Luton Town to Wrexham in 1983:

> I was going from a First Division club to a Fourth Division club – and it was a culture shock as well. I was used to a better training facility, I would say probably better players, but once you start then, training with your new team, within time, you become one of them. I was used to being, OK, maybe a main reserve player at Luton, but I was still hanging out with Mal [Donaghy] and other international players, whereas when I was twenty-one I went. I found then my level, I found that a culture shock.[187]

Martin Russell commented in a magazine after moving from Second Division Leicester City to Fourth Division Scarborough in 1989 that 'I just had to have regular league football. There was nothing permanent at Filbert Street, playing behind closed doors and in midweek games.'[188] Although Russell was later able to move back to a higher level of football, joining Middlesbrough in 1990, by the following year he was back in Ireland with Irish League side Portadown, winning the Northern Ireland PFA Player of the Year in

1992, and claimed around this time that 'at that stage I could see no future for myself in English football'.[189] When asked about the need to play first-team football when interviewed for this study, he felt that at Manchester United in the 1980s, he …

> would have regarded it [the competition] as strong when you consider things … the likes of David Platt, who got released, and he couldn't get into the team because of the likes of Mark Hughes, Norman Whiteside being ahead of him. In midfield it was difficult for a young player to get ahead of the likes of the Arnold Muhrens, Bryan Robsons, Remi Moses, Ray Wilkins, all world-class players at the time so, yeh, competition was difficult. I played a lot of reserve football with these lads, so it was again, valuable experience, but to actually get the first-team chance at the time seemed difficult, yeh.[190]

For Brian Mooney, who won Preston North End's Player of the Year in 1988–89 and was part of Liverpool's squad earlier in the 1980s, remaining at one of English football's top clubs was frustrating when he could have been part of another First Division team's starting eleven:

> When I went over [in 1983], they were probably the top club in Europe, I was mostly in the reserves, like we were winning the reserves' Central League nearly every year and then during the summer they'd be signing a big bunch of international players so it was hard to break through, but the competition was very severe to get into that particular team at the time. I suppose, towards the end of my career at Liverpool I got very frustrated, being in the reserves, I was there nearly … it would have been my fifth season there, I was there like four and a half seasons, frustrated playing in the reserves all the time. I suppose the reserves played midweek, there was no game at the weekend for them, so the whole club is geared to playing the game at the weekend in those days and then you were playing midweek and you were off for the weekend.[191]

Some other players, such as Barry Prenderville, have expressed regret about the way that possible transfers were dealt with, with his club, Coventry City, blocking a move to Hibernian after a successful loan spell.[192] Players at lower-league clubs at times face the threat of loan players from those at a higher league level, as Dean Kelly explains of his time at Oldham Athletic:

> The competition was very tough, like you're playing League One so you get a lot of people from Championship and Premiership coming on loan to the likes of Oldham and Division One teams, so I was getting a few starts with Oldham, then they got a fella on loan from Sunderland, and he was playing ahead of me, so it's hard that way, when you think you're doing well and you get a fella on loan from a club at a higher level, he's gonna play, so that can be difficult.[193]

Being sent on loan to a club with a much lower standard of football could be demoralising for some players, as Raymond Campbell notes of his time at Hereford United:

> I really struggled, I didn't want to be there … at that time I didn't see the point, I thought Forest were just loaning me out maybe to get Hereford to maybe sign me permanently and I didn't want to go. I thought the football was poor, it was the Fourth Division then I think Hereford were in though it was just hump it up and I was playing wide-right and I just didn't see the ball … the ball was up in the air most of the time and I went back to Forest reserves and the ball was on the deck and it was a totally different style of football.[194]

Being released could be a traumatic experience, and the reasons at times depend on a club's changing circumstances. John McClelland felt that his release from Cardiff City in 1974 was more to do with the club's financial situation rather than his progress on the pitch:

> Cardiff had got relegated, I had played in the reserves as centre-forward when somebody got injured and then I got in the first

> team at centre-forward, and I played six or seven games in the first team. They got relegated, but looking back, it was probably budgets, there might have been a clause in my contract, I don't know, you don't know that, so they called me in and said I hadn't progressed quickly enough. So I remember, there was about ten of us, outside the manager's office, and I was the youngest, had played more games, and everybody thought I was going to get a new contract. In fact I was the first in, and they told me I wasn't going to make it, they'd be releasing me – they don't say free transfer – and I remember going out and people saying, 'How are you getting on?' I started crying. The older players had long-term contracts, so they couldn't get rid of them, the younger players were always on a one-year contract, so once there's a budget thing, just get rid of all, get rid of everybody whose contracts were up.[195]

A change in manager could also see the end of a player's career at a club. Michael Carvill's release from Charlton Athletic in 2007 by new manager, Alan Pardew, was abrupt and left the player stunned:

> Alan Pardew just took over the job about three weeks and we were training and I remember sitting in the dressing room and my youth team manager being promoted to the reserve team manager, the assistant coach. Mark Robson came in and he says, 'Mickey, the gaffer wants you upstairs.' I just had a really bad feeling in the pit of my stomach, he said it in front of all the boys as well so maybe I was a bit embarrassed because I thought, 'You don't get called into the manager's office very often and not unless something [is up]'. So I went up and he just brought me in, literally sat me down. Before I could even sit he just said, 'I'm letting you go.' Straight away, straight away. And I froze, I didn't know what to say to him. Looking back now, I wish I would have stood my ground and said [something]. I hadn't really had a go at him because it was just, 'Well, I'm letting you go, I'm bringing in my own players and clearing out the squad.' I wasn't the only one to go. He said, 'We're clearing out the squad, there's

> a cheque next door, collect it' and he goes, 'Don't come back in the morning' … and he goes, 'Do you want to train today?' And I didn't know anything else so I said, 'Yeh, of course I'll train', and I remember training and it's stupid, when I look back now, I remember thinking, 'Maybe if I train well today, he'll change his mind', or something like that there. Things like that go through your head, and I just remember coming in after training … had about three or four pairs of boots, just put them in a wee bag, it was like, I didn't even say goodbye I was that embarrassed, I just said it to people I could trust, I just said, 'I've been released there, so I'll see you later' 'n' all, and I remember two boys driving me home, dropping me off.[196]

As Harding notes, 'managers have been known to sack and demote players with apparent randomness' and 'the player must deduce the reasons for himself through a series of significant encounters, nods and ambiguous signs'.[197] In addition, 'players often find themselves out of favour with an incoming manager, another occupational hazard for the professional', while many of those 'with little time to make mistakes will opt for the finished article rather than gamble on an untried youngster'.[198] Moving to a team halfway through the season when others were well established could be difficult, as Andy Waterworth states of his move to Hamilton Academical from Lisburn Distillery early in 2008:

> I think because the team was playing so well and I came in in January, there's nothing else needed, I maybe came in at the wrong time and then everybody just had their numbers, their places, their mates … they didn't really need me [at that time], this was like a project for long-term.[199]

Roderick has illustrated how professional footballers' decisions regarding relocation impact on family life and has noted a change in how some players' wives are now more focused on their own career aspirations rather than simply following their husbands from club to club, with those such as Ann Lee and Suzy Barnes eager to follow

Andy Waterworth celebrates a goal for Glentoran versus Coleraine in 2011. Having returned from Scotland in 2008, he has gone on to become a prolific scorer at Linfield, having joined the club in 2013. Picture: © Inpho

their own career paths.[200] More players are now showing a tendency to commute longer distances to their clubs or live apart from their partners for periods during the week.[201] Transferring between English clubs has evidently also caused disruption to Irish players' morale and form. Players who moved their families to England and bought homes also faced the threat of transfer and further uprooting if they failed to establish a place in the starting eleven. Just over a year after moving his wife and child over from Dublin and buying a house in Nottingham, Roddy Collins was transferred to Newport County in Wales from Mansfield Town in August 1987.[202] He failed to play in any additional football league matches after the 1987–88 season, and later returned home to Ireland and stated in a television documentary that he was 'in deep despair' during his time there, with his playing time curtailed by injury.[203] Needless to say, relocating has proved difficult for players' other family members; Stephen Hunt's wife, Joanne, stated in a radio broadcast in 2012 that 'it's such an unpredictable job that way … that's the side that's hard'.[204] Michael McHugh felt that moving house after signing for Scarborough from Bradford in the early 1990s with only a one-year contract 'wasn't ideal' with a wife and young child and instead travelled the ninety-minute journey back and forth to his new club every day.[205] According to Martin Russell:

> It does take you a little bit to get, to feel part of the new club, and bar [Manchester] United, I think I was only over a year at each of the other ones so you feel more like a visitor in terms of that. You haven't settled down long enough so it's probably a difficult part. It wasn't so bad for me at the time, I had only kids when I came back to Ireland, but for anybody that had kids and getting schools and stuff like that it would be an issue there … a lot of hassle, uprooting and stuff.[206]

Senior players, as well as teenage migrants (see above), have also expressed a desire to move to a welcoming club while transferring between English teams. Aaron Callaghan illustrated his relief and the importance of a comfortable environment in a magazine interview after he signed a three-year contact with Crewe Alexandra in 1991, having left Stoke City: 'It was a bit of security. The wages aren't great here, but OK. It's a homely club though.'[207] The work of Kuper and Szymanski has illustrated how as late as the twenty-first century, even the richest clubs – such as Real Madrid and Chelsea – were still neglecting to employ relocation consultants to assist top players with movement issues such as finding them suitable housing and schools for their children, although a few other teams – such as AC Milan and Ajax – had better policies in place in this regard.[208] Many top clubs (such as Liverpool) now have club liaison officers to help players settle in their new environments but it is likely that lower-league teams have less efficient player relocation strategies in place.[209]

INTERNATIONAL FOOTBALL

While, as will be shown later, the majority of post-war Irish football migrants did not get to represent their country at senior international level, for those who do, the experience can have a lifelong impact, particularly if qualification for a major tournament is secured. Success for the Republic of Ireland at international level has been hindered by a variety of factors, not least the selection process, with both Alfie Hale and Damien Richardson expressing disappointment about this.[210] Getting released for international matches could be problematic for some players, as Mick Meagan recalls in relation to his time as an international player between 1961 and 1969:

> In those days, as you know, the club didn't have to release you, and I'd say, probably, there was ten times I know, that I wasn't being released because the club didn't have to. They'd pay you the fee, the match fee, which was only £35. I probably would have liked to have played more, but in those days that's the way it was – the club would say, 'No, you're not going.'[211]

Although he felt that he enjoyed his time as manager between 1969 and 1971, he states that he was 'never cut out to be a manager, never' although it was Meagan who was the first manager of the side given the power to choose his own players.[212] However, the Republic of Ireland did not qualify for the World Cup Finals until 1989. Along with bad luck in missing out on the 1982 competition in Spain through some scandalous refereeing decisions, organisational difficulties were a common feature of their preparation for much of the late twentieth century and indeed into the 2000s, culminating in the infamous Saipan incident in 2002, which was news headlines in Ireland with Taoiseach Bertie Ahern being asked to resolve the row between manager, Mick McCarthy, and captain, Roy Keane, in the build-up to the Japan–South Korea finals. For Alan Bairner, the debate was 'clear evidence of sport's ability to supersede almost all other domestic and international matters.'[213] Despite these problems, Paddy Mulligan felt that:

> From a footballing standpoint, I mean, before they appointed a manager [in 1969], they were shambolic, because there was a committee picking the team. And they could pick anybody. 'Oh I'll pick my man there, I'll pick mine.' No balance in the team, no nothing. They might pick six midfielders, six forwards, you wouldn't know what you were going to do, so that would have been horrible, but as regards the travelling arrangements, forget about the travelling arrangements, this is something that happened, but by and large apart from that, things were fine. Look, we could all be picky and say this wasn't right, that wasn't right, and something else wasn't right, but look, you're there to play football, put everything else aside, go and play the football, that's why you're there, you can count your lucky stars that you are playing for the Republic of Ireland, that's as far as I would be concerned. So I've no time for these lads that moan and groan about this, that and the other, and they tweet this and tweet that and this is wrong ... negativity. Professional footballers are the best at making excuses, that 'it's not my fault, and how can I get out of this', instead of meeting the problem head on: 'I don't want to get out of this, this is the way it's going to be.'[214]

According to Matthew Taylor, 'the presence of all four UK sides at the 1958 World Cup in Sweden could be read as a belated acceptance of the international game and the end of Britain's era of insularity'.[215] The build-up to Northern Ireland's final appearances was seemingly relatively quiet in comparison to the Republic's preparation problems, although playing on Sunday was not an entirely satisfactory arrangement for the IFA and goalkeeper, Harry Gregg, in particular, with the Munich disaster survivor only deciding to participate in the 1958 tournament having cleared his conscience through a telephone conversation with a vicar.[216] For defender, John McClelland, who was part of the 1982 and 1986 campaigns, playing in the World Cup was part and parcel of being a professional footballer, and he felt that 'you're so busy working, just to get over the line, or not be embarrassed, or let your country down, or let yourself down, you

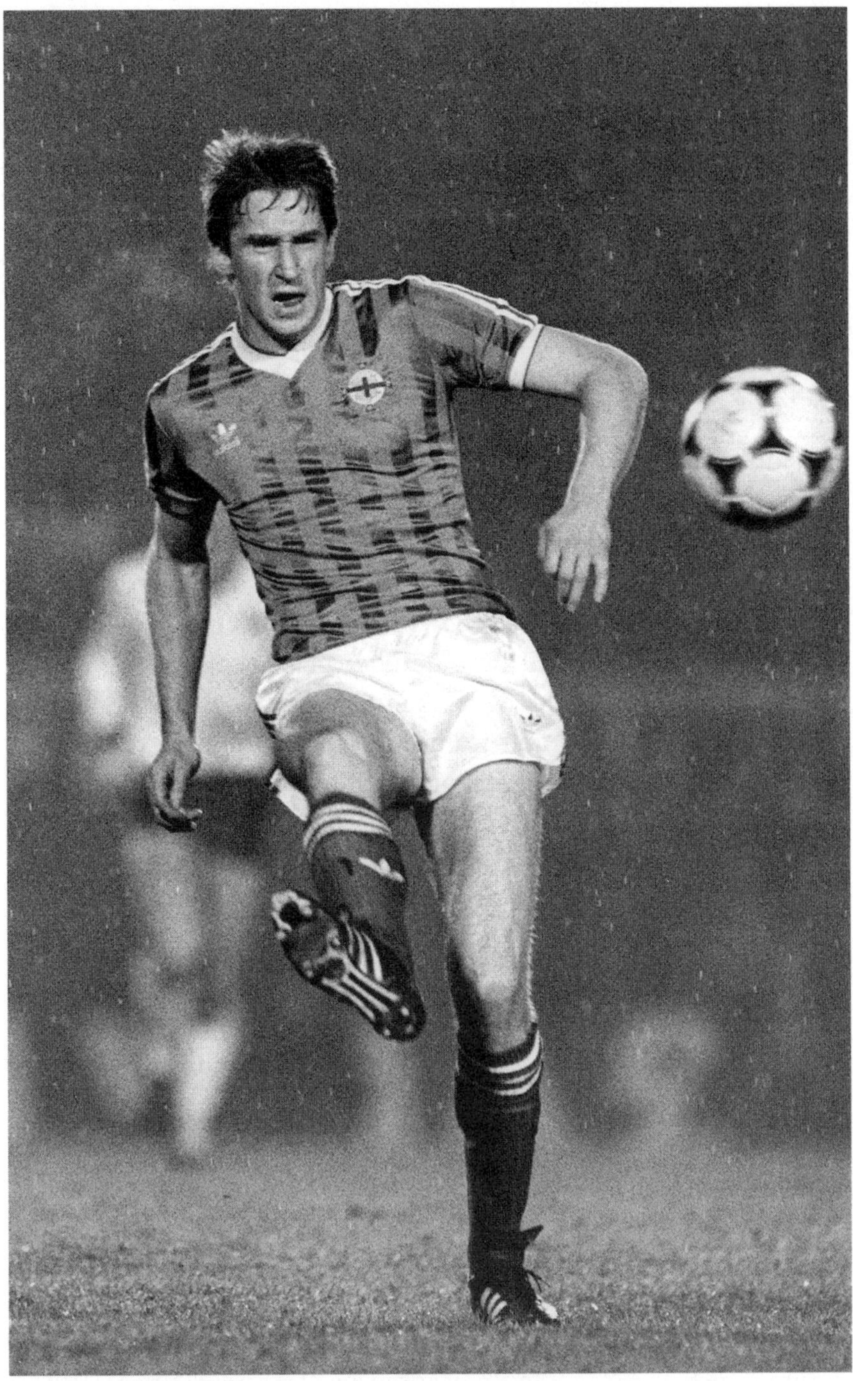

John McClelland played in two World Cup finals for Northern Ireland and won the First Division championship with Leeds United in 1992. Picture: © Inpho

don't see the big picture'.[217] For a World Cup player, the experience can continue long after a career has come to an end, as he states:

> You think, well, that's what I do – represent – and I know I represent Northern Ireland everywhere I go – even now, when I'm out of football that long. But I feel I have that responsibility, all the time – it's not a responsibility, it's not something that's heavy to me, I'm proud to do it, and I think that's what you do.[218]

CONCLUSION

As Hunter Davies wrote in 2001, 'inside a club, inside a dressing room, basic things are much the same, despite the externals having changed so drastically' over the years.[219] This chapter has illustrated the views of a number of Irish-born players on life as a professional footballer. Roderick's assessment of the tough culture of football clubs has been confirmed by a number of players interviewed for this study, and what he has described as 'passages of vulnerability' – when players lose their first-team places or are injured – have been discussed.[220] What would be termed bullying in other occupations is seen as 'banter' and appears to be part and parcel of dressing-room life. How much the cultural difference of being an Irish professional footballer has changed across the period covered here still remains to be seen, as while financially football has exploded since the 1990s, the dressing-room culture of many clubs has not changed greatly, and being wealthy does not shield players from being lonely and putting up with anti-Irish jokes. As Hickman has noted, 'Despite the European location of Ireland, and despite their white skin colour, the Irish are an example of a group subject to racism.'[221] There is some evidence to suggest this is also the case within football, although the majority of players interviewed appear to see stereotypical name-calling as being part of the dressing-room culture. This is not something that developed during the Troubles, however, with pre-war migrant, Jimmy Dunne, once stating that he felt uncomfortable during a spell at Arsenal in the 1930s as he was referred to as 'Paddy' by his team mates.[222] Despite these challenges, professional football has provided many Irish-born footballers with a standard of living and the realisation of a dream, which would not have been available to them in Ireland.

In many ways, Irish-born players are similar to other footballing migrants, but while Irish and English culture is in many ways alike, close familial ties and certain attitudes to Irish people mean that moving across the sea is tough. For those who do break into first-team football, there are many aspects of the game that can raise a player to the greatest sporting heights, but all the while they are treading a thin line between success and failure and carrying the constant threat of a loss of form or an injury that will mean a lack of progress or the end of a career. There are also the problems of dealing with the competition from other players and the expectations of managers and having to relocate. Despite this, the satisfaction levels for those who establish themselves can lead to unforgettable memories, a high standard of living and worldwide recognition. Being a professional footballer is not a constant high, however, and the lack of support systems and the cut-throat nature of the industry have again been highlighted. As Billy Humphries has stated, the old cliché, 'you're only as good as your last match', is a fairly accurate summary of the insecurity of the game.[223] Chapter 5 examines the experiences of a number of players who have ventured outside the English game to other professional football leagues.

CHAPTER 5

Migration to Scotland, Europe and North America

> I took it with a pinch of salt … I mean, Celtic fans would see you in the street and give you a bit of abuse and have a joke, and say, 'How did you play against Aberdeen?' [You'd ask] 'How did Charlie Nicholas do, [how did] Davie Provan and Paddy Bonner get on?' and within ten minutes, they'd say, 'Ah you're not bad for a Protestant, you're all right, have a good one' and they'd be giving the guy that gave you stick, stick. You know the way the guy that actually gave you stick, they were on his back! So I never took it as a personal thing, in a way.[1]
>
> John McClelland, 29 January 2014

INTRODUCTION

Irish-born football migrants have generally moved to England rather than other countries in attempting to further their careers. Given the similar culture and lack of language difficulties and close proximity, this is understandable, but Scotland has also been a popular destination, although not to the same extent. The sectarian nature of Scottish football, and the impact this has had on some Irish players, is assessed in this chapter. Pre-war migration to European clubs by Irish-born players was rare. Movement to continental Europe has been a more recent phenomenon, particularly for younger players going on loan, but the overall numbers for these players have not challenged those for player migration to Britain from Ireland in any serious manner. This does not mean that the players analysed in this book did not move to clubs outside Britain, however. The movement of Irish-born players to the American Soccer League (ASL), which lasted for a decade from 1921 to 1931, is discussed. North America also became a more popular destination for some players with the brief success of the North American Soccer League, which ran from 1968 until 1984. More recently, a few Irish-born players have also moved to play in the Major Soccer League, founded in 1996. An even smaller number of players have moved to other continents, such as Australia, while some players have migrated to South Africa. This chapter therefore generally discusses the movement of Irish-born players to Scotland, continental Europe and North America and the views of a number of players who made these moves are offered.

PRE-SECOND WORLD WAR MIGRATION TO SCOTLAND

By the early 1890s, 194,807 or 4.8 per cent of Scotland's population was Irish-born, while the figure for England and Wales was only 1.6 per cent.[2] As noted earlier, Irish players have been migrating to play for Scottish clubs since the late nineteenth century. In the period from 1890 to 1939, at least seventy-two Irish-born footballers played in the Scottish First Division. On average, the players recorded played for 1.5 Scottish clubs and spent 4.1 seasons in Scotland while the age of migration to a club there was twenty-four. Forty-nine of these players were born in present-day Northern Ireland, illustrating the strength of links between clubs there and Scotland, while nineteen of these were born in Belfast. Fourteen players migrated from Belfast Celtic (seven) and Glentoran (seven), which was almost 20 per cent of the overall number. Glasgow Celtic initially recruited and gave first-team league football to eleven of the overall figure while Glasgow Rangers signed and later gave first-team league football to five players from Irish clubs, which is probably lower than would be expected. Forty-nine players returned to Ireland having played in Scotland although they did not all stay there after this.

Newry-born Willie Maley was part of the Celtic set-up in 1888, having played for Cathcart Hazelbank Juniors and Third Lanark and appears to have been the first Irish-born player to appear in the Scottish First Division, although it seems he did not migrate as a footballer. Similarly, some other early Irish-born players did not migrate as footballers, but were resident in Britain having moved there earlier in their lives.[3] Sunderland, Sheffield United and Clapton Orient player, Peter Boyle, migrated to Coatbridge from Carlingford as a child with his family in the 1870s.[4] There, he played Gaelic football before joining Albion Rovers and moving to Sunderland in 1896.[5] Some players, like Boyle, moved to English league football via Scottish clubs, although the first Irish 'football migrant' to transfer directly from an Irish League club to a Scottish team appears to have been the aforementioned Belfast man Tommy 'Ching' Morrison, who had previous experience of the game at Burnley before returning to Glentoran. He joined Celtic from Glentoran in the 1894–95 season and later returned to Burnley after three seasons in Scotland.[6] He was suspended for two months by the Scottish Football Association in 1895 having been reported for questioning decisions, hacking and abusing opponents, violent conduct and giving cheek to the referee during a Celtic versus Liverpool friendly in Liverpool in September of that year.[7] Garnham has noted the greater physicality of the game in Ireland in comparison to that in England at that time, with John Peden earning a reputation for rough tackles in some sections of the English press.[8]

In turn, a few of these players joined Scottish clubs from those in England in the early twentieth century, including Charlie O'Hagan, Matt Reilly, Frank Thompson and Joe Toner.[9] Less common was movement of Irish-born players from America, although Omagh-born Robert Logan McDonald joined Rangers in 1928 from ASL club Bethlehem Steel.[10] Some players with experience of lower-league football were recruited by professional clubs while employed in Scotland. Coleraine-born Sam English, who went on to play for Rangers, Liverpool and Hartlepools United, was a shipyard worker on the Clyde when he attracted Rangers' attention in 1931.[11] More commonly, Irish-born players who joined Scottish clubs were usually recruited from Irish clubs.

As shown in Table 5.1, in the period from 1888 to 1899 only five Irish-born players were identified as joining top-flight Scottish league clubs. 1900 to 1909 saw this figure increase to nine while between 1910 and 1919 there were nineteen. Although Scotland's First Division continued through the war, the Second Division did not and wages were reduced, while a number of clubs outside the central region of Edinburgh and Glasgow – Aberdeen, Raith Rovers and Dundee – stood down to save travel expenses.[12] However, the number of Irish-born players joining Scottish top-flight clubs between 1914 and 1918 was low, with only seven noted. From 1920 until 1929 there were twenty-four Irish football migrants noted as moving to Scottish First Division clubs. This only slight rise from the previous decade differs significantly to migration to England (106) and may be indicative of the poor financial state of the game in Scotland in that decade which, as will be shown later, saw a large exodus of Scottish players to the American Soccer League. Admittedly, data for England covers all divisions. In the 1930s there were only fifteen Irish-born players noted as moving to Scottish Division One clubs.

Table 5.1 Number of Irish-born footballers who migrated to Scotland (and played in the First Division), by decade, 1888–1939.

Years	Present day Northern Ireland	Present day Republic of Ireland	Unidentified place of birth recorded only as 'Ireland'	Overall Number
1888–99	3	1	1	5
1900–09	5	3	1	9
1910–19	11	6	2	19
1920–29	21	3	0	24
1930–39	8	4	3	15
Overall Total	**48**	**17**	**7**	**72**

Source: Steve Emms and Richard Wells, *Scottish League Players' Records. Division One 1890/91 to 1938/39* (Nottingham: Tony Brown, 2007).

IRISH FOOTBALL MIGRANTS IN TOP-FLIGHT SCOTTISH LEAGUE FOOTBALL, 1945–2010

Using the best sources available, it was possible to compile sufficient data to draw a number of conclusions about those appearing at the highest level of Scottish club football, i.e. the old First Division in the 1945–75 period and in the Premier Division from 1975 to 1998. The

Scottish Professional Football League was formed in 2013 after the Scottish Premier League and Scottish Football League merged. The Scottish Premier League was formed in 1998 as a breakaway from the Scottish Football League.[13]

Table 5.2 Number of Republic of Ireland- and Northern Ireland-born football migrants to Scotland by decade, 1945–2010 (who played in Scottish Football's top division). In 1975 the Premier League replaced the old First Division and in 1998 this became known as the Scottish Premiership.

Years	Republic of Ireland	Northern Ireland
1945–55	9	7
1956–65	2	5
1966–75	0	3
1976–85	3	4
1986–95	5	15
1996–2005	24	15
2006–10	16	8
Total	**59**	**57**

Source: Richard Beal and Steve Emms, *Scottish League Players' Records, Division One 1946/47 to 1974/75* (Nottingham: Tony Brown, 2004); Derek Gray and Steve Emms, *Scottish League Players' Records, 1975/76 to 1999/2000* (Nottingham: Tony Brown, 2002).

Table 5.2 illustrates the estimated number of Republic of Ireland and Northern Ireland football migrants who have played in top-flight Scottish football in the period 1945–2010. At least fifty-seven Northern Ireland and fifty-nine Republic of Ireland born footballers played in the Scottish First Division prior to 1998 or in the Scottish Premier League as it was known afterwards. While a decline was noted in figures for players migrating and playing league football after 1955, it was in the late twentieth century that figures for both countries' football migrants to this level of football reached their peak, which may be an indication of the impact of foreign players on the English Premier League. Thirty-one of these Northern Ireland-born players also experienced English league football while thirty-seven Republic of Ireland-born players also did so. Some post-war players, such as Gerry Burrell, entered English league football via Scottish clubs. A number of players, including Barry Prenderville and Robbie Keane, also went on loan to Scottish clubs but this has been a more recent trend.[14]

Unsurprisingly, Glasgow Celtic initially recruited the most players (sixteen or 27.11 per cent), although some came from English clubs. Shelbourne (six players or 10.16 per cent) was the leading Republic of Ireland-based supplier of these players. The average number of clubs was 1.65 while the average length of seasons played was found to be 4.3. The majority of players (forty or 70 per cent) were born in Dublin. A few players from areas in the north-west of Ireland with strong Scottish connections have managed to break into Scottish league football, such as Sligo-born Sean Fallon, who moved to Celtic in 1949, and Donegal-born Packie Bonner, who was the last player to be signed by Jock Stein, having been invited to Celtic Park by Fallon for a trial.[15] Despite the strong cultural links between west Donegal and Scotland, with seasonal migration of agricultural workers prominent in the nineteenth century, Bonner struggled with homesickness after joining the club in 1978 despite living with his aunt and uncle in Glasgow. He stated in a 1990s' publication that 'my time was spent waiting for the post, hoping that letters would arrive. When they did I saved them for the bus journey to Celtic Park', again illustrating a major problem which has faced Irish football migrants in both England and Scotland.[16]

Some other Irish-born players have also struggled to settle in Scotland. Andy Waterworth, who joined Hamilton Academical in 2008, felt if he had been born in Scotland and grown up in that environment, he would have lasted a lot longer in Scottish football than he did, such was the level of isolation he felt away from his family and close friends.[17] Indeed, Shane Supple, who had a spell on loan at Falkirk while at Ipswich Town, has noted how it was hard to maintain close friendships within the game due to the migratory nature of a career in professional football.[18]

Bonner was not the first football migrant born in Donegal to play in top-flight Scottish football, with Ramelton-born Patsy Gallagher joining Celtic in 1911, although he appears to have migrated as a child.[19] Buncrana-born players, Bernard Cannon and Hugh Doherty, also appeared for Celtic in the 1940s while Chris Fletcher, who was also born in the same town, moved to Kilmarnock via Southend United in 1955. Arranmore Island-born Michael Gallagher also had spells with Scottish clubs Alloa, Hibernian and Ayr United, and more Donegal-born football migrants have appeared in Scotland's top division than those from any other Irish peripheral county.[20]

The majority of Northern Ireland-born football migrants to Scotland in the 1945–2010 period (twenty-two or 39 per cent) were born in Belfast. Distance between Northern Ireland's east coast and Scotland help explain this, with early post-war football migrant, Gerry Burrell, being approached by a St Mirren scout present in Belfast in 1947. Burrell had joined Dundela from Belfast Celtic as he felt he had a better chance of getting a game there. Having made arrangements with his club manager at Dundela, Bobby Doyne, to travel to Scotland, he was very much on his own as he set off for Glasgow after he received his boat tickets in the post:

> I remember coming off the boat … I didn't know where the hell I was, to tell you the God's honest truth so when I met this policeman, I said to him, 'I want to go to Paisley' and he thought I was kidding him on because I don't know, there was a hell of a lot of Irish people in Paisley and Glasgow. So he told me to go in to the bus station, and I got on the bus and I didn't even know the fare. And the conductor came up to me and said, 'A pound' and I said 'OK'. So I gave him a pound and I got on the bus and I told him I was a stranger and I said, 'Could you let me off in Paisley?' He said, 'I can go no further than Paisley, I'll let you off at the top of the town.' So off we went, I got on the bus to Paisley, and I didn't know where the hell I was, to tell you the truth.[21]

He was signed by manager Bobby Rankin the following day after ringing home to again discuss the move with his father. He soon made friends with Celtic player Charlie Tully, a fellow Belfast man, and was looked after by a doctor from Fermanagh who was also at St Mirren, a club which he felt did everything to make him feel at home.[22] Linfield was found to be the leading source club (six players or 10.5 per cent) while Glasgow Rangers were found to have initially recruited the most players (ten or 17.54 per cent) although Celtic followed closely behind with eight (14 per cent). The average number of clubs per player was found to be 1.89 and the average length of seasons played was 6.28, which illustrates that these players have generally had longer spells in Scottish top-flight football than their Republic of Ireland-born counterparts.

SECTARIANISM AND IRISH FOOTBALL MIGRANTS

In July 2015, Rotherham defender Kirk Broadfoot was banned for a record ten matches, ordered to undertake an education programme and fined £7,500 by the FA for sectarian abuse of James McClean during a match against Wigan Athletic.[23] Many Irish-born players have been subjected to sectarianism from opponents and supporters in British football but this appears to have been the first time any significant action was taken. While Norman Whiteside got on very well with other club mates from the Republic of Ireland at Manchester United despite their differing religious and cultural backgrounds, Neil Lennon claimed that he received sectarian abuse from one of the more senior players during his time as an apprentice at Motherwell, with jokes about 'Irishness' common in the dressing room.[24] Both Barry Prenderville and Shane Supple admitted they noticed a different atmosphere while playing in Scotland, particularly among rival supporters.[25] Prenderville also felt that he was poorly advised about the sectarian nature of life in Scotland and was initially left puzzled after experiencing strong anti-Irish abuse there.[26]

There is evidence that this is also a problem at underage level. He first received sectarian abuse while playing in the 1993 under 16 Milk Cup final for Cherry Orchard versus Rangers. Prenderville admitted that it was the first time he was called a 'Fenian' and stated: 'I wasn't brought up with that sort of thing – in Dublin, people aren't, the general population … the average boy … fifteen, sixteen, seventeen-year-old boy in Dublin is not brought up with that … they know that they like Celtic and not to like Rangers but that's probably about it'.[27] However, he felt that in terms of sectarianism, Scotland was 'as bad as Northern Ireland probably in ways'.[28] John McClelland was also surprised by the level of religious tension:

> I think in England it's different, 'cause you've probably got a rival club, but obviously it wasn't a flag thing and a Catholic–Protestant thing, it's just the rivalry of the game, you've got your derby games, so it's wasn't the utmost intensity. But I've said to people, I think that's what makes Rangers and Celtic so special, that's what makes the game so special, it's not just football, it's bigotry, it's religion, it's hatred, it's everything – you want passion when you play football … because that's what makes it the special game. So, what you like about it can be the things you don't like about it, but that's what makes it that game. I didn't realise how bigoted it was, it's more bigoted than Northern Ireland from what I remember, because I just got on with life, because Whiteabbey was a mixed village, and my mother used to go to mass … so there wasn't any bigotry, in my view, just good people and bad people. So I was very surprised how … well, you know Rangers and Celtic … different sides of the city … and people presumed I was a bigot.[29]

As Richard B. McCready has stated, in Scotland, 'the prevalence of sectarianism may not be as great as has often been believed but there is no doubt that it was significant' and in relation to the Old Firm rivalry, he notes that 'the entrepreneurial instincts of the Scots, and indeed the Irish, recognised that sectarianism was good for business'.[30] The work of Joseph Bradley, in particular, has highlighted the sectarian nature of some Scottish football clubs and Scottish society in general.[31] Bradley believes that 'in the years after the Reformation, Scotland developed a strong anti-Catholic culture which infused many aspects of social and political life'.[32] However, 'the arrival of Irish Catholic immigrants to Scotland during the nineteenth and twentieth centuries added a radical aspect to traditional antagonism'. In particular, in tracing the origins of the Celtic–Rangers rivalry, Bradley states that from Glasgow Celtic's early beginnings in 1887, the club had strong Catholic and Irish links as 'all the club's founders were expatriate Irishmen or of Irish stock and the new club's support was drawn largely from the swelling Irish community in Glasgow'.[33] This can be contrasted to Rangers, founded in 1872–73 by the McNeil family from Gareloch and other locals interested in the game, as the club began 'in terms more normally associated with football, that is, as a purely sporting and athletic institution'.[34]

Although a Protestant team, Bradley states that 'a combination of factors enabled Rangers to encapsulate, or become the main focus of, a Protestant sporting identity'.[35] He feels that Celtic's early success, in having won the Scottish league and cup, the Glasgow Cup and the Charity Cup by 1893 brought resentment from 'society at large' and as both clubs enjoyed domestic success by the early 1890s, 'Rangers, through their ability to halt this "Irish" dominance of Scottish football, assumed a pre-eminent role in defending native prestige'.[36] The biggest reaction to Celtic's early success came from Rangers, 'and a strong Protestant nationalist-like identity was thus forged within the club'.[37] Bradley believes that 'this identity would not have been possible without the presence of the Celtic club' and was 'a reflection of much of the larger society's attitude towards the Catholic Irish in general'.[38]

As Matthew Taylor has stated, 'the "Old Firm" reflected, and in time reinforced, the divisions and polarities of Glasgow and Scottish society more generally'.[39] With the identities associated with these Glasgow clubs closely linked to Northern Ireland politics, former players on both sides have received death threats, with a summit taking place between club representatives in 2011 to address the issue of sectarianism.[40] Taylor has stated that 'it acquired a harder political edge in Belfast' with the rivalries between the Catholic club Belfast Celtic and the Protestant-backed Linfield and Glentoran teams, all of which were heavily linked, from 1912 onwards, with Home Rule politics, but sectarian violence at matches had also been notable in Glasgow prior to this.[41]

Both Northern Ireland and Republic of Ireland born footballers have played a part in Rangers' and Celtic's success, with former Northern Ireland captain John McClelland winning two Scottish

League Cups with Rangers before going on to star in the Leeds United team that won the last First Division Championship before the inauguration of the Premier League.[42] For McClelland, as a player who had first-hand experience of the Celtic–Rangers rivalry, the religious divide within Scottish football was not something he was overwhelmed by:

> I took it with a pinch of salt … I mean, Celtic fans would see you in the street and give you a bit of abuse and have a joke, and say, 'How did you play against Aberdeen?' [You'd ask], 'How did Charlie Nicholas do, [how did] Davie Provan and Paddy Bonner get on?' and within ten minutes, they'd say, 'Ah you're not bad for a Protestant, you're all right, have a good one' and they'd be giving the guy that gave you stick, stick. You know the way the guy that actually gave you stick, they were on his back! So I never took it as a personal thing, in a way.[43]

As a seven-year-old, Packie Bonner could name the Celtic 1967 European Cup winning team from a picture which hung in his godfather's house and has noted the 'strong Glasgow Celtic tradition in Donegal'.[44] As Bonner himself has written, Celtic have had some Protestant supporters, while he has also stated that as his career developed, he tried to treat the Old Firm clash like any other match, illustrating how players actively involved as professionals have to employ a different attitude to that of spectators.[45] Sectarianism within the game is obviously not a one-sided problem and, as Seán Ryan has shown, Northern Ireland players were said to be unhappy with Roy Keane's abuse of them during the tense World Cup qualifying decider at Windsor Park in 1993.[46] Protestant Norman Uprichard, who was banned by the Gaelic Athletic Association from playing Gaelic football as a teenager in the 1940s as he had also played soccer, stated that he received sectarian abuse from Everton's Dublin-based supporters while later playing in matches at Goodison Park. He was also keen to mention, however, that he always had a good relationship with the club's Dublin-born players, who were Roman Catholics, and 'had as many Catholic friends in Lurgan as Protestant'.[47]

IRISH-BORN PLAYERS IN MAJOR EUROPEAN LEAGUES: GERMANY, ITALY, FRANCE AND SPAIN

Irish football migrants to European clubs in the pre-Second World War period were few, although an exception was Tommy Davis who was suspended for three months by the FA in 1935 after he broke a contract with French club FC Metz to join Oldham Athletic, having initially moved to France from New Brighton in 1934.[48] A professional league had been set up there in 1932, and despite British players being the 'dominant non-French national grouping during the first two years of professional football in France' (making up around 40 per cent of 'foreigners' in the league's initial season), by the mid-1930s migration of British-based players to France had declined.[49] According to Matthew Taylor, 'many of those who travelled to France were on the margins of the professional game in England', while 'the problems of adapting to a different style of football and a new way of life' are of key significance in explaining why this decline occurred.[50] By the 1938–39 season there were only five British players in top-flight French football, a figure which was less than 2 per cent of the overall number of players.[51] Jim Donnelly, a Mayo man who joined Blackburn Rovers in 1920 from the Royal Artillery and who later had spells in Yugoslavia with Grajanski and Gunes in Turkey after an eleven-year career in England, was another exception among pre-war Irish football migrants to Britain in that he also moved to European clubs.[52] Naturally, some Irish-born players had toured Europe with their clubs, with Charlie O'Hagan noting how he had played in Austria and Germany with Tottenham Hotspur 'a few years before the big guns had caused earthquakes in the heart and the coastlines of the continent'.[53] Indeed, prior to the First World War, Barnsley, Blackburn Rovers, Burnley, Everton, Manchester United, Oldham Athletic and Sunderland had all played tour matches against European clubs.[54]

Figures for Irish football migrants from both the Republic and Northern Ireland who moved to England in the 1945–2010 period indicate that the vast majority of these 917 men did not play outside the United Kingdom and Ireland. Of the 500 Republic of Ireland-born migrants who played league football in England, just fifty-six players or 11.2 per cent, and sixty-nine or 16.5 per cent of the 417 Northern Ireland-born players, also played outside of Irish and British football leagues. Despite this, it is possible to offer a wider analysis of the experiences of a number of players who have also moved outside Britain. Writing in 1984, one journalist praised League of Ireland club Shamrock Rovers, whom he claimed had 'shunned the traditional market place and put the advantage in their favour'.[55] In selling players Pierce O'Leary, Liam Buckley and Alan Campbell to Canada, Belgium and Spain respectively in that decade, it was noted that 'Rovers met the clubs and negotiated on an equal footing'.[56] He added that the three players in question had 'proved their mettle in their new environment'. Despite the transfer fees being of 'a respectable nature', the club's attempts to bypass the British market were not consistently replicated by them or other Irish clubs and the idea never caught on.[57] Nor did these players enjoy any great longevity in their adopted countries: O'Leary moved to Glasgow Celtic from Vancouver Whitecaps after three years in 1984, and Buckley signed for Spanish club Racing Santander from the Belgian club KSV Waregem in 1986, before joining Swiss club FC Montreux-Sports the following year. He returned to Shamrock Rovers in 1989.[58] Campbell left Racing Santander in 1986 after two years there to play for Club Deportivo Logroñés before moving to Belgium in 1987 to play for Berchem. In 1989 he moved to Scotland where he played for Dundee and Forfar Athletic.[59] None of these three footballers played league football in England but they all received senior international honours, although this career pathway was not one generally taken on by football migrants from either the Republic or Northern Ireland.

As Enda Delaney has stated, Irish emigration to European Union countries excluding Britain increased in the period from 1988 to 1992, with greater opportunities for free movement brought on by different treaties, particularly the Single European Act of 1987. Greater focus on European languages within second- and third-level Irish educational institutions in the last two decades of the twentieth century and the recognition of educational and other qualifications within Irish and European labour markets assisted this growth.[60] Although most Irish-born players moving to European clubs in the period covered in this study did so without additional European languages or third-level qualifications, as will be shown, it was the late twentieth century when moves to continental clubs became more common among Irish-born players. However, the number of players who did so remained minimal in comparison to those moving to England and Scotland. Delaney has also noted how 'a greater variety of destinations' was an important aspect of 'the "new wave" of Irish emigration of the 1980s and early 1990s'.[61] This was also the case in terms of Irish football migration to Europe, although there is no great evidence of any major influx of Irish-born players into European football clubs, illustrating again the nature of professional football in comparison with work requiring educational qualifications, and Britain as a primary location for Irish football migrants. It also highlights how Britain continued to be seen as the main destination for Irish players, while as David Hassan has highlighted of more general workers in a 2007 article, 'the pattern of movement demonstrated by the "new" Irish migrants to the near continent is typically short term'.[62]

In addition, he has stated that many of the recent Irish migrants to Europe have been graduates who 'are well paid, mobile professionals working in the finance, banking, IT and recruitment sectors' while others have been employed as part of the military or for reasons related to international diplomacy. Some migrants have no academic qualifications and pursue employment in catering, while 'a not insignificant number are university students undertaking seasonal work' or 'a "gap" year'.[63] Most Irish-born footballers who have moved to European clubs have obviously been professionals and therefore would not fall into the above categories, although many are similar in that they could generally be described as temporary migrants. Irish-born footballers have, like their British counterparts, to borrow Lanfranchi and Taylor's phrase, 'tended to be sojourners rather than settlers' within European football.[64] Most Irish-born players who relocated to European clubs usually did not settle there, although, as will be seen, there were some exceptions.

Generally, Irish-born players have not featured heavily in Italian football, or indeed in the other three major European leagues in Spain,

France and Germany.[65] Lanfranchi and Taylor have calculated that in the fifty years after the Second World War, 'fewer than a hundred players have been drawn from British football to the major European leagues' and 'Britain has witnessed nothing like the diaspora of native football talent which has affected most other European nations'.[66] They also note that an ability to adapt to their new country of residence was crucial to the success of players such as John Charles, while those who did not like the lifestyle and culture of the club, like Jimmy Greaves, struggled to settle.[67] In the period from 1945 to 1995, the presence of British and Irish footballers in these major European leagues grew from just six players in the 1945–54 period to fifty-two during 1985–95. The majority of these players featured in Italy's top division, with twenty-nine noted, despite a ban on foreign imports being imposed by the Italian league's governing body between 1966 and 1980. French clubs attracted twenty-three British and Irish players in the period 1945–95, while twenty-one went to Spain to play their football there and only fifteen moved to Germany, although admittedly the Bundesliga did not begin until 1963.[68]

By the early 1990s Germany was proving to be the most popular destination of Irish migrants to Europe, but again, this was not reflected in terms of Irish football migration.[69] Irish-born players moving to Germany were scarce in the period covered here. There were a few exceptions, such as Republic of Ireland international Noel Campbell, who spent eight seasons at SC Fortuna Köln in the 1970s having moved from St Patrick's Athletic in 1971. He had been recommended to the club by a trial player from the League of Ireland, Ben Hannigan, and had previously lived abroad as a teenager at Arsenal, without making a league appearance. Campbell stated in a newspaper interview that he 'was an old hand as far as living somewhere else … in Germany, the language was a bit of a barrier but I got over that fairly quickly'. He was glad to be given the opportunity to play full-time as a professional and embraced the social scene at the club, although they only played one season in the Bundesliga during his spell there.[70] He returned to Ireland in 1980 having struggled with injury, joining Shamrock Rovers. In 2004, Joe Kendrick joined TSV 1860 Munich from Newcastle United through the assistance of the latter club's scout, Charlie Woods, although his stay lasted only briefly, and he returned to England to play for Darlington after one season in which he was injured, having failed to make an appearance in the Bundesliga.[71]

Irish-born players appearing in Italian league football, which was restructured in 1929, have been few, with Liam Brady the most successful of these.[72] Having rejected an offer to sign for Manchester United in July 1980, he joined Juventus from Arsenal and also appeared for Sampdoria, Inter Milan and Ascoli in the period 1980–87 before returning to England to finish his career at West Ham United.[73] Juventus team mates Roberto Bettega and Dino Zoff both spoke in a television interview of his ability to learn and adapt at the Turin club. Juventus manager at the time, Giovanni Trapattoni, felt the reason for his ability to adapt was because he was 'a Latin-type player' who had 'no problem joining in'.[74] There he won two Scudettos and was the team's top goalscorer for two seasons, and he himself stated that he was devastated about the manner in which he was told that he had to leave the club to make way for the president's favourite, Michel Platini, with the club only allowed two 'foreign' players at that time.[75] Brady, said to be 'virtually a national idol' by the end of his first season in Italy, famously converted the penalty which won the club the 1981–82 Scudetto, earning even more admiration from Juventus supporters as he had been forced to move.[76] One reporter described the lifestyle Brady enjoyed in 1981:

> He earns a six figure salary, three or four times what he took home from Highbury (one of England's richest clubs) and the bonuses – awarded for league points and trophies – are up to four times better than those in England. Fiat, which holds a controlling interest in Juventus, provide Brady's luxury saloon car which goes with the job. Italian supporters' clubs also bid to outdo each other with breath-taking generosity towards their players. Jewellery and valuable lampshades are typical expressions of appreciation. Watching Brady train with his team mates, I met an hotelier who was offering the Juventus player two days in his hotel in the Bay of Naples in July for each goal scored.[77]

John Foot has categorised British and Irish players in Serie A as 'those who played just a few games, who soon found out that Serie A (or B) was not for them'; 'those who lasted a season or two, without making much impact'; 'relative successes' and finally those who could be deemed 'unqualified successes'. He states that along with Brady, only three others who began their careers in English league football could be placed in the final category. These were John Charles, Eddie Firmani and Gerry Hitchens.[78]

The much-travelled Robbie Keane would be part of the first category, along with players such as Lee Sharpe and Franz Carr, having had a short spell at Inter Milan the 2000–01 season. Pre-war Northern Irish football migrant Paddy Sloan, who joined Manchester United from Glenavon and later appeared for Tranmere Rovers and Arsenal, joined AC Milan in 1948 and went on to play for a number of other Italian clubs before returning to England in 1951, would probably fall into the second group along with others such as Gordon Cowans, Paul Rideout, Des Walker and Paul Ince. Sloan was an exception among Northern Irish players in moving to an Italian club in the period covered here, although he has not been included in Table 5.3 as he was a pre-war migrant to England.[79] 'Relative successes' would include Trevor Francis, Ray Wilkins, Graeme Souness and David Platt.[80]

Some other Irish-born players attracted interest from European clubs on the back of club and international performances, with Gerry Armstrong joining Real Mallorca from Watford in 1983 having scored Northern Ireland's winner against Spain in the 1982 World Cup finals before returning to England to join West Bromwich Albion in 1985.[81] The number of other Northern Ireland migrants who moved to Spain were few, but Jim Hagan enjoyed two seasons with Celta Vigo in the late 1980s, making fifty-nine appearances in La Liga football having joined from Birmingham City. Hagan won Overseas Player of the Year in 1988 and returned to Larne the following year, and he later had a season in Sweden at IK Oddevold in the early 1990s.[82] Having returned to Ireland from England in 1985, Martin Bayly moved to Spain in 1989 to play for Figueres, while other Republic of Ireland-born footballers to play in both Spain and England in the late twentieth century include Ashley Grimes (Osasuna) and Kevin Moran (Sporting Gijon), while Steve Finnan (Espanyol) and Ian Harte (Levante) moved there in the 2000s.[83]

Hassan has noted how France has featured heavily within Irish emigration to Europe, with approximately 15,000 Irish people residing there in 2007.[84] However, Irish footballers have not generally been drawn there. A few have appeared for French clubs, perhaps most notably Frank Stapleton, who joined then Ligue 2 side Le Havre in 1988 from Derby County, having previously had spells at Ajax and Anderlecht (on loan).[85] A few Northern Ireland-born footballers also played in France, with Philip Gray appearing for both AS Nancy and Fortuna Sittard (Holland) in the late 1990s before returning to England. Michael Hughes also moved to France where he played for RC Strasbourg for four years in the early 1990s before returning to England, although he also had loan spells at West Ham in this period.

IRISH FOOTBALL MIGRANTS' OVERALL RATES OF MOVEMENT TO EUROPEAN CLUBS, 1945–2010

Table 5.3 Republic of Ireland- and Northern Ireland-born football migrants to England, 1945–2010, who also played for European clubs in the same period.

Years	Republic of Ireland-born football migrants	Northern Ireland-born football migrants
1945–55	0	0
1956–65	1	1
1966–75	2	1
1976–85	4	5
1986–95	5	3
1996–2005	9	2
2006–10	4	8
Total	**25**	**20**

Sources: 'Northern Ireland Footballing Greats' Retrieved from http://nifootball.blogspot.ie/ [accessed 6 May 2016]; 'The Wild Geese' Retrieved from http://irishfootballersineurope.blogspot.ie/ [Accessed 26 April 2016]; *Charles Buchan's Football Monthly*, 1951–74; *Soccer Magazine*, 1984–1996; *Irish Independent*, *Sunday Independent*, *Evening Herald* 1945–2010 and *Irish Press* 1945–1995.

The figures for British and Irish players given above by Lanfranchi and Taylor can be further broken down more specifically to give an indication of the numbers of Republic of Ireland and Northern Ireland born players with experience of English league football who moved to European clubs. As shown in Table 5.3, in the period from 1945 to 2010 a total of twenty-five of these Republic of Ireland-born players also played for European clubs. In the decades immediately following the Second World War, figures remained quite low. Peter Fitzgerald, who joined Dutch champions Sparta Rotterdam in 1959, actually migrated before playing for an English league club. Fitzgerald had played an exhibition match for the club against a British Military XI and was offered 'part-time playing terms' as well as a job said to be worth between £25 and £30 a week, while Waterford received around £5,000 for his services.[86] Eric Barber also appeared briefly for Austrian side Weiner Sportclub having joined the club in 1970 but was an exception among Irish football migrants in relocating there. Barber had made the move through a Vienna-based agent although he returned home after a short spell after a conflict of interest over how a knee injury he suffered should be treated.[87]

He was, along with Fulham's John Conway, who joined Swiss club FC Winterthur in 1975, the only Republic of Ireland-born player with English league experience who moved to a European club in this period. The 1976–85 period saw an increase in these players' moves to European clubs with Maurice Daly and Pat Walker moving to Sweden while Liam Brady and Don Givens went to Italy and Switzerland respectively in these years. These four players enjoyed lengthy spells in their new countries of residence. Daly, capped twice by the Republic of Ireland in the 1970s, appears to have been exceptional in that he took up the opportunity to gain some third-level education qualifications. He became a computer systems analyst having been offered a place on a degree course in the University of Stockholm as well as a coaching position at IKF Vaesteraas. He also obtained coaching badges in Sweden and played and managed Skultana in the Swedish Second Division and moved his family over.[88] Others were discouraged from moving by the lack of overall migration to European clubs from Britain in the 1970s, with Paddy Mulligan stating that 'it wasn't the done thing in those days'.[89]

Figures for those moving increased gradually in the 1986–95 period, with five noted, but it was in the 1996–2005 period that the figures for Republic of Ireland-born players moving to non-British European clubs peaked with nine registered, although admittedly some of these were only as loans, such as John O'Shea's spell at Royal Antwerp. In the 2006–10 period four more migrations took place, ranging from those at the top level (Steve Finnan) to those less prominent in the English game (John Andrews, Richie Ryan and Cillian Sheridan).

Similar patterns were noted with regard to Northern Ireland-born players who moved to England and non-British European clubs, although lesser numbers of players moved than those from the Republic, with only twenty noted. The first of these, Johnny Crossan, was exceptional in that he moved to Sparta Rotterdam from Coleraine in 1959 after he was banned from English football over a contract dispute which saw him also temporarily unable to play in the Irish League.[90] Like Fitzgerald above, he had not played English league football at that stage, but after his ban was lifted by the Irish League he went on to play for Sunderland, Manchester City and Middlesbrough, having previously played for Standard Liege against Rangers and Real Madrid in the European Cup. Crossan, like Fitzgerald, was not a full-time professional in Holland, and both took up part-time positions as shipyard workers and were helped by the fact that 'three or four players' spoke English. The club trained four nights a week, while they were joined in the league by former Welsh international Trevor Ford.[91] This work was undertaken in the shipyard business owned by a man with an interest in the club, a not dissimilar arrangement to that involving former Waterford United and Irish Olympic team striker, Mick Bennett, while playing with Belgian club KE Wervik in the early 1990s, who 'could have been full-time, but opted instead, to relieve possible boredom, by working in the furniture factory of wealthy chairman Andre Olivier'.[92]

While Fitzgerald felt that the big difference between Irish and Dutch football was 'the tremendous enthusiasm of the people' and that Dutch football was 'somewhere between First and Second Division standard in England' and was said to be happy with the move, later

Irish football migrant, Frank Stapleton, was less complimentary about the game there.[93] He had moved to Ajax in 1986 but felt that the atmosphere at matches just wasn't the same as in England, and scored only one goal for the club in his injury-hit spell there, illustrating the contrast in standards of those moving abroad from an Irish club in comparison to an English one.[94] Stapleton had to live in an hotel there and could not get time to view any houses, although he did stress that the players 'were very friendly and helpful and they all spoke good English'.[95] None of these Irish-born footballers stayed for very long in Holland, with Fitzgerald joining Leeds United in 1960 while Crossan moved to Sunderland in 1962. Stapleton returned to England in 1987, joining Derby County, although as noted earlier, he later moved to France.[96]

In 1968, Sunderland's John Parke moved to Belgian side Mechelen at the end of his English league career, while the 1976–85 period saw figures for Northern Ireland-born football players joining non-British European clubs surpass those from the Republic of Ireland for the first time with five players involved in moves of this nature. After playing for Aston Villa, Brighton & Hove Albion and Cambridge United, Sammy Morgan, who attended the same primary school as George Best, moved to Rotterdam in 1978 to play for local club Sparta and he later joined Groningen before returning to England.[97] Derek Spence joined Sparta Rotterdam in 1982 and later played in Hong Kong. Northern Ireland-born players joining Mediterranean clubs in the period covered here were scarce, although Tommy Cassidy joined Apoel Nicosia of Cyprus in 1983 where he won a league championship as manager before exposing corruption in the game and leaving the club.[98] Steven McAdam also had a spell in Cyprus after moving to EPA in 1981 from Wigan Athletic, signed by former Manchester United manager Frank O'Farrell, as his career in England came to an end having been blighted by injuries.[99] The aforementioned Gerry Armstrong also moved in this period.

Over the following two decades there were just five migrations to European clubs, with three in the 1986–95 period and just two in the years between 1996 and 2005. Noel Brotherston, who joined Motala in Sweden in 1989, sampled Scandinavian club football after his English league career had ended. Sammy McIlroy had a spell at Swedish club Orgryte in 1986 in the latter stages of his career while he also played in Austria from 1988 to 1990 with Vfb Modling before returning to English clubs each time.[100] For some players such as Paul Ramsay, Finland offered an alternative cultural and playing experience to England.[101] Although he did not actually leave England for a European club by transfer, Seamus Heath took up the offer to play summer football in Finland with TPS Turku having approached Luton Town manager David Pleat about having something to do after the season had ended in 1979:

> He got back to me within two days saying, 'I've a chairman from a Finnish club coming over, he's here today, will you go and meet him at the hotel?' And as an eighteen-year-old, I went and met him. And that he offered me the chance to go and play in the summer, an eighteen-year-old, doubling my wages tax free, with a car and all, was just unbelievable. So I went to Finland, and then obviously, worked hard, did well, made contacts and friends, and the rest was history. I was there for nine seasons and a lot from there has stuck with me for life, meaning, even in my own home, the culture I brought back, sauna in my own house, I don't have any carpets, all wooden floors, so I learned even from there, their culture that I've embraced, that I've brought back home here.[102]

Heath also felt that the language barrier was never a problem as most Finnish people spoke English, while playing during the summer meant that he missed the harsh weather:

> I used to go every April and come back in October, so as I was going there the bad weather was ending, when I was leaving, the bad weather was just starting ... If I thought their climate was milder, I'd have lived there for the rest of my days. I have friends, English friends, living there, and they embraced it and adapted – I wasn't prepared to adapt through the winter months, because people don't realise the alcohol problems in Scandinavia and the suicide that comes from the winter ... dark days and nights.[103]

Seamus Heath is now an IFA Development Officer and continues to play the game having enjoyed a professional career in Ireland, England and Finland. Picture: Seamus Heath collection.

It was in the 2006–10 period that the numbers of Northern Ireland-born players moving to non-British European clubs peaked in the period covered here, and in this way patterns of migration differed slightly to the Republic, with eight noted. Three of these were loans to Belgian clubs, with Jonny Evans, Darron Gibson and Craig Cathcart, like John O'Shea, all moving temporarily as part of Manchester United's young player development system. Daryl Smylie, who failed to make the breakthrough at Newcastle United despite a loan spell at Stockport, moved to Sweden in 2007 where he signed a permanent deal with Jönköpings Södra IF in 2011 after spells with three different clubs there. A few players have attempted to resurrect their English careers abroad, with Roy Carroll leaving Derby County to join Danish side Odense in 2009 and later moving to Crete club OFI Crete and then Greek team Olympiakos before returning to England to Notts County.[104] Although he was not part of those migrating to Europe in the 1945–2010 period, Kyle Lafferty played for a number of continental clubs including FC Sion of Switzerland and Italian side Palermo after leaving Rangers when the club experienced an economic meltdown in 2012. He later returned to Norwich and was instrumental in Northern Ireland's successful Euro 2016 qualifying campaign, although Carroll generally had to be content with a place on the bench with Michael McGovern, then of Hamilton Academical, preferred as goalkeeper.[105]

IRISH-BORN PLAYERS' MOVEMENT TO NORTH AMERICA

As noted earlier, Irish emigration to North America declined in the opening decades of the twentieth century. While legislation implemented in the USA between 1921 and 1924 ensured that the number of immigrants from Free State Ireland had decreased from an average of 25,000 annually in the middle of this decade to over 14,000 in 1930, it was the Wall Street Crash of 1929, and the worldwide economic depression which subsequently followed, that was the main reason why Irish emigration to North America declined in the 1930s.[106] The Second World War and its immediate aftermath saw Britain emerge as the main destination for the majority of Irish emigrants.[107]

Despite the division of Ireland into the Irish Free State and Northern Ireland following the Anglo-Irish Treaty of 1921, as Diarmaid Ferriter has stated, 'emigration remained a central feature of the Irish experience in the 1920s and 1930s, making a mockery of much of the rhetoric of the pre-independence era, which had depicted it as solely a consequence of foreign occupation'. In the years between 1926 and 1936, almost 167,000 Irish people emigrated.[108] The *Commission on Emigration* noted how Irish emigrants to the USA had been motivated by a demand for labour there, and in turn, an absence of this in Ireland, while there was no difficulty with the language for most Irish emigrants.[109] Similarly, it found that there was 'a minimum of personal and social adjustment' in moving across the Atlantic, while family connections were also a help in making the move.[110] With high levels of unemployment in the 1970s and early 1980s in Britain, 'an increasing proportion of Irish emigrant flow' was again directed towards the USA.[111] However, as Kevin Kenny has noted, 'although substantial numbers of Irish people came to the United States in the 1950s and 1980s, they made up only a small percentage of total Irish emigration and a tiny percentage of American immigration in the second half of the twentieth century'.[112]

IRISH-BORN FOOTBALLERS IN THE AMERICAN SOCCER LEAGUE, 1921–31

By the late nineteenth century, 'sports of all kinds had become a major cultural phenomenon in the United States'.[113] Basketball, college football and baseball were attracting significant support, with [American] football emerging 'as a modified form of soccer and rugby'.[114] Association football or soccer was also beginning to gain popularity there by the 1890s. While there had been football migration to the USA in the years from 1894 to 1921, the first professional soccer league there, the American League of Professional Football, lasted only briefly in 1894.[115] Although there is evidence that some players were Irish, none appear to have migrated through clubs in the English Football League, instead being selected from local leagues in the USA.[116] Lanfranchi and Taylor have stated that the American Soccer League, which was in operation from 1921 until 1931, was 'the first attempt to create a competition comprising the best teams in the country'. It was also 'effectively a multi-ethnic and multinational league, drawing on American-born European personnel but also importing significant numbers of Austrian, Hungarian, Swedish, Irish, English but, above all, Scottish footballers'.[117] One reporter noted after the opening weekend in September 1921 how the league was 'franchised and encouraged by the national organisation [then known as the United States Football Association], [it] is to put up a staunch fight to place the game on what its American supporters believe to be its proper place'.[118] The aforementioned Thomas Cahill, said to be 'the father of American soccer', was reported as being 'the guiding spirit of the League', while it was also noted that 'there is a good deal of money behind the enterprise'. Soccer, the reporter felt, had 'never really appealed to the United States, any more than baseball has appealed in England'. He also noted the precarious nature of competitive professional soccer in the USA.[119]

Under an Immigration Bureau ruling, non-American players were allowed into the USA as 'artists', with footballers being classed alongside 'musicians, actors and others entering the country to display special accomplishments'.[120] Taylor notes that 'the loss of registered players to the emerging leagues in the USA during the 1920s and France in the 1930s became a highly contentious issue among club and [English] League officials, mainly because no agreement or transfer payment was necessary'.[121] By 1923, it was being reported in the Irish press that 'unsatisfactory labour conditions' in England and Scotland had been a major factor in this movement, with 'scores of crack footballers' taking up positions at American clubs.[122] In particular, the Bethlehem Steel team was said to have been 'made up almost completely of players who have come over from the British Isles since the close of the last soccer season', with the 'paying of sizeable sums' and 'the increased public interest in soccer in the United States' fundamental to this migration.[123]

While acknowledging the problems in tracing all of these ASL recruits' birthplaces and nationalities, Lanfranchi and Taylor have identified that Scottish players were the dominant nationality in terms of figures for European footballers playing in the ASL, reaching a peak of eighty-three in the 1927–28 season. Migratory links with the USA, 'with Scots numerous in the towns and factories in which the ASL was based', along with poor working conditions and low wages in Scotland's football leagues, help explain this.[124] This season was also when the number of Irish players there was at its highest, with twelve migrating that year. This can be explained by Philadelphia Celtic's recruitment of eleven Irish players in 1927, and this club will be discussed in more detail below. As shown in Table 5.4, at least thirty-seven Irish-born footballers played in the ASL and these figures for migration gradually rose from just one Irish player present in 1921 until the end of the decade when their migration ceased, when after peaking at twelve in 1927, only two were recorded as migrating in 1928. None were recorded as having done so afterwards. Although there were nine Irish-born players who moved in 1924, the figure had dropped to four in 1925 and was at six in 1926. This sudden increase in 1924 can be partially explained by the fact that three Irish-born players moved from non-Irish clubs to the ASL that year.[125]

Table 5.4 Irish-born players' migration to the American Soccer League, 1921–31.

Year	Total
1921	1
1922	1
1923	2
1924	9
1925	4
1926	6
1927	12
1928	2
1929	0
1930	0
1931	0
Overall Number	**37**

Source: Colin Jose, *American Soccer League, 1921–1931: the golden years of American soccer* (Maryland: Scarecrow Press, 1998).

The rise of Irish-born players moving to the ASL to twelve in 1927 correlates with the more general movement of British players, which reached its peak in the 1926–29 period, with a decline in migration afterwards as a result of 'America's internal "soccer" war, together with the agreement to respect contractual rights on both sides of the Atlantic and the financial impact of the Wall Street crash'.[126] Despite financial problems in the Irish League in the early 1920s with the temporary withdrawal of Belfast Celtic and the permanent movement of Bohemians and Shelbourne to the new Free State League discussed in Chapter 3, there was no huge exodus of Irish-born players to the

USA, illustrating that most did not view this league as a popular option and that active recruitment in Ireland by ASL clubs was less common than by British clubs.[127] As noted earlier, a total of 106 Irish-born footballers were recruited by English clubs and played first-team league football in England in the 1920s.[128] While the number of Irish players in England remained low in comparison with those from England, Scotland and Wales, England remained the principal destination for Irish footballers in this decade.[129]

As shown in Table 5.5, rates of migration of Irish players to the ASL from British clubs remained low, with only eight moving from English league clubs and four from those in Scotland. Among the first of these was Belfast-born Mickey Hamill, who left England in May 1923 'for a tour in the States' and a position as player-coach at Bridgeport, Connecticut, although it appears he later played out the 1923–24 season with Manchester City before returning to the USA on a more permanent basis.[130] Along with Hamill, just nine other Irish-born football migrants who played professionally in England's football leagues were identified as having played in the ASL at some point in their careers.[131] Two did not move from British or Irish clubs but appear to have already been playing in North America, albeit at a lower level than the ASL, and the source club of one Irish-born player could not be traced. A few Irish-born players who moved to America, including Hamill and Mick O'Brien, played in both Scotland and England.

The greatest movement of Irish-born players to the ASL came from Ireland rather than leagues in England or Scotland, with twenty-three players moving to the USA from Irish clubs. Fifteen of these were located in present-day Northern Ireland, particularly the Belfast and north-east area, which at that point had a stronger concentration of professional clubs than in Dublin. Nine players were recruited from Glentoran, with the Belfast club similarly supplying the most Irish-born players to English league clubs in the pre-Second World War period, illustrating the strength of their links with English clubs and evidently those further afield.[132] It was in this decade that Irish players began to gain attention from non-British clubs through their achievements at home. Tommy 'Tucker' Croft was recruited to the

ASL as a result of his growing reputation. Queen's Island had won the Irish League and Cup in the 1923–24 season and Croft was said to have signed for the American team, Fall River, while in Scotland for an inter-league match. He had scored the winner for Ireland against England in Belfast in October 1923 'after as fine a piece of individual play as one would see', which undoubtedly raised his reputation.[133] Another top club, Belfast Celtic, had more success in keeping their players. They apparently withstood the efforts of Philadelphia's agent to recruit 'the whole front line … en bloc, namely McGrillen, Ferris, Curran and the brothers Mahood' in August 1926, although McGrillen later moved to Bethlehem Steel in 1928.[134]

Only seven moved to the ASL from the Irish Free State and prior to 1927 there does not appear to have been any direct movement from the league there. Six of these joined Philadelphia Celtic in 1927 having been targeted by Fred Magennis, the owner of Philadelphia Celtic between 1926 and 1927. A few others, such as Lennox of Brideville, were eager to go too but had already signed contracts in Ireland and appear to have been less reluctant, or have had less nerve, to break them.[135] Irish-born players were calculated to have played for an average of 2.44 clubs and spent, on average, 2.6 seasons in the ASL. Most of these were not high-profile players. Only nine players won international caps, with Mick O'Brien featuring for both Irish national teams while one player, George Graham, a Derry man, was capped by Canada.[136]

Table 5.5 Irish-born players' migration to the American Soccer League by club, 1921–31.

Country	Number
Northern Ireland	15
England	8
Irish Free State	7
Scotland	4
Canada/USA	2
Unknown Source	1
Overall Total	**37**

Source: as Table 5.4.

THE GEOGRAPHICAL TRAJECTORIES OF IRISH-BORN MIGRANTS TO THE ASL

Kevin Kenny has stated that 'the primary cause of Irish emigration in the first half of the twentieth century was much the same as in the late nineteenth century, ongoing problems in agriculture and the landholding system combined with retarded urbanization and industrialization'.[137] Aspiring footballers looking for professional clubs in Ireland were generally not drawn from agricultural backgrounds and were mainly brought up in or around the island's two biggest cities, Dublin and Belfast, with a higher concentration of clubs and greater opportunities to learn the game. While not all the birthplaces of Irish-born migrants to the ASL could be traced, at least eight were born in Belfast and two outside the city in Newtownards, while Ballyclare, Derry, Omagh, Enniskillen, Kilcock, Waterford and Dublin were also positively identified as places of birth. Kenny has noted that 'regionally, the pattern of Irish emigration in the first half of the twentieth century displayed a striking similarity to the dominant pattern throughout the nineteenth century, with the north-central counties of Leitrim, Cavan, Monaghan and Roscommon, along with County Mayo, having the heaviest departure rates'.[138] None of the Irish-born players whose places of birth could be identified who appeared in the ASL were born in these counties. Therefore Irish football migrants differed significantly in this regard, again illustrating the differing nature of the social backgrounds of Ireland's professional footballers in comparison to more general migrants.

The ASL's clubs were generally located along the east coast, with the eight teams involved in the initial season of 1921–22 – Philadelphia Field Club, New York, Todd Shipyards, Harrison FC, J&P Coats, Fall River United, Holyoke Falcos and Jersey City Celtic – based in this area.[139] In the first half of the 1900s, as Kenny states, 'the American Irish remained an overwhelmingly urban people' and 'they also retained their preference for living in the Northeast and Midwest'.[140] Admittedly, although movement to Philadelphia was greatest, New York clubs did recruit Irish players at various stages in the ASL's lifespan, and the fact that most ASL clubs were located along the north-east would indicate that these players had a greater choice of clubs there as opposed to moving to other areas in the USA.

By the early 1900s 'instead of being concentrated in menial labour, as they had been for much of the nineteenth century, the American Irish now worked in the skilled trades', and 'most Irish-American workers were skilled rather than unskilled, and they disproportionately concentrated in the best paid and most highly unionized trades'.[141] On the eve of the ASL in 1920, New York had a population of 203,450 Irish-born residents while Philadelphia had a total of 64,590 persons who were born in Ireland. Boston was home to 57,011 Irish-born people while Chicago's Irish-born population was slightly lower at 56,786.[142] Despite this region being the dominant destination for most players, the number of Irish-born footballers employed in the USA in the opening decades of the twentieth century could hardly be said to be a reflection of the Irish-American population in the east coast area to any great extent, illustrating the contrasting nature of migration for professional soccer purposes and how North America remained on the periphery of soccer migration as opposed to the 'core' area of Britain.

The summer of 1927 was said to have been when Irish-born players' interest in a move to the ASL was at its highest, with $20 apparently being offered per match and work equivalent to $24 a week available.[143] At least two of these players' moves to the ASL that year were motivated by the low level of payment available to them during the close of the soccer season in Ireland and throughout the summer, despite repeated warnings in the press about the precarious nature of contracts with American clubs and poor treatment of players.[144] Irish professionals Hugh Reid, Bob Maguire and William Pitt, who had gained experience of soccer in America, were also said to be acting as recruiting agents for ASL clubs.[145]

The largest grouping of Irish football migrants at any one time were based in Philadelphia, the majority of these having been brought together by Fred Magennis, who had a specific aim to create a team of Irish players. Despite this, as Steve Holyroyd has stated, whether or not he brought them together as a marketing ploy or simply out of national pride is unclear.[146] This type of attempt to create an ethnic identity among ASL clubs was not uncommon. The success of a tour made by Austria's top team, Vienna Hakoak, in 1926 saw them lose most of their best players to Brooklyn Wanderers and New York Giants, two Jewish-owned ASL clubs, while the owners of Bridgeport Hungaria and Indiana Flooring of New York also attempted to create teams with strong national ties, recruiting Hungarian and Swedish players respectively.[147]

Nineteen Irish-born players joined Philadelphia clubs at some point during the league's ten years in existence, and ten of these were in the Philadelphia Celtic squad at the beginning of the 1927–28 season. Although Philadelphia Field Club, in reality comprised of Bethlehem Steel players, had won the inaugural ASL championship in 1922, by the mid-1920s Philadelphia teams had continuously ended the season with a losing record.[148] Magennis had bought the Philadelphia ASL franchise in 1926 and intended to reinvigorate the now Philadelphia Celtic team by putting together a selection made up of Irish footballers.[149] Irish League players William Stewart, Arnold Keenan, William Pitt, Dave Rainey, Hugh Reid and Bob Maguire were recruited in 1926, while goalkeeper Alex McMinn, said to have been at Stockport County and born in Ireland, was signed in 1927.[150] Those recruited in the latter year from the Free State League included the captain of Dublin club Shamrock Rovers, Bob Fullam, and his team mates Dinny Doyle and Alfie Hale senior, along with Brideville's Michael Maguire and Paul O'Brien and Bray Unknowns' Larry Kilroy.[151]

Despite these hopes, by the end of September 1927, their playing arrangements had fallen through after only a few matches, with Magennis said to have walked out on the team at Wilkes-Barre. He had apparently signed a contract agreeing to pay each of the players $50 a week, with the result that they were left unpaid after he disappeared, and according to one source, the team had to spend two days and two nights in a railway station having been left stranded and evicted from their hotel.[152] The club was later folded by the American Soccer League after it emerged Magennis had attempted to sell all the players to Boston club Fall River Marksmen.[153] With the collapse of Magennis's venture, by the end of October 1927, these Irish players had to look elsewhere for professional football. Left without a club, Doyle joined Fall River while Kilroy, Hale, Maguire and William Burns transferred to Coates FC of Rhode Island.[154] *Football Sports Weekly*'s reporter on the subject hoped that the episode would be 'a timely warning to our players' and 'may be the means of putting a stop to the wiles of unscrupulous adventurers who are domiciled in "the land of the Almighty Dollar" and also a few nearer home'.[155]

GENERAL PLAYING CONDITIONS IN THE ASL AND REMIGRATION

In any case, some players clearly found it difficult to settle. By 1924, 'some of the Scots to whom the lure of the dollar was stronger than that of the "sixpence"' were said to be 'anxious to get home', with one reporter of the view that the climate might not have been to their liking.[156] In particular, Mick O'Brien played just seven matches for Brooklyn Wanderers in 1926 before returning to England, with the player said to be unhappy about the playing conditions in the American league.[157] He was suspended by the American club for 'violation of contract, insubordination and indifferent playing' in December 1926 despite being signed on a five-year contract said to be worth £15 a week.[158] Similarly, in 1930 Irish-born player, Harry Chatton, spoke well 'of the standard of play in the States', but preferred 'the conditions governing the game in the Home Countries'.[159] Even those hoping to recruit players were forced to admit the league was not as strong as England's First Division. In 1928, New York Giants' manager George Moorehouse, a former Tranmere Rovers player, stated that 'first class American football is about on a par with England's Second Division League', illustrating the gulf in the standard of play across the Atlantic.[160] Not every player was unhappy with the conditions there. Although there is some evidence of a dispute with one of his ASL clubs, Mickey Hamill stated that during his two-year spell in Boston, he had made many friends and felt that the game was progressing well there.[161] Liverpool's David McMullan stated that the game was 'good and fast', although the pitches were smaller and did not have as much grass as in England.[162]

The rates of return of these Irish footballers differed slightly to general patterns noted in studies of Irish migrants to the USA. As Kenny has stated, in the late nineteenth century, while over 50 per cent of East European and Italian migrants to the United States returned home 'after only a few years', approximately 10 per cent of Irish emigrants went back home, as 'there was usually little or nothing to go back to in Ireland', with 'American wakes' customary as 'when they left, they left for good'.[163] In total, nineteen of these thirty-seven Irish-born players (almost 51 per cent) were positively identified as returning to Ireland after playing in the ASL.

The movement of prominent players such as Irish international Mickey Hamill in 1924 from Manchester City to Fall River Marksmen had led the English Football League's Management Committee to bring in measures to prevent migration, and in 1926 they stated that players who left English clubs would not be allowed to re-join the league until the conditions under which they left and the reasons why they were returning were investigated.[164] Following pressure from a number of Central European countries to have the United States Football Association expelled from FIFA in 1927 over the poaching of European footballers and the breaking of contracts, and 'similar complaints from Scotland and Ireland', the ASL and the USFA 'agreed on an immediate end to negotiations for foreign players' until FIFA's annual congress at Helsingfors that year.[165] While the USFA had also indicated they might leave FIFA, the European threat dissipated before the forthcoming congress. Article 17, which stated that 'national associations which have membership with the Federation [FIFA] shall recognise each other's suspensions', was strengthened to 'avoid the problems of players jumping contracts'.[166] At the congress, 'a special commission to control the migration of players from one country to another was decided upon', while it was also agreed that professional players looking to be reinstated as amateurs had to wait one year after the receipt of application before they could play.[167]

The following year, the English and Scottish Associations drew up an agreement with the United States Football Association (USFA) 'to respect each other's registrations and suspensions' after the British Associations' withdrawal from FIFA, while the IFA's relations with the USFA had also improved considerably at this point.[168] The IFA therefore generally acted as part of the Home Countries of England, Scotland and Wales in terms of broader agreements regarding movement to the ASL, although figures paled in significance to those of British players' migration.[169] The FAIFS took a more independent stance following deteriorations in relations with the Home Countries after the split with the IFA.

This transatlantic migration was to become a concern for Northern Ireland's clubs and the IFA given that most occuring on the island took place from the Irish League. In 1924 Queen's Island player, Tommy Croft, was suspended by the Irish League club as his departure to United States' team Fall River was 'said to have extended the trouble to Belfast'.[170] On returning, Croft was asked to attend a meeting of the IFA's Senior Protests and Appeals committee in August 1925 and claimed he had violated his contract with Queen's Island because 'he had a wife and three children to look after' while his wages at the club were only £2 per week.[171] He admitted he had not given the club any notice before leaving for the USA but, with his family still living at home, he was hoping to now remain in Ireland and stated that it depended on him getting 'a living wage'.[172]

Although he stated that he had a contract with Fall River for 1926, it was 'not a binding agreement', illustrating the inconsistent nature of ASL contracts at that point. The committee decided to 'severely caution' the player and instructed him to re-sign for Queen's Island.[173] Having then attempted and failed to get a move to England, he returned to America in September 1925 to take up what was said to be 'a really good offer'.[174] He was again suspended by Queen's Island in November of that year.[175] At this point the IFA had not begun to apply fines and suspensions to returning ASL players, but this changed shortly afterwards, and these got heavier for those who had stayed abroad longer.

In the initial years of Irish players departing the Irish League for the ASL, the IFA were more reluctant to impose heavy penalties on migrants. In December 1925, Hugh Reid applied for reinstatement at Glentoran through the IFA having 'violated his professional status' by joining Bethlehem Steel in March of that year, playing two matches in May. He claimed that he had told Glentoran that he was leaving for the USA and 'left them on good terms' and that his contract had expired. Bethlehem Steel had released him when he notified them of his intention to return home, and the IFA's committee decided to suspend the player for 'one month of the offences committed'.[176]

By the late 1920s the IFA were becoming increasingly frustrated with player movement to the ASL, and had contacted FIFA and the USFA about their suspending of ASL migrants William Pitt, William Reid and Eddie Maguire for breach of contract.[177] Fines and punishments were increased for lengthy absentees. Tommy Croft again returned home in 1928 and was asked to provide 'a certified copy of the matches he played whilst in America', which, along with applying for reinstatement and appearing at a meeting of the IFA's Senior Protests and Appeals committee, was required before reinstatement was considered.[178] In October 1928 he was given the choice of a fine of twenty-five guineas, which was equivalent to £26.5.0, or undertake a forty-eight-week suspension.[179] He was given a reduction of £5 having paid the fine on 7 December.[180]

William Reid did not apply to the IFA for reinstatement until 1930, and, like Croft, he explained that his move was motivated by the money on offer, which was $45 a week as opposed to the £1 he would get at Irish League club Willowfield. He also justified his move by stating that he had a wife and two children to look after. Reid was fined £50 by the IFA and suspended until the fine was paid.[181] It would appear that the sending home of remittances was a feature of some players' migration, like more general migrants, although there is less evidence that families at home joined these players in the USA.[182] An exception appears to have been Mickey Hamill's wife, who joined him in New York in 1924, although he later returned to Belfast in 1926 having bought a pub there.[183]

In October 1931 William Pitt was also ordered to pay a fine of £50, with Newry Town to be given first preference on his services, having applied for reinstatement.[184] Having paid the fine, he was allowed to join Glentoran.[185] These fines were quite high in comparison with those given to non-migrating Irish League players at this time. In August 1931, Thomas Hutton, 'an unsigned professional', was given a fine of £3.10 or an alternative of four weeks' suspension for taking part in a match during the close season, while Thomas Wilson of Dundela was fined ten shillings or as an alternative, two weeks' suspension, 'for violation of his professional status'.[186]

The FAIFS intervention in Irish players' movement to the USA was rather limited to some extent given that fewer numbers moved from their league. They did, however, endorse the removal of a suspension on Paddy Robinson by Shelbourne in September 1926 after he had returned from the ASL.[187] They also confirmed the suspension of William Burns by Shelbourne in August 1927, and stated that their secretary, J.A. Ryder, had corresponded with 'the American Association' regarding the movement of players to Philadelphia Celtic. The Council also agreed that they would take 'suitable steps to safeguard the interests of Free State clubs and migration'.[188] However, after the Philadelphia debacle, it appears that no other Free State players made the move to the ASL, thus ensuring that the FAIFS did not have to intervene, and there is scarce evidence of suspensions imposed by the other Free State clubs who lost players. In November 1927, Shelbourne removed Burns' suspension while 'the Association granted the permission sought on condition that he gave satisfactory evidence that he was prepared to carry out his contract with his club'.[189] This policy differed significantly to that employed by the IFA.

The insecure nature of contracts in the ASL undoubtedly influenced the decision to return. With the collapse of Philadelphia Celtic in 1927, Bob Fullam, said to be 'just as big an idol over there as he was in the Free State', later joined Holley Carburetors of Detroit. However, he returned to Dublin in May 1928 to take his place for Shamrock Rovers against Belgian club Berchem, the Irish club apparently having paid his fare home.[190] Paul O'Brien, Hale, Kilroy and Burns had all returned home a few months into the season, while Doyle and Maguire stayed on with Fullam.[191] One player who was content to play at a lower level was Alfie Hale senior, who joined Tipperary club Cahir Park of the North Munster League on his return in January 1928, despite the offer of a trial with Hull City, but the vast majority of returning Irish players attempted to again play at a high level in Ireland.[192] In returning to his previous club,

Fullam was not exceptional among European football migrants to the ASL.[193] As Lanfranchi and Taylor have highlighted, 'remigration was the norm' and 'returning to former clubs was not uncommon'.[194] One newspaper noted in April 1930 the impact of former American club players in the English and Scottish cups semi-finals, with Alex Jackson of Huddersfield, formerly of Bethlehem and Jimmy Howison (ex-New Bradford), then at Hull City, prominent in the English ties.[195]

Some Irish migrants to the ASL stayed in North America. George Graham, who returned to Toronto Ulster United after playing for Philadelphia, Fall River and Brooklyn, later died in Toronto in 1966.[196] Some others settled in Britain, with Robert Logan McDonald, who played for Bethlehem Steel for a number of seasons, dying in Scotland in 1955 having joined Rangers in 1928.[197] However, Irish footballers who moved to the ASL knew that, as well as a more familiar environment, a decent standard of football was still available if they did return to Ireland and they would be reinstated relatively quickly if they complied with football authorities' regulations. As Taylor also notes, 'the tightening of US immigration controls during the first half of the 1920s was probably more important in encouraging European players to visit rather than settle'.[198] He sees the rejection of the New York Giants' offer of £23 a week by Everton star Dixie Dean in July 1928 as impacting greatly on 'the ASL challenge'. In addition, after 1928, 'US soccer was ravaged by an internal dispute which, combined with the impact of the Wall Street Crash, caused a significant drop in football immigration'.[199] In January 1929, football league authorities in England and Scotland also set up a 'working agreement' with the United States Football Association with regard to respecting registrations and suspensions.[200]

According to David Goldblatt, the ASL's decline was due to a row between the United States Football Association and the ASL in 1928, with a number of ASL clubs participating in the USFA's Open Challenge Cup despite being warned not to do so by the ASL.[201] Three clubs left the ASL and were instrumental in the organisation of the East Coast League, but, as Goldblatt states, 'the quality of play and the attention of the sport's audience was too thinly spread. Two poor leagues could not match the interest created by one good one.'

Although the league was later re-formed as a single competition, the Depression impacted greatly on clubs with an industrial background, with Fall River and Bethlehem Steel collapsing by the early 1930s, and the ASL had completely folded by 1933.[202]

IRISH-BORN FOOTBALLERS' MIGRATION TO THE USA, 1945–2010

Just twenty-three or 4.6 per cent of the 500 Republic of Ireland-born players who played English league football between 1945 and 2010 also played in North America. Similarly, Northern Ireland-born players did not move to North America in any great numbers in the period covered here, but a higher rate was noted, with thirty-four or 12.26 per cent of the 417 football migrants to English league football experiencing professional football in North America. Prior to the inauguration of the North American Soccer League (NASL) in 1968, some post-war Irish football migrants had appeared sporadically in North American soccer. For example, Danny Blanchflower appeared as a guest for Toronto City in 1961 while Peter McParland did likewise with Toronto Inter-Roma in 1965 in the Eastern Canada Soccer League.[203] Although these players appeared there only briefly, as Delaney has stated, 'relative to the size of the outflow to the United States, travel to Canada has remained a minor yet important element of Irish emigration, especially in the case of Northern Ireland'.[204] This section will focus primarily on Irish football migrants' brief involvement in the United States Soccer Association's league of 1967 and in the NASL which ran from 1968 to 1984.

The organisation of the United Soccer Association's league, in 1967, saw the introduction of Latin American and European clubs as participants.[205] Two Irish-based teams, Shamrock Rovers and Glentoran, competed in this tournament, staged in the summer of 1967, using names of American teams Boston Rovers and Detroit Cougars respectively, with Glentoran invited to play after Linfield had failed to take up the offer of a place in the competition.[206] According to Lanfranchi and Taylor, this league saw teams 'assigned to specific cities and even given new names; some effort was made to align them with appropriate ethnic communities'.[207] While the movement of GAA teams 'on tour' has been well assessed by Mike Cronin and David Toms amongst others, the trials of Irish soccer teams abroad has attracted scarce academic attention.[208]

Kevin Kenny has stated that in the twentieth century, 'the combined metropolitan areas of Boston, Chicago and New York were home to between 54 and 58 per cent of all Irish immigrants to the United States'.[209] Boston Rovers were based in the Massachusetts area for the duration of the USA league, but in general Irish football migrants have not gravitated towards professional soccer clubs in the above cities in any great numbers, and the 1967 team's stay was only temporary. In fact, Philadelphia was the city which attracted the most Republic of Ireland-born players during the NASL years, with five registered there as players in 1978 alone.[210] Four Northern Ireland-born footballers played for Tulsa Roughnecks in the late 1970s and early 1980s, with the club's Oklahoma location illustrating no major link between general migratory trends from Northern Ireland and those for professional football reasons, while an equal number also appeared for San Diego clubs.[211]

Along with Shamrock Rovers – though this was not the first Rovers team to go travelling abroad as in 1961 the club also played in a New York tournament – some other League of Ireland clubs were also able to afford tours at that point, with Bohemians travelling to Spain for an eleven-day trip in 1967.[212] The 1967 Rovers squad also included two Brazilian players, Carlos and Gilson Metidieri, and a few guest players, such as goalkeeper Pat Dunne of Plymouth Argyle.[213] On arriving in Boston in May of that year, they were greeted by the Boston Fire Department band and the city's mayor, John Collins. Each player received a gift copy of *The History of Boston* and participated in press interviews but, as team member Paddy Mulligan states, 'As a player you don't pay too much attention to that sort of thing … you were out there to play football for the seven weeks and you didn't want any distractions at all.'[214] A welcoming committee was made up of a Boston soccer club managed by Clondalkin man Niall Staunton. They then moved on to their headquarters in Lynn where they began training each day to acclimatise.[215] They also attended a 'Soccer Clinic' where the public was admitted free 'to have the rules of the game and tactical situations explained to them', illustrating the challenge local administrators faced in attracting support.[216] One Irish migrant, based in Toronto, took it upon himself to organise a supporters club for the team, but match attendances were relatively small, with the 7,000 spectators present at the first match versus Detroit Cougars lower than the projected attendance of one organiser who hoped to 'have attendances of about 8,000 at the games'.[217] Mulligan recalls that 'the people in Boston were great to us because we were based in Boston for the seven weeks, and they were just fabulous ... it was great to meet people from home because it was a fair oul trek in those days'.[218] The team were given a Volkswagen van for transport and trained every day provided they weren't travelling, although they were allowed to go out on the town by manager, Liam Tuohy. Mulligan remembers the tour as being 'a great experience', with officials such as John Adams ensuring that 'everything was paid for and you were getting paid as well'.[219]

Boston Rovers and the Detroit Cougars were joined in the USA league by eleven other non-American clubs taking on local names.[220] The only other club involved which was made up of part-time players, Glentoran, were located in Detroit's Tiger Stadium for their home matches while Rovers were based at the Manning Bowl in Lynn, Massachusetts with two groups of six clubs playing each other home and away, with the top two proceeding to the semi-finals.[221] The Cleveland Stokers team was made up primarily of Stoke City players while Wolverhampton Wanderers appeared as Los Angeles Wolves and Sunderland as Vancouver Royal Canadians. Scottish clubs were also involved, with Dundee United playing as Dallas Tornado, Aberdeen Dons appeared as Washington Whips and Hibernians as Toronto City.[222] Cagliari Calcio played as Chicago Mustangs that year, although the team also included a few non-Italians, such as former England striker Gerry Hitchens, who had played for a number of Italian clubs.[223] Dutch club ADO Den Haag played as San Francisco Gales and South American clubs were also involved with Bangu Athletic club from Brazil playing as Houston Stars and CA Cerro of Uruguay appearing as New York Skyliners.

Some Irish-born footballers appeared as part of their English clubs' lineups, with John Parke and Martin Harvey (Sunderland) and Derek Dougan (Wolves) taking part in the short-lived league, which was won by Los Angeles Wolves, who beat Washington Whips in the final on 14 July 1967 in Los Angeles.[224] Boston Rovers' campaign was hindered by injuries while the part-time nature of their status was evident in their lowly final position at the bottom of their group.[225] However, it did give them the opportunity to play against opponents of the calibre of Jim Baxter, as Mulligan stated.[226] In addition to the USA league, a rival league known as the National Professional Soccer League (NPSL) was operational in 1967. A general failure to attract support was evident and the USA league merged with the NPSL to form the North American Soccer League (NASL) in 1967, which ran from 1968 to 1984.[227]

IRISH-BORN PLAYERS IN THE NASL

According to Lanfranchi and Taylor, the NASL 'faced the perennial dilemma that while there were insufficient North American players of the required quality, an over-reliance on foreigners would reinforce the notion of football as an "un-American", or foreign game.'[228] Clubs relied heavily on imports as had been the norm during previous attempts to develop professional soccer leagues, although there was also the first real attempt to 'Americanize' the competition. The New York Cosmos' signing of Pelé in 1975 was 'an important turning point' in that it 'encouraged the signing of better foreigners and further marginalised the North Americans', and 'the tension between the policies of importing aliens and using native talent was never resolved.'[229] By the 1980s the league was hindered by declining attendances and revenues but 'in the end the collapse of the NASL was the result of financial mistakes made by the league administration and the club owners.'[230]

Table 5.6 illustrates the numbers of Republic of Ireland and Northern Ireland born players appearing in the NASL in the years between 1968 and 1984. As shown, in the early years, 1968 was the peak year for these players' presence, with a total of nine (five from the

Table 5.6 Republic of Ireland and Northern Ireland born players appearing in the NASL, 1968–84.

Year	Republic of Ireland	Northern Ireland
1968	5	4
1969	1	0
1970	0	0
1971	0	1
1972	1	1
1973	0	2
1974	3	1
1975	3	5
1976	4	6
1977	2	5
1978	10	9
1979	7	5
1980	3	7
1981	5	7
1982	3	7
1983	3	5
1984	3	5

Source: Colin Jose, *North American Soccer Encyclopedia* (Haworth: St Johann Press, 2003).

Republic and four from Northern Ireland) until the mid-1970s. A few of the 1968 players – Joe Haverty (Kansas City Spurs), David Pugh, Paddy Mulligan (Boston Beacons), Barry Brown (Detroit Cougars), Walter Bruce (Detroit Cougars) and Peter McParland (Atlanta Chiefs) – had experienced soccer in America in 1967. Mulligan was motivated by the idea of becoming a full-time professional, as he had not had the opportunity to go to England at that point, although he had had offers as a young player but his parents wouldn't let him go.[231] He recalls the first year of the NASL as being 'crazy stuff', particularly with regard to the players being recruited. One eastern European centre-half partner asked him if he 'would be happy to do all the running' before backtracking when confronted by the former Shamrock Rovers player. He added that:

> There were quite a few players at Boston Beacons. I didn't understand how they were bought into the club but then when I got to know the running of the club and who was doing the buying, I wasn't too long to figure it out. Some of these people had lots of money to go and spend but they'd no real knowledge of professional football, not by a long shot.[232]

Mulligan felt that manager Jack Mansell, who had played for Brighton & Hove Albion, Cardiff City and Portsmouth from 1948 until 1958, 'was very, very good on the game, but then his hands were tied with the lack of quality that he had'.[233] Given the cosmopolitan nature of the league, Mulligan was of the opinion that 'it was entertaining and interesting to say the least, to meet up with all the different players from all the different cultures … [but] you were an international [standard] team in name only, I'm afraid'.[234] The club played their home games at Boston Red Sox's Fenway Park, with a huge dressing room and warm-up area available. He felt that the venue was …

> incredible … a different world altogether, from Milltown, Shamrock Rovers' ground, or from Tolka Park … that was a real eye-opener for me. I'd played in Europe, with Rovers, the dressing rooms at Rapid Vienna and Real Zaragoza were fine, but this was just typical America – it just made you a better person and a better player during the six-month experience.[235]

At times the conditions could be too much for some Irish players, with red-haired David Pugh collapsing after twenty minutes during 108 degrees Fahrenheit heat (42 degrees Celsius) during a heavy defeat in Kansas city.[236] With the club in decline at the end of the season, Mulligan returned to Ireland and later went on to have a successful career in England, having been encouraged to pursue a full-time career in professional football by his USA and NASL experiences.

In 1969, there was only one Republic of Ireland-born player who appeared in the NASL, with Eric Barber playing for Kansas City Spurs, and no Northern Ireland-born representatives; the following year there were none from either country. By 1974, the total had risen to four overall and two years later there were ten present. A drop to seven was experienced in 1977 but by the following year this had peaked at nineteen, with figures for Republic of Ireland-born players at a higher level (ten) than for Northern Ireland-born players (nine). This may be linked to the 'turning point' noted above after Pelé's arrival in 1975.

Lanfranchi and Taylor have shown that figures for British players in the NASL also peaked in 1978 at 214.[237] The Football League brought in a number of regulations towards the end of the decade to control transatlantic player movement from Britain, with an agreement made between the English league governing body and the NASL regarding transfers and loans. Some chairmen and managers remained distrustful of NASL clubs, however, and in 1979 British clubs could no longer loan players to the NASL after this was prohibited with a dispute between LA Aztecs and Derby County over George Best's registration significant in this decision.[238] After 1978, figures for Irish-born players never reached the total of nineteen again and by 1984 only eight Irish-born players were present, with three of these born in the Republic and five in Northern Ireland. Generally, figures for Northern Ireland-born players were higher on an annual basis. Some players were evidently put off from taking part in the NASL during the summer months with the need to take a break after a hard season in English and international football, with Mulligan turning down an offer from New England Tea Men, who were then managed by Noel Cantwell, to return in 1978, so that he could go home to Ireland from West Bromwich Albion to recuperate.[239] Similarly, Alfie Hale turned down an offer from Dennis Viollet, who was assistant coach at the Washington Diplomats for a spell in the 1970s, as he did not want to relocate at that stage in his then League of Ireland career.[240]

Lanfranchi and Taylor have noted that 'in all but one season after 1973 over 35 per cent of NASL players were North Americans' but 'only a small proportion of these footballers played on a regular basis'.[241] They also state that 'of the foreign players, Britons dominated from the start', particularly those from England, although 'by the late 1970s, a trend away from British imports was being observed', with West German, Yugoslav and Dutch players becoming more numerous.[242]

Some Irish-born players were at the end of their professional career when they moved, such as former Arsenal, Blackburn Rovers, Millwall, Celtic and Bristol Rovers player and Republic of Ireland international, Joe Haverty, who, in the latter stages of his career at Shelbourne, had brief spells at Chicago Spurs in the NPSL in 1967 and at Kansas City Spurs in the 1968 NASL season before returning to Dublin to play for Shamrock Rovers.[243] A few others, such as Belfast-born Brian Quinn, who joined LA Aztecs in 1981 as a twenty-one-year-old after being released by Everton without making a league appearance, were still relatively young when migrating. He spent the majority of his professional career in the USA.[244]

The frequency with which Irish-born players appeared ranged from a few months (Brendan Bradley, for example, played for three months with Toronto-Metros Croatia in 1976) to continuous seasons in some cases, with George Best appearing on a yearly basis from 1976 until 1981 with three clubs – Los Angeles Aztecs (1976–78), Fort Lauderdale Strikers (1978–79) and San Jose Earthquakes from 1980–81.[245] Bradley had been recruited through a Dublin-based agent while playing in the League of Ireland and recalls the excitement of playing in the same team as Eusebio, although like many players in the league the former European Footballer of the Year was past his best at that stage. While Bradley was not fond of flying he enjoyed his time there but had to return home at the start of the domestic football season with Finn Harps.[246] A small number of players who had no experience of English league football as players were able to appear continually in the league in the immediate years before its collapse, with Dublin-born Fran O'Brien present each season between 1978 and 1984, making a total of 187 appearance with three clubs, Philadelphia Fury, Montreal Manic and Vancouver Whitecaps.[247] Similarly, Northern Ireland-born goalkeeper, Bill Irwin, was ever-present in the league in those years, appearing a total of 176 times for four clubs, Washington Diplomats, Dallas Tornado, Portland Timbers and Golden Bay Earthquakes.[248]

Along with the aforementioned Brian Quinn, these two players were generally exceptional in their length of career in the USA. The average spell of a Republic of Ireland football migrant in the NASL

Seen here in action for Finn Harps, **Brendan Bradley** is the all-time leading goalscorer in the League of Ireland. Along with a short spell at Lincoln City, he also played in the North American Soccer League in the 1970s. Picture: Declan Doherty (*Donegal News*).

was 1.6 seasons while Northern Ireland football migrants averaged 2.33 seasons. The average age of migration of a Northern Ireland-born player to the NASL was 26.2 while this was noted as 26.8 for Republic of Ireland-born migrants, illustrating how these players generally moved at a later stage in their careers to those moving to England from Ireland in the 1945–2010 period (average of nineteen years old) and Scotland (twenty-one years generally). In addition, the average number of seasons played in the NASL was also much lower for both sets of players than the average of 6.5 playing seasons (Republic of Ireland-born players) and 6.6 playing seasons for Northern Ireland-born players in the English Football League and Premiership, as will be examined more fully in Chapter 7. As noted earlier in this chapter, Northern Ireland-born players had an average length of career in top-flight Scottish football of 6.28 seasons, with those born in the Republic averaging 4.16 seasons in the 1945–2010 period. Again, this was much longer than the average number of seasons in the NASL. The vast majority of Republic of Ireland football migrants to the NASL were born in Dublin, with a few exceptions, such as San Diego Jaws player John Minnock who was born in Tullamore, County Offaly and Waterford-born Maurice Slater, who played for Washington Diplomats.[249] Those from Northern Ireland were mainly born in Belfast.

John Giles has written that while player-manager at Vancouver Whitecaps from 1981 to 1983, 'the standard was surprisingly high' although he later returned to England to manage West Bromwich Albion.[250] Republic of Ireland-born migrants to England from 1966 to 1975 who also played in the NASL included Giles (Philadelphia Fury, Vancouver Whitecaps), Tony Dunne (Detroit Express), Ray Treacy (Toronto Mets), Terry Conroy (Cleveland Stokers), Tony Macken (Washington Diplomats, Dallas Tornado), Jimmy Conway (New England Tea Men), Jimmy Holmes and Mick Martin (Vancouver Whitecaps) and Don O'Riordan (Tulsa Roughnecks). With the exception of Don O'Riordan, these players were all capped at senior international level, illustrating the greater career opportunities in America for these men as opposed to non-capped players, although there were some exceptions. As noted by Lanfranchi and Taylor, 'even the more modestly rewarded players enjoyed a lifestyle and a standard of living which was unattainable at home'.[251] Three Republic of Ireland-born players – Pat Byrne, Eddie Byrne and Fran O'Brien – had moved 'from Bohemians for a fee variously quoted between £28,000 and £100,000' to Philadelphia Fury in 1978 according to one contemporary source, while one of these players was said to be 'earning £1,000 a month with a free car and a free flat'.[252] Only Pat Byrne would later experience playing English league football, spending two seasons at Leicester City from 1979 until 1981 before moving to Scottish club Hearts and also earning eight international caps. However, it was world superstars such as Johan Neeskens and

Pelé who could command the highest figures in the NASL, with the Dutchman receiving $2 million per annum from New York Cosmos from 1979 to 1984, while Pelé's contract with the same club was 'worth between $4 and $5 million for eighty-five matches over three years' and made him 'the highest paid team athlete in the world'.[253]

Moving to the United States of America allowed some players to make more money than was available in England, and it also provided a pathway into coaching. In 1985 Limerick-born Joe Waters was said to have trebled his Grimsby salary at Tacoma in the Major Indoor Soccer League (MISL) (which lasted from 1978 to 1992) while working as a part-time coach and also had the luxury of flying 'virtually everywhere'.[254] Brian Quinn also now resides there having moved into a coaching role and become a US citizen and international player in the early 1990s.[255] Similarly, by the summer of 1986 Steve Heighway was heavily involved in coaching in the USA, having left Liverpool in 1981 to join the Minnesota Kicks while he later played professional indoor soccer in Philadelphia.[256] Unlike Quinn, however, he later returned to Britain, taking up a role as head of youth development at Liverpool in 1989 before returning to the USA to coach in 2007 and again returning to Liverpool's Academy in 2015.[257]

Like Quinn, a few other Northern Ireland-born players have experienced professional success as footballers in America. Having both begun their careers at Glentoran, Vic Moreland and Billy Caskey had loan spells at NASL club Tulsa Roughnecks in 1978 before signing together for Derby County and then re-joining the American club in 1980 and winning the NASL Soccer Bowl in 1983. Despite returning to Glentoran in 1985, Caskey also had a spell in the USA playing in the MISL in the mid-1980s, while Moreland stayed in the US and won the MISL Championship in 1987 with Dallas Sidekicks as captain and the American Soccer League with Fort Lauderdale Strikers in 1989.[258]

Recent Republic of Ireland internationals to experience the game there include Robbie Keane (LA Galaxy) and Kevin Doyle (Colorado Rapids), illustrating the success of Major League Soccer in attracting top-level players in the latter stages of their careers, although Paddy Mulligan has suggested that this type of migration is more akin to 'a retirement fund … it's the same with Schweinsteiger going to Man. Utd'.[259] Darren O'Dea (Toronto), Shane McFaul (Virginia Beach) and James O'Connor (Orlando City) have also migrated there having failed to settle in England. Current Northern Ireland manager Michael O'Neill had a short spell at Portland Timbers in 2001.[260] Steve Morrow played for Dallas Burn during the 2002–03 season having moved on a free transfer from QPR, illustrating how some players are happy to see out their careers there.[261]

ASIA, SOUTH AFRICA, AUSTRALIA AND NEW ZEALAND AS DESTINATIONS

Northern Ireland-born players did not move to Asia in any great numbers, although exceptions include Patrick Sharkey, Derek Spence, Jim Hagan and Allen McKnight.[262] Republic of Ireland-born footballer, Timothy Dalton, had moved to Hong Kong's short-lived club Earnest Borel by the summer of 1993 on a 'lucrative' one-year deal, stating at the time that 'the overall standard wasn't terrific' but that 'the lifestyle and treatment is absolutely wonderful'.[263] A few Northern Ireland-born players also experienced professional football in South Africa: Bobby Braithwaite joined Durban City after four seasons with Middlesbrough in 1967, while Exeter's George Spiers joined Port Elizabeth after a spell in England. Republic of Ireland-born Eoin Hand spent two seasons with South African club Arcadia Shepherds in the mid-1970s after finishing his playing career in England.[264]

A few Northern Irish-born players have also moved to Australia, with Jimmy O'Neill joining Hakoah of the Victorian State League in 1965 after a career with Sunderland and Walsall while George Best had a short spell with Brisbane Lions in 1983.[265] Terry McCavanagh joined New Zealand club Eastern Union via Coleraine in 1960 after a brief career at Notts County, although he appears to have been an exception in terms of players moving there from Northern Ireland.[266] For some, a move to an Australian club could allow them to continue with football in a new environment. Dublin-born Derek Ryan, who was released from Wolves after four seasons and had few other options within the English game but to play non-league for Uxbridge (while also taking up a job with British Home Stores), moved there in the 1980s.[267] In May 1988, the twenty-one-year-old was playing with Sydney club Ku Ring Gai while working during the day in a sports shop in Willoughby, although he returned to Ireland the following year after his work permit ran out, a factor which, along with the distance involved and the standard of play in Australia, has probably been significant in the overall lack of Irish footballers who have relocated there.[268] As Delaney has noted, along with Australia, 'New Zealand and South Africa were also destinations for twentieth-century Irish emigrants, even if at a lower rate than before 1921'.[269] Despite this, these areas were not heavily frequented by Irish footballers in the period covered in this book, with British football leagues remaining the primary destination throughout the late nineteenth, twentieth and early twenty-first centuries.

CONCLUSION

This chapter has illustrated some of the patterns of movement for Irish-born football migrants who have joined clubs outside England's football leagues. An analysis of the sectarian nature of Scottish football has been offered from the point of view of a number of players with experience of the game there. It has been shown that some professionals, such as John McClelland, while enjoying the buzz generated while playing in a less than friendly atmosphere at times, have not been unduly concerned about religious affiliations and associated abuse while playing the game and developing their careers. With Rangers' recent promotion to the Scottish Premier League more interest may again be shown in these clubs by top international players as was evident during Graeme Souness' era at the club (1986–91), when 'some serious salesmanship' allowed him 'to reverse the tradition of the best Scottish players moving to England' temporarily, although it is difficult to again see them or Celtic competing at the top level of European football unless finances improve.[270]

This chapter has also offered an assessment of movement to alternative non-UK destinations, which Irish-born players have found to be increasingly necessary as a result of foreign player migration into the traditional centre for British and Irish players, English league football. While Irish football migration to European clubs was not particularly common in the immediate post-war decades, player movement to less prominent European clubs has become more notable in the late twentieth and early twenty-first century, highlighting an increase in accessibility due to the development of new club networks. An increase in flight paths between the United Kingdom and less frequented areas around Europe to some extent has been a factor in this, along with, more significantly, a loosening of restrictions on clubs' fielding of foreign players in correlation with European Union legislation. It has also illustrated that the numbers of Irish players moving abroad to non-British clubs, and to top-flight football clubs in Scotland, have been relatively low in comparison with figures for those who have moved to England and played league football there. It is also doubtful that any of the other four major European leagues will see an influx of Irish footballers in the near future given the difference in language and culture and styles of play.

Hassan has noted how 'Northern European cities with a strong commercial and economic base attract most Irish migrants who are seeking (or more commonly have secured) employment with major international corporations located in the central business district'.[271] Coincidentally, a number of Irish-born players have had spells with clubs in Belgium and Holland, but with no great success. Irish-born players in Europe have generally not achieved the levels of success which the aforementioned stars of Manchester United, Liverpool and Arsenal enjoyed in the late twentieth century, with the exception of Liam Brady, although it could be argued that he was a world-class performer who adapted well to the culture of Italian football. Irish-born footballers have therefore been similar to British players in favouring a culture and way of life with which they are most familiar.

Some players have used European and American clubs, rather than British ones, as a means to pursue a career in the game, with the examples of Noel Campbell and Brian Quinn illustrating that experience of English league football is not necessary to gain international recognition, although generally speaking, these players have been the exception rather than the rule. The arrival of international players such as Kevin Doyle, Sean St Ledger, Andy O'Brien and Jermain Defoe at Major League Soccer clubs in recent years has also illustrated how some established players have seen this leagues as an opportunity to experience a different lifestyle and earn additional money while they could still be playing English league football, although some lesser players have also used soccer in America as the basis for starting a career in coaching. Liam Miller's move from Hibernian to Perth Glory in 2012 has generally not been reflective of the migratory patterns of Irish-born players, although, as noted, a number have taken on the challenge of non-European or American soccer leagues.[272] What Irish-born players have generally gone on to do when their professional careers have ended is assessed in the next chapter, along with the difficulties they have faced in attempting to enter a more traditional and, for many, a more mundane type of workplace.

CHAPTER 6

Post-playing Careers

> Of that era [the 1960s], all the guys who finished up their careers would have had a good wage and maybe got the remnants or the start of the maximum wage being abolished, got the benefits of that. They would have got enough money through the union membership and a sort of retirement fund to say 'well, I can open a business' and most of them opened a pub or something like that … they would go into some business … but unfortunately what happened with [around] 97 per cent of them is that they met a guy and [he] said, 'Look, I know how to run a business, with my expertise and your money, we'll go well together.' Unfortunately, [around] 97 per cent of them went broke, and the situation is then, they're left with no money, no education, nothing.[1]
>
> Alfie Hale, 27 September 2013

INTRODUCTION

Neal Garnham has noted in his study of Ireland's first professional players that 'a very few players could find employment as club trainers, coaches, or officials; the number of opportunities was always tiny'.[2] As will be shown, this situation had improved by the late twentieth century. This chapter illustrates that the majority of Irish-born players who moved to England in the 1945–2010 period attempted to remain in the game in some capacity after retiring. Changes in the post-playing career routes undertaken by retired players indicate that while more modern careers such as agent and sports science-related work are now available, the number of players who complete second-level education and attain third-level degrees remains low, given that most Irish-born players migrate as teenagers. Despite more emphasis on educating young recruits, the level of qualifications available at clubs has been problematic for those seeking to further their education outside the game. Education is not a priority for clubs or young players. In addition, financial difficulties and a change in identity have left many players facing tough mental challenges on retirement from football. The majority of Irish-born players in the post-war period have chosen to remain in football at various levels from Premier League management to matchday hosts after retiring from playing. Fewer numbers of those analysed left the game completely over this period. The work of the Professional Footballers' Association in assisting players in their post-playing career choices has certainly been beneficial to some and there is now more public awareness, and acceptance, of players' mental health issues. Despite this, less is known about lower league players in this regard as they generally do not attract media attention to the same degree as top-flight players have done.

THE POST-PLAYING CAREERS OF IRISH-BORN PLAYERS IN ENGLAND, 1888–1939

Early Irish football migrants differed from more general Irish migrants in showing a tendency to return to the country of their birth. Returning home was 'rare' in the nineteenth century although Irish seasonal workers in Britain were more inclined to do so than migrants who moved to the United States of America.[3] Writing in 1904 of those who had moved to cross-channel clubs, one Belfast reporter felt that 'the majority will, I am certain, return'.[4] Some 133 of the 286 pre-Second World War Irish football migrants who played in English league football were identified as returning to Ireland, although they did not all continue to play the game on arriving home. Some, such as Billy Gillespie, who took over as Derry City manager in 1932, stayed only temporarily before returning to live in England.[5] Mason has noted in his major study of English football that after retiring, early professional footballers generally took up positions as shopkeepers, public house licencees or football managers or 'whatever job the player held before he became a professional'.[6] In some ways, Irish football migrants were no different although there is less evidence for the latter category. A few players became managers (Peter Doherty, Johnny Carey, Elisha Scott), coaches (Alex

Stevenson) and scouts (Bob Fullam, Jimmy Ferris and Billy Behan), while some availed of new positions created within the Irish Free State in the post-1922 years. Southport player Paddy Clarke became an employee with the newly formed Electricity Supply Board, which was established in 1927, on returning in 1932.[7]

Former New Brighton, Sheffield United, Arsenal and Southampton player Jimmy Dunne became a coach with Bohemians having finished his playing career in Ireland with Shamrock Rovers, although he died suddenly aged forty-four in 1949.[8] Some players, such as Newton Heath's John Peden and Derby County and Reading player Sid Reid, who both ran sweetshops, took up positions in retail, with Jack McCandless running a shop in Coleraine before succumbing to the eventual effects of a gas attack while serving in the First World War.[9] Mickey Hamill ran a pub, the Centre Half, on the Falls Road before drowning in the river Lagan in 1943.[10] Similarly Matt Reilly ran a pub in Dublin.[11] Tom Priestly, who joined Chelsea from Linfield in 1933, became a school principal in Lambeg and Hugh Blair, who had spells at Manchester City, Swansea and Millwall, became a teacher in Liverpool, but the numbers taking up positions in education were minimal.[12] Although Mason has noted a few players taking up coaching positions in colleges in the pre-First World War period, 'the number of openings in football itself was not very large' at that time, and this continued for much of the twentieth century.[13]

A few others tried their hand at journalism, including Lawrie Cumming, who had spells at English and Scottish clubs and later became a founder member of the Scottish Football Writers' Association in 1965.[14] Charlie O'Hagan became editor of the short-lived *Football Sports Weekly* for a period in the 1920s while also retaining an interest in coaching, taking up positions in Seville and Rotterdam before moving to the USA.[15] Unusually for an Irish-born football migrant, he had experience of coaching abroad and boasted in 1926 that his football and travel experiences were 'perhaps unequalled in the history of the game'.[16] However, it is Patrick O'Connell, the former Manchester United captain, who is said to have saved FC Barcelona from folding during the Spanish Civil War by taking the club on a tour of Mexico and New York, who remains the most famous Irish-born player to take charge of a continental club. He also managed Racing Santander, Real Oviedo and Real Betis.[17] Political turmoil in Ireland led at least one player to move to a new workplace in a different Irish city during the 1920s. Harry Buckle, who returned from Coventry City of the Southern League to Belfast Celtic in 1911, later moved to Cork-based club Fordsons in the early 1920s having endured sectarian abuse in the Belfast shipyards where he had worked part-time.[18] Mason has noted how former England internationals George Wall and Micky Bennett returned to industrial work after retiring from the game and has stated that 'individual personality' was also a factor in the post-playing career choices of early professionals.[19]

While former Celtic and Woolwich Arsenal player, Patrick Farrell, was said to have lived comfortably after retiring, O'Connell, who later fell upon hard times, was less fortunate, as was John Kirwan, an FA Cup winner with Spurs, who was forced to seek a grant of £10 from the IFA in 1924 to improve his circumstances.[20] Archie Goodall, somewhat unusually, became a theatre entertainer and appeared in a strongman tour.[21] Some players received benefit matches from their clubs, although this depended on the length of time spent there, with the *Belfast Telegraph* noting Burnley's intention to give Tommy 'Ching' Morrison a match of this nature in 1902, which, the newspaper stated, he deserved, as he had been 'faithful' to them.[22] In 1954 Real Betis arranged a benefit match for O'Connell although he died five years later and was buried in an unmarked grave in London.[23] In contrast, former England international James Forrest, who won the FA Cup three times, later became a successful businessman and on dying in 1925 left an estate worth £5,845, although he appears to have been almost unique among early professional footballers in England in this regard.[24]

IRISH-BORN FOOTBALL MIGRANTS' POST-PLAYING CAREERS, 1945–2010

Despite the limited amount of research on the post-playing careers of professional footballers in Britain throughout the twentieth century, a number of changing trends have been noted by Harding in his work on the social life of these men. He states that 'prior to the 1960s and 1970s, opportunities to remain in and around the professional game, unless you were a player, trainer or manager, were scarce'.[25] Former top professionals such as John Charles, Wilf Mannion and Tommy Lawton, had 'all either met with bad luck or shown poor judgement in preparing for their eventual retirement'.[26] Players' earning ability was drastically reduced by the maximum wage which was not lifted until 1961 with the help of Professional Footballers' Association chairman, Jimmy Hill.[27] Two years later George Eastham's case against his club, Newcastle United, who initially refused to allow him to move to a London team, was settled in the High Court, with Justice Wilberforce condemning the system of retain-and-transfer, although Taylor believes that the modified version left footballers 'some way short of freedom of contract'.[28] Introduced in 1964, this new method of option contracts allowed clubs 'to renew a player's contract as long as it was for the same period and on equivalent terms as those previously offered', while free transfers were also to be granted 'by clubs not wishing to take up its option and players in the process of being transferred were to continue to receive their contracted terms'.[29]

Former players who later became successful businessmen such as Dave Whelan, Johnny Hayes, Ron Harris and Mick Channon, were probably the exception rather than the norm. Harding has noted factors such as 'class, education and inclination' providing a hindrance to the majority of players in developing similar post-football business-type acumen.[30] As Alfie Hale has noted about the 1960s:

> Of that era, all the guys who finished up their careers would have had a good wage and maybe got the remnants or the start of the maximum wage being abolished, got the benefits of that. They would have got enough money through the union membership and a sort of retirement fund to say 'well, I can open a business' and most of them opened a pub or something like that … they would go into some business … but unfortunately what happened with [around] 97 per cent of them is that they met a

> guy and [he] said, 'Look, I know how to run a business, with my expertise and your money, we'll go well together.' Unfortunately, [around] 97 per cent of them went broke, and the situation is then, they're left with no money, no education, nothing.[31]

He also stated that 'some of them became successful on the radio and television. But they were a tiny minority. Most of the guys had nothing. You had the great Wilf Mannion – he ended up sweeping the streets.'[32] For Republic of Ireland internationals playing in the 1986–2002 period, post-career prospects were helped significantly by the country's qualification for four major tournaments and the television-related financial boom of the Premier League.[33] A 2010 assessment by Miguel Delaney of the post-playing careers of the seventy Republic of Ireland retired international footballers who played from 1986 to 2002, found that the majority of these have attempted to stay in football. He has established that 'twenty have some form of punditry or media work as their main income; thirty-five are in coaching or management; two are in some way involved in football administration' and therefore 81 per cent are 'still directly involved in the framework of the sport'.[34] While not all Irish-born, a contrast can certainly be seen with some of those who struggled to cement a place at international level and played at lower levels around this time.

One former Irish international player who missed out on the opportunities which came with the Jack Charlton years of 1986–95 was former Oxford United defender David Langan, who failed to make the Euro '88 squad despite appearing in the qualifiers. After his career ended, he depended on state benefit and is now registered as disabled due to injuries sustained as a player. While suffering from alcoholism and finance-related problems, he slept in the basement of the town hall in Peterborough and has worked in a dry-cleaning delivery service, as a milkman, a security officer, town hall beadle and is now assistant in a mayor's office. Langan was given a testimonial dinner by the FAI in 2008, although he has written that he is unhappy about the way the money has been distributed.[35] Langan's case illustrates the fine line between those who were able to cash in on the Premier League boom and those who narrowly missed out, although it is difficult to be precise about how common his post-career employment situation is among professional footballers.

This is partly because a large number of these Irish football migrants' post-playing careers have not been identified as some footballers who played for only one or two seasons and were not capped internationally are now extremely difficult to trace. In addition, many recent players, particularly those who migrated and signed as professionals in the last two decades, are still playing. However, it was possible to identify the post-playing careers of 188 Republic of Ireland and 197 Northern Ireland-born footballers who played professionally in the English Premiership and Football Leagues in the period from the end of the Second World War until 2010.

Table 6.1 Post-playing careers of Republic of Ireland and Northern Ireland-born players, 1945–2010.

Occupation	Republic of Ireland-born	Northern Ireland-born
Football industry and other occupations (combined)	118 (62.76%)	134 (68.02%)
Business/Sales	32 (17.02%)	25 (12.69%)
Industrial work	13 (6.91%)	15 (7.61%)
Education	5 (2.65%)	6 (3.04%)
Medical	4 (2.12%)	4 (2.03%)
Security/Policing	3 (1.59%)	4 (2.03%)
Other	13 (6.91%)	9 (4.56%)
Total	**188 (100%)**	**197 (100%)**

Source: Soccer Magazine; 'Northern Ireland Football Greats', http://nifootball.blogspot.ie/2006/07/welcome.html [accessed 24 March 2017].

Table 6.1 provides a breakdown of occupational categories for these footballers' post-playing careers. Of the 188 footballers born in the Republic of Ireland whose post-playing careers have been positively identified for this study, 118 players or 62.76 per cent attempted to stay in the game at various levels, many while combining work such as management, coaching and scouting with other jobs such as newsagent, publican and media work. In a 1967 interview, then

Millwall player, Eamon Dunphy, stated that coaching badges were 'a form of security against football injury' and 'a passport to anything in the soccer game'.[36] Although Dunphy did not pursue a full-time career in coaching and became a respected journalist, many retired Irish-born players became involved as managers or coaches ranging from international level to non-league. However, none could be said to have enjoyed the length of career or success of Sir Alex Ferguson or Arsène Wenger and the vast majority, such as Liam Tuohy, appear to have combined these positions with other work at some stage.[37] A number of those returning to Ireland have shown a tendency to manage at League of Ireland and Irish League level and some, such as Turlough O'Connor and Alfie Hale, have combined this with successful business interests. Hale stated that having tired of working in sales for a number of companies on returning home, he decided to open a sports shop near Waterford city centre, having noted the success of a business where footballers collected their training gear in a back street near Villa Park:

> When I went to Aston Villa, the first thing they did is they gave me what they call a 'chit' – a piece of paper, an order. They said, 'Go down there and get a tracksuit and a pair of boots for yourself, kit yourself out.' I went down to some side street, not far from the ground, around Aston. A guy called Lesley Smith, a former player, had a shop, and they told me, 'He'll look after you.' And they were looking after the former player themselves. So I went down, got the boots and gear. It was only a terraced house, and he had converted it into a shop – this is back in the '60s. And this fella was flying – Birmingham City were coming to him, Wolves were coming to him, Coventry City were coming to him, and the Villa gave him all his business – and at the side of a terraced house.[38]

Despite being told by some locals that his business, set up in Barrack Street, was not located centrally enough to succeed, Hale had gathered a lot of experience in his other jobs and figured with his contacts he would be OK. He was soon able to afford a place in the middle of

Alfie Hale scored sixty-four league goals in 158 matches in England before returning to League of Ireland football and has also had a highly successful business career. Picture: Alfie Hale collection.

the city through the demand for sports gear and his energetic work ethic. He studied a number of business and sports books, and having seen many players, such as Bobby Moore, lose much of what they had earned in the game, avoided taking on a business partner:

> In terms of those sports books that I read, in relation to business management, they say, 'well don't ever go into business with some other guy', you know the guy who knows the business and you have the money. There's an old saying in business: 'Man with money meets man with experience, man with experience ends up with money and man with money ends up with an experience'. And that's what happens. For example, if you're the kid that made all the money and I'll be your manager, three years down the road, I've spent it all, or else shifted it away somewhere else

> and you're left bust ... now, I'm still educated, you've nothing left. What your career of fifteen years has given you ... it's gone down the Swanee and no education to fall back on.[39]

Like Hale, O'Connor struggled to settle in England, at London club Fulham and, denied the opportunity to move back to Ireland by the Craven Cottage side, he apparently went home and refused to return when the club withheld his registration, although it is unclear how unusual this type of player-power manoeuvre was among Irish football migrants in the pre-Bosman era.[40]

The post-playing careers of 197 Northern Ireland footballers were positively identified and 134 players or 68.02 per cent have attempted to stay in the game. Similarly Northern Ireland-born players have become heavily involved in management and coaching after retiring from playing.[41] Five Republic of Ireland-born players were found to have been employed as scouts while others have probably worked informally in this capacity to some degree.[42] At least thirteen Northern Ireland-born players have taken up this role, including Gerry Burrell, who was approached by Linfield about the job, having returned to the shipyards on the advice of his wife after finishing his full-time professional career in England in the late 1950s.[43] He continued to hold his scouting position until he was eighty-six years of age.[44]

While management, coaching and scouting positions have been common within football for much longer, television punditry also provides employment for some more high-profile players. Former Northern Ireland stars such as Terry Neill, George Best and Gerry Armstrong have worked in television while Danny Blanchflower became a columnist for the *Sunday Express* after retiring, as well as managing.[45] The use of agents by players over the past three decades now means that retired players can find work in this capacity. At least ten Republic of Ireland-born players have used their experience in the game to give financial and personal advice as agents.[46] As Harding has stated, many football clubs have now become 'more akin to social centres' with more job opportunities available to players such as club radio and television channel hosts, matchday tour guides and 'football in the community' officers.[47]

Gerry Burrell pictured (*left*) with **Kenny McKeague**. Having returned from English league football, he worked as a scout for Linfield until the age of eighty-six. Picture: Linfield FC.

A lack of higher-level education among most Republic of Ireland-born players means that involvement in the medical profession has been minimal (2.12 per cent) with only three footballers – Tony McCarthy, Fred Murray and Richie Partridge – becoming physiotherapists while only one, Kevin O'Flanagan, was noted as a doctor. The volume of Northern Ireland-born players who became involved in medical matters has also been small (2.03 per cent).[48] Harding describes 'the leisure industry' as also having changed the lives of former players as ex-athletes can be used as fitness instructors, coaches and organisers of games.[49] Republic of Ireland-born Tadhg Purcell and Richie Kennedy have gained employment as personal trainers while a small number of Northern Ireland-born migrants, including Michael Carvill, have also become involved in the scientific aspects of football, illustrating the new types of employment opportunities available to modern-day players who undertake third-level education.[50]

NON-SPORTS-RELATED CAREERS

A few players became involved in security and policing, but these figures were also minimal, with just over 1 per cent of the Republic of Ireland-born migrants' total identified in this category, while slightly over 2 per cent of Northern Ireland-born migrants sought employment in this sector. Dublin-born Hugh Atkinson's decision to become a policeman highlights the lack of security for many lower league players. The former Wolves, Exeter, York City and Darlington player had joined West Midlands Police by April 1987 after struggling to recover his place after a broken leg. He illustrated his frustration with professional football when he stated at the time that 'it was decision time. It couldn't go on any longer.'[51] The traditional post-football position of publican has been taken up by a small number of former Irish internationals.[52] Business and sales was found to be the second highest post-playing career category outside football-related work for players after retiring from English football, with 17 per cent of Republic of Ireland-born migrants and 13 per cent of those from Northern Ireland taking up positions in this sector. A number of former players have become bookmakers and newsagents while a few others developed businesses such as retail chains and insurance agencies.[53] Some other players from both countries found that lower-paid industrial-based jobs were necessary to make ends meet with plasterer, docker, forklift driver, construction worker and panel beater all identified as means of post-playing employment. Almost 7 per cent of Republic of Ireland-born players became involved in industrial work while almost 8 per cent of those born in Northern Ireland did so. As will be shown later, the number of players who took up educational positions was low. The remainder of players not identified in these categories included a small number who became involved in religious organisations – such as Philip Mulryne, Stuart Elliott and Dennis Keating – and those in other forms of employment such as the postal service, park supervision and male modelling.

PROFESSIONAL FOOTBALL AND PART-TIME WORK

Even prior to retirement, many footballers in the latter part of the twentieth century were still poorly paid at lower-league level and have earned higher wages in careers outside professional football. Derry city-born Felix Healy joked in 1988 that he had been earning more as a pop singer at home than as a full-time professional footballer at Port Vale.[54] Other lower-league players mixed a variety of employment positions to make ends meet after their football league contracts were terminated or when they failed to agree new terms. Following a career at Tottenham Hotspur, Bournemouth and Sheffield United, Tom Heffernan retired from non-league football and took up a position as a bread man in 1993, admitting in a magazine interview that 'the unsocial hours didn't help getting to games'.[55] He had previously worked as a hospital nurse and painter and decorator.

Although 1990s' Nottingham Forest players, Tommy Gaynor and Roy Keane, both endured spells of unemployment prior to transferring from Ireland, this is not to say that Irish players who did not complete their education had no work experience or trade outside football.[56] Northern Ireland's Peter McParland worked as a barman and in a timber yard after he had left school in the early 1950s and some players who joined from the League of Ireland continued to work part-time prior to moving to England, such as 1980s' migrants Roddy Collins, who worked as a plasterer and Liam O'Brien, a welder by trade prior to becoming a full-time professional with Manchester United.[57] Some gave up more secure and sometimes more lucrative positions in order to become full-time professional footballers. Damien Richardson recalled that Shamrock Rovers had got him a job while he was playing part-time for them in the early 1970s:

> I was working in a place called Motor Manufacturers up on the Naas Road with the Mercedes and Volkswagen assembly plant. Money was extraordinarily good, it was a very highly unionised position and the unions ran it very, very strictly. The pay at the time was extraordinary, so the combination of very good pay

> at Shamrock Rovers, very good pay at Motor Manufacturers … and I was in clover as they say. And when I went to England I actually had to take a drop in wages to go full-time. At the time, with the combination of job and football I was making about £60 a week which was extraordinary, and I went and signed, I remember, for £47 a week for Gillingham. But money has never entered into anything I ever done anyhow, so that didn't matter – £47 was still very good money, at that time, with appearance money it pushed it up, but it was the fact of being full-time.[58]

He also admitted that he was never afraid of the risks of a career in football.

> Football was never a danger to me, it was almost my greatest friend, it was always a constant companion, so there was never, ever, any moment that I ever doubted my involvement in football, even when difficult times came later in my career. It was never the game that caused the difficulties, the game was something I was in love with.[59]

Some professionals appear to have had little idea of what to do outside sport when their contracts were not renewed or they were forced to eke out an existence outside the English Football League. Waterford-born goalkeeper Timothy Dalton said he hoped to get a career in a leisure centre when overlooked for a new contract by Notts County in 1986.[60]

THE PROSPECT OF RETIREMENT

Despite the public farewells afforded to Steven Gerrard and Barcelona's Xavi at the end of the 2014–15 season by their long-term clubs, not every professional footballer can hope to receive a grand send-off the day they finish playing the game, and for many, it is a gradual process. As Roderick has stated, 'As they approach their final career statuses, players lower expectations to the point that their departures are not wholly unexpected and, for many, retirement provides a degree of relief from the employment conditions and the merciless physical demands of this sport.'[61] Some players such as Mick Meagan have been able to gradually adapt by taking up roles as player-managers in Ireland, although he states that he fully expected to have to work elsewhere when he finished in England and 'there was no big deal about it'.[62] There is some evidence that being an ex-professional makes it harder to gain the acknowledgement of employers that a post-playing career is necessary. Damien Richardson has stated that the toughest time of his career was when he was released by Gillingham in 1981 after a difference of opinion with his manager. He eventually was offered work as a window salesman by a friend, but his local stardom had left him with a problem:

> The difficulty I had in getting employment was, I'd done a lot of radio work, I was well-known in the area, in the county [Kent], and everybody thought I was just grand. So nobody offered me anything. People were almost afraid to come and offer me something, so for two years I did nothing – and in doing nothing, [it] was a dangerous thing, a very dangerous thing.[63]

He later returned to the club as manager in 1989, again taking a significant pay cut to do so. In summing up the challenges facing players when their contracts are terminated, he also stated that:

> The divorce rate among professional footballers when they retire is 45–50 per cent, something like that, you go from a life where you've been cocooned and surrounded by adventure, by admiration, and all of a sudden, one Monday morning, you're normal again, and a lot of players, in those days, the vast majority of players, found it very difficult to handle.[64]

For Richie Sadlier, the prospect of retirement came earlier than expected as he struggled to recover from a hip injury he received in 2002, and when it came, almost two years later, aged only twenty-five, it was hard to deal with:

> I found it really hard because I still hadn't dealt with retirement. I was miserable, I was angry, I was feeling sorry for myself, really badly, and I wasn't talking to anyone about it. So I was just glad that I had stuff to do, I was glad for the structure that it [media work] gave me. Because, it was so … in a weird sense … it was an eighteen month injury so it wasn't an overnight thing but in the same way when I'd finished it felt like it was an overnight thing, I was totally unprepared for it. But it was hard, because it was so weird, it was so strange having to do anything … I'd gotten to terms with the parameters of being a footballer, the discipline, the dos and the don'ts, and all the things that come with it. It's totally unique, it's different from any other job that you're going to do, so it was difficult. Yeh, it was a total culture shock, being anything other than a footballer, because I'd never been anything else – I went from school to being a footballer. I remember at the time when I finished I did a thing on Sky Sports and they said, 'Well, what's it like?' It was the day after I retired, and I said, 'Well to be honest, this is the first day I've woken up as an adult with nowhere to be.' Like if I didn't get out of bed this morning, no one would have rang to see where I was. So that lack of being part of something, that kinda freaked me out a little bit.[65]

EDUCATION, REST AND SPARE TIME

Part of the problem for retiring players is that outside of football, most footballers in Britain have few other qualifications. An assessment of the playing careers of the 188 players born in the Republic of Ireland has shown that only five (2.65 per cent) were deemed to have undertaken careers outside football in the educational sector, whether as teachers, lecturers or education officers. Only seventeen (9.04 per cent) were found to have obtained university degrees at some point. Of the 197 Northern Ireland-born players identified, eighteen or 9.13 per cent are thought to have college degrees. At least six former Northern Ireland-born players (3.04 per cent) took up teaching careers having retired from the game. In the immediate post-Second World War years, many English and Scottish league clubs offered the opportunity of learning a trade on a part-time basis along with the opportunity to play professional football, with the *Irish Independent* noting this in February 1959, although naturally this became less necessary as the wages available in the game increased in the following decade.[66] Some other players had continued their industrial training after migrating, with Gerry Burrell given the chance by St Mirren to finish his apprenticeship as an electrician in Harland and Wolff's Glasgow base in the late 1940s.[67] Many other players also undertook apprenticeships in trades before migrating, with Harry Gregg working as a joiner in Coleraine before becoming a professional footballer.[68] Other 1950s' migrants, Danny Blanchflower and Terry Neill, were also keen to have alternative careers before turning professional, with the latter stating in his autobiography:

> I never set out to be a footballer. From an early age I fully expected my life to follow the same pattern as that of so many in Belfast, finishing up as a fitter, engineer or draughtsman in the shipyard, in Short's aircraft factory or in one of the engineering concerns in that corner of Ulster.[69]

Others were under no illusions that their only chance of escaping a life of drudgery lay in football. Charlie Hurley stated: 'I was fairly decent at school. But the only way out of my standard of life was through sport.'[70]

Alfie Hale felt that attitudes to education from clubs, players and parents were all part of the problem:

> I didn't do my Leaving Cert., I went straight to work at sixteen. There was no education after you left school and it was a question that you had to work to support the family. So college or secondary education never came into it. As far as the clubs were concerned, in England, it was a definite no-no because the clubs never took on board anybody's education. In fairness to the clubs, the players, 85 per cent of them would say they're not

> going to school anyway … [they generally said], 'I'm not going back to school, I want to play football' even though they had a lot of time on their hands. So you could say the club were remiss in not setting up something, but they got no encouragement either by the parents or by anybody else.[71]

As Mick Meagan has said:

> Well, being honest, they [clubs] wanted footballers. They weren't sort of worried of making you a barrister or [providing] education. So that's one thing probably that I thought was a little bit … they should have had a school for you after training, night school or something like that, where you went in and spent two hours, to keep you out of harm's way. Now if you were unlucky enough to pick up the wrong company, you were in trouble. Lucky enough, the lads I dealt with were good lads.[72]

Despite this, many aspiring footballers with no second-level qualifications at that time were part of a wider trend within Irish society, as by the middle of the 1950s approximately two-thirds of young school-leavers in the Republic of Ireland were aged fourteen, while the following decade only one-fifth of Irish Republic-born migrants in Britain were thought to have attended secondary school in their native country.[73] Shortly after the introduction of free secondary school education in the Republic of Ireland in 1966, one survey of Irish migrants taken in the early 1970s highlighted that 75 per cent had finished their education having only completed primary school.[74] Delaney has noted that 'the fragmentary data available underline the unskilled nature of the Irish emigrant flow after 1921' although there is also evidence that 'a long-established tradition of graduates did exist'.[75] Similarly, by the late twentieth century, Irish emigrants were drawn more from 'the enlarged ranks of the middle class' and 'at very least they would usually have completed secondary education, and a significant minority were graduates'.[76]

Educational opportunities at secondary school level were somewhat better north of the border in the decades after the Second

World War, and by the 1980s, Northern Irish emigrants in Britain were shown to have a greater level of education qualifications than those from the Republic, although it is difficult to clarify exactly if this was the case with those who migrated for football purposes.[77] As mentioned earlier, free education had been available in Northern Ireland since 1947, while selection for places in grammar schools, based on the eleven-plus examination, was also introduced.[78] However, the amount of time available off the playing field has been a problem for many players, with thoughts often turning to home life.[79] Richie Sadlier has stated he took it upon himself to get into education as a senior professional footballer, and has since completed a master's degree in psychotherapy having initially undertaken a Bachelor of Science degree in sports science and coaching:

> When I was about twenty-one, I think the first thing I signed up to do was a computer course for beginners. I never turned on a computer or I never shut down a computer because I never liked playing computer games and I never had a job that required a computer and I left school before computers became the thing. And I knew … I was starting to book flights on a computer and I knew it would be handy to be able … I thought that's as much as I'll ever be able to do with a computer. So it was a computer course for beginners – and I'm talking beginners, I knew nothing, nothing. And that was the first thing I did. And then I started the degree course then when I was twenty-two, maybe twenty-three, in the summer of '02, partly because I thought I might retire, partly also because it's the thing that I set out to do when I first went over – I always said I'd do something education-wise because you've loads of time, just loads of time. I didn't have kids, I wasn't married, I didn't have any other time-consuming things beyond training so it was the best thing for me to do.[80]

Encouragement from family members has been shown to benefit some players' post-career choices. Having returned to Northern Ireland from Nottingham Forest in 1988 as a twenty-year-old, Raymond Campbell was encouraged to become a physical education

Richie Sadlier in action for Millwall in 2001. Since retiring from football through injury he has become a successful television match analyst and psychotherapist. Picture: © Inpho

teacher by his brother, stating that 'if he hadn't have, I could have been doing anything, I could have been on a building site or something but I definitely didn't want to do that, so I was very lucky'.[81] He also felt that his football background helped him get a job. Brian Mooney felt that his father had instilled a strong belief in him about the importance of education, and on returning to Dublin in the 1990s, he took up a degree having joined Shelbourne on a part-time basis.[82] These influences are important because, as Roderick has stated, many players' 'world views have been shaped by people within the game, such as club directors, managers and coaches, for whom second careers post-football are not a central concern'.[83]

As shown by Seamus Kelly, 'dressing room culture can marginalise players interested in engaging with educational discourse' while, as Seamus Heath found, commitments to non-football-related qualifications generally came second to football, with exams in the early summer at times clashing with club tours abroad.[84] Attitudes towards the value of education have been slow to evolve within professional football and it is debateable whether they have changed much since the early 1970s when Tottenham Hotspur manager, Bill Nicholson, stated that 'it's a football brain that matters and that usually doesn't go with an academic brain. In fact I prefer it when it doesn't. I prefer players not to be too good or clever at other things. It means they concentrate on football.'[85] As Bourke has shown in her 2003 study of the career development of Irish teenage players, 'A large proportion of intending professionals opt to forego career advice in school and rely on external social networks to advance their career.'[86] Similarly, Roderick concluded from his study of professional players that they 'developed informal networks of people "inside the game" to whom they turned, when for example, their position in the first team was under threat, or when they realised that they were no longer in their manager's plans'.[87] Some players are also inclined to use their contacts in the game to assist in gaining employment outside of it. In particular, Mick Meagan felt that he had been lucky to gain a position in a hospital after retiring from English league football in the late 1960s, through the help of former Manchester United goalkeeper Pat Dunne.[88]

A few players have realised education's benefits and managed to delay their full-time professional football careers until they had some qualifications outside the game. At least four Republic of Ireland-born players have been identified as waiting until they had finished their secondary school education before migrating to England, but given the fact that most football league apprenticeships traditionally started at sixteen, the vast majority of players appear to have neglected to do this.[89] There were some exceptions, however. Former 1960s' Third Division player and Northern Ireland international, Hubert Barr, did not play first-team league football until he had gained his teaching qualifications, and knew he had these to fall back on.[90] However, like most players interviewed here, nobody at his club (Coventry City) advised him of the risks of a career in football. Education was not given any great emphasis by the club as 'there wasn't very much in a way … that was the early days … football came first, and everything else came after that'.[91] Only a small number from both countries, including John O'Neill, Ken O'Doherty, Tony McCarthy, Seamus Kelly and Kevin Moran, have waited to finish third-level education before transferring to English clubs.[92] Northern Ireland-born O'Neill, for example, finished his 'A' levels and completed a Batchelor of Science degree at Loughborough University before joining Leicester City from Derry Athletic in 1976.[93] As Harding has stated, unlike top professional athletes in America, 'the majority of British footballers have, until recently, shunned formal education almost completely'.[94]

Some Irish clubs do advise players to complete their exams. Richie Sadlier waited to do his Leaving Certificate before moving to England, having taken on board the advice of his schoolboy club, Belvedere:

> Well, I was very well briefed by the Belvedere coaches, they said that something like fifty … I'm guessing-maybe forty-eight … players from Belvedere have gone to England and signed for a club and two maybe made a career out of it … But they said, 'Listen, the failure rate is huge here, it's huge.' So I was given really good advice. In the summer of fifth year [at school], in the summer of '95, Millwall offered me a two-year contract and I said no to it because I wanted to stay and do my Leaving Cert.,

> that was the advice that Belvedere gave me. [They said], 'If they want you now they want you in a year.' Which is a ballsy thing to do at that age, to say no to a contract, because you just don't know what's going to happen until the following year, but at the time I just thought, 'It just makes far more sense to stay and do my Leaving.' I was all right in school and I knew I would get an honours Leaving Cert., so I stayed and I got that, and then I went over.[95]

The offer of a move to England could lead to those undertaking the Leaving Certificate to neglect their studies, with Michael McHugh stating that he knew six months before these examinations that he would be moving, with the result that he probably let his studies 'slip a wee bit', although he later became an account technician having returned home from English football.[96]

What to do off the pitch has been problematic for many players, with training often finishing early and players left to their own devices when they exit the club gates. Brian Kerr, Republic of Ireland manager between 2003 and 2005, stated in a 2000 interview that Irish youth team players spent their spare time at their clubs playing snooker and watching television and felt that 'very few of them are being educated about life, about books. Their concentration levels are very poor.'[97] While education is now commonplace in many football academies, a few players have questioned whether it is of any real value. It is still questionable whether the courses offered to teenage recruits are of any major benefit to careers outside the game and whether clubs are truly concerned about trainees' prospects outside of football, and if this aspect of football has changed very much since the 1950s and 1960s recollections of players mentioned above.

Raymond Campbell, who participated in the trainees' education system offered by Nottingham Forest in the late 1980s, stated that 'the club didn't put any barriers on you … if you didn't go, you didn't go and that was it … it was very lenient in that way'.[98] Despite some claims that the system for young players has improved with the introduction of the scholar system in 1999, some players interviewed felt that it was still not enough.[99] Shane Supple was eager to complete the education offered at his club Ipswich Town's Academy but found that his B. Tech. diploma in sports qualifications were of little help when he retired from professional football and returned to Ireland. He felt that the academy education system 'was standard enough' and that 'there was nothing much expected of us really, just to turn up'.[100] Like Shane Supple, on returning to Ireland Michael Carvill found his academy qualifications were insufficient to get into college although he admitted that the choice to do 'A' levels was also there and regretted not doing those rather than a sports course he undertook.[101] While stating that his recruiting club, Southampton, was 'first class' in helping young players settle, former Northern Ireland international Alan Blayney felt that the education qualifications available

> … wouldn't really have got you very far … I think it was a case where the PFA, I think, sent guidelines out to the clubs that they have to send you to university and things like that, so I think that's kind of a big part of it, they [the club] would probably rather you be training, but they kind of have to send you to university. But young footballers, they just want to be playing football, they don't want to be going to school for three or four hours in an afternoon and things like that … you're training all morning, after that you're tired, you don't want to go and sit in school for another two or three hours.[102]

Given the emphasis placed by clubs on rest and recovery, it is understandable that they would not be over-encouraging of players having a more balanced life away from the club, and as Mick Meagan has noted, players develop a mentality which encourages them to shy away from anything that will interfere with their football.[103] Roderick has stated that 'the structures of football engulf players to such an all-encompassing extent that they unwittingly collude in fashioning for themselves blindness to alternative sources of self-identity and self-enhancement'.[104]

He has also noted that 'there are few vocations where professional status is so inextricably dependent on the athleticism of the body'.[105] This means getting as much rest as possible outside of training and matches. Former Republic of Ireland international Stephen Hunt admitted in his newspaper column in 2014 that he would drive 800 yards to the training ground just to save his legs while at Reading:

> I wasn't being flash, I just felt I had to rest. My life was dedicated to rest and then more rest. I would never go out and when I say 'go out', I don't mean a night out, I mean out. I never left the house. All I did was train and rest, train and rest … it is all about rest and if you want to make it as a footballer, you have to understand that. It's such a mundane thing in so many ways, but I would say that more players fail to break through because they don't understand that.[106]

There is some evidence that education courses offered by clubs to young recruits have had little variety, with David Miskelly stating that at Oldham Athletic in the 1990s, 'you were basically only allowed do leisure and tourism at that time' and 'it was something I wasn't interested in', although he admitted that this structure has now changed.[107] He found it 'quite tough' attending as he would have preferred to do a course in business studies.[108] Michael Carvill was forced to give up the university education he had started after his contract was not renewed, illustrating the problems of gaining education as a player given the migratory nature of professional football.[109] Football will, of course, generally take priority for most professional players while still in the game. Barry Prenderville was accepted for a physiotherapy degree while at Oldham Athletic in his mid-twenties but decided to move home after he got a good contract offer as he wasn't playing first-team football in England.[110]

Some managers have undertaken steps themselves to improve players' education, with Damien Richardson working in co-operation with a local school liaison officer to help ensure younger footballers' educational needs were being met during his term as Gillingham manager from 1989 to 1992, although he admits that qualifications available to players have generally been inadequate within the game.[111] Educational neglect is not something that is unique to Irish football migrants. The conferring of Sunderland striker Duncan Watmore with a first-class degree attracted media interest in December 2015, illustrating how associations between professional footballers and the third-level education awards are still something that is perceived as a novelty.[112] More research needs to be undertaken on the role of a family background in education in the decision to take up these studies, before, during and after professional football careers, although Kuper and Szymanski's analysis of a sample of thirty-four England players' fathers have shown that eighteen of these footballers 'were sons of skilled or unskilled manual labourers', reflecting the authors' view that 'football still recruits over-whelmingly from the traditional working classes'.[113]

THE WORK OF THE PROFESSIONAL FOOTBALLERS' ASSOCIATION

As Harding has shown, some players have, 'over the last couple of decades', been able to receive assistance from the Professional Footballers' Association to pursue 'careers in all forms of life' with advice and grants available after they retire.[114] This funding was initiated in 1967 'with a view to providing assistance to any member or ex-member wishing to undertake vocational training'.[115] A number of players interviewed for this study have stated that they were always aware of the PFA – which is a fee-paying service 'for those at Conference National level or higher' – and its representatives' presence at their training grounds and have received advice on post-career options.[116] As Dean Kelly notes, this can come in a number of forms:

> There would be a rep there … when you sign you get all these booklets and there's [telephone] numbers for reps and things and you can get in contact with them and ring them. And basically just talk to the captain of the team and the manager and he'll give you the number and sort everything out. You are told that there are people there to talk to.[117]

Most players interviewed spoke very highly of the organisation and were clearly grateful for the financial help received to undertake post-

Barry Prenderville in action for Shelbourne in 2003. He retired from the game through injury at the age of thirty and is now Soccer Development Officer at the National University of Ireland in Maynooth. Picture: ©Inpho

career educational courses and training.[118] Barry Prenderville stated that he received assistance in the organisation of his mortgage while at a football league club and also in gaining funding for post-career courses undertaken, where up to £5,000 was available. Despite this, he struggled with a number of employment positions after his early retirement from the game through injury, working as a taxi driver, postman and estate agent before eventually gaining employment in football as a development officer at the National University of Ireland in Maynooth.[119] He felt that:

> You can't expect anybody to come out and give you anything because you played football. I'd say a lot of fellas say, 'well I'll

> just go into something because I played football and that will open a door' – it doesn't and you have to go out and get your qualifications. If you want to work in a bank you'll still have to go and get your qualifications, nobody's going to [hand it to you]. And in some ways, you're sort of hampered, because you're ten to fifteen years behind everybody else in that job.[120]

Seamus Kelly has also spoken of the PFA's assistance in funding a number of college courses he undertook having retired from professional football in Britain in the early 2000s.[121] According to Seamus Heath, who also received assistance for courses, most players wouldn't think too much about retirement:

> In my era, you thought football went on forever. And you don't realise 'till now when you're advising other people how quickly it goes in. No, from my experience, from 1979 to 1990, there wasn't advice, you just played. You thought it was going on forever, and that was it.[122]

Mick Meagan admitted that, like a number of his fellow players in the 1950s and 1960s, he had neglected to take out a pension scheme, although one of his former clubs, Everton, help their former players through the Everton Foundation.[123] Another lesser-known organisation for retired ex-footballers is the charity X-Pro, which caters for all of those who have worked in professional football, whether as players, coaches, physios or club staff, and aims to provide legal, financial, physical and psychological services.[124] In 1995 a trust fund was launched in Manchester to help former Republic of Ireland players who had fallen on hard times, with Terry Conroy one of the main organisers of the event. Around 100 players were said to have joined, but the extent of its success is unclear.[125] There is some indication that governing bodies for football in other countries have set up funds for former players, with former Argentina captain Antonio Rattin involved in the organisation, *Asociacion Mutual Casa del Futbolista*, which helps retired players and oversees matches for veteran players in his country.[126]

THE RETURN TO LEAGUE OF IRELAND AND IRISH LEAGUE FOOTBALL BY IRISH-BORN FOOTBALL MIGRANTS

Research on the post-playing careers of Irish-born footballers indicates that of 262 Republic of Ireland-born players' places of settlement positively identified from the 1945–2010 period, 146 players or 55.72 per cent have returned to the Republic of Ireland while 102 or 38.93 per cent have chosen to remain in England and Wales. This means just 5.35 per cent of the total have settled outside these countries. Of the countries of settlement of 250 Northern Irish-born, lesser numbers of players have decided to return home. Some 116 players or 46.4 per cent have returned to Northern Ireland while 100 or 40 per cent have stayed in England and Wales, which may be a reflection of the Troubles (1968–98). The work of Johanne Devlin Trew (2010), based on ninety-two 'returned and non-returned migrants from Northern Ireland', has illustrated how some interviewees for her study expressed an uneasiness with returning to live there until the early twenty-first century and that 'developing a sense of belonging' to Northern Ireland has been difficult irrespective of religious denomination.[127] Hubert Barr admitted when interviewed for this book that he initially did not want to go back there because of the violent conflict after retiring from the game in the early 1970s although, with the country presently more stable, he and his wife now reside in Northern Ireland.[128] Seamus Heath returned to Belfast in the late 1980s prior to the ceasefires of 1994 although his family later made the decision to move outside the city, as his Welsh-born wife was not used to the political situation there:

> If we'd have stayed in Belfast, she'd have went back home. The bits that were sad, for example, you'd probably hear, Europa Hotel, bomb going off, I'd go up the stairs, look out the skylight and go, 'Oh, just blown Europa up.' Now I'm saying that just in casual talk, that's how we did it [to cope with the Troubles]. For my missus, that was a shock to her system. We'd a shop in the Ormeau Road and five doors down was the bookie's massacre

> [in February 1992 when the Ulster Freedom Fighters killed five people and injured nine in retaliation for the Teebane Bombing], where they came in one day and killed almost everybody. My missus couldn't hack it, so we had to get away, so we moved out to the country to give our kids a wee chance.[129]

Being released, injuries which meant the end of a full-time professional career, homesickness, offers to play in Irish leagues and the desire to make a new start were some of the reasons cited by those interviewed as to why they decided to return to Ireland.[130] Brendan Bradley stated he just didn't like living in England and returned home from Lincoln after only a year.[131] Some former players became disillusioned with football in England and were eager to get home, with Shane Supple citing some other professionals' poor attitudes to the game and a lack of team spirit as problematic, while Brian Mooney was unhappy with the way an injury he received was treated.[132] Michael McHugh returned home while still in his twenties, having become 'fed up' with the managerial disorganisation of his new club, Scarborough, after joining them from Bradford City and he wanted to get home and 'start afresh' despite offers of trials with other English clubs.[133] Roderick has written that 'for the majority of players, the conjunction of ageing and injury, in a situation where discomfort and pain are accepted features of football life, finally brings about an end to their careers'.[134] As shown above, some players have decided to cut short their professional careers in England when they might have continued in more satisfactory circumstances. Players' relationships with families and girlfriends have also influenced the decision to return home. Barry Prenderville felt that, as a young single man at the time, the fact he didn't get to meet someone and get married over there influenced his decision not to stay in England, with Brian Mooney stating, 'I think another aspect of it is a lot of lads who did well would have met girls over there and settled down and [they] would have had a more stabilising effect on them.'[135]

Table 6.2 Number of Irish-born football migrants identified as having returned to Ireland to play League of Ireland or Irish League football, 1945–2010.

Years of migration	Number positively identified as having returned to live in the Rep. of Ireland	Number and percentage of those identified who returned to football in Ireland	Number positively identified as having returned to live in Northern Ireland	Number and percentage of those identified who returned to football in Ireland
1945–55	20	18 (90%)	28	21 (75%)
1956–65	17	17 (100%)	16	15 (93.75%)
1966–75	17	16 (94.11%)	10	9 (90%)
1976–85	15	14 (93.33%)	22	16 (72.72%)
1986–95	43	40 (93.02%)	17	14 (82.35%)
1996–2005	31	25 (80.64%)	20	20 (100%)
2006–10	3	1 (33.3%)	3	3 (100%)
Overall Total	**146**	**131 (89.72%)**	**116**	**98 (84.48%)**

Sources: As Table 5.6.

As shown in Table 6.2, of those 1945–2010 players who could be positively identified as having returned to the Republic of Ireland and Northern Ireland having finished their careers in England, the majority from both nations returned to Irish League or League of Ireland football, although data for the 2006–10 period indicates a large number still playing. Almost 90 per cent of the 146 Republic of Ireland-born players who returned to Ireland took up careers in League of Ireland or Irish League football, while 84 per cent of the 116 born in Northern Ireland did the same, which is indicative of a desire to continue playing at a lower professional level in the country of their birth before they finally retire from playing the game, and an interest on the part of League of Ireland and Irish League clubs to recruit native players with proven experience of English football.

Some players from both countries evidently came back to play for their home-town clubs, such as Bobby Burke, who spent one season at Burnley in the 1950s before joining Ballymena United.[136] Some others such as Billy Dickson, who left Glenavon to join Notts County in

1946 and later returned to the Irish League club after twelve seasons in England with clubs including Chelsea, Arsenal and Mansfield Town, returned to the clubs they had migrated from.[137] Some were influenced by friendships within the game in their choice of Irish-based club along with a club's reputation, with John Giles, Eamon Dunphy and Ray Treacy returning in the 1970s in an attempt to develop Shamrock Rovers into a force in European football.[138] While more general studies of Irish emigration indicate that the 1970s saw 'a significant reversal in Irish demographic history' with 'the numbers immigrating into independent Ireland exceeding those leaving', there is no real indication the above figures (while covering only those players who could be positively identified as returning) reflected this overall pattern in this decade, or that Irish professional football benefited hugely from the improved prosperity of the economy at that time.[139] Although the number of high-profile players who return to professional football in Ireland has lessened significantly since the late twentieth century, a few players continue to do so, with Keith Gillespie's move to Longford Town in 2011 coming through the encouragement of his agent and what the former Northern Ireland international saw as 'the chance to get off the dole, and back in the game'.[140]

Not all Irish football migrants were put off coming back to live in Northern Ireland by the Troubles. Financial considerations affected the choice to move north or south in some cases, with Martin Russell stating, in regard to his move back to Ireland to play for Irish League club Portadown in 1991:

> I was probably able to just get by in terms of week to week stuff. [I was] able to pay towards the mortgage with the money that was in the Irish League at the time, that was, I think, the attraction of going there. At the time, [in] the League of Ireland, down south, there wasn't the sort of investment going into the clubs, it was the north. That sort of has changed, and changed again in the time I've been back, where some of the clubs down here ended up paying a lot of money to players and then went bust. But I was able to get by on a few quid coming through Portadown.[141]

Alan Blayney pictured in action for Linfield. A former Northern Ireland international, having returned to Ireland in 2007, he was voted Ulster Footballer of the Year in 2011 and has captained Linfield to domestic league and cup success. Picture: © Inpho

This decision appears to be part of a wider trend of League of Ireland players moving to the Irish League in the early 1990s.[142] Similarly, Alan Blayney's release from Oldham Athletic while in his late twenties saw him given the opportunity of football in the League of Ireland with Bohemians at a time before League of Ireland clubs ran into financial difficulties in the late 2000s, and he felt that the prospect of a salary was better than going on trials at lower-league English clubs.[143] Blayney went on to have a more successful career in Irish League football having returned to live with his family in Belfast, winning the Ulster Footballer of the Year in 2011.[144] Michael Carvill favoured a return to Northern Ireland on leaving Wrexham rather than playing in the Conference, which he describes as 'just another dog-eat-dog league', and has instead embraced life in the Irish League:

> [I] returned home to Linfield, and I really, really enjoyed it and it's good to be back, and I love travelling down to training, and

David Miskelly in action for Portadown in 2013 having returned from Oldham Athletic after a shoulder injury hampered his full-time involvement in professional football. Picture: © Inpho

> it's so weird for me, travelling to training, coming home and seeing my mum and dad, talking about it, because at sixteen I never had that, they never [saw me], they rang me all the time, but it's repetitive, it was so weird. And then my mum and dad came and watched me [in the Irish League] and all, and I'd go out with friends after the match. It was just what you miss about home, because, [it was] a mad gap, sixteen to twenty-one, I've missed out on what all my mates were doing, having the time of their lives. It's good to be back, I really, really enjoyed it.[145]

Similarly, Billy Humphries fitted in smoothly on his return to the Irish League. He joined Ards for a third time in 1968 having left

Swansea. He began to take night classes which led to a full-time job in personnel management:

> In my first year back with Ards, George Eastham was the manager and during my first spell at Ards he was the manager there as well at that time. I sort of just got into it, and that particular season [1968–69] we won the Irish Cup so I more or less sort of eased into [Irish League football]. I was named the Sports Writers' Player of the Year and then I got two Ulster Footballer of the Year titles and I won two Ards Player of the Year awards as well.[146]

Former Oldham goalkeeper David Miskelly felt that beginning work again along with playing in the Irish League after returning from England 'was a culture shock, but at the end of the day if you don't knuckle down and you don't go into work, then your quality of life suffers'.[147]

Most players who returned to play did so while balancing work commitments, while, as noted, only a small number took the opportunity to pursue educational qualifications. As Brian Mooney notes, re-adjusting to football in Ireland can be tough:

> I would have always tried to be very professional – when I came back to League of Ireland [this continued]. I think there's a lot of lads that come back from England, they think League of Ireland's going to be easy – it's not easy, it's a very, very tough league and I think they get a sort of rude awakening when they come back. I found it tough enough and it's a very physical league so I would have knuckled down and would have trained, and because I was off in the day – I wasn't working at that stage – I would have done some extra training myself, because I would have been into that routine.[148]

Without the schedule of training in the morning and a daily professional set-up, Denis Behan found it strange, and time management was problematic:

> My last game was at Southampton, 36,000 [present], I came back to Limerick and there was like 680, you know, a wall around it, a stand that held 1,500 people sitting, dressing room that was the size of my sitting room here, you know it's a big culture shock. [You] can't swap a jersey at the end of the game because they've only one set for the year, all this kind of thing, they seem insignificant but … when you're used to it, it is tough. We'd train Monday, Tuesday, off Wednesday, Thursday, match Friday, and then come in again on Saturday and Sunday. But going from getting up in the morning and going to training, to waiting 'till six o'clock for training, was a massive kind of cultural change for me so I had to find something to do, to spend my time during the day.[149]

Raymond Campbell felt that adapting to the Irish League and a different lifestyle, managing work along with dietary requirements, training and fitness levels, travelling and playing requires a lot of dedication to the game.[150] Similarly, Seamus Heath felt that making the switch from training in the morning to the evening could be difficult, with the usual morning training buzz missing until the evening, with the result that it could affect a player's moods and make sleep difficult after the high of late-night training.[151] He has also stated that a number of players he knew have suffered from weight problems and drinking because they don't know what to do with their time.[152] A less professional environment could mean additional difficulties. Barry Prenderville felt that he was never the same player after an ankle operation while in his mid-twenties, having injured his ankle when he returned to play in the League of Ireland:

> I think if I'd had that injury when I was in the UK I would have got to the bottom of that, because you were in the League of Ireland, the backup wasn't there really … so I had my operation and that was it. I had a stabbing pain, I was taking a lot of anti-inflammatories for training and never really recovered and I suppose that was my toughest time because I couldn't be as good as I wanted to be.[153]

Brian Mooney seen here in action for Republic of Ireland's B team in a 4–1 win over England B in 1990. He returned to education while continuing to play League of Ireland football after leaving English football. Picture: © Inpho

The *Commission on Emigration* noted that 'many emigrants to Great Britain intend to return to Ireland later in life, although the intention may weaken in course of time'.[154] Gerard Leavey, Sati Sembhi and Gill Livingstone have described 'the myth of return' as 'the unfulfilled expectation or desire of the migrant to return to their country of origin' and have illustrated how 'the myth provides the individual with both a strategy for both maintaining identity and affirming belonging in a community which stretches from home land to new land'.[155] A common theme throughout Irish studies of migrants returning home has been the struggle to adjust and to establish relationships, as noted by Gmelch (1986, 1987), McGrath (1991), Ní Laoire (2007, 2008) and Ryan (2008) in their work.[156] Enda Delaney has illustrated how, in studies of the post-war years, 'the "myth" of return is a common feature of all migrations, Irish or otherwise' but 'as the number of years spent abroad increased, marriage, the availability of housing, the purchase of property, as well as lifestyle and income aspirations, all worked against the realization of the eventual homecoming'.[157] Additionally, 'once children started school, it was even more difficult to contemplate the prospect of the upheaval involved in returning to Ireland'.[158] These factors have also affected Irish football migrants in their post-English football decisions. Seamus Heath also felt that in regard to settling in England post-career,

> I just think sometimes people embrace it and maybe have a family and maybe their wife's family's there and they're in it, but the other side of it [is] … home is home. I was fortunate that when I said I would like to go back home to live, my wife said, 'Yeh, I'll come with you.' Now if she had to have said, 'I'm not going' … it depends how you settle, do you have a house … sometimes players when they finish say, 'Oh I never bought a house yet' and then get attracted to the home. I just looked at myself and thought I had more opportunities of maybe coaching, business [in Northern Ireland], which has proven right but I didn't know that at the time.[159]

Despite this, not every player made a clear-cut decision to settle in England or Ireland, with Damien Richardson noting that, although he returned to Ireland to manage after his term in charge of Gillingham had ended, he would have no problem going back to England to live:

> I loved my time there, I was there for twenty-three, twenty-four years … [we] go back on a regular basis, my wife wants to go back full-time to England, so I've great admiration for England and English people, and I would willingly live there. I've been very lucky that I'm equally at home in either country.[160]

Statistics for Northern Ireland-born players whose places of settlement were identified here also illustrate that 13.6 per cent of 1945–2010 players took up permanent residence outside Britain and Ireland. They also showed slightly more diversity in relocating outside of Europe to places such as South Africa and New Zealand as well as North America and Australia. These were generally positions in management or coaching although there were some exceptions: former Manchester City player Frank McCourt became a prison guard in Vancouver, Eric Ross became an estate agent in the same city while Dave Clements became a candyfloss vending executive in Denver.[161]

A NEW IDENTITY?

Post-retirement remains a problem for many players in terms of their identity, the excitement the game provides for players and its related lifestyle. As Roderick has stated, 'One might well argue that professional football is a vocation or perhaps, *a calling*.'[162] He also noted how 'talent in football is accorded special value among certain groups in society and retains, for some, an aura of mystery: some players possess talent which is hard for others to fathom.'[163] Brendan Bradley, who retired in the late 1980s, felt that 'when you stop playing, it sort of comes like a bombshell … you still miss it yet.'[164] Similarly, Damien Richardson was of the opinion that 'there's a degree of escapism about football … I still miss being a player dreadfully … there's nothing better than being a professional footballer, being a player.'[165] Some players, such as Seamus Heath and Mick Meagan, continue to play at an amateur level after retiring from professional football. As Raymond Campbell states, football is an addiction:

> It's in my blood, to be honest, with all the camaraderie … I'm still playing at the minute, training with the boys, the craic, the feel-good aspect of it, you know, the competitiveness is still there, with the team that I'm playing for [Northern Ireland Veterans], you know it's just the general buzz of the game. I very rarely watch it, but I still really enjoy playing it.[166]

Quite recently, the mental health issues affecting those still playing, as well as those who have been forced to consider life outside the game, have been highlighted in the media, with Clarke Carlisle, Warren

Aspinall, Dean Windass and Lee Hendry all admitting to suffering from depression.[167] Former Republic of Ireland international, Jason McAteer, has also spoken publicly of his post-career problems and while now recovering after seeking help, he has admitted to taking 'six or seven baths a day' just 'for something to do'.[168] The deaths of Agostino Di Bartolomei, Gary Speed and Robert Enke have also illustrated how top-level players are at risk, while Stan Collymore's problems with depression were dismissed by his manager at the time. Northern Ireland-born player Steven McAdam's tragic death in 2004, having suffered from ME, led his family to question the healthcare system when dealing with mentally ill patients.[169]

With an increase in campaigns to promote awareness of depression within Irish society in recent years, the Professional Footballers' Association of Ireland and player welfare associations within other sports have been keen to lend their support, with Bohemians FC wearing the 'Lean on Me' logo on their shirts during a Setanta Cup game in 2012.[170] As Seamus Kelly has stated, 'speak-up campaigns' are now in place within professional clubs in an attempt 'to alleviate these barriers and facilitate anonymous consultation with expert medical and counselling personnel' although he admits this acceptance of mental health issues has historically not always been the case within the football industry.[171]

The case of David Langan is certainly a pitiful one, and some comparisons can be drawn with former players who suffered from drink-related problems including George Best, Garrincha and Gazza, although Langan was obviously more of a journeyman player than these former greats. There are also echoes of the case of pre-war England trial player, Jim Dillimore.[172] While Langan's case has been well publicised, less is known about lower-league Irish- (and British-) born players who have been forced to seek employment outside of the game and have battled with addictions. Part of the reason for this is the social stigma attached to problems such as alcoholism, gambling or depression, and the fact that their difficulties are not highlighted in the media as they may be deemed not worthy of attention.[173] Therefore, the case of David Langan may be more common than is publicly known.

Despite this, not every player who has retired early or failed to earn enough in the game to be financially secure for the rest of their lives is unhappy about the way their career turned out. Former Millwall player and London Underground employee, Robbie Ryan, who played in the 2004 FA Cup final, has stated in a newspaper interview that 'I'm happy now. My job is a good one. I've got a nice life. I've got lovely memories from football but I've moved on.'[174] A few players, including Shane Supple and Ciaran Lyng, have attempted to maintain a high level of performance in other sports after retiring from English football by playing Gaelic football at inter-county level, although Supple is no longer involved with his county team and has returned to play soccer in Dublin with Bohemians along with Gaelic football for St Brigid's.[175] When asked to compare playing for Dublin with Ipswich Town, he indicated a closer identity with team-mates within Gaelic football:

> It's different and similar – we still have big crowds, sometimes bigger than soccer, but it's not weekly, which is hard. Soccer is a different game for a goalkeeper, you're not as busy in Gaelic which is frustrating but you have more identity with the Dublin players than those in England.[176]

Returning to Gaelic football is not a new phenomenon, with Tyrone underage star Mickey McCay, who had a spell at Leicester City in the early 1970s without playing a league game, returning to Tyrone GAA and featuring in the 1975 All-Ireland minor final. However, the decision by Supple and Lyng to switch sports is generally the exception rather than the norm among the 917 post-war Irish-born players who have experience of professional league football in England.[177] An analysis of 436 teenage players who were selected for Republic of Ireland under 16 squads between 1997 and 2009 has shown that just six of them (1.37 per cent) joined Gaelic football clubs after deciding they had no future in professional football.[178]

Although he admits he was 'totally unprepared' for retirement and that it was 'a total culture shock being anything other than a footballer', Richie Sadlier expressed similar sentiments to those of Ryan about his present career, stating that 'you're never not a footballer in people eyes' but 'I don't see myself in those terms anymore which is the important bit'.[179] He also admits to having 'a fierce amount of variety' in his life at the moment. Finding a daily structure appears to be an important part of making the switch to a non-playing career, as Sadlier recalls:

> [Immediately after retiring] you're not part of a group – I was at school, and then I was part of a football team. So there's a load of people involved in both, and you have to be places. There's a responsibility, you're part of a team, and you're going to be missed if you're not there, and all your focus, particularly in football and what you ate and where you went, who you hung around with, your sleep pattern, everything is dictated by the fact that you're a footballer, and what people talk to you about, 95–99 per cent of the conversation, the topic would be about football, because most people just see you … 'you're Richie the footballer' and that's the box you're put into and that's fine and then you go from that and you're not and you're something else … what do you do (laughs)? That's hard like, that's really hard, because it's all so consuming.[180]

Dealing with new career prospects, making adjustments and accepting a change in identity is perhaps crucial to overcoming the move from playing career to retirement. This is partially because clubs and agents generally organise day-to-day matters for many first-team players, particularly at the highest levels. In fact, some clubs actively discouraged players from thinking too much about what would happen when their careers were finished, as Sadlier notes:

> [It] would have been a token gesture if anyone at the club mentioned it. [It] would be, 'Do you fancy doing anything in the evening, a course or anything?' Just to say that they'd said it. I remember when I was worrying that I mightn't recover from my injury, and I said it to my agent, my agent said it to the chairman, the chairman said it to the manager, and I was called in the next

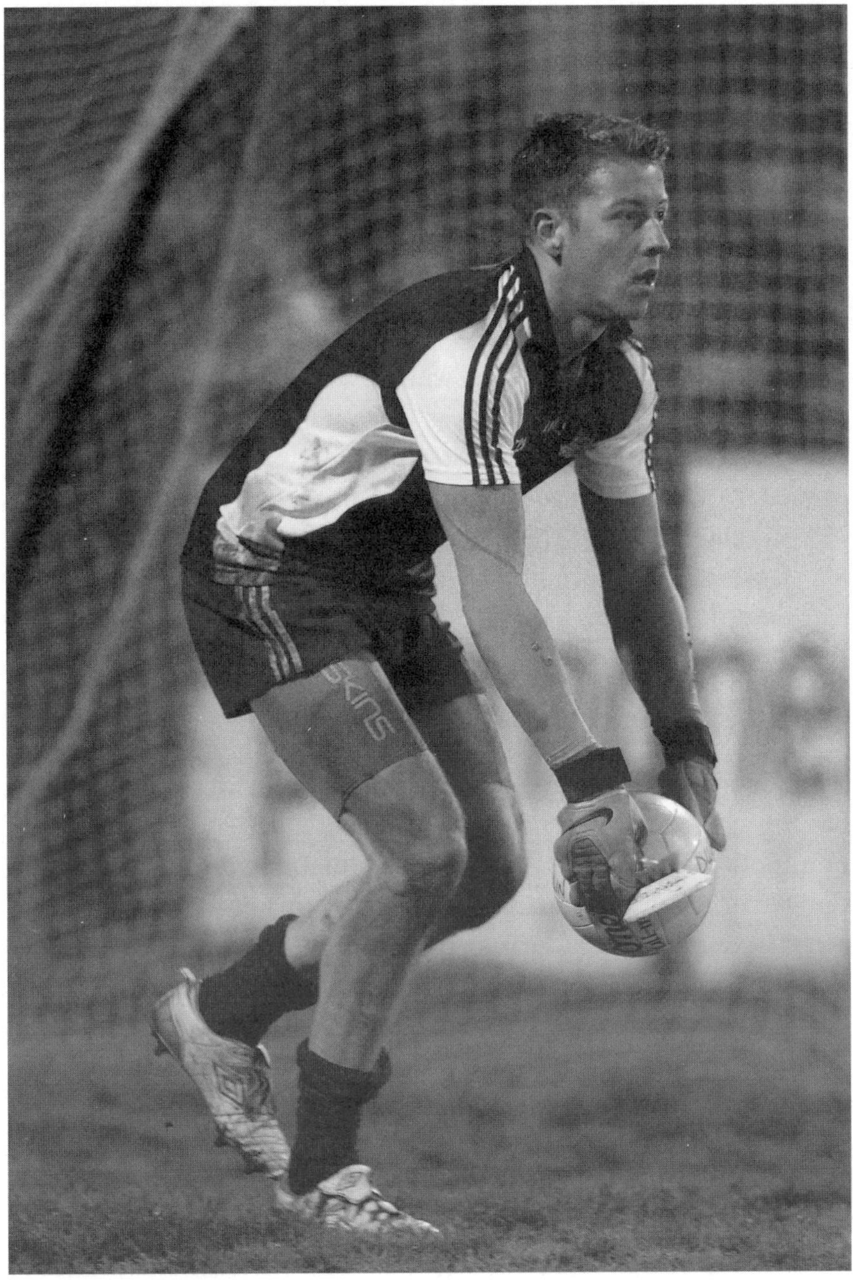

Shane Supple has fulfilled a life-long ambition to play for Dublin's Gaelic football team and won an All-Ireland medal in 2013 having returned home from England after becoming disillusioned with professional football there. Picture: © Inpho

> day and I was given a bit of a telling off, going, 'Stop thinking of life after football, this is what your focus should be on, you'll be fine.' So it was actively discouraged, because the thinking within a football club is … and going back to when you're sixteen and you're told, 'You've got to believe you're the one, in this group, you've got to believe that you're the one that's going to make it', so it doesn't allow a huge amount of effort or conversation around post-playing careers … I would do all these things on the off chance that I'm one of the nineteen or twenty that's not going to make it, and even when I was a pro facing the possible scenario of retirement, I was discouraged from discussing the possibility of retirement. So if you're going to prepare for life after football, you've got to do it on your own terms away from the club. It's not in their interests to really make you aware of the fact that this is all going to end one day, they want your focus on Saturday and that's it.[181]

CONCLUSION

As shown by Barrett and Mosca, the problem of social isolation has been a recurring feature of the noted experiences of returning non-football migrants.[182] Therefore, maintaining an identity within the game has probably been beneficial to many players, although some have felt it necessary to no longer primarily see themselves as footballers. The work of Brown and Potrac has shown how the emotional trauma of de-selection can be traced to a total focus on developing as a player, the result of which is 'a one-dimensional identity based around their footballing performances' and scarce interests outside the game on retirement.[183] Irish-born players have also had, like those scholars interviewed, 'varying degrees of success' in adapting to their new identities after retiring.[184] Post-career, most Irish-born players have stayed relatively near home, and have generally looked to take up positions related to football. Kuper and Szymanski have noted the importance of players' 'status as an icon' in clubs' recruiting of managers and believe that 'popular ex-players often get the job because they are easily accepted by fans, media and players'.[185] This attitude has been beneficial to some Irish-born players in finding post-career work, with the 2007 sacking of Republic of Ireland manager, Steve Staunton, illustrating the frailties within the FAI's recruitment structures at the time, and the culture of giving posts to former stars which prevails within football.

While the work of the PFA in assisting those who retire must be commended, the responsibility for placing greater emphasis on education and post-career options and making players more aware of the failure rate, and post-career choices, lies with those running football clubs. Some Irish schoolboy clubs, such as St Kevin's Boys and Belvedere, are remarkably open in their advice to players and parents about the low rates of trainees breaking into professional football.[186] Some players interviewed have also stated that their English clubs made it very clear to them just how slim the chances of getting a future professional contract were while they were serving trainee terms.[187] However, clubs themselves may need to look at their education structures and offer players more concrete alternatives when they are not actually on the training ground or involved in matches, given the amount of free time available.

Eamon Dunphy wrote in 2013 that professional football in the 1960s was 'a way of life that induced boredom … after a couple of hours' training each morning professional footballers faced long, empty days with very little to do'.[188] The case of Keith Gillespie, who went bankrupt, largely through financial mismanagement, indicates that structures for players outside some professional football clubs have changed little since Dunphy's time, and that providing constructive activities off the field is still neglected.[189] In turn, preparing for the future is not something that is given huge consideration by either clubs or players. The lack of educational qualifications common among Irish footballers would indicate that most have little choice in attempting to stay in the game in some capacity after retiring. Perhaps it is time for a lowering of expectations among players hoping to remain in football after retiring, and for more effective career guidance from the clubs themselves to those they are recruiting into the game.

CHAPTER 7

The Decline of Irish-born Football Migrants in Top-flight English League Football

> What can they offer people to stay, the League of Ireland clubs? They can't even offer a one-year contract, like that's the highest contract you can get, League of Ireland, one year.[1]
>
> Interview with Dean Kelly, 13 January 2014

INTRODUCTION

Despite its glamorous image on television and in the media, as has been shown, professional football can be a ruthless business, and since the Second World War, the numbers of Irish-born players who have played at the highest levels of club football in England, and at senior international level, are outweighed by those featuring in lower leagues and remaining uncapped at that level. The majority of Irish-born football migrants who moved to England in the period from 1945 to 2010 have not played in the Premier League or former First Division or for their country. Levels of Republic of Ireland-born players appearing in top-flight English football and at international level have dropped since the 1976–85 period while a decrease in those playing at the highest level of English league football has also been noted since 1986–95 for those born in Northern Ireland. The number of players who do not manage to establish an average term of professional career, by footballing standards, is high and a number of those with experience of English league football interviewed as part of this study have called for a more efficient structure to be put in place to cater for aspiring young Irish players before they move abroad, and when they return home. This chapter also identifies how many of these players had pre-migration experience of a professional set-up through being contracted by League of Ireland or Irish League clubs and explores if this was found to lengthen players' careers in the English game after migration as opposed to those who did not experience this before moving.[2] This theme is particularly relevant given recent media debates regarding whether young Irish players should delay their movement to English clubs.[3]

THE ATTRACTION OF ENGLISH FOOTBALL

Sports sociologist Richard Elliott's reasons for Irish footballers' migration to English league football has illustrated some crossover with Delaney's assessment of more general migrants' reasons for choosing Britain as a place of employment. A lack of opportunities to play professional football at an adequate level in Ireland, the availability of a higher standard of football in England, geographical distance, a similar culture and a tradition of migrating there means that the route to England to progress as a professional footballer is 'a well-developed and potentially self-sustaining one'.[4] In addition, while non-EU players have at times struggled to obtain work permits to play in Britain and have needed to illustrate international status, Irish-born players have been free from this restriction with, on paper, little difference between players born in Dublin and London, for example, in this regard.[5]

As a spectacle, soccer in Ireland in the early twenty-first century struggles to attract the attention given to it until the 1970s. As stated earlier, the advent of live televised English football on Sundays initially impacted on interest levels in the domestic game, given that Sunday afternoon was the day for League of Ireland football, while the best Irish players are usually playing abroad.[6] In 1992, then Bohemians president Brendan Duffy and a League of Ireland delegation were able to secure a decision in their favour from a UEFA committee in regard to gaining compensation from English clubs Arsenal and Huddersfield Town, who had signed amateur players from Bohemians. This came as part of a UEFA 'principles' ruling, inaugurated in 1990, which meant that the previous club could seek compensation for training and development if the players, aged between fourteen and thirty, went on to become professionals.[7]

Irish clubs are now more adequately compensated for the loss of players via compensation under a FIFA ruling, implemented in 2001, although professional football in Ireland still struggles to compete with the interest levels given to Gaelic football and rugby as spectator sports and to generate sufficient revenue to provide an alternative to the attraction of the English Premier League.[8] At the same time, with the permanent absence of a proper professional structure hindered by a lack of finance and the GAA's strong parish and county identity to some degree, movement to Britain remains the best choice for these players.

THE STRENGTH OF FOREIGN TALENT

While traditionally Manchester United, Liverpool and Arsenal (particularly in the late 1970s) have been renowned for their Irish players, by 2010 John O'Shea, Darron Gibson and Jonny Evans of Manchester United were the lone Irish-born players appearing for any of these clubs in the Premier League, illustrating the strength of foreign talent there.[9] In fact, there were just twenty Republic of Ireland-born players featuring in the English Premier League during the 2010–11 season, while only seven players were born in Northern Ireland.[10] In his assessment of the recruitment of foreign players into the English league between 1946 and 1995, Patrick McGovern has shown that 'since the [English] league recommenced in 1946, the vast majority (87.4%) of non-English players came from the "Celtic fringe" of Scotland, Northern Ireland and the Irish Republic', with Scottish players making up the largest contribution.[11] However, 'after the 1960s, the volume of Scottish and Irish signings declined until it eventually fell below that coming from overseas after the mid-1980s', and in the period from 1976 until 1995, recruits into the English league became 'increasingly international in nature'.[12] This trend has continued to the present day, with the failure of the England football team to achieve victory in the World Cup since 1966, or European Championship, being linked by PFA chief executive Gordon Taylor, former England manager Roy Hodgson and a number of sports writers to the reduction in the pool of homegrown talent available as a consequence of clubs' tendencies to import foreign players, rather than give locally born players a chance.

Although the ban which had effectively been in place since 1931 on bringing non-British footballers into English football was removed in 1978 and led to the signing of players such as two of Argentina's World Cup stars, Ricky Villa and Ossie Ardiles, by Tottenham Hotspur, there was some opposition shown by the PFA.[13] Despite this, Matthew Taylor has stated that 'it is possible to detect the beginnings of what might be called the "Europeanisation" or "internationalisation" of British professional football' at this time.[14] He also feels that 'the 1990s witnessed a considerable influx of foreign players and coaches at British clubs', and the number of non-British players registered with Premier League clubs grew from eleven in its opening season (1992–93) to over 400 by August 2000.[15] The 1995 Bosman ruling 'was undoubtedly significant' in assisting increased player movement while higher financial gains for players at English clubs, which came with satellite television deals and affluent owners willing to spend big, meant that Britain went from being 'an oasis of foreign talent into a prime destination for the modern football migrant'.[16]

By the end of the 1990s, the Premier League had grown to a stature comparable to Serie A and La Liga in the global market, and homegrown talent has increasingly struggled to cement first-team places in England's top flight. Hugh McIlvanney, formerly of the *Sunday Times*, revealed in 2013 that the percentage of English footballers starting matches in the English Premier League between 27 March and 24 April that year (30.79 per cent) was the lowest ratio of native players represented in each of the top five leagues in Europe.[17] By 2015, the English Premier League's percentage of 'expatriates' or percentage of 'squad members who play outside the association where they began playing football' was calculated to be 59.9 per cent and was second only to Cyprus (66.4 per cent), with Chelsea having the highest 'percentage of expatriates by club' in England at 83.3 per cent, while the lowest percentage was recorded at Bournemouth (33.3 per cent).[18] In contrast, the Bundesliga's overall average was just 45.9 per cent. English Premier League clubs had a percentage of only 0.40 'debutant players' or 'players without previous experience in adult leagues launched by their employer club since the start of the year' in 2015, illustrating the general failure of clubs to bring through homegrown players.[19] In addition, the percentage of English Premier League 'squad members who played at least three seasons between the age of 15 and 21 for their employed club' dropped from 17 per cent in 2009 to just 11.7 per cent in 2015.[20]

Although this theory behind international failure has been refuted by Kuper and Szymanski, there can be little doubt that increased competition for positions in Premier League teams has also led to the squeezing out of Irish players who may have been able to command places in teams in the First Division during the 1980s, prior to the Premier League's establishment.[21] The volume of foreign players in the First Division was minimal in the early part of this decade, with only thirty-three registered in September 1980.[22] For example, an assessment of Brighton & Hove Albion and Manchester United's squads for the 1983 FA Cup final illustrates that seven Irish-born players, along with three other Irish internationals, were involved in these clubs at the time, while Irish homegrown talent as well as British-born Republic of Ireland internationals had a strong influence in Liverpool's success at various stages of the 1980s.[23] According to Richie Sadlier:

> Back in that time, you were only competing with the best of Britain and maybe some others. Now you're competing with the best of Africa, South America … there's nowhere that's beyond the reach of the Premier League, so it's much more difficult, simple numbers wise, to be the best in the world, rather than to be the best among Britain and Ireland. In its simplest terms,

> the talent pool is a hundred times the size of what it was twenty years ago for the lads that were playing then.[24]

Similarly, Barry Prenderville was of the opinion that:

> You're now competing with the whole world, I mean it's the biggest, the richest league in the world, so you're dealing with scouts that are doing South America, they're doing North America, they're doing Europe, they're scouting the world, Chinese, Japanese players, the best of them … so that's the only reason [for the declining number of Irish players in the Premier League]. There's some good Irish players out there, but it's nothing to do with the quality. There maybe was better quality, you know, maybe fifteen years ago, in the Irish squad, but I think it's cyclical as well, I think that goes in cycles. It's unfortunate, but it's the same for England, they haven't got many players playing in the Premier League either, they have a very small pool as well.[25]

Seamus Heath has stated that with the academy systems now in place and the amount of training talented underage players can get per week, an aspiring Irish-born player would need to be in England at the age of twelve to have any chance of competing with those being developed by their clubs in terms of making it into the Premier League, although he admitted there are some exceptions.[26] He cites the example of a top Irish League club, Cliftonville, whose under 13 structure gives young players training for two hours, twice a week with a match at the weekend, while those who are part of Everton's under 12 squad train four nights a week, get two afternoons out of school and play a match at the weekend.[27] Hubert Barr noted how his great-grandson who resides in England was already on the books of a Championship club, despite still being at primary school, and was training there three times a week during the school holidays.[28] Raymond Campbell also noted how young Irish-born players were at a disadvantage in this regard, as they only get over to England during school holidays.[29]

Some players were of the view that street football has now more or less disappeared in Ireland and this may have impacted on the talent being produced. Hubert Barr, who learned his early football 'up an entry and a big garage at the end of it … booting the ball against the garage to score a goal', admitted that he sees few children playing football on the streets in his native town of Ballymena these days – 'there just isn't any of that about now' – and that this lack of practice is probably a factor in the decline in top-flight players being produced in his country.[30] Alan Blayney felt that today, parks were generally empty of kids playing football, unlike when he grew up in the 1980s and that 'it's just like a computer-game generation, they all want to just sit in the house and play computer games'.[31] Brendan Bradley similarly felt that nowadays children 'were all in[side] playing these games, and it's not the right thing … not just because of football, but it's their health as well'.[32] Increased lifestyle choices have also affected children's interest levels in the game, according to John McClelland.[33] Similarly, along with a lesser standard of coaching than was available in England, Shane Supple felt that the Celtic Tiger of the late 1990s and early years of the new millennium, which saw the Republic of Ireland briefly become a more affluent society, may have had a negative effect on professional player production.[34] Billy Humphries felt that an increase in facilities had led to the decline of street football, although he doubted if coaching was any more beneficial to players' development than playing in the streets, as young players were prone to get bored with being coached all the time.[35] Coaching styles in European football, as opposed to those in Britain and Ireland, have probably also impacted on the progress of young players. Brian Mooney gave his opinion:

> I think the whole way the game's coached in England and Ireland is completely different to the continent and I think that they concentrate on more technique on the continent whereas over in England it's more physical, big physical athletes rather than touch players so I think that might have something to do with it.[36]

THE DECLINE OF IRISH-BORN PLAYERS IN TOP-FLIGHT ENGLISH FOOTBALL

Table 7.1 Republic of Ireland-born Premier League/pre-1992 First Division and senior international players, 1945–2010.

Period	Overall Total	Overall Percentage appearing in Premier League/old First Division	Number/Percentage of Senior Internationals
1945–55	95	46 (48.42%)	51 (53.68%)
1956–65	41	21 (51.21%)	28 (68.29%)
1966–75	41	22 (53.65%)	23 (56.09%)
1976–85	33	23 (69.69%)	17 (51.51%)
1986–95	90	31 (34.44%)	24 (26.66%)
1996–2005	148	40 (27.02%)	48 (32.43%)
2006–10	52	8 (15.38%)	9 (17.30%)
Total	**500**	**191 (38.2%)**	**200 (40%)**

Source: As Table 1.2 above.

The decline in the number of Irish-born players featuring at the highest levels of English football, and being capped at senior international level, is illustrated in Tables 7.1 and 7.2. While the numbers of Republic of Ireland-born players recruited per decade and playing in the football leagues has increased from ninety-five in the 1945–55 period to 148 during 1996–2005, the rates of these players appearing in top-flight football has dropped from 48.42 per cent in the early period to 27.02 per cent in the latter. Similarly, while the percentage of players recruited in the years from 1945 to 1955 who were capped by the Republic at senior international level was almost 54 per cent, this had decreased to 32.43 per cent for those who signed in the 1996–2005 period. The percentage of Republic of Ireland-born players who played top-flight English football was greatest in the 1976–85 period (69.69 per cent) although this was also when the overall number signed per decade was much lower (thirty-three). More recent figures for the first half of the decade after 2005 have also shown little improvement, with a decline in the number of those playing Premier League football (15.38 per cent) and appearing at senior international level (17.3 per cent).

Table 7.2 Northern Ireland-born Premier League/pre-1992 First Division and senior international players, 1945–2010.

Period	Overall Total	Overall Percentage appearing in Premier League/old First Division	Number/Percentage of Senior Internationals
1945–55	102	49 (48.03%)	34 (33.33%)
1956–65	67	33 (49.25%)	36 (53.73%)
1966–75	61	27 (44.26%)	33 (54.09%)
1976–85	49	21 (42.85%)	23 (46.93%)
1986–95	41	19 (46.34%)	25 (60.97%)
1996–2005	82	17 (20.73%)	36 (43.90%)
2006–10	15	1 (6.66%)	8 (53.33%)
Total	**417**	**167 (40.04%)**	**195 (46.76%)**

Source: As Table 1.2 above.

Figures for Northern Ireland-born players indicate that while the number of players signed and playing league football in the 1945–55 period (102) had dropped to forty-one in the 1986–95 period, eighty-two players were signed professionally and played league football in the 1996–2005 period. However, like those born in the Republic of Ireland, the number of those appearing at the highest levels of English club football had dropped significantly, falling from 48 per cent in 1945–55 to 20.73 per cent in the 1996–2005 period, illustrating the growing international competition to gain a place in Premier League teams. Despite this, figures for those capped internationally per period actually increased since 1945–55, rising from 33 per cent at this time to a peak of almost 61 per cent during the 1986–95 period and dropping again to 43.90 per cent of those signing between 1996 and 2005. More recent figures over the 2006–10 period show a slight rise in those migrating and gaining senior caps but only fifteen players have signed professionally and played league football in this period. This is perhaps reflective of the fact that the pool of players available to Northern Ireland selectors has not been as large due to the country's smaller size.

The average length of career for a Republic of Ireland-born player who migrated between 1945 and 1995 (work on 1996–2010 is incomplete as a number of players are still playing) was found to be 6.5 playing seasons, while Northern Ireland-born players had an average career length of 6.6 playing seasons in the English Premier and Football Leagues. While both figures are quite similar, this highlights the relatively short career of a professional footballer in comparison with other occupations and is in fact shorter than the average career length identified by Gearing of eight and a half years.[37] Recent research indicates that the average stay of a player at an English Premiership club in 2015 was only 2.82 years.[38] Republic of Ireland-born players (1945–95) signed for an average of 2.32 clubs in the English leagues, excluding loans. Northern Ireland-born players in this period signed for an average of 2.47 English Premiership or Football League clubs. Woolridge's analysis of 908 English league players appearing between 1946 and 1985 has demonstrated that just over 45 per cent played for only one club while almost 24 per cent had two clubs during their careers.[39] Therefore Irish-born players in the 1945–2010 period differed slightly in this regard.

CHANGES IN THE PROCESS

Enda Delaney has noted that 'an over-riding characteristic of the emigrant profile was the relative youth of the persons who left twentieth-century Ireland', with the majority of these under thirty years old.[40] Joyce Woolridge has illustrated how from 1955 onwards, more players were making their league debuts as teenagers as 'the profession was experiencing a distinct turn to youth, a policy which was promoted before the Second World War, but gained new momentum during peacetime reconstruction'.[41] An assessment of the ages of players born in the Republic of Ireland who migrated between 1945 and 2010 has shown that the average age of turning professional, i.e. signing with the club and entering the British work force, was 19.3. The average age at which a footballing migrant born in Northern Ireland who moved to England during the same time period signed professionally was found to have been slightly older (19.87 years of age). As shown in Table 7.3, the average age of Republic of Ireland migrants turning professional in this period had dropped from 22.11 in 1945–55 to 19.54 years of age during 2006–10, indicating that players are now being recruited and signing professionally earlier than the initial period. In Northern Ireland, this figure has dropped from an average age of 22.27 years old in the 1945–55 period to 18.2 in 2006–10. Despite this, most English Premier League squads are now generally made up of players in their mid-twenties. Recent work undertaken by the International Centre for Sports Studies Football Observatory has highlighted that the average age of a Premier League squad member on 1 October 2015 was 26.9.[42]

Table 7.3 Average age of Republic of Ireland and Northern Ireland-born players signing as English Premier League/Football League professionals per decade, 1945–2010.

Years	Republic of Ireland-born players	Northern Ireland-born players
1945–55	22.11	22.27
1956–65	20.24	19.7
1966–75	19.17	19.68
1976–85	18.78	19.53
1986–95	18.51	18.4
1996–2005	17.97	18.34
2006–10	19.54	18.2

Source: As Table 1.2 above.

While changes in technology have meant that young migrants can now have more daily contact with those at home, and there is less Anglo-Irish tension since the end of the Troubles, some of those with experience of professional football in England have stated that younger players should reconsider their early migration as trainees.[43] Martin Bayly and Gary Howlett, who returned to the League of Ireland in the 1980s and 1990s respectively after playing in the English Football League, were of the opinion in magazine interviews that players should wait until they are older before migrating.[44] This is not an entirely new idea, with *Irish Independent* reporter Seán Ryan stating in 1973 that 'the truth is that very few of the starry-eyed boys who go over to serve apprenticeships with English clubs at the tender age of fifteen are coming through to first team football'.[45] He noted that eight out of sixteen Irish players who were 'regulars' with First Division clubs in the 1971–72 season had experience of the Irish League or League of Ireland before migrating, while in Division Two there were more 'recent exports from Irish clubs prevailing over former [Irish-born] apprentices'.[46] In 1975, then FAI Director of Coaching, John Jarman, claimed that English clubs were behaving like 'raiding vultures in a free shop window of Irish youth soccer' and stated that 'kids of all ages are pursued in Ireland and often all sorts of incentives are being offered by unscrupulous people. Money is changing hands and up to £1,000 is being offered by clubs if players make the grade.'[47]

Jarman also felt that 'youngsters should only be able to sign professionally for clubs within thirty miles of their home town until they are able to decide about their futures', while too much emphasis was being put on winning rather than on developing young players' 'real talents'.[48] Home Farm's Don Seery, said to be 'a prominent figure in the Irish soccer world' at that time, felt that parents were to blame for letting their sons move while too young and that young players should not be allowed to migrate until they were seventeen, 'at which stage the boy would have had some education'.[49] Rumours that Home Farm players as young as twelve were being approached by English clubs undoubtedly were also a cause of concern to some of those running Irish soccer, but little action was taken at this time, with schoolboy players from other clubs, such as Martin Russell, being invited for coaching in England in their early teenage years.[50]

Although he chose not to sign as an apprentice, Barry Prenderville stated that he was 'tremendously homesick' after joining Coventry City and had earlier come home from Manchester United after only a few weeks there. He felt that, in hindsight, it would perhaps have been better to have had some League of Ireland experience, and a college degree, before moving to England.[51] In citing the case of the Norwegian club Rosenberg who refuse to sign teenagers not linked to education, he felt that those running association football in the Republic of Ireland should get together and discuss this early migration and has suggested an age cap of eighteen on players going across to England. In addition, he stated that if FIFA made more money available to clubs, they could develop their own players and link this with education until they are in their early twenties and have degrees. Then, if players are good enough to migrate, the clubs would also benefit financially through selling them on and the money could be reinvested in the game at grassroots level, while the migrants would also get proper wages.[52]

There is evidence to support the view that migrating at a later age makes settling in a lot easier. Damien Richardson, who migrated to join Gillingham in his early twenties, had no problems settling in at his new club, with the transition being 'very, very smooth', illustrating the difference between moving as a teenager and as an adult with a wife and children.[53] Hubert Barr, who migrated to Coventry City as a young adult, also felt that his life experience and the fact that he was older than most teenage migrants was beneficial in settling down at his club.[54] John McClelland felt that 'probably you've more about you and you know how to socialise more at twenty-two and twenty-three … you know how to entertain yourself … at seventeen, you haven't got a lot of money anyway'.[55] For those with a young family staying behind in Ireland, such as Dean Kelly, who joined Oldham Athletic in 2010, settling in could be more difficult.[56]

Under current FIFA rules, players are not supposed to migrate until they are eighteen if they are not guaranteed education, but with clubs now providing academy education they can still move at sixteen. Raymond Campbell felt that Irish football's governing bodies needed to act to do something about teenage migration and he would have made a better career for himself if he hadn't moved as a sixteen-year-old:

> There needs to be some kind of legislation put in place. I would have loved to have stayed, children mature at different levels, and they mature at different rates as footballers as well. I mean there was boys who peaked earlier than I did, as regards to their height and their strength and all that kind of thing. When I went over, I was only seven and a half stone when I went to England … there's grown men who were sixteen as well, you know, English boys, who had beards and everything. I wasn't matured

> physically, or probably psychologically as well, at that age. But when I hit twenty, twenty-one, when I came back home, and I stayed home for a wee while, grew up a wee bit, life skills and all that kind of thing, I was ready to go back over again, and I really regretted coming back home. I would have loved to have went over at this age … nineteen, twenty, twenty-one, I was ready to go back over again because I'd matured, obviously, a lot more – I was only a child at sixteen.[57]

While, as noted earlier, he managed to go to university and get a degree, he was on the verge of returning to England while at Linfield after Everton put in a bid, only for his club to demand a higher fee and the move fell through.[58] At that point, he felt he was much better prepared for English football: 'I was a better player, a far better player, coming over here and playing the Irish League football toughened me up a wee bit and I mean I did become a better player, but it just didn't happen then.'[59] Some players, such as former Republic of Ireland goalkeeper David Forde and Denis Behan have managed to return to England having failed to make the grade earlier and after having had a spell in League of Ireland football.[60] Behan was of the opinion that moving having finished exams was more beneficial to a player mentally and physically, as by moving as a seventeen-year-old,

> I was nearly a grown man as such, because my next step would have been college anyway and leaving home, so that part of it is key because to be honest with you, it's a bit of ammo when you do go to England, that you have a bit of education behind you, you have some form of fallback, it gives you that safety net, you can give it your all when you're over there and if it doesn't work out, well you're over here as second prize then, you know.[61]

Despite this, he felt that 'initially work in football was tough at seventeen … if I knew then what I know now it would have been a different story'.[62] Having returned to Ireland after a spell at Brentford as a trainee, he later moved back to English league football after establishing himself as a pivotal player in Cork City's first team.

He stated that the difference between moving as an adult and as a teenager was 'huge' as 'you're going into a setup where you're dealing with men' and as a more established player having been signed to do a job 'with a bit of status' as opposed to being part of an underage system. Simple things like having a car as an adult were also beneficial to him in England, and this is something which has not always been available to younger players.[63] Damien Richardson's confidence was boosted when signing for Gillingham by the fact that manager Andy Nelson had threatened to resign if the transfer was not put through, as he knew that Nelson had great faith in him from the beginning and this made him more determined not to let him down.[64] Mick Meagan felt that he would have benefited from an extra couple of years in the League of Ireland as a teenager rather than moving to Everton where he played in their third team for a number of years, although he admits that the chance might not always be there if a player decides to wait in Ireland, while the standard of the League of Ireland was a lot better in the 1950s than it is today.[65]

However, one of the problems for many young migrants returning home to Ireland having not broken into first-team football is that the university acceptance system is generally based on points obtained in the Leaving Certificate for those in the Republic of Ireland and A level examinations for those in the United Kingdom. These exams are usually undertaken at the age of seventeen or eighteen. Many who sign as trainees with British clubs will have migrated as sixteen-year-olds without undertaking these exams. In recent years, opportunities for mature students to return to college in Ireland have improved, but acceptance on a university course still usually requires sufficient points from the Leaving Certificate or A levels and a wait until a student is in their early twenties before admission. This means that returning migrants are faced with undertaking these exams at an older age if they wish to gain entry into university if they have not completed them before migrating.

Raymond Campbell felt that he was too young when he moved to Nottingham Forest as a teenager. He returned home to have a successful career with a number of Irish League and League of Ireland clubs. Picture: © Inpho

THE SIGNIFICANCE OF PRE-MIGRATION EXPERIENCE OF IRISH PROFESSIONAL FOOTBALL FOR IRISH-BORN FOOTBALL MIGRANTS

Table 7.4 Number and percentage of Irish-born footballers who played English league or Premier League football having earlier migrated from League of Ireland or Irish League clubs, 1945–2010.

Years of Migration	Rep. of Ireland football migrants	Northern Ireland football migrants	Number and percentage who moved from a League of Ireland or Irish League club (ROI migrants)	Number and percentage who moved from a League of Ireland or Irish League club (NI migrants)
1945–55	95	102	70 (73.6%)	76 (74.5%)
1956–65	41	67	18 (43.90%)	46 (68.65%)
1966–75	41	61	21 (51.21%)	41 (67.21%)
1976–85	33	49	14 (42.42%)	27 (55.1%)
1986–95	90	41	36 (40%)	12 (29.29%)
1996–2005	148	82	35 (23.64%)	12 (14.63%)
2006–10	52	15	23 (44.23%)	2 (13.33%)
Overall Total	**500**	**417**	**217 (43.4%)**	**216 (51.79%)**

Source: As Table 1.2 above.

As shown in Table 7.4, in the period from 1945 until 2010, a total of 217 or 43.4 per cent of the 500 Republic of Ireland-born players noted above moved to England from League of Ireland or Irish League clubs. In Northern Ireland, the number who migrated from Irish League or League of Ireland clubs was proportionally greater, with 216 players (51.79 per cent) identified as having undertaken this route, although, as noted earlier, the overall figure (417) was not as high. The percentage rate per decade of Republic of Ireland-born players moving from League of Ireland or Irish League clubs was highest in the 1945–55 period (74 per cent), while this type of migration was also highest in the same period for Northern Ireland-born players with 75 per cent of migrants identified as having completed moves to England in this way. After this, Republic of Ireland-born players' figures dropped before rising again in the 1966–75 period, then decreased again until the 2006–10 period. The percentage of Northern Ireland-born migrations from Irish League or League or Ireland clubs decreased steadily until the 2006–10 period (13 per cent), although this was when the overall number was at its lowest (15). Admittedly this was also the shortest span analysed. This decline is also, however, reflective of the greater use of the trainee system as a more recent means of recruitment, as noted above.

In some cases, particularly in the immediate post-war era (1945–55), a small number of players moved from cross-border clubs, such as Republic of Ireland-born players Bud Aherne, Robin Lawler and Billy O'Neill (Belfast Celtic), while Noel Kelly, James Lawler, Con Martin and Paddy Watters (Glentoran) and James Kelly (Glenavon) also transferred to England. Fewer Northern Ireland-born players moved to England from clubs south of the border in those years, with only Newry-born Peter McParland noted, having joined Aston Villa from Dundalk in 1952. This is perhaps illustrative of the strength of the Irish League over the League of Ireland at that time, and more Northern Ireland players (102 as opposed to 95) migrated from Northern Ireland in that period. This pattern of Republic of Ireland-born players moving to England from Irish League clubs did not continue throughout the twentieth century however, with only sixteen (3.2 per cent) of the 500 migrating this way, and the last player to do so appears to be Dublin-born Terry Conroy, who moved from Glentoran to Stoke City in 1967. This reduction in cross-border player movement may have been influenced by the onset of the Troubles.

Of the 417 Northern Ireland-born players, only twelve (2.87 per cent) were noted as having moved from League of Ireland clubs, and Dundalk, with its close proximity to the border between Northern Ireland and the Irish Republic, supplied four of these. Derry city-born Jim McGroarty was found to be the last of these migrants, moving from Finn Harps to Stoke City ten years after Conroy had joined the English club. Irish League clubs continuously provided more players via transfer than those in the League of Ireland until the 1986 to 1995 period. After this, in line with general overall trends, there were more transfers to England from clubs south of the border, illustrating perhaps a shift in scouting networks and a general improvement in League of Ireland clubs and greater opportunities for Republic of Ireland-born players as the twentieth century progressed.

As noted earlier, 6.5 playing seasons was found to be the average career length in English league football for a Republic of Ireland-born football migrant who moved in the period from 1946 until 1995, while Northern Ireland-born players' career lengths was found to be slightly longer, at 6.6 playing seasons.[66] Republic of Ireland-born players who had migrated from a League of Ireland or Irish League club in the same period had an average career length of 6.2 playing seasons, while those who moved from other clubs were found to have an average career length of 6.7 years. In addition, Northern Ireland-born migrants who moved from Irish League or League of Ireland clubs spent, on average, 6.5 seasons in English league football while those who had moved without experience of this had an average length of career of 7.5 years. Therefore, the average length of playing career for both sets of nationalities was found to be quite similar but with a slight discrepancy shown in the case of those who moved from Northern Ireland without having been contracted to an Irish League or League of Ireland club. This figure may have been offset by the exceptionally long careers of a number of these players in England such as Pat Rice, David McCreery, Sammy McIlroy and Alan McDonald. More significantly, it illustrates that in terms of the average length of career in English league football, there was no huge difference historically between moving from a League of Ireland or Irish League club and moving through the trainee system, as a junior player or through other means.

However, the downside to waiting is that many aspiring teenagers would feel they would miss their chance if they did not join as trainees in their mid-teenage years. Coming to a suitable solution to the problem is difficult, as Shane Supple notes:

> I think it's hard, I would have loved to have done my Leaving Cert., but if you take that chance, it could be gone then, the opportunity to go to England might be gone, it's difficult. I think the FAI need to look at doing something for that sixteen to eighteen-year-old lad, whether its setting up an academy with the top twenty-five players, keep them here, there's quality coaching, they get decent games, whether its travelling over to

> England every couple of weeks or some teams coming over from England to play against them, and obviously they get to do their education and finish up. If they looked at something like that, which is something I think they should do, that would be a step forward.[67]

In July 2015, in the aftermath of the launch of a national under 17 league in the Republic, former international Niall Quinn echoed this view when he stated that 'there has to be a system put in place – you could call them academies, nurseries, whatever you want – to give our footballers, our young footballers, an education, an elite football education as a first'.[68] For some players, getting to England as a teenager is seen as paramount to having a fair chance of making it in English football. Hubert Barr felt that:

> If they're really going to make it, they should be going over as young as possible because it's a routine over there and you have to get into that routine, being at the club's behest and plans all the time, they're the bosses. And you're training every day and I think really, the younger you make it [the better] – within reason, I don't mean six-year-olds and seven-year-olds, but certainly in the teens.[69]

Alan Blayney also felt that getting to England early was critical in a young player's development:

> I think now, you need to get over as quickly as possible to get in the face of it because most people now will not touch you if you're over twenty. If you've been playing in the Irish League, they'll think, 'Well he mustn't be any good, why is he playing in the Irish League?', you know that type of thing. But in respect of your education and homesickness and things like that, and how you're growing up, I think it would definitely be a good idea to go when you're maybe about eighteen, nineteen, twenty … I think sixteen is sometimes very young for a boy to be just leaving his family and going to a completely different country.[70]

Denis Behan felt that players brought up in England also had a strong advantage:

> You're coming from facilities [in Ireland] that are not as good, over to them, they're going to be training nearly every day of the week, whereas you're not. You're trying to take the place of somebody so they're going to have to put you up in digs, pay probably more wages than what the other ones have been on – this is the lower leagues I'm on about – and they have to take a chance on you whereas they know they've a player who's been with them for a while, they know what he's about, and they know that they can make money off him, whereas they take a chance on somebody in Ireland … coming off what is a poor set-up at the moment.[71]

In fact, Richie Sadlier stated in 2013 in his newspaper column that, with regard to playing in the League of Ireland, 'nobody I knew grew up aiming to play in it, and anyone who did could forget plans of going any further'.[72] While he accepts that players are now gaining more experience in this domestic league before moving abroad, he also feels that 'as long as credibility can only be earned by emigrating, football in Ireland will always remain in its current state' and 'the entire system is geared towards selling the best to clubs in the UK'.[73] When questioned in an interview for this study on whether young players could be advised to stay in Ireland until they get older, he felt that staying in school is, in any case, pointless for some players aspiring to become footballers, unless they genuinely want to learn and their families have some understanding of the importance of education. He also stated that it would be pointless trying to convince a football-mad teenager to 'start thinking like a mature adult' and 'the people that stay are generally the people that haven't been asked to go'.[74] At a 2015 charity event, Roy Keane, when interviewed by Matt Cooper, was of the opinion that it suited him not to move to England at sixteen, signing for Nottingham Forest instead as an eighteen-year-old, although he stated that it depended on different players with regard to when the time was right to move across the

Irish sea.[75] Brian Kerr, in a 1998 newspaper interview, felt that those from traditional working-class areas were not going to be interested in education anyway, and were never going to spend their time off the pitch studying:

> The days are long for them and it's easy to see how they could get to be good at snooker or backing horses, but no matter what you say they don't exactly be jumping up and down about the prospect of going to school. Maybe it's a cultural thing. Fellas who play football aren't going to get hundreds of points in the Leaving Cert. Football is the main chance. Not many come through from Foxrock and Shankill and Killiney. The players we get are from Coolock, Tallaght, Brookfield, those places. They're not worrying about getting on to *University Challenge* teams. It's worth the risk to them to give it a few years anyway.[76]

Despite the efforts of Johnny Giles in the late 1970s to develop Shamrock Rovers into a strong set-up which could provide professional football of a significant standard to prevent talented Irish youngsters leaving for England, his project amounted to nothing.[77] Some Irish-born players, such as Seamus Kelly, Chris Fagan and Paul Corry, have managed to move to English clubs having completed the scholarship system at University College Dublin, inaugurated in 1979.[78] According to former UCD manager, Martin Russell, delaying a move to England meant that Corry had his educational qualifications to fall back on:

> We've had some success, you remember Paul Corry going to sign as a seventeen-year-old – he'd been offered a one-year professional contract at Burnley who were in the Premiership at the time, and Paul decided to come to UCD and do his three-year degree course, went there in 2012 and at the end of that to Sheffield Wednesday, in the Championship, but he went as a first-team candidate as opposed to going to Burnley as a youth team player, so he left a bit older, he left with his qualifications, that he can fall back on. He knows that if things don't happen, he has put the work in education and he's in a good position as a twenty-one, twenty-two-year-old.[79]

Since returning to Ireland in the early 1990s, **Martin Russell** has established himself as a respected manager in the League of Ireland. Picture: © Inpho

With a more balanced lifestyle through football and studying, on returning to Ireland, Seamus Kelly actually noticed an improvement in his form, indicating the value of combining education with football at the highest level in Ireland, although returning players' interest levels in education will, of course, vary.[80]

Despite some of these former players' strong views on the importance of education, there are no current plans in place between the FAI or the IFA and their respective governments to put in operation a wide-ranging system to provide significant education and football structures for young players to encourage them to stay in Ireland before moving to England. Some players, such as Roy Keane and Paul Byrne, have benefited from FÁS schemes in terms of gaining moves to England afterwards on the back of these courses, initiated in 1989 and connected with League of Ireland clubs. However, the level of education on offer is unlikely to enable participants to gain a broad choice of university entry with emphasis mainly placed on sport, recreation and computer qualifications.[81] With the current state of the Irish economy, these structures are unlikely to change for some time, while League of Ireland football remains in a precarious state. As Dean Kelly asked, 'What can they offer people to stay, the League of Ireland clubs? They can't even offer a one-year contract, like that's the highest contract you can get, League of Ireland, one year.'[82]

Similarly, the establishment of REAP (Reinvention, Education, Appraisal and Preparation) in 2002, to help young players released by English clubs on their arrival back in the Republic of Ireland, through the efforts of Darragh Sheridan, a former Aston Villa trainee, and Eoin Hand, then career guidance officer at the FAI (with the support of the FAI and the PFA), lasted only briefly in the last decade and the system for dealing with returning players remains inadequate, although English clubs do help in getting players set up with teams in Ireland.[83] Raymond Campbell hopes to see the IFA establish a set-up for returning players as there is currently none in place within Northern Ireland.[84] In addition, other Northern Ireland-born players, Michael Carvill and Andy Waterworth, felt that the system in their country for dealing with those who dropped out of English football is inadequate, despite securing places with Irish League clubs on their return from Britain.[85] In particular, Carvill felt that more should be done to improve the image of soccer in Ireland and its professional leagues:

> I've enjoyed my time back home, but there's so much more to be done over here, and when you're over in England you realise that, because of the amount of squads, teams, academies they have over there compared to us. I just think it's a wee bit sad, boys travelling over and back. The only option for a good footballer now … everybody's [got] the same aspirations … go to England, and of course Scotland, or Wales, get across, that makes you a good player. [Whereas] if they developed it right here, they could turn … maybe form an all-Ireland league, or something like that there, they could really make it [the League] something to be proud of, because over here you're seen as a failure. If you

> go to England, and you come back, you're deemed as not good enough, because you came home, where it should be: 'I want to play here, because I want to stay in this country and I want to have my life in this country' and I just don't think it's really there for anybody, and that's for young players, included [at the moment].[86]

Since returning to Belfast, Carvill has combined with former Linfield team mate, Waterworth, to establish a coaching academy for young players, while both have completed degrees at the University of Ulster in Jordanstown.

Returning players' confidence can also be hugely affected, as John McClelland recalls: 'You feel a bit of a stigma because people say "oh that failed footballer returned home"', although he himself later returned to England to have a successful career in professional football.'[87] Despite this, movement of Irish-born players has been much more successful than has been acknowledged in terms of improving the quality of players' lives, and rates of those who have not had Premier League/First Division or international careers can be deceptive to some extent. Association football in Britain has provided Irish football migrants with the opportunity to fulfil a childhood dream while travelling and learning the game in a social and cultural environment which has traditionally been more conducive to the development of young players than at home, not just in terms of coaching but in levels of professionalism.

It has also helped nurture a lifelong passion for the game and allowed many players to remain involved at various levels, and in turn to pass on the knowledge of the game that they have gathered and to share their experiences. Although Andy Waterworth admitted that it was difficult as a full-time professional in Scotland when he wasn't playing well and there was nothing else to occupy his mind, he was in no doubt about his love for the game:

> I love the game. I love everything about it, I love the feeling obviously when you're playing, I love the coaching side, I love the technical side. I have to say I do love the game, it's my

> number one love and passion in life. I don't want to be out of it when I finish playing, I want to be coaching, [or] whether it's journalism, whatever I can get my hands on, I'll be doing it. The game's given me so much joy, as a player, supporter, whatever, so I love everything about it.[88]

Denis Behan felt that despite the pressure and discipline discussed earlier in this book, it was still a job like no other:

> There's a great saying I heard once, 'the minute you start getting paid for something, it stops becoming something you love', because you're told where to go, when to do it, you can't go out on a Saturday night, you can't do this on a Sunday, you can't do that on a Monday, so you kind of fall out of love with the game, as such it becomes a job, but when you sit back and take stock of it, it's definitely a privileged position.[89]

Similarly, Damien Richardson stated:

> It's a wonderful privilege to go and play a game of football. I always say it's a child's game, you become a child again – if I go in training, I'm a child, I go play a game, I even still play five a side. It keeps me young, it keeps me dealing with young people as a coach and manager, but most important of all, it's the very essence of the game that I first saw professionally at seven years of age, it's still the same game.[90]

CONCLUSION

As shown above, the achievements of Irish-born footballers have varied and players have had diverging levels of success, ranging from those who were capped internationally at senior level and won the highest honours in club football to those who played for only a few seasons but were able to earn a living in the game, albeit very briefly in some cases. In addition, the problem remains with sending young players, as opposed to more experienced adults, overseas and there have been calls for those governing Irish soccer to intervene to curtail this early movement. The reality is, despite improvements in the Football Association of Ireland's development scheme for emerging talent and the implementation of elite playing squads, it would be extremely difficult to discourage youngsters, many of whom have low levels of interest in gaining educational qualifications, from pursuing their dreams of playing in the Premier League. Improvements have also taken place in structures for young footballers in Northern Ireland, but the same problem remains.

This comes despite the increase in worldwide talent in the English football leagues and the decline in opportunities for homegrown talent to break into Premier League clubs' first teams, and as shown here, the fact that the majority of Irish-born players have not played in the top division or for their countries. The *Commission on Emigration* stressed the need for Ireland to become more competitive with Britain 'in matters relating to employment'.[91] In professional football terms, this has not improved, and appears unlikely to do so for the foreseeable future. Ireland also remains a source of cheap footballing labour although provisions have been put in place to ensure Irish clubs now gain more financial benefits. It would be incorrect to see Irish-born players in the same category as Taylor and Lanfranchi's 'football mercenaries' who 'change countries as soon as they get a better offer' as the vast majority have remained in Britain or returned back to Ireland.[92] More research needs to be undertaken on the views of those running the Premier and Football League, and those involved in the highest level of football league administration in Ireland, in relation to player movement. Along with the opinions of those at the head of football recruitment in clubs in both Ireland and Britain, the support systems in place to ensure the smoother transition of players to their new places of settlement, and in returning to their homeland, would also need to be investigated in order to shed more light on the future of Irish footballing migrants.

Conclusion

This book is based on four key themes. Firstly, it has illustrated how twentieth-century infrastructures for soccer in the Republic of Ireland generally favoured players in Dublin in their attempts to progress to the highest levels of the game, although recent developments have meant that young players from more regional areas now have a greater chance of gaining the attention of English scouts. Similarly, those living in Belfast have had more opportunities to develop as young players than in more outlying areas of Northern Ireland such as Fermanagh. In highlighting this, it has also discussed the historical social challenges many young Irish players have faced in even gaining the attention of English clubs, although opportunities to get 'spotted' have increased dramatically over the past few decades. In particular, it has illustrated the strength of clubs and scouting networks in the Belfast area in the early twentieth century, with English clubs apparently putting more value on their talent than those from other Irish cities such as Dublin. Given that the Irish Free State League was not established until 1921, this is understandable.

While it would be too simplistic to blame the GAA as having stolen soccer's thunder in Ireland through its 'Ban' and propagation of the view of its native sports as befitting the 'true Irishman', and the organisation's strong parish and county identity, the fact remains that regional variations in the choice of sport available to young Irish people have probably affected rates of production of football migrants to some degree.[1] As noted earlier, the lack of player movement to England from Kerry comes down to more than its peripheral location on the map of Ireland. However, this problem is not unique to Ireland, with Raphael Honigstein noting that many young German players in rural areas were neglected until more widespread coaching and scouting structures were developed in the early 2000s.[2]

While the number of Irish-born players who would have made a career in England had environmental and social conditions been different is impossible to quantify, it might be more beneficial to look at government policies towards the promotion of certain sports, particularly within the Irish education system, and a full-length analysis of the amount of funding given to various codes in the period covered here awaits publication. Similarly, the development of physical education within Irish schools, and the policy of some schools, and physical education teachers, of focusing almost solely on their preferred sport as opposed to offering a more balanced education for students, awaits further investigation. As shown here, soccer struggled to gain a place in many secondary and primary schools in both the Republic and Northern Ireland for much of the twentieth century. It is certainly debateable whether or not talented players would have succeeded in securing moves to English league football clubs no matter where in Ireland they were from, and the evidence presented here suggests that the odds have been stacked against many youngsters, although opportunities have recently improved.

Despite the prominence of the Dublin and District Schoolboys' League in producing football migrants on a national level, and its appeal as a magnet for young players from regional Ireland, broadcaster Eamon Dunphy stated in 2015 that there was too much emphasis on winning medals in schoolboy football, with the result that smaller players are neglected as coaches focus on winning, unlike in other European countries such as Germany, where the emphasis is apparently on enjoyment at underage level. He also feels this may be a reason for the Republic of Ireland's decline at international level, as quality players are not developing as too much emphasis is placed on fielding bigger, stronger players in the quest to win schoolboys' leagues and cups.[3] In comparison, Belgium's progress in recent years has been attributed to a coordinated focus on coaching in schools, clubs and national teams and an emphasis on enjoyment rather than winning at underage level and the development of young players at home rather than abroad.[4] A lack of coaching has undoubtedly hindered players' development in Ireland, although some would argue that natural talent and hard work can compensate for technical development and that 'the cream always rises to the top'.

However, the fact remains that those growing up in Dublin and Belfast have generally been the ones from Ireland to break into English football. As shown in the case of John Jarman's efforts in the 1970s, without sufficient funding it was a tough task to try to implement a structure for grassroots football and a coaching system throughout the Republic of Ireland similar to that in place in England and in some continental countries. Coaching structures in Northern Ireland were undoubtedly quicker to gain development, although, again, social conditions differed and some more rurally based players in counties such as Fermanagh struggled to gain the attention of international selectors and English league clubs, although this has changed slightly recently.

Jarman's efforts were generally hindered by the lack of finance available to the FAI, and it was not until the Jack Charlton era that soccer really took off throughout the Republic of Ireland, with sponsorship improving, but the example of areas such as Westport illustrate that interest had been there in rural areas. One might ponder whether, if qualification had been gained for major international tournaments in the decades preceding the 1988 European Championship in West Germany, progress would have been any quicker in securing a firmer place for soccer within Irish society, but this is another question that is impossible to answer. Whether or not the game in Northern Ireland was boosted by qualification for three World Cup finals in the twentieth century is also unclear and also requires more research, although it did not lead to an increase in the number of Northern Irish players breaking into English league football in the 1960s or 1990s in the wake of these achievements by the national team. Despite the late implementation of competitive structures, particularly in rural areas outside Ulster, localised leagues and cups had been present since the late nineteenth century, albeit sporadically in most counties, but a major problem had always been in keeping them going on an annual basis and the lack of attention given to non-affiliated clubs and associations by both the FAI and IFA.[5]

Secondly, in assessing the movement process, it has also been shown how, like more general Irish migrants, Irish-born footballers have faced tough challenges in settling into English culture, although some have adapted better than others. This ability to adapt appears to be crucial in breaking into English league football, but statistically, moving at a later age does not improve the length of a player's career in the game there. In the case of Northern Ireland-born migrants as opposed to those from the rest of Ireland, it is clear that initially in the post-war era, there was more demand shown for those north of the Irish border by English clubs, and it was not until the late twentieth century that Republic of Ireland-born players in England began to outnumber their Northern Irish-born counterparts. While English football is now dominated by foreign players at its highest levels, it would be interesting to see what impact, as noted by Seamus Kelly, new compensation rules have had on English clubs' reluctance to buy Irish-born players, and subsequently the lack of prowess of the Republic and Northern Ireland's national teams.[6] However, 2016 has seen both nations compete in the finals of a major tournament together for the first time, and with some notable victories.

Written in 1976, Eamon Dunphy's *Only a Game?* was a stern warning to any young player hoping to succeed in professional football.[7] Despite this and other biographical assessments of the difficulties in securing a career in the game, the system for dealing with those who are deemed not talented enough to make it, or fall out of love with professional football, remains inadequate in many countries. The opportunities of a career in professional soccer in England, as shown in this book, have become increasingly slim for aspiring players in both the Republic of Ireland and Northern Ireland, but the hope of truly fulfilling one's sporting potential in a professional setting remains a dream for many Irish youngsters. Despite this, as shown in the case of Shane Supple, the professional game is no mere fantasy even if the breakthrough has been made and a professional contract and first-team league football has been secured at an English club. As Alfie Hale stated when interviewed, little has changed since his playing era in terms of the high levels of aspiring Irish footballers who go to England for trials and don't establish themselves within first-team football there.[8] This book has highlighted the cut-throat nature of professional football although the game is by no means unique in comparison with other professional (and some amateur) sports in this regard. Irish-born football migrants have struggled heavily with homesickness and some have been subjected to discriminatory comments as a result of their nationality, but as noted earlier, this is not unique to them. However, many of these players have added greatly to the game's rich history and development. As MacRaild states, 'on a human level, Britain has drawn huge benefits from the willingness of Irish people to settle there', while these football migrants have also added to the game's culture and strengthened the close links between the two islands.[9] In addition, they have also proved inspirational to many people.

The factors influencing the decision to head to Britain were generally very similar whether the destination club was to the north or the south of the English–Scottish border, although the more sectarian nature of the Scottish game has been highlighted. On the other hand, while players' moves were generally motivated by the desire to play football professionally at a decent level and be paid for their talents, the move to either the USA or continental Europe generally seems to be very different in nature, with, additionally, the ASL and NASL set in a very different environment to major leagues in Europe to which some Irish players migrated. Culturally, however, the transition to playing in North America appears to have been easier than migration to clubs in continental Europe, with similar language and traditions obviously a reason for this.

Given the nature of professional soccer as an occupation and the timeframe around which the game developed, Irish footballers' migration to North America differed to that of most Irish migrants in that it generally did not take place during the key period of Irish emigration there, i.e. between the Great Famine and the First World War. The temporary nature of Irish players' settlement in the United States in the 1921–31 period has been discussed and has illustrated that this movement was the result of push and pull factors, particularly the opportunity to earn higher wages playing the game than those available in Britain's and Ireland's football leagues at that time. While the attraction of Philadelphia Celtic has also been noted, the club's decline meant that a number of Irish players who had travelled to take up positions there found themselves having to move to clubs which had more internationalised playing squads. This attempt in 1927 to develop a team with a distinct Irish identity was not successful, and lasted only briefly, with financial difficulties evident. However, it had also highlighted the lack of control Ireland's soccer bodies and clubs had over this transatlantic movement, from north and south of the border. Reintegration was generally not a problem for returning migrants hoping to get back into professional soccer in Ireland once they had complied with league authorities. Similarly, the NASL has provided some Irish footballers with the opportunity to develop their talent outside Britain and Ireland, and a few of these players were able to carve out long-term careers in the professional game there.

This book has shown how movement to non-British clubs has contrasted with more general trends of Irish migration discussed by Delaney, particularly in terms of destinations. Given the low age of school-leaving among prospective Irish football migrants, most players will have no foreign languages or third-level qualifications and the unique nature of professional football as a career has been highlighted. The early 2000s have also seen a slight shift among Premier League clubs in terms of loaning inexperienced players, some of whom are now tending to loan to European clubs in countries such as Belgium rather than to lower-league English clubs. Despite these changes, and the decreasing numbers of Irish and British players in Premier League squads, it is hard to see English league football being replaced as the core destination for Irish-born migrants hoping to pursue a professional career in the game.

Thirdly, the experiences of Irish-born footballers in Britain appear representative of broader migrational trends in many ways, with Delaney stating that 'there was no universal historical experience of being Irish in post-war Britain', but the unique nature of a career in professional football must also be noted.[10] According to MacRaild, 'the lives of the Irish in Britain were varied and rich, even though a stark contrast between achievement and animosity so often marked out their lives'.[11] This is also true of Irish football migrants. It has been shown that some football migrants were glad to have their clubs cater for them on arrival, lessening the difficulties in cultural adaption, although others failed to adapt and settle no matter how much attention they received. The differences in professional as opposed to part-time football have been discussed, and it has been shown that Irish players have been more than able to hold their own away from home. Almost all players interviewed admitted that it was mental toughness, rather than outstanding talent, that enabled them to pursue a career in England, although one suspects that this view was down to modesty about their own abilities. A love for the game was also critical in succeeding, according to more than one player, while the ability to sacrifice what would be deemed normal aspects of growing up was also identified as being crucial to breaking through trainee systems. Good morale and the help of other Irish players, and managers and coaches, not to mention local Irish communities, have also been of importance in developing their careers. While it is difficult to define how much the experience of being a professional footballer has changed over the period covered in this book, as Hunter Davies has stated of the game more generally, 'the fears, the tensions, the dramas, the personality clashes, the tedium of training, the problems of motivation, injuries, loss of form, the highs and the lows, new people coming through, old stars beginning to fade, that sort of stuff goes on, and will go on, forever'.[12]

This study has focused mainly on a sample of twenty-four footballers from both the Republic and Northern Ireland, and attempted to use their experiences of life as young trainees, professionals and retired players, to examine how Irish football migrants have coped away from home. Admittedly, this is only a small fraction of the overall numbers who played league football in England in the period covered here. In addition, it has not been possible to examine the stories of every single player in the overall list of players who played league football, but every effort has been made to focus on some of the key themes affecting their careers. However, there are countless others who have travelled to Britain and have failed to break into first-team league football, whether as trainees, trialists or reserve players, and as yet, their stories remain largely untold, and their names largely unrecorded.

Fourthly, and finally, it has been shown that many Irish football migrants have looked to stay within the football industry after retiring from the game or having their contracts ended, while professional clubs and governmental systems in Ireland have failed to provide adequate services to cope with this career transition, although there is some evidence that attempts have recently been made to improve this situation. Professional soccer in England provides an alternative to a somewhat flawed football system in both codes in Ireland where player welfare is often neglected, but the social perception remains that true satisfaction within Irish soccer for a player appears to lie solely in 'making it' in English football. As highlighted, the stigma of failure for those who come back too soon from the English game haunts many young players and, like the GAA in historically not catering properly at a psychological level for players who are omitted from teams at an elite level, soccer's governing bodies have also struggled to provide the proper structures to look after those who have failed to break into first teams in England's football leagues.[13] Admittedly, the Gaelic Players' Association and the PFA, and PFAI, have made much progress in this regard in recent years, but this provision of assistance has been a relatively modern development. An inadequate education system within many English clubs has meant that university entry is difficult on returning home, although a general lack of interest in schoolwork is evident among many young players, with the distraction of the dream of a Premier League career greatly impacting on many players' interest in studying.

Movement to England generally comes at a time in their life when, biologically, many lack the maturity or attention spans to sit down and study for lengthy periods. The Irish education system has also been unhelpful in that, unlike the opportunities offered to talented athletes in the USA, for example, there is little available to these scholars to combine education with professional sporting opportunities at home once they finish secondary school. Hence the majority of Irish footballers and athletes must look abroad for a career in professional sport should they wish to concentrate fully on this. Thankfully, however, in recent years, third-level education in Ireland has become more accessible to those wishing to study as mature students, and this has allowed some returned football migrants to gain university qualifications after a career in the game.

Post-retirement issues remain a problem for many players, but structures for assisting those who have fallen on hard times or who lack the ability to fit into what would be deemed a more normal working environment require further development. Given the huge adrenaline and excitement of daily life as a player, and the camaraderie which comes with it, adapting to a job that is a lot more mundane is a difficult task for many, and it requires a change in identity and thought processes, and a lessening of daily expectations in many cases. With the scarcity of academic writing on the post-playing careers of non-Irish professional footballers, a broader comparison is difficult in this regard. Most of what we know about professional players' post-career experiences comes from sociologists rather than historians. In particular, Brown and Potrac have suggested that coaches and managers within professional football academies try to 'develop the whole person as opposed to the standardized mechanistic athlete', while they also recommend the establishment of intervention programmes to assist players in developing skills to cope with retirement.[14]

A number of themes discussed here, such as the influence of scouting and education, the impact of foreign players, and post-playing careers, also apply to British players, and clubs there clearly see the island of Ireland as a natural part of their cultural hinterland despite the Republic and Northern Ireland's location. Even today, the Republic of Ireland national team gets considerable coverage in the United Kingdom and is sometimes treated as if another home nation. Therefore, this book has presented a number of issues which offer a base for a wider development of the experiences of British players in relation to those from Ireland, as well as those from outside the United Kingdom and Ireland, while acknowledging how Irish players differ, as Damien Richardson noted when interviewed.

While this book has also attempted to outline the geography of Irish-born footballing migrants and professional player production per county, more work needs to be undertaken on the geography of sport in Ireland and how this has shifted since the late Victorian era. As John Bale stated in 1989, 'despite its fundamentally geographical character, sport was not traditionally thought of as a subject worthy of serious geographic enquiry'.[15] This is unfortunately still true of sport's acceptance as a genuine topic worthy of teaching and funding in the majority of history departments within Irish universities today, despite the increasing amount of academic research undertaken in the last fifteen years.

Despite a small number of works of note such as Kevin Whelan's 1993 article on the geography of hurling and Mike Cronin, Mark Duncan and Paul Rouse's *The GAA: county by county* (2011), the question remains, how does one judge the strength of a county in any particular code?[16] Is it by national or provincial titles, number of clubs per population and size of county or individual club success? Should it be defined by international caps or provincial team selection? Can a comparison of the number of registered players and pitches per sport in each county be made? Success in sport can be consistent or cyclical, or can simply disappear in some cases. Until more work has been undertaken on sport's role within Irish society and its relationship with particular areas and national identity, the difficulties of making straightforward connections between geographical regions and the various codes available to Irish sportspeople will remain.

More research also needs to be undertaken on those who migrated from Ireland to develop careers in other professional sports, particularly rugby, cricket and Australian rules football, so that a more comparative analysis can emerge. Similarly, little has been written academically about Irish women taking up positions within English clubs as players. As Kevin Kenny has stated, 'the theme of emigration is central to any understanding of modern Ireland and its history'.[17] This book has attempted to situate the experiences of Irish football migrants within wider studies of the Irish diaspora and within the growing academic historiography of Irish sport. It has also offered a history of local and national structures for young soccer players, and the challenges they have faced, through an examination of the game's development at schools and grassroots level. It is hoped that it has shed some light on what has been, at a governmental level, a largely neglected aspect of Irish emigration and that it will also be of some value to anyone considering a career in professional football abroad, while raising a number of important issues which those young players travelling across the Irish Sea, and their families looking on anxiously, ought to be aware of in pursuit of the dream of playing professional football in England.

Notes

INTRODUCTION

1 Interview with Barry Prenderville, 12 July 2013.
2 Matthew Taylor, *The Association Game: a history of British football* (Harlow: Pearson/Longman, 2008), p. 50 and p. 66.
3 'NIFG: Billy Gillespie', http://nifootball.blogspot.ie/2006/12/billy-gillespie.html; 'NIFG: Jimmy Dunne', http://nifootball.blogspot.ie/2006/11/jimmy-dunne.html [accessed 21 Jan. 2017].
4 Conor Curran, *Sport in Donegal: a history* (Dublin: The History Press, 2010), p. 9.
5 Cormac Moore, *The Irish Soccer Split* (Cork: Cork University Press, 2015), p. 71.
6 See Michael Joyce, *Football League Players' Records, 1888 to 1939*, 3rd edn (Nottingham: Tony Brown, 2012) and Barry J. Hugman (ed.), *The PFA Premier & Football League Players' Records, 1946–2005* (Harpenden: Queen Anne Press, 2005); *The PFA Footballers' Who's Who 2005–6* (Harpenden: Queen Anne Press, 2005); *The PFA Footballers' Who's Who 2006–7* (Edinburgh: Mainstream, 2006); *The PFA Footballers' Who's Who 2007–8* (Edinburgh: Mainstream, 2007); *The PFA Footballers' Who's Who 2008–9* (Edinburgh: Mainstream, 2008); *The PFA Footballers' Who's Who 2009–10* (Edinburgh: Mainstream, 2009); *The PFA Footballers' Who's Who 2010–11* (Edinburgh: Mainstream, 2010).
7 Donald M. MacRaild, *The Irish Diaspora in Britain, 1750–1939*, [2nd edn] (London: Palgrave Macmillan, 2011), p. 1.
8 The term 'Irish-born' will be generally used to describe those players who were born in the Republic and Northern Ireland.
9 Norman S. Barrett (ed.), *Purnell's New Encyclopedia of Association Football* (Maidenhead: Purnell & Sons Ltd, 1980), p. 84; Brian Glanville, 'Noel Cantwell', http://www.theguardian.com/news/2005/sep/09/guardianobituaries.football [accessed 30 March 2016]; 'NIFG: Danny Blanchflower', http://nifootball.blogspot.ie/2006/08/danny-blanchflower.html [accessed 30 March 2016].
10 Phil Soar, Martin Tyler and Richard Widdows, *The Hamlyn World Encyclopedia of Football*, 4th edn (London: Hamlyn, 1984), p. 108.
11 'BBC On this Day: 1968: Manchester United win the European Cup', http://news.bbc.co.uk/onthisday/hi/dates/stories/may/29/newsid_4464000/4464446.stm [accessed 30 March 2016].
12 Soar, Tyler and Widdows, *The Hamlyn World Encyclopedia of Football*, pp. 77–8 and pp. 117–20. Other Irish-born football migrants to taste success in European club competitions at English clubs included Paddy Mulligan, John Giles, Martin O'Neill, Mal Donaghy, Denis Irwin, Roy Keane, John O'Shea and Steve Finnan.

13 Stephen F. Kelly, *The Hamlyn Illustrated History of Liverpool, 1892–1998* (London: Hamlyn, 1998), p. 146 and p. 164; Norman Barrett, *The Daily Telegraph Football Chronicle* (London: Carlton Books Ltd, 1993), p. 208. Whelan also won the League Cup with Liverpool in 1982, 1983 and 1984.
14 'NIFG: Norman Whiteside', http://nifootball.blogspot.ie/2006/11/norman-whiteside.html [accessed 30 March 2016].
15 'Republic of Ireland into top 30 in world rankings', http://www.rte.ie/sport/soccer/2016/0204/765315-ireland-up-to-top-30-in-world-rankings [accessed 25 March 2016].
16 Alan Bairner, 'Irish Sport', in Joe Cleary and Claire Connolly (eds), *The Cambridge Companion to Modern Irish Culture* (Cambridge: Cambridge University Press, 2005), pp. 190–205, p. 190.
17 Martin Roderick, *The Work of Professional Football: a labour of love?* (London: Routledge, 2006) p. 174.
18 Ibid., p. 22.
19 MacRaild, *The Irish Diaspora in Britain*, p. 8.
20 Graham Davis, 'The Irish in Britain, 1815–1939', in Andy Bielenberg (ed.), *The Irish Diaspora* (Harlow: Pearson, 2000), pp. 19–36.
21 Interview with Barry Prenderville, 12 July 2013.
22 Deirdre McMahon, 'Anglo-Irish Treaty', in Connolly (ed.), *Oxford Companion to Irish History*, paperback edition (Oxford: Oxford University Press, 2004) p. 16; Joost Augusteijn, David Fitzpatrick, Peter Hart and Charles Townshend, 'Anglo-Irish War', in ibid., p. 17; McMahon, 'Irish Free State', in ibid., pp. 280–81 and 'Republic of Ireland', in ibid., p. 508.
23 McMahon, 'Ireland Act', in ibid., p. 275.
24 Enda Delaney, *Irish Emigration Since 1921* (Dundalk: The Irish Economic and Social History Society, 2002), p. 10.
25 Matthew Taylor, 'Football, Migration and Globalisation: the perspective of history', pp. 1–21, at p. 2, http://www.idrottsforum.org/articles/taylor/taylor070314.pdf [accessed 16 April 2016].
26 Delaney, *Irish Emigration Since 1921*, p. 1.
27 Ibid., pp. 8–11.
28 Ibid., p. 9.
29 Ibid., p. 7.
30 Donald M. MacRaild and Malcolm Smith, 'Migration and Emigration, 1600–1945', in Liam Kennedy and Philip Ollerenshaw (eds), *Ulster Since 1600: politics, economy and society* (Oxford: Oxford University Press, 2013), pp. 140–59, p. 156; Delaney, *Irish Emigration Since 1921*, p. 30.
31 Neal Garnham, *Association Football and Society in Pre-partition Ireland* (Belfast: Ulster Historical Foundation, 2004), pp. 177–96.
32 Peter Byrne, *Green Is the Colour: the story of Irish football* (London: Carlton Books, 2012), p. 200.
33 'Blatter Backs Republic's Stance', http://news.bbc.co.uk/sport2/hi/football/internationals/7917738.stm [accessed 19 April 2013].

34 See, for example, Pat Jennings, *Pat Jennings: an autobiography – one of the world's greatest goalkeepers* (London: Granada, 1984), pp. 185–86. Jennings, a Roman Catholic brought up in the nationalist town of Newry, while stating that players of differing religious backgrounds generally got on well with each other in the Northern Ireland squad, admitted that 'being a Catholic was no popularity boost' while playing at Northern Ireland's home ground, Windsor Park and he was abused by supporters of his own team.

35 'The Irish FA: spectator behaviour', http://www.irishfa.com/the-ifa/sporting-laws1 [accessed 30 March 2016].

36 Neal Garnham, 'Soccer', in Connolly (ed.), *Oxford Companion to Irish History*, pp. 545–46.

37 D.H. Akenson, 'Emigration', in Connolly (ed.), *Oxford Companion to Irish History*, p. 179.

38 Taylor, 'Football, Migration and Globalisation: the perspective of history', p. 2.

39 Garnham, *Association Football and Society*, p. 72. Garnham states that a Scottish club approached a Glentoran footballer in 1889 and a year later, one English club's agent was actively seeking players in Belfast for recruitment.

40 Matthew Taylor, *The Leaguers: the making of professional football in England, 1900–1939* (Liverpool: Liverpool University Press, 2005), pp. 204–5.

41 Pierre Lanfranchi and Matthew Taylor, *Moving With the Ball: the migration of professional footballers* (Oxford: Berg, 2001), p. 146 and p. 150.

42 Robin Peake, 'The Migrant, the Match Fixer and the Manager: Patrick O'Connell, a typical professional footballer of his time?', unpublished master's thesis, University of Ulster, 2010.

43 See Conor Curran, 'Irish-born Footballers in the English Football League, 1888–1939', paper given at the annual conference of the British Society of Sports History, University of Edinburgh, 3 Sept. 2016.

44 Mike Cronin, *Sport and Nationalism in Ireland: Gaelic games, soccer and Irish identity since 1884* (Dublin: Four Courts Press, 1998); Garnham, *Association Football and Society*; Tom Hunt, *Sport and Society in Victorian Ireland: the case of Westmeath* (Cork: Cork University Press, 2007); Conor Curran, *The Development of Sport in Donegal, 1880–1935* (Cork: Cork University Press, 2015); 'Networking Structures and Competitive Association Football in Ulster, 1880–1914', *Irish Economic and Social History*, vol. 41, pp. 74–92; David Toms, *Soccer in Munster: a social history, 1877–1937* (Cork: Cork University Press, 2015).

45 Moore, *The Irish Soccer Split*; Mark Tynan, 'Association Football and Society in Ireland during the Inter-war period, 1918–39', unpublished PhD thesis, National University of Ireland, Maynooth, 2013.

46 Conor Curran and David Toms (eds), 'Going Beyond the "Garrison Game": new perspectives on association football in Irish history', special edition of *Soccer & Society*, http://www.tandfonline.com/doi/full/10.1080/14660970.2016.1230344 [accessed 26 April 2017].

47 Patrick McGovern, 'The Brawn Drain: English league clubs and Irish footballers, 1946–1995', *British Journal of Sociology*, no. 36, vol. 32 (2000), pp. 401–18.

48 Seamus Kelly, 'The Recruitment, Assessment and Development of Professional Soccer Players in the UK and Ireland', unpublished research project (2011) and 'The Migration of Irish Professional Footballers: the good, the bad and the ugly', in Richard Elliott and John Harris (eds), *Football and Migration: perspectives, places, players* (London: Routledge, 2014), pp. 76–92. I am grateful to Seamus for granting me access to his work. See also Ann Bourke, 'The Road to Fame and Fortune: insights on the career paths of young Irish professional footballers in England', *Journal of Youth Studies*, vol. 5, no. 4 (2002), pp. 375–89 and 'The Dream of Being a Professional Soccer Player: insights on career development options of young Irish players', *Journal of Sport & Social Issues*, vol. 27, no. 4 (2003), pp. 399–419 and Richard Elliott, 'Football's Irish Exodus: examining the factors influencing Irish player migration to English professional leagues', *International Review for the Sociology of Sport*, vol. 49, no. 3 (2014), pp. 1–15.

49 Lanfranchi and Taylor, *Moving With the Ball: the migration of professional footballers*; Paul Darby and David Hassan (eds), *Emigrant Players: sport and the Irish diaspora* (London: Routledge, 2008).

50 John Bale and Joseph Maguire, *The Global Sports Arena: athletic talent migration in an interdependent world* (London: Frank Cass, 1994).

51 Tony Mason, *Association Football and English Society, 1863–1915* (Brighton: Harvester Press, 1980); David Russell, *Football and the English: a social history of association football in England* (Preston: Carnegie, 1997).

52 Taylor, *The Association Game*, pp. 303–6.

53 Pierre Lanfranchi, Christine Eisenberg, Tony Mason and Alfred Wahl, *100 Years of Football: the FIFA centennial book* (London: Weidenfeld & Nicolson, 2004); David Goldblatt, *The Ball is Round: a global history of football*, paperback edition (London: Penguin, 2007), pp. 101–5.

54 David Goldblatt, *The Game of our Lives: the making and meaning of English football*, [paperback edition] (London: Penguin, 2015), pp. 200–10.

55 *Commission on Emigration and other Population Problems, 1948–54: Reports* (Dublin: The Stationery Office, 1955), p. 2, p. 258 and pp. 260–61. The Commission had published advertisements in the press in April 1948 inviting 'evidence from persons or bodies' with an interest in the inquiry. Along with forty-nine 'witnesses' being utilised for their views, the following organisations were consulted: An Ríoghacht, Athlone Commission on Emigration, Coiste-Ghairm Oideachas Chonndae Liathdroma, Coiste Oideachas Gairme Beatha Chonndae Shlighigh, Comhdaíl Náisiúnta na Gaeilge, Cork Workers' Council, County Cork Committee of Agriculture, Cumann Caomhanta na Gaedhealtachta, Dublin Unemployed Workers' Association, Foras Mhuiridhe na hÉireann, Irish Club, London, Irish Conference of Professional and Service Association, Irish Countrywomen's Association, Irish Employers' Bureau, Irish Farmers' Federation, Irish Housewives Association, Irish Labour Party (Ballydaly branch, Cork), Irish Nurses' Organisation, Irish Tourist Board, Irish Women Workers Union, Macra na Feirme, Mellifont Conference on Depopulation and Council of National Action, Muintir na Mara, Muintir na Tíre, National Liberal Club, London, Swinford Parish Council, University

Women Graduates' Association (Dublin branch) and Women's National Council of Action. The following government departments also submitted memoranda of evidence: Agriculture (Fisheries branch), Education, External Affairs, Industry and Commerce, Lands, Social Welfare, Bord na Móna and the Electricity Supply Board.

56 Ibid., p. 5.

57 Patrick Sullivan (ed.), *Patterns of Migration*, vol. 1 (Leicester: Leicester University Press, 1992); Enda Delaney and Donald MacRaild (eds), *Irish Migration, Networks and Ethnic Identities Since 1750* (London: Routledge, 2007).

58 Tim Pat Coogan, *Wherever Green Is Worn: the story of the Irish diaspora* (London: Arrow, 2000), p. 127.

59 Diarmaid Ferriter, *Ambiguous Republic: Ireland in the 1970s* (London: Profile Books, 2012), pp. 320–22.

60 Ruth Dudley Edwards, *An Atlas of Irish History*, [3rd edn], with Bridget Hourican (London and New York: Routledge, 2005), p. 239.

61 Garnham, *Association Football and Society*, p. 94.

62 Wray Vamplew, 'Successful Workers or Exploited Labour? Golf professionals and professional golfers in Britain, 1888–1914', *Economic History Review*, vol. 61, no. 1 (2008), pp. 54–79 and 'Close of Play: career termination in English professional sport, 1870–1914', *Canadian Journal of History of Sport and Physical Education*, vol. 15, no. 1 (1984), pp. 64–79; Mason, *Association Football and English Society*, pp. 117–23.

63 Gavin Brown and Paul Potrac, '"You've Not Made the Grade, Son": de-selection and identity disruption in elite youth level football', *Soccer & Society*, vol. 10, no.2 (2009), pp. 143–59.

64 Jerome Berthoud and Raffaele Poli, 'L'Après-carrière des Footballeurs Professionnels en Afrique du Sud', *STAPS: Revue Internationale des Sciences du Sport et de l'Éducation Physique*, no. 94 (2011), pp. 25–38.

65 Luke Jones and Jim Denison, 'Challenge and Relief: a Foucauldian analysis of retirement from professional association football in the United Kingdom', *International Review for the Sociology of Sport*, http://journals.sagepub.com/doi/abs/10.1177/1012690215625348 [accessed 27 Dec. 2016].

66 Tony Judt, *Postwar: a History of Europe since 1945*, [2nd edn] (London: Vintage Books, 2010), p. 782.

67 Ibid., p. 783.

68 John Merriman, *A History of Modern Europe: from the Renaissance to the present*, [3rd edn] (New York and London: W.W. Norton & Company, 2010), p. 780.

69 Paul Darby, *Gaelic Games, Nationalism and the Irish Diaspora in the United States* (Dublin: UCD Press, 2009).

70 Patrick R. Redmond, *The Irish and the Making of American Sport, 1880–1935* (Jefferson: McFarland & Company, 2014), p. 194.

71 Martin Roderick, *The Work of Professional Football*; 'A Very Precarious Profession: uncertainty in the working lives of professional footballers', *Work, Employment and Society*, vol. 20, no. 2 (2006), pp. 245–65; 'Domestic Moves: an

exploration of intra-national labour mobility in the working lives of professional footballers', *International Review for the Sociology of Sport*, vol. 48, no.4 (2012), pp. 387–404; 'An Unpaid Labour of Love: professional footballers, family life, and the problem of job relocation', *Journal of Sport and Social Issues*, vol. 36, no.3 (2012), pp. 317–38; David Stead and Joseph Maguire, '"Rite De Passage" or Passage to Riches? The motivation and objectives of Nordic/Scandinavian players in English league soccer', *Journal of Sport and Social Issues*, vol. 24, no.1 (2000), pp. 36–60; Jonathan Magee and John Sugden, '"The World at their Feet"': professional football and international labor migration', *Journal of Sport and Social Sciences*, vol. 26, no. 4 (2002), pp. 421–37.

72 See, for example, Paul Rowan, 'Grealish an Excellent Servant for Ireland', *Sunday Times* (Sport), 28 April 2013, p. 11.

73 See Ferriter, *The Transformation of Ireland*, pp. 465–66. Ferriter states that in the decade immediately after 1951, 412,000 people emigrated from Ireland, and 'in 1956 and 1957 Ireland was alone in Europe in being a country where the total volume of goods and services consumed fell'.

74 Joyce, *Football League Players' Records.*

75 Hugman (ed.), *The PFA Premier & Football League Players' Records, 1946–2005*, p. 5.

76 Liam Brady, *So Far So Good … A Decade in Football* (London: Stanley Paul, 1980); Norman Whiteside, *Determined Norman Whiteside* (London: Headline, 2007), pp. 57–58.

77 Matthew Taylor, 'From Source to Subject: sport, history and autobiography', *Journal of Sports History*, vol. 35, no. 3 (2008), pp. 469–91, at p. 469.

78 *Shoot!*, 11 July 1970.

79 Andy Pringle and Neil Fissler, *Where Are They Now? Life after soccer - over 2,000 players* (London: Two Heads, 1996).

80 Steve Emms and Richard Wells, *Scottish League Players' Records. Division One 1890/91 to 1938/9* (Nottingham: Tony Brown, 2007); Richard Beal and Steve Emms, *Scottish League Players' Records: Division One 1946/47 to 1974/75* (Nottingham: Tony Brown, 2004); Derek Gray and Steve Emms, *Scottish League Players' Records: Premier Division and Premier League 1975/76 to 1999/2000* (Nottingham: Tony Brown, 2002).

81 Colin Jose, *American Soccer League, 1921-1931: the Golden Years of American Soccer* (Maryland: Scarecrow Press, 1998); *North American Soccer League Encyclopedia* (Haworth: St Johann Press, 2003).

CHAPTER 1. THE GEOGRAPHY OF IRISH SOCCER MIGRANTS

1 Interview with Damien Richardson, 13 Aug. 2013.

2 Enda Delaney, *The Irish in Post-war Britain*, [paperback edition] (Oxford: Oxford University Press, 2013), p. 7.

3 John Bale, 'Sport and National Identity: a geographical view', *The British Journal of Sports History*, vol. 3, no. 1 (1986), pp. 18–41.

4 Ibid., pp. 25–40.
5 Ibid., pp. 32–33.
6 Joyce Woolridge, 'A New Breed: some observations about the careers of professional footballers in England, 1946–1985', *Soccer & Society*, vol.11, no. 5 (2010), pp. 522–36, at p. 524.
7 Ibid., p. 534.
8 Gary Neville, 'North of England Falls off Map in Football's Changing Geography', *Irish Independent*, 26 Sept. 2015.
9 Bale, 'Sport and National Identity', pp. 32–33.
10 R.J. Morris, 'Urban Ulster Since 1600', in Kennedy and Ollerenshaw (eds), *Ulster Since 1600*, pp. 121–39, p. 128.
11 Liam Kennedy and Philip Ollerenshaw, 'Preface', in Kennedy and Ollerenshaw (eds), *Ulster Since 1600*, vii.
12 Garnham, *Association Football and Society*, p. 69 and p. 73.
13 Ibid., p. 11.
14 Ibid.
15 Liam Kennedy and Philip Ollerenshaw, 'Introduction', in Kennedy and Ollerenshaw (eds), *Ulster Since 1600*, pp. 1–11, at p. 2.
16 Garnham, *Association Football and Society*, p. 63; *Belfast Newsletter*, 24 Oct. 1878.
17 Garnham, *Association Football and Society*, pp. 45–7.
18 Ibid., p. 5.
19 Ibid., pp. 201–2.
20 *'Ireland's Saturday Night' Football and Athletic Annual 1909–10* (Belfast, 1910), p. 50.
21 Ibid., p. 51.
22 Garnham, *Association Football and Society*, p. 88.
23 *Belfast Telegraph*, 3 Feb. 1902.
24 *Sport*, 28 May 1921.
25 Garnham, *Association Football and Society*, pp. 35–6.
26 *Ireland's Saturday Night*, 18 April 1896.
27 Ibid., 10 April 1897.
28 *Belfast Telegraph*, 3 Feb. 1902. See also 3 Jan. 1898.
29 Ibid., 23 April 1906.
30 Sport, 17 Nov. 1883.
31 Garnham, *Association Football and Society*, p. 4, p. 6 and p. 17.
32 Ibid., p. 48.
33 Ibid., p. 46.
34 Ibid., pp. 5–6.
35 Joyce, *Football League Players' Records, 1888 to 1939*, p. 113.
36 'NIFG: Archie Goodall', http://nifootball.blogspot.ie/2006/12/archie-goodall.html [accessed 1 Nov. 2016].
37 *Sport*, 17 March 1900.
38 Joyce, *Football League Players' Records*, p. 70 and p. 282.
39 *Derry Journal*, 1 March 1893; Joyce, *Football League Players' Records*, p. 155, p. 211 and p. 237.

40 *Derry Journal*, 1 March 1893.
41 Joyce, *Football League Players' Records*, p. 128 and p. 167.
42 Ibid.
43 Delaney, *Irish Emigration Since 1921*, p. 13.
44 Ibid., p. 38.
45 *Census 2006, Principal Demographic Results* (Dublin: The Stationery Office, 2007), p. 13, http://www.cso.ie/en/media/csoie/census/documents/Amended,Final,Principal,Demographic,Results,2006.pdf [accessed 18 May 2014].
46 Dave Hannigan, *The Garrison Game: the state of Irish football* (Edinburgh: Mainstream, 1998), pp. 17–18.
47 Delaney, *Irish Emigration Since 1921*, p. 13.
48 Ibid., pp. 13–14.
49 Dermot Keogh, *Twentieth Century Ireland: revolution and state building*, revised edition (Dublin: Gill & Macmillan, 2005), p. 36.
50 These figures have been calculated in relation to when the players actually made their debuts in English league football; cup ties and European matches have not been included in the data.
51 See 'Waterford United: club information', http://www.waterford-united.ie/club-info [accessed 12 April 2015]. I am grateful to David Toms for drawing my attention to this.
52 Interview with Alfie Hale, 27 Sept. 2013.
53 *Irish Independent*, 5 June 1946.
54 *Kilkenny People*, 6 March and 10 April 1948.
55 'Kilkenny GAA Roll of Honour', http://www.kilkennygaa.ie/page/Roll%20of%20honour [accessed 7 March 2016].
56 Patrick McGovern, 'The Irish Brawn Drain: English league clubs and Irish footballers, 1946–1995', Working Paper, University College Dublin, Centre for Employee Relations and Organisational Performance, no. 28 (1999), p. 7.
57 *Sunday Independent*, 22 April 1956.
58 Ibid.
59 Ibid.
60 Ibid., 13 Sept. 1959; *Irish Independent*, 23 Oct. and 2 Dec. 1959.
61 Interview with Paddy Mulligan, 13 Nov. 2013.
62 Interview with Damien Richardson, 13 Aug. 2013.
63 *Irish Press*, 22 Jan. 1972.
64 *Times Pictorial*, 12 Sept. 1953; *Irish Independent*, 3 Jan. 1968.
65 'Cherry Orchard FC: our club story, our history', http://www.cherryorchardfc.yourclub.ie/history [accessed 4 Feb. 2017].
66 Toms, *Soccer in Munster*, p. 8.
67 Interview with Alfie Hale, 27 Sept. 2013.
68 *Sunday Times* (Sport), 28 April 2013, p. 11.
69 Ibid.
70 John Fallon, 'Schoolboys' Chief Defiant after FAI Pass "80km" Rule', http://www.independent.ie/sport/soccer/schoolboys-chief-defiant-after-fai-pass-80km-rule-29587192.html [accessed 27 March 2017].

71 *Irish Examiner*, 8 Oct. 1937.
72 *Sunday Independent*, 20 March 1960.
73 Interview with Richie Sadlier, 23 July 2013.
74 Interview with Barry Prenderville, 13 July 2013.
75 See Hugman (ed.), *The PFA Footballers' Who's Who 2010–11*, p. 89, p. 124, p. 208 and pp. 257–8.
76 Shamrock Rovers have won the trophy a record seventeen times, with other Dublin-based clubs Shelbourne (12), Bohemians (11), St Patrick's Athletic (7), Drumcondra (5), St James's Gate (2) and Dolphin (1) also claiming victories. In 1985 the Premier Division was inaugurated.
77 See, for example, Mike Cronin, Mark Duncan and Paul Rouse, *The GAA: county by county* (Cork: The Collins Press, 2011) for a full discussion of how the GAA has managed to foster this identity.
78 Gavin Mellor, 'Professional Football and its Supporters in Lancashire circa 1946–1985', unpublished PhD thesis, University of Lancashire, 2003; Alan Metcalfe, 'Football in the Mining Communities of East Northumberland', *International Journal of the History of Sport*, vol.5, no. 3 (1988), pp. 269–91.
79 *Irish Examiner*, 29 Dec. 1973.
80 Interview with Damien Richardson, 13 Aug. 2013.
81 Interview with Paddy Mulligan, 12 Nov. 2013.
82 Interview with Billy Humphries, 14 Jan. 2014.
83 Interview with Brendan Bradley, 16 Jan. 2014.
84 Interview with Mick Meagan, 11 Nov. 2013.
85 Ibid.
86 Interview with Alan Blayney, 13 Jan. 2014.
87 Interview with Mick Meagan, 11 Nov. 2013.
88 Diarmaid Ferriter, *The Transformation of Ireland, 1900–2000* (London: Profile Books, 2004), p. 388.
89 Ibid.
90 Interview with Mick Meagan, 11 Nov. 2013.
91 *Limerick Chronicle*, 8 Aug. 1981; interview with Alfie Hale, 27 Sept. 2013 and interview with John McClelland, 29 Jan. 2014.
92 Interview with Paddy Mulligan, 12 Nov. 2013.
93 Interview with David Miskelly, 21 Jan. 2014.
94 Interview with Dean Kelly, 13 Jan. 2014.
95 Interview with Paddy Mulligan, 12 Nov. 2013.
96 Interview with Mick Meagan, 11 Nov. 2013.
97 Interview with Damien Richardson, 13 Aug. 2013.
98 Interview with Billy Humphries, 14 Jan. 2014.
99 Taylor, *The Association Game*, p. 124.
100 Interview with Seamus Heath, 26 Sept. 2013.
101 Interview with Brendan Bradley, 16 Jan. 2014.
102 *Sunday Independent*, 2 Sept. 1973.
103 Curran, *The Development of Sport in Donegal*, p. 93 and p. 165.
104 Delaney, *Irish Emigration Since 1921*, p. 13.

105 Ibid., p. 38.
106 *Ulster Herald*, 8 Sept. 1973.
107 Interview with Alan Blayney, 13 Jan. 2014; interview with Brendan Bradley, 16 Jan. 2014.
108 Garnham, *Association Football and Society*, p. 18; 'NIFG: Gerry McElhinney', http://nifootball.blogspot.ie/2007/01/gerry-mcelhinney.html [accessed 12 April 2015]. An All-Star is an award given annually to those deemed to have been the best players in their positions over the All-Ireland Gaelic football and hurling championship season. Other football migrants who have played both codes include Bud Aherne, Niall Quinn, Shane Long (hurling); Norman Uprichard, Gerry Armstrong, Mal Donaghy, Pat McGibbon, Neil Lennon, Anton Rogan, Con Martin and Kevin Moran (Gaelic football).
109 Interview with David Miskelly, 21 Jan. 2014.
110 'Eoin Bradley Remains Glenavon Player with Coleraine Return Reports Wide of Mark', http://www.bbc.com/sport/football/38451434 [accessed 30 Jan. 2017].
111 Interview with Seamus Heath, 26 Sept. 2013.
112 IFA Papers, Youth International Committee Minutes, 1948–63. D/4196/ F/1, 10 Nov. 1955.
113 IFA Papers, Finance Committee, D/4196/ R/3, 28 Aug. 1958.
114 IFA Papers, Rules Revision and League Sanction Committee, D/4196/ T/5, 14 Nov. 1961 and 22 Aug. 1963.
115 *Ulster Herald*, 3 March 1973 and 8 June 1974.
116 *Fermanagh Herald*, 15 March 1986.
117 Ibid., 19 April 1986.
118 Interview with Raymond Campbell, 10 Dec. 2013.
119 Interview with Seamus Heath, 26 Sept. 2013.
120 Interview with Raymond Campbell, 10 Dec. 2015.
121 'Glentoran FC Academy', http://www.glentoran.com/academy [accessed 21 Jan. 2017]; 'Linfield Academy', http://www.linfieldfc.com/academynews.aspx?id=15631 [accessed 21 Jan. 2017].
122 See, for example, *Fermanagh Herald*, 17 July 1976.
123 Interview with David Miskelly, 21 Jan. 2014.
124 Ibid.
125 'Lisburn Youth Football Club: about us', http://www.lisburnyouth.co.uk/about-us [accessed 22 Jan. 2014].
126 Donald M. MacRaild and Malcolm Smith, 'Migration and Emigration, 1600–1945', in Kennedy and Ollerenshaw (eds), *Ulster Since 1600*, pp. 140–59, at p. 146.
127 Delaney, *Irish Emigration Since 1921*, pp. 13–14.
128 Taylor, *The Leaguers*, p. 89.
129 *Sport*, 26 March 1921.
130 *Sport*, 27 Sept. and 25 Oct. 1894.
131 *Football Sports Weekly*, 14 Nov. 1925.
132 Ibid., 1 Oct. and 12 Nov. 1921.
133 Interview with Raymond Campbell, 10 Dec. 2015.
134 Interview with Michael Carvill, 8 Oct. 2013.

135 Ibid.
136 Interview with John McClelland, 29 Jan. 2014.
137 Ibid.
138 I am grateful to John Duffy for this information.
139 Interview with Billy Humphries, 14 Jan. 2014.
140 *Belfast Telegraph*, 9 Jan. 1899.
141 'Linfield Academy Trip to Murray Park', http://www.linfieldfc.com/academy news.asp?id=13953 [accessed 25 July 2015].
142 *Belfast Telegraph*, 3 Feb. 1902.
143 Ibid., 21 April 1902.
144 Lanfranchi and Taylor, *Moving With the Ball*, p. 4.
145 Malcolm Sutton, 'An Index of Deaths from the Conflict in Ireland: geographical location of the deaths', http://cain.ulst.ac.uk/sutton/tables/location.html [accessed 16 April 2016].
146 See, for example, John Sugden and Alan Bairner, *Sport, Sectarianism and Society in a Divided Ireland*, paperback edition (Leicester: Leicester University Press, 1995); David Hassan, Shane McCullough and Elizabeth Moreland, 'North or South: Darron Gibson and the issue of player eligibility within Irish soccer', *Soccer & Society*, special issue: 'Why Minorities Play or Don't Play Soccer: a global exploration', vol. 10, no. 6 (2009), pp. 740–53. For an assessment of the impact of the 'Troubles' on other sports, see Ferriter, *The Transformation of Ireland, 1900–2000*, p. 650.
147 *Irish Independent*, 1 June 1972.
148 Mike Cronin, 'Playing Away from Home: identity in Northern Ireland and the experience of Derry City Football Club', *National Identities*, vol. 2, no. 1 (2000), pp. 65–79, p. 71.
149 IFA Papers, Council Meeting Minutes, 30 Nov. 1971 and 27 May 1975 and '1975 British Home Championship: Northern Ireland Football Project', http://home.online.no/~smogols/ifcp/archive/northernirelandarchive/britishhomechampionship/bhc1975.htm [accessed 16 Oct. 2015].
150 Thomas Bartlett, *Ireland: a history* (Cambridge: Cambridge University Press, 2010), p. 522; Ferriter, *The Transformation of Ireland*, p. 630.
151 Interview with Seamus Heath, 26 Sept. 2013.
152 Ibid.
153 Interview with John McClelland, 29 Jan. 2014.
154 Neil Lennon, *Man and Bhoy*, [paperback edition] (London: HarperSport, 2007), p. 43.
155 Interview with Brendan Bradley, 14 Jan. 2014.
156 'NIFL Premiership', http://en.wikipedia.org/wiki/NIFL_Premiership [accessed 7 Aug. 2013].
157 'The Official Website of the Danske Bank Premiership', http://premiership.nifootballleague.com [accessed 29 Sept. 2013].
158 *The Malcolm Brodie Northern Ireland Soccer Yearbook* (Belfast: Ulster Tatler Group, 2014), p. 76.
159 *Shoot!*, 24 Jan. 1970, p. 35.

160 Garry Doyle, 'Irish Demise at Arsenal Shows Ireland Are in Danger of Being Left Behind', http://irishpost.co.uk/irish-demise-at-arsenal-shows-ireland-is-in-danger-of-being-left-behind [accessed 6 May 2016].

161 See McGovern, 'The Irish Brawn Drain', p. 14; Hannigan, *The Garrison Game*, p. 24.

162 'Rolls of Honour', http://www.gaa.ie/about-the-gaa/gaa-history/rolls-of-honour/0/0/0/2 [accessed 12 Oct. 2013].

163 *Irish Independent*, 9 Feb. 1971.

164 *Anglo-Celt*, 11 Dec. 1965.

165 Ibid.

166 *Sunday Independent*, 13 Aug. 1967.

167 Ibid.

168 *Anglo-Celt*, 27 Aug. and 21 Oct. 1966; Daire Whelan, *Who Stole our Game? The fall and fall of Irish soccer* (Dublin: Gill & Macmillan, 2006), p. 51. *Match of the Day* began in 1964 while *The Big Match* was introduced four years later.

169 *The Kerryman*, 8 May 1971.

170 Ibid.

171 Ibid., 19 June 1971 and 29 Jan. and 12 Feb. 1972. Eighteen teams were said to have affiliated to the junior league.

172 Ibid., 2 May 1975.

173 Interview with Alfie Hale, 27 Sept. 2013; *The Kerryman*, 2 May 1975.

174 *The Kerryman*, 2 May 1975.

175 Curran, 'Networking Structures and Competitive Association Football', pp. 74–92.

176 Curran, *The Development of Sport in Donegal*, p. 189.

177 *Connacht Tribune*, 12 May 1928.

178 Ibid., 22 Sept. 1928.

179 Ibid., 27 March 1948.

180 *Sligo Champion*, 19 June 1954; 'Men's League History', http://inform.fai.ie/League/Clubs/portals/MAFL/mayomensleaguehistory.aspx?ClubIDa=1283 [accessed 12 Sept. 2013]; *Donegal Democrat*, 10 May 1972 and 6 June 1996; 'History of the Roscommon and District League', http://www.sportsmanager.ie/uploaded/8525/history_from_beginning_up_to_2006pd [accessed 11 Sept. 2013].

181 *Anglo-Celt*, 18 May 1935 and 24 May 1958.

182 Ibid., 10 Sept. 1966; *Longford Leader*, 26 Jan. 1973; 'Meath and District League: providing a structured system for clubs in Meath', http://www.yellowtom.ie/155446 [accessed 25 Oct. 2013]

183 *Meath Chronicle*, 11 Dec. 1971.

184 *11 a-side*, vol. 2, no. 6 (1994), p. 23.

185 'Kildare and District Football League', http://www.kdfl.ie/about.htm [accessed 11 Sept. 2013]; *11 a-side*, vol. 2, no. 6 (1994), p. 25.

186 'Soccer Clubs Leagues in Leitrim', http://www.leitrimcoco.ie/eng/Services_A-Z/Community_and_Enterprise/Community-Soccer-Programme/Soccer-Clubs-Leagues-in-Leitrim.html [accessed 11 Sept. 2013].

187 'Leitrim Genealogy Centre', http://www.leitrimroots.com [accessed 27 Dec. 2013].

188 'Schoolboys Football Association of Ireland', http://www.sfai.ie [accessed 14 Oct. 2013]; 'Clare Schoolboys/Girls Soccer League', http://www.cssleague.ie [accessed 14 Oct. 2013]; 'Meath and District League: Providing a Structured System for Clubs in Meath', http://www.yellowtom.ie/155446 [accessed 25 Oct. 2013]; *Sunday Independent*, 13 Feb. 2011; 'Midlands Schoolboys/Girls League', *http://www.msleague.ie/* [accessed 14 Oct. 2013]. The SFAI claims to cater 'for close on 100,000 players from more than 1,000 clubs'.

189 *Connacht Tribune*, 28 Dec. 1935; *Limerick Leader*, 8 Feb. 1936; interview with Alfie Hale, 27 Sept. 2013.

190 Interview with Mick Meagan, 11 Nov. 2013.

191 *Sunday Independent*, 1 Oct. 1933; *Irish Press*, 13 May 1937.

192 *Sunday Independent*, 6 Jan. 1957.

193 *Irish Examiner*, 1 Oct. 1937; *Irish Independent*, 23 April 1954.

194 *Kilkenny People*, 17 April 1948.

195 *Westmeath Examiner*, 4 May 1946; *Anglo-Celt*, 4 July 1959 and 10 Aug. 1963.

196 *Longford Leader*, 19 June 1948.

197 *Sligo Champion*, 3 Nov. 1951.

198 'Schoolboys Football Association of Ireland: Kennedy Cup – Past Winners', http://www.sfai.ie/ [accessed 14 Oct. 2013].

199 *Derry People and Donegal News*, 20 March 1976.

200 Interview with Mick Meagan, 11 Nov. 2013.

201 *Connacht Sentinel*, 29 April 1929.

202 Curran, *The Development of Sport in Donegal*. For an overview of this conflict, see, in particular, Chapter 7.

203 *Derry People and Donegal News*, 28 Aug. 1976 and 7 May 1977. The latter report stated that the pitch had been vandalised for the seventh time, with glass broken on the playing surface, goalposts smashed and cars used to cut up the playing surface.

204 *Connaught Telegraph*, 6 Nov. 1948; *Western People*, 13 Nov. 1948.

205 *Connaught Telegraph*, 11 Dec. 1948.

206 *Sligo Champion*, 26 Sept. 1953.

207 Interview with Alfie Hale, 27 Sept. 2013.

208 Interview with Michael McHugh, 29 Oct. 2013.

209 Ibid.

210 Ibid.

211 Interview with Gerard Mooney, 4 May 2013.

212 'Eoin Hand Welcomes New Regulations for Scouts and Trials'; http://www.fai.ie/football-services-a-education/player-a-club-services/100500-eoin-hand-welcomes-new-regulations-for-scouts-and-trials.html [accessed 5 May 2013]. According to the FAI's website, this figure is higher as they note the presence of fifty-two registered scouts working for thirty-two British clubs in Ireland.

213 'NIFG: From School to Full', http://nifootball.blogspot.ie/2007/01/from-schoolboy-to-full.html [accessed 24 May 2016].

214 IFA Papers, Youth International Committee Minutes, D/4196/A/6, 20 Nov. 1951.
215 *Fermanagh Herald*, 19 Dec. 1959.
216 'NIFG: From School to Full'.
217 Oliver Kay, *Forever Young: the story of Adrian Doherty, football's lost genius* (London: Quercus, 2016), pp. 52–65.
218 Roy Keane (with Eamon Dunphy), *Keane: the autobiography* (London: Michael Joseph, 2002), pp. 8–9. Keane claims that selection for the Republic of Ireland under 15 team was 'a prize that to us seemed reserved for stars on the Dublin schoolboy scene'. See also Steven Gerrard, *Gerrard: my autobiography* (London: Transworld Publishers, 2006), pp. 44–45.
219 *Irish Independent*, 20 March 1947.
220 *Sunday Independent*, 10 Jan. 1954.
221 *Irish Press*, 20 April 1959.
222 *Connacht Sentinel*, 20 Oct. 1964.
223 Ibid.
224 *Irish Press*, 6 Feb. 1971.
225 *Irish Examiner*, 23 March 1973.
226 *Donegal News*, 27 Sept. 1975.
227 *Connacht Tribune*, 12 and 26 Dec. 1975.
228 Ibid., 26 Dec. 1975.
229 *Derry People and Donegal News*, 18 Jan. 1992.
230 Ibid., 19 Oct. 1991.
231 Ibid.
232 Interview with Michael McHugh, 29 Oct. 2013. See also *Derry People and Donegal News*, 9 Dec. 1978. The reporter lamented the fact that only one Donegal player had been selected for the national youth squad and questioned whether 'the Dublin mafia was back in control'.
233 *Derry People and Donegal News*, 30 March 1992.
234 Interview with Damien Richardson, 13 Aug. 2013.
235 See McGovern, 'The Irish Brawn Drain', p. 13 and Burke, 'The Road to Fame and Fortune', p. 381 and p. 389. See also '2013 St Kevin's Boys Club', http://www.skbfc.com/2013-tournament-the-best-yet [accessed 25 Oct. 2013] and 'Home Farm FC Host Under 16 Tournament this Weekend', *http://www.fai.ie/domestic-a-grassroots/17-district-leagues/103629-home-farm-fc-hosts-u16-tournament-this-weekend.html* [accessed 25 Oct. 2013].
236 *Irish Press*, 28 June 1946.
237 Ibid., 23 April 1935.
238 *Irish Independent*, 7 Dec. 1955.
239 *Mayo News*, 4 Nov. 1967; *Sligo Champion*, 1 Jan. 1971.
240 *Derry People and Donegal News*, 20 July 1991.
241 Curran, *The Development of Sport in Donegal*, pp. 164–70.
242 *Derry People and Donegal News*, 4 April 1992.
243 See 'One-on-One: Your Questions Answered by Shay Given', *Four-Four-Two Magazine*, no. 216 (June 2012), pp. 8–13 and *Donegal News*, 20 Jan. 1973.

244 Packie Bonner, *The Last Line: my autobiography* (London: Ebury Press, 2015), p. 283; *Derry People and Donegal News*, 2 May 1992.
245 *Derry People and Donegal News*, 20 July 1991.
246 Bourke, 'The Road to Fame and Fortune', p. 378.

CHAPTER 2. SCHOOLS' SOCCER AND COACHING IN IRELAND

1 *Football Sports Weekly*, 26 June 1926.
2 Garnham, *Association Football and Society*, p. 93.
3 *Football Sports Weekly*, 6 Aug. 1927.
4 Ibid., 26 June 1926.
5 *Irish Independent*, 9 Aug. 1946.
6 Taylor, *The Association Game*, p. 219.
7 Neil Carter, *The Football Manager: a history* (London: Routledge, 2006), p. 107.
8 *Football Sports Weekly*, 6 Aug. 1927.
9 Garnham, *Association Football and Society*, pp. 23–26.
10 Neal Garnham, 'Ein Spiel in zwei Nationen: fussball in Irland, 1918–1939', in Christian Koller and Fabian Brändle (eds), *Fussball zwischen den Kriegen: Europa 1918–1939* (Münster: Lit Verlag, 2010), pp. 65–86, p. 75.
11 *Ulster's Saturday Night*, 4 May, 17 and 24 Aug. 1895.
12 Malcolm Brodie, *The History of Irish Soccer* (Glasgow: Arrell Publications, 1968), pp. 74–75.
13 *Sport*, 23 Aug. 1924.
14 Joyce, *Football League Players' Records*, p. 220.
15 Ibid., p. 213.
16 Ibid., p. 71.
17 Ibid., p. 189.
18 *Ulster's Saturday Night*, 9 Feb. 1895; Emms and Wells, *Scottish League Players' Records: Division One 1890/91 to 1938/39*, p. 206.
19 *Sport*, 27 Sept. 1924.
20 Ibid.
21 IFA Papers, Council Minutes, 28 April 1925 and 26 March 1929.
22 Ibid., 12 Nov. 1928 and 30 Oct. 1934.
23 Ibid., 26 Nov. 1935.
24 Ibid., 27 Oct. 1959.
25 *Strabane Chronicle*, 12 Sept. 1964; *Anglo-Celt*, 6 March 1965.
26 'NI Schools FA', http://www.irishfa.com/grassroots/ni-schools-fa [accessed 12 Oct. 2013].
27 'History of NIBFA', http://www.nibfa.org/?tabindex=5&tabid=913 [accessed 12 Oct. 2013].
28 'Super Cup NI 2016-Entries Close Feb 2nd', http://supercupni.com/latest-news/details-for-supercupni-2016-formerly-the-milk-cup-have-been-released.html [accessed 4 June 2016].

29 'History of the Milk Cup', http://www.nimilkcup. org/index.php?option=com_k2&view=item&layout=item&id=27& Itemid=90 [accessed 12 Oct. 2013].
30 'Hughes Insurance Foyle Cup: About', http://www.foylecup. com/About.aspx [accessed 12 Oct. 2013].
31 Whiteside, *Determined Norman Whiteside*, pp. 32–35. The Boys' Brigade was a movement founded in Belfast in 1888 for the development of young men. See Garnham, *Association Football and Society*, p. 17.
32 *Ireland's Saturday Night*, 11 April 1896.
33 Joyce, *Football League Players' Records*, p. 201.
34 Ibid., p. 258.
35 *Football Sports Weekly*, 12 Sept. 1925.
36 Brendan Power, 'The Functions of Association Football in the Boys' Brigade in Ireland, 1888–1914', in Leanne Lane and William Murphy (eds), *Leisure and the Irish in the Nineteenth Century* (Liverpool: Liverpool University Press), pp. 41–58, p. 41; 'About the Boys' Brigade in Belfast', http://www.belfastbb.org.uk/ [accessed 28 April 2016].
37 Emms and Wells, *Scottish League Players' Records. Division One 1890/91 to 1938/39*, p. 165.
38 Interview with Alan Blayney, 13 Jan. 2014; interview with David Miskelly, 21 Jan. 2014.
39 Peter Doherty, *Spotlight on Football* (London: Art and Education Publishers, 1947), pp. 113–15. See also IFA Papers, Council Minutes, 27 Sept. 1932. Proposals by a Mr Mercer of Glentoran to have a coach organised for schools' football do not appear to have made any huge impact at this time.
40 IFA Youth International Committee Minutes, D/4196/ F/1, 6 July 1948.
41 Ibid., 7 Dec. 1948.
42 Ibid., and 22 March 1949.
43 IFA Papers, Council Meeting Minutes, D/4196/A/6, 29 Nov. 1949; 'Sir Walter Winterbottom', http://www.theguardian.com/news/2002/feb/18/guardianobituaries.football1 [accessed 23 Sept. 2015].
44 IFA Council Meeting Minutes, A/6, 29 Nov. 1949.
45 Ministry of Education Papers, Ed/13/36.
46 IFA Youth International Committee Minutes, 22 June 1949.
47 IFA Coaching Committee Minutes, D/4196 Q/1, 21 June 1950.
48 Ibid., 3 Jan. and 19 April 1951.
49 Ibid., 29 Aug. 1951 and 19 April 1952.
50 IFA Youth International Committee Minutes, 8 Oct. 1953.
51 IFA Council Meeting Minutes, 24 Oct. 1950.
52 Norman Uprichard (with Chris Westcott), *Norman 'Black Jake' Uprichard* (Stroud: Amberley, 2011), p. 13.
53 George Best, *Blessed: the autobiography* (London: Ebury Press, 2001), p. 25; Terry Neill, *Revelations of a Football Manager* (London: Sidgwick & Jackson, 1985), p. 29.
54 IFA Papers, Council Meeting Minutes, D/4196/A/5, 30 Dec. 1947.

55 Ibid., 24 Feb. 1948.
56 N.C. Fleming, 'Education Since the Late Eighteenth Century', in Kennedy and Ollerenshaw, *Ulster Since 1600*, pp. 211–27, at p. 222.
57 'Discrimination and Education', http://cain.ulst.ac.uk/issues/discrimination/gibson1.htm [accessed 10 March 2016]. In 1981, the first school to integrate Catholics and Protestants in Northern Ireland, Lagan College, was opened. Schools in Northern Ireland are now defined as 'controlled' (generally Protestant-run), 'maintained' (Catholic), 'voluntary' (grammar schools in the Protestant or Catholic tradition but with some pupils enrolled from either community) or 'integrated', schools which have a balanced number of pupils and staff from both communities.
58 Jonathan Bardon, *A History of Ulster* [updated edition] (Belfast: Blackstaff Press, 2005), pp. 595–96.
59 IFA Council Meeting Minutes, 29 June 1954.
60 Ibid.
61 Ibid. See, for example, *Irish Independent*, 22 Dec. 1949.
62 Northern Ireland Ministry/Department of Education Papers, ED/13/1/2745, Association Football in Grammar Schools, 1954.
63 *Sport*, 23 Aug. 1924.
64 Ibid.
65 Northern Ireland Ministry/Department of Education Papers, ED/13/1/2745, Association Football in Grammar Schools, 1954.
66 *Sport*, 27 Sept. 1924.
67 Northern Ireland Ministry/Department of Education Papers, ED/13/1/2745, Association Football in Grammar Schools, 1954.
68 *Charles Buchan's Football Monthly*, May 1966, p. 10.
69 Interview with Hubert Barr, 7 Jan. 2014.
70 Interview with Billy Humphries, 14 Jan. 2014.
71 Garnham, *Association Football and Society*, p. 23.
72 John Sugden and Alan Bairner, *Sport, Sectarianism and Society in a Divided Ireland* (paperback version) (Leicester: Leicester University Press, 1995), p. 55.
73 Northern Ireland Ministry/Department of Education Papers, ED/13/1/2745, Association Football in Grammar Schools, 1954.
74 Ibid.
75 Liam O'Callaghan, *Rugby in Munster: a social and cultural history* (Cork: Cork University Press, 2011), p. 118.
76 Northern Ireland Ministry/Department of Education Papers, ED/13/1/2745, Association Football in Grammar Schools, 1954.
77 IFA Papers, Council Meeting Minutes, D/4196/A/6, 28 March 1950.
78 Northern Ireland Ministry/Department of Education Papers, ED/13/1/2745, Association Football in Grammar Schools, 1954.
79 IFA Annual General Meeting, 29 May 1954.
80 Ibid., 28 June 1980.
81 Ibid., 28 May 1955 and 26 May 1956.

82 IFA Papers, T/5, Miscellaneous, Referees and Coaching Committee, 13 Aug. and 5 Dec. 1958.
83 IFA Annual General Meetings, 31 May 1958 and 31 May 1959.
84 Ibid., 28 May 1960.
85 Ibid., 29 June 1963 and 27 June 1964.
86 IFA Referees and Coaching Committee Minutes, 11 March 1964 and 31 Jan. 1967.
87 Malcolm Brodie, *100 Years of Irish Football* (Belfast: Blackstaff Press, 1980), p. 120.
88 *Ulster Herald*, 14 Jan. 1967.
89 *Fermanagh Herald*, 23 Aug. 1969.
90 IFA Miscellaneous, Referees and Coaching Committee, 2 Oct. 1967.
91 IFA Annual General Meeting, 30 April 1971; *Irish Independent*, 23 March 1971.
92 IFA Annual General Meeting, 30 April 1971.
93 *Ulster Herald*, 29 May 1971.
94 *Strabane Chronicle*, 10 and 17 July 1971.
95 Ibid., 1 July 1972.
96 *Fermanagh Herald*, 6 Nov. 1976 and 20 Dec. 1986.
97 IFA Annual General Meeting, 30 May 1975.
98 Ibid., 30 April 1976.
99 *Derry People and Donegal News*, 14 April 1986; *Ulster Herald*, 21 March 1992.
100 *Ulster Herald*, 15 May 1993.
101 Ibid., 28 May 1994.
102 *Fermanagh Herald*, 18 July 1992.
103 Delaney, *Irish Emigration Since 1921*, p. 30.
104 Cronin, *Sport and Nationalism in Ireland*, p. 125.
105 Goldblatt, *The Ball Is Round*, p. 105.
106 FAI Junior Committee Minutes, P137/28-9, 24 Feb. 1938 and 2 Sept. 1943.
107 FAI Minutes, P137/31, Junior Committee Annual Report, 1944–45.
108 Interview with Alfie Hale, 27 Sept. 2013; *Ulster Herald*, 14 Jan. 1905; see Cronin, *Sport and Nationalism in Ireland*, p. 84.
109 See Garnham, *Association Football and Society*, p. 29 for the introduction of 'the Ban'.
110 See Curran, *The Development of Sport in Donegal*, pp. 217–21 for its impact in Donegal.
111 Interview with Mick Meagan, 11 Nov. 2013. See also *Sunday Independent*, 21 Dec. 1960.
112 Interview with Mick Meagan, 11 Nov. 2013.
113 See *Limerick Leader*, 8 Aug. 1981; Brady, So Far So Good, pp. 11–13; John Giles, *A Football Man: the autobiography* (Dublin: Hachette Books Ireland, 2011), pp. 41–44; *Charles Buchan's Football Monthly* (July 1958), p. 36 and ibid., Oct. 1959, pp. 6–7; *Shoot!*, 26 Sept. 1970; interview with Damien Richardson, 13 Aug. 2013.
114 See in particular, Brady, *So Far So Good*, pp. 11–13. Brady was expelled from his Christian Brothers school for captaining the Republic of Ireland international

schoolboy team in a match versus Wales instead of playing in a Gaelic football schools' game.

115 Interview with Alfie Hale, 27 Sept. 2013.
116 *Anglo-Celt*, 18 Nov. 1966.
117 'Doherty, Paddy', http://www.hoganstand.com/Down/ArticleForm.aspx?ID=8758 [accessed 30 Jan. 2017].
118 Peter McParland, *Going for Goal: my life in football by Aston Villa's flying Irishman* (London: Souvenir Press, 1960), p. 10.
119 Interview with Raymond Campbell, 10 Dec. 2013.
120 *Sunday Independent*, 29 Nov. 1964.
121 Lennon, *Man and Bhoy*, pp. 41–43.
122 Ibid.
123 *Strabane Chronicle*, 1 June 1974.
124 Ibid., 16 March and 6 April 1974.
125 Toms, *Soccer in Munster*, pp. 30–34.
126 *Irish Independent*, 12 June 1970.
127 Ibid.
128 Interview with Seamus Kelly, 22 Aug. 2013.
129 *Sunday Independent*, 21 Dec. 1952.
130 *Irish Independent*, 15 May 1959.
131 *Football Sports Weekly*, 14 Nov. 1925.
132 Ibid.
133 'FAI Schools: About Us', http://www.fais.ie/about-us [accessed 20 Oct. 2013].
134 *Irish Press*, 4 Feb. 1969.
135 Ibid.
136 Ibid., 27 April, 1948.
137 *Irish Independent*, 5 Oct. 1948.
138 *Western People*, 1 Oct. 1949; *Irish Press*, 4 May 1950.
139 *Sunday Independent*, 14 May 1950.
140 *Connaught Telegraph*, 12 May 1951.
141 *Irish Examiner*, 30 Aug. 1951.
142 Ibid., 30 Aug. 1951.
143 *Irish Independent*, 6 April 1953.
144 *Connaught Telegraph*, 4 July 1953.
145 Ibid., 11 June 1953; *Irish Independent*, 10 Sept. 1953.
146 *Irish Independent*, 5 Aug. 1953.
147 Ibid., 27 Jan. 1954; *Irish Press*, 28 Sept. 1954. Livingstone and Stevenson were full-time coaches but were not in charge of Inter-League selections.
148 *Sunday Independent*, 22 April 1956.
149 *Irish Independent*, 5 Nov. 1957.
150 Ibid., 4 Aug. 1958.
151 *Munster Express*, 9 May 1958.
152 *Irish Press*, 31 May 1960.
153 Ibid., 1 Jan. 1963.
154 Ibid.

155 *Irish Independent*, 31 March 1965.
156 *Connacht Sentinel*, 13 June 1967; *Meath Chronicle*, 29 July 1967.
157 *Irish Independent*, 26 June 1968.
158 Ibid., 21 June 1969.
159 *Irish Press*, 4 March 1969.
160 Thomas A. O'Donoghue, 'The Attempt by the Department of Defence to Introduce the Sokol System of Physical Education into Irish Schools in the 1930s', *Irish Educational Studies*, vol. 5, no. 2 (1985), pp. 329–42; Mike Sleap, 'A Survey of Physical Education in Irish Post-Primary Schools', *The Irish Journal of Education*, vol. xii, no. 2 (1978), pp. 107–18, p. 108.
161 O'Donoghue, 'The Attempt by the Department of Defence', p. 342.
162 Ibid.
163 Ibid.; *Irish Press*, 4 March 1969.
164 *Irish Press*, 4 March 1969.
165 *Irish Independent*, 25 April 1966.
166 Byrne, *Green Is the Colour*, p. 219.
167 Ibid.
168 Sleap, 'A Survey of Physical Education in Irish Post-Primary Schools', pp. 115–16.
169 Ibid.
170 Ibid., p. 117.
171 Interview with Mick Meagan, 11 Nov. 2013.
172 *Irish Press*, 18 Nov. 1970.
173 *Irish Independent*, 16 June 1970.
174 Ibid., 16 June and 1 Dec. 1970.
175 Ibid., 18 Nov. 1970.
176 *Sunday Independent*, 18 April 1971.
177 *Irish Press*, 12 April 1972.
178 *Irish Independent*, 10 May 1973.
179 Ibid.
180 *Irish Press*, 4 Aug. 1973.
181 *Irish Examiner*, 29 Dec. 1973.
182 *Irish Press*, 10 Dec. 1973.
183 *Connacht Tribune*, 5 July 1974; *Sligo Champion*, 19 July 1974; *Donegal News*, 3 Aug. 1974; *Irish Independent*, 29 Aug. and 28 Nov. 1974; *Irish Press*, 30 Dec. 1974.
184 *Irish Examiner*, 4 Sept. 1975.
185 *Irish Press*, 21 Oct. 1975.
186 Ibid., 4 Sept. 1975.
187 *Irish Examiner*, 4 Sept. 1975.
188 *Donegal News*, 27 Sept. 1975; *Sligo Champion*, 14 Nov. 1975.
189 *Sligo Champion*, 14 Nov. 1975.
190 *Irish Press*, 30 April 1976.
191 *Irish Examiner*, 23 July 1977.
192 Ibid., 17 Jan. 1977.
193 *Irish Press*, 12 Jan. 1977.

194 *Soccer Magazine*, no. 5 (1985), p. 22.
195 Dave Hannigan, *The Garrison Game: the state of Irish football* (Edinburgh: Mainstream, 1998), pp. 20–27.
196 Richard Giulianotti, *Football: a sociology of the global game* (Cambridge: Polity Press, 1999), p. 37.
197 Cronin, *Sport and Nationalism in Ireland*, p. 129.
198 *Sunday Independent*, 13 Feb. 2011.
199 *Soccer Magazine*, no. 48 (1989), p. 26.
200 Ibid., no. 47 (1989), p. 3.
201 Ibid., no. 33 (1988), p. 10.
202 Ibid., no. 59 (1990), p. 25.
203 Ibid., no. 96 (1995), p. 26.
204 *11-a-Side*, vol. 2, no. 5 (1994), p. 3.
205 *Donegal News*, 22 Aug. 1992; *Soccer Magazine*, no. 68 (1992), p. 18; *Irish Press*, 16 March 1979.
206 'Coca-Cola', http://www.fifa.com/about-fifa/marketing/sponsorship/partners/coca-cola.html [accessed 24 March 2016].
207 *11-a-Side*, vol. 1, no. 1 (1993), p. 44.
208 Interview with Denis Behan, 6 Dec. 2013.
209 Ibid.
210 *11-a-Side*, vol. 1, no. 1 (1993), pp. 16–19.
211 Ibid., pp. 6–9.
212 *Irish Times*, 10 April 2003.
213 'RBAI Football Champions', http://www.rbai.org.uk/index.php?option=com_content&view=category&layout=blog&id=89&Itemid=372 [accessed 3 May 2016].
214 Ibid.; 'Sport and Games', http://www.methody.org/School-Activities/Sport-Games.aspx [accessed 3 May 2016]; 'Football Results 2015–16', http://www.methody.org/School-Activities/Sport-Games.aspx [accessed 3 May 2016].
215 *Leinster Express*, 21 Dec. 2006.
216 'Emerging Talent', http://www.fai.ie/domestic/take-part-programmes/emerging-talent [accessed 6 Aug. 2015].
217 *Leinster Express*, 21 Dec. 2006; interview with Martin Russell, 11 July 2013.
218 'Enrolment Fees', http://www.irishfa.com/kit/model/11/player-development-programme [accessed 12 Oct. 2013].
219 'Small-sided Games Strategy 2013–14', *http://www.irishfa.com/fs/doc/Irish_FA_Small-Sided_Games_Strategy_120613.pdf* [accessed 3 Dec. 2015].
220 'Grassroots', http://www.irishfa.com/grassroots/primary-school-coaching-programme [accessed 3 Dec. 2015].
221 'IFA Launches Youth Football Strategy', http://irishfa.com/news/item/10103/ifa-launches-youth-football-strategy [accessed 3 Dec. 2015].
222 Interview with Seamus Heath, 26 Sept. 2013.
223 Hunter Davies, *The Glory Game: the new edition of the British football classic* (Edinburgh: Mainstream, 2001), p. 270; interview with Seamus Heath, 26 Sept. 2013; interview with Raymond Campbell, 10 Dec. 2013.

CHAPTER 3. THE MOVEMENT PROCESS

1 Interview with Richie Sadlier, 23 July 2013.
2 See Joyce, *Football League Players' Records, 1888 to 1939*.
3 *Derry Journal*, 28 Oct. 1902.
4 Garnham, *Association Football and Society*, p. 77; *Ireland's Saturday Night*, 11 June 1904.
5 *Belfast Telegraph*, 28 Oct. 1903.
6 Ibid.
7 Ibid.
8 *Ireland's Saturday Night*, 11 June and 13 Aug. 1904.
9 Garnham, *Association Football and Society*, p. 79.
10 Ibid.
11 Irish Football League Papers, Committee Minutes, D4511/1/31. Season 1914–15, Fourth Committee Meeting; Taylor, *The Leaguers*, p. 204.
12 Irish Football League Papers, Committee Minutes, D4511/1/31, Season 1915–16.
13 David Fitzpatrick, *Irish Emigration, 1801–1921: studies in Irish economic and social history 1* (Dundalk: Dundalgan Press, 1984), p. 5.
14 MacRaild, *The Irish Diaspora in Britain*, p. 3.
15 Taylor, *The Association Game*, p. 121.
16 *Football Sports Weekly*, 12 and 19 June 1926; 'NIFG: Bernard Donaghey', http://nifootball.blogspot.ie/2008/06/barney-donaghey.html [accessed 1 Nov. 2016]; 'NIFG: Jack Doran', http://nifootball.blogspot.ie/2006/11/jack-doran.html [accessed 1 Nov. 2016]; 'NIFG: Joe Enright', http://nifootball.blogspot.ie/2006/11/joe-enright.html [accessed 1 Nov. 2016]; 'NIFG: Harry Hampton', http://nifootball.blogspot.ie/2006/12/harry-hampton.html [accessed 1 Nov. 2016]; 'NIFG: Johnny Houston', http://nifootball.blogspot.ie/2007/01/johnny-houston.html [accessed 1 Nov. 2016]; 'NIFG: Bert Smith', http://nifootball.blogspot.ie/2006/12/bert-smith.html [accessed 1 Nov. 2016]; 'NIFG: Jack Wright', http://nifootball.blogspot.ie/2007/10/john-wright.html [accessed 1 Nov. 2016]; Garnham, *Association Football and Society*, pp. 93–94.
17 Dónal McAnallen, 'The GAA and the Great War', paper given at 'Sport and the Great War' Conference, Public Record Office of Northern Ireland (PRONI), 5 Nov. 2016, https://www.youtube.com/watch?v=mk4d9Tr2eto [accessed 12 March 2017].
18 Andrew Toland, 'PRONI's Football Archives', paper given at 'Going Beyond the "Garrison Game": new perspectives on association football in Irish history' Symposium, PRONI, 17 Feb. 2017.
19 *Football Sports Weekly*, 10 July 1926.
20 Garnham, *Association Football and Society*, p. 171.
21 *Ulster Herald*, 9 Jan. 1915.
22 Taylor, *The Association Game*, p. 120.
23 Garnham, *Association Football and Society*, pp. 167–74.
24 Taylor, *The Association Game*, p. 122.
25 Garnham, *Association Football and Society*, p. 18.

26 David Fitzpatrick, 'Militarism in Ireland, 1900–1922', in Thomas Bartlett and Keith Jeffery (eds), *A Military History of Ireland* [paperback edition] (Cambridge: Cambridge University Press, 1997), pp. 379–406.
27 Joyce, *Football League Players' Records*, p. 107.
28 Ibid., p. 289.
29 T. Ryle Dwyer, 'Guests of the State', in Dermot Keogh and Mervyn O'Driscoll (eds), *Ireland in World War Two: diplomacy and survival* (Cork: Mercier Press, 2004), pp. 107–25, pp. 109–10.
30 Ibid.
31 *Sport*, 19 Nov. 1887.
32 Joyce, *Football League Players' Records*, p. 63.
33 Ibid., p. 268; 'Residents of a House 7 in Mall Street (Ballyshannon, Donegal)', http://www.census.nationalarchives.ie/pages/1911/Donegal/Ballyshannon/Mall_Street/476960 [accessed 24 March 2017]; 'NIFG: Bert Smith'.
34 *Belfast Telegraph*, 3 Jan. 1898.
35 *Football Sports Weekly*, 7 Nov. 1925.
36 Ibid. See also the careers of William Gilmer, J. Mitchell, Tim Kelly and Davy 'Boy' Martin.
37 Taylor, *The Leaguers*, pp. 206–7.
38 Ibid., p. 206; Irish Football League Papers, Management Committee Minutes, D4511/1/31, 16 Dec. 1920 and 12 Oct. 1921.
39 Taylor, *The Leaguers*, p. 206.
40 Garnham, *Association Football and Society*, pp. 194–95.
41 *Sport*, 18 March 1922; Garnham, *Association Football and Society*, p. 178.
42 *Sport*, 25 March 1922.
43 Ibid.
44 Ibid., 6 May 1922.
45 Bardon, *A History of Ulster*, p. 467.
46 Ferriter, *The Transformation of Ireland*, p. 282.
47 *Sport*, 12 Aug. 1922.
48 Ibid., 14 Oct. 1922.
49 Ibid.
50 Ibid., 20 Jan. 1923.
51 Ibid., 2 June 1923.
52 Ibid., 1 March 1924.
53 Ibid., 10 May 1924.
54 Ibid., 24 May 1924.
55 Jonathan Bardon and Stephen Conlin, *Belfast: 1000 Years* (Belfast: Blackstaff Press, 1985), p. 24.
56 Aaron Ó Maonaigh, 'Who Were the Shoneens? Irish militant nationalists and association football, 1913–1923', in Conor Curran and David Toms (eds), 'Going Beyond the "Garrison Game": new perspectives on association football in Irish history', *Soccer and Society* http://www.tandfonline.com/doi/abs/10.1080/14660970.2016.1230339.

57 Ibid.

58 David Toms, 'Darling of the Gods': Tom Farquharson, Irish footballing migrant', *Soccer & Society*, vol. 16, no. 4 (2015), pp. 508–20, p. 511.

59 *Irish Press*, 18 Nov. 1949; Tom Feeney, 'Dunne, James (Jimmy)', *Dictionary of Irish Biography*, http://dib.cambridge.org/viewReadPage.do;jsessionid=B1CB0DC3C71B72FC8A9FEEAA054A68DB?articleId=a2857 [accessed 24 March 2017]. I am grateful to Aaron Ó Maonaigh for drawing my attention to this.

60 Toms, 'Darling of the Gods', p. 516.

61 Taylor, *The Leaguers*, pp. 206–7.

62 Ibid.

63 *Football Sports Weekly*, 26 Sept. 1925.

64 Fitzpatrick, *Irish Emigration, 1801–1921*, pp. 24–25.

65 *Sport*, 23 Sept. 1922; *Football Sports Weekly*, 7 Nov. 1925; Joyce, *Football League Players' Records*, p. 183.

66 Bob Wilson, *You've Got To Be Crazy: on goalkeepers and goalkeeping* (London: Weidenfeld & Nicolson, 1989), p. 41.

67 *Sport*, 30 Sept. 1922; Joyce, *Football League Players' Records*, p. 183.

68 *Sport*, 30 Sept. 1922.

69 Joyce, *Football League Players Records*, p. 195.

70 Ibid., p. 88.

71 *Football Sports Weekly*, 4 Feb. 1928.

72 *Sport*, 25 March 1922.

73 *Football Sports Weekly*, 6 Aug. 1927.

74 'NIFG: Jack Brown', http://nifootball.blogspot.ie/2006/08/jackie-brown.html [accessed 1 Nov. 2016].

75 'NIFG: Tom Waddell', http://nifootball.blogspot.ie/2008/08/tom-waddell.html [accessed 1 Nov. 2016].

76 Fitzpatrick, *Irish Emigration, 1801–1921*, p. 9.

77 'Residents of a House 4 in Victoria Terrace (Larne, Antrim)', http://www.census.nationalarchives.ie/pages/1901/Antrim/Larne/Victoria_Terrace/996636 [accessed 23 March 2017]; 'Residents of a House 62 in Cumberland Street (Wood Vale Ward, Antrim)', http://www.census.nationalarchives.ie/pages/1911/Antrim/Wood_Vale_Ward/Cumberland_Street/163769 [accessed 23 March 2017]; 'Residents of a House 26 in Flora (Pottinger) (part of Down)', *http://www.census.nationalarchives.ie/pages/1911/Down/Pottinger_part_of_/Flora/221051* [accessed 23 March 2017].

78 'Residents of a House 8 in Court Street (Newtownards Urban, Down)', http://www.census.nationalarchives.ie/pages/1911/Down/Newtownards_Urban/Court_Street/268061 [accessed 24 March 2017]; 'Residents of a House 2 in Castleton Avenue (Duncairn, Antrim)', http://www.census.nationalarchives.ie/pages/1911/Antrim/Duncairn/Castleton_Avenue/139821 [accessed 24 March 2017]; 'Residents of a House 41 in Castlewellan (Castlewellan, Down)', http://www.census.nationalarchives.ie/pages/1911/Down/Castlewellan/Castlewellan/235408 [accessed 24 March 2017].

79 'Residents of a House 91.1 in Upper Grand Canal Street (Pembroke West, Dublin)', http://www.census.nationalarchives.ie/pages/1901/Dublin/Pembroke_West/Upper_Grand_Canal_Street/1287956 [accessed 24 March 2017]; 'Residents of a House 11 in Jones's Terrace (Drumcondra, Dublin)', http://www.census.nationalarchives.ie/pages/1901/Dublin/Drumcondra/Jones_s_Terrace/1272488 [accessed 24 March 2017]; 'Residents of a House 27.1 in Capel St. (North City, Dublin)', http://www.census.nationalarchives.ie/pages/1911/Dublin/North_City/ Capel_St_/36594 [accessed 24 March 2017].

80 'Residents of a House 6 in Mill Street (Enniskillen East, Fermanagh)', http://www.census.nationalarchives.ie/pages/1911/Fermanagh/Enniskillen_East/Mill_Street/516056 [accessed 24 March 2017]; 'Residents of a House 6 in Duncreggan Road (Londonderry Urban (1), Londonderry)', http://www.census.nationalarchives.ie/pages/1911/Londonderry/Londonderry_Urban_1_/Duncreggan_Road/627759 [accessed 24 March 2017].

81 The family details of the following players were assessed: Tony Bird, Hugh Blair, Harry Buckle, Sydney Cobain, Joe Connor, Bill Corkhill, Bill Delea, Bernard Donaghey, Charlie Dowdall, Alf Downey, Harry Duggan, William Emerson, Tom Farquharson, Hugh Flack, Archie Goodall, Harry Graham, Bob Griffith, Mickey Hamill, Alfie Harland, Val Harris, William T. Hobbs, Davy Lyner, Jimmy McCambridge, Billy McCleery, Andy McCluggage, English McConnell, Bobby McCracken, Frank McGloughlin, Paddy McIlvenny, Fred McKee, John McKenna, Daniel McKinney, Hugh Leonard Meek, Billy Millar, Billy Mitchell, Pat Nelis, Joe O'Beirne, Patrick O'Connell, Billie O'Hagan, Charlie O'Hagan, Sid Reid, James Wilson Robinson, Pat Robinson, Dave Rollo, Sam Russell, Billy Scott, Elisha Scott, Jack C. Slemin, Joe Toner, John Marshall Wilson.

82 'Residents of a House 8 in Court Street (Newtownards Urban, Down)'; 'Residents of a House 41 in Castlewellan (Castlewellan, Down)'.

83 Garnham, *Association Football and Society*, p. 96.

84 Pamela Dixon and Neal Garnham, 'Drink and the Professional Footballer in 1890s England and Ireland', *Sport in History*, vol. 25, no. 3 (2005), pp. 375–89, at p. 381.

85 Garnham, *Association Football and Society*, pp. 95–96.

86 Mason, *Association Football and English Society*, pp. 90–91.

87 Ibid., p. 92.

88 Conor Curran, 'The Social Background of Ireland's pre-World War I Association Football Clubs, Players and Administrators: the case of south and west Ulster', *International Journal of the History of Sport* (ID: 1304381 DOI:10.1080/09523367.2017.1304381).

89 Curran, *The Development of Sport in Donegal*, p. 192.

90 Hunt, *Sport and Society in Victorian Ireland*, pp. 186–87.

91 Garnham, *Association Football and Society*, p. 97.

92 Ibid.

93 Curran, 'The Social Background of Ireland's pre-World War I Association Football Clubs, Players and Administrators'.

94 Taylor, *The Association Game*, p. 186.

95 Ibid.
96 Ibid.
97 Ibid.
98 Ibid., pp. 190–91.
99 Byrne, *Green Is the Colour*, p. 169.
100 'NIFG: Johnny Carey', http://nifootball.blogspot.ie/2006/08/johnny-carey.html [accessed 17 March 2017].
101 Taylor, *The Association Game*, p. 192.
102 Garnham, *Association Football and Society*, p. 87.
103 *Charles Buchan's Football Monthly* (July 1959), p. 21 and (March 1963), p. 15.
104 Interview with Alfie Hale, 27 Sept. 2013.
105 Interview with Damien Richardson, 13 Aug. 2013.
106 Interview with Brendan Bradley, 16 Jan. 2014.
107 Roderick, *The Work of Professional Football*, p. 100 and p. 112.
108 *Charles Buchan's Football Monthly* (Feb. 1956), p. 35 and (May 1960), p. 30.
109 *Shoot!*, 21 March 1970.
110 Interview with Dean Kelly, 13 Jan. 2014.
111 Interview with Richie Sadlier, 23 July 2013.
112 Interview with Alan Blayney, 13 Jan. 2014.
113 Interview with David Miskelly, 21 Jan. 2014.
114 Interview with Barry Prenderville, 12 July 2013; interview with Brian Mooney, 30 Sept. 2013.
115 Interview with Seamus Heath, 26 Sept. 2013.
116 Seamus Kelly, *The Role of the Professional Football Manager* (London: Routledge, 2017), Chapter 6. I am grateful to Seamus for granting me access to a draft of his work prior to publication.
117 Ibid.
118 John Harding (with Gordon Taylor), *Living To Play: from soccer slaves to socceratti – a social history of the professionals* (London: Robson Books, 2003), p. 52.
119 Interview with Billy Humphries, 14 Jan. 2014.
120 Interview with Brian Mooney, 30 Sept. 2013.
121 Interview with Barry Prenderville, 13 July 2013.
122 Harding, *Living To Play*, p. 72.
123 Interview with Shane Supple, 8 July 2013.
124 Interview with Richie Sadlier, 23 July 2013.
125 Interview with Seamus Kelly, 22 Aug. 2013.
126 Ibid.
127 Interview with Dean Kelly, 13 Jan. 2014.
128 Interview with Seamus Heath, 26 Sept. 2013.
129 Interview with Michael McHugh, 29 Oct. 2013.
130 Interview with Martin Russell, 13 July 2013.
131 Interview with Richie Sadlier, 23 July 2013.
132 Ibid.
133 Harding, *Living To Play*, p. 55.

134 Carter, *The Football Manager: a history*, p. 84.
135 Hugman, *The PFA Premier & Football League Players' Records, 1946–2005*, p. 8.
136 McGovern, 'The Brawn Drain', p. 9.
137 Paul Keane, *Gods vs Mortals: Irish clubs in Europe – a front row seat at ten of the greatest games* (Kells: Irish Sports Publishing, 2010), pp. 13–15.
138 *Shoot!*, 25 Oct. 1969.
139 Ibid.
140 Delaney, *Irish Emigration Since 1921*, p. 18.
141 McGovern, 'The Brawn Drain', p. 10.
142 Ibid., p. 11.
143 Fitzpatrick, *Irish Emigration, 1801–1921*, p. 33.
144 Joyce, *Football League Players' Records.*
145 Peake, 'The Migrant, the Match Fixer and the Manager', p. 37.
146 Lanfranchi and Taylor, *Moving With the Ball*, p. 42.
147 Hugman (ed.), *The PFA Premier & Football League Players' Records, 1946–2005; The PFA Footballers' Who's Who, 2005–6; The PFA Footballers' Who's Who, 2006–7; The PFA Footballers' Who's Who, 2007–8; The PFA Footballers' Who's Who, 2008–9; The PFA Footballers' Who's Who, 2009–10; The PFA Footballers' Who's Who, 2010–11.*
148 Fitzpatrick, *Irish Emigration, 1801–1921*, p. 33.
149 Interview with Richie Sadlier, 23 July 2013; interview with Seamus Kelly, 22 Aug. 2013; interview with Seamus Heath, 26 Sept. 2013; interview with Denis Behan, 6 Dec. 2013.
150 Interview with Paddy Mulligan, 13 Nov. 2013.
151 Interview with Barry Prenderville, 12 July 2013.
152 Interview with Shane Supple, 8 June 2013.
153 Interview with Alfie Hale, 27 Sept. 2013; interview with David Miskelly, 21 Jan. 2014.
154 Davies, *The Glory Game*, p. 21.
155 Neville, 'North of England Falls off Map in Football's Changing Geography'.
156 Interview with Seamus Heath, 26 Sept. 2013.
157 Kelly, 'The Migration of Irish Professional Footballers', p. 77.
158 *Soccer Magazine*, no. 56 (1990), p. 26; 'Republic of Ireland Players in Britain', *Irish Times*, 2 Dec. 2002, 8 March 2004, 24 March 2008.
159 Interview with Damien Richardson, 13 Aug. 2013.
160 *Soccer Magazine*, no. 56 (1990), p. 26.
161 Interview with Damien Richardson, 13 Aug. 2013.
162 Interview with Seamus Kelly, 22 Aug. 2013.
163 *Soccer Magazine*, no. 28 (1986), p. 28 and no. 29 (1987), p. 12.
164 Davies, *The Glory Game*, p. 39.
165 Ibid., pp. 30–31.
166 Ibid., no. 92 (1994), pp. 10–11.
167 Lanfranchi and Taylor, *Moving With the Ball*, p. 82.
168 Ibid., p. 55, p. 61 and pp. 64–65.

169 See, for example, Catherine Woods, Finian Buckley and Melrona Kirrane, *Career Transitions in Young Footballers: a study of how young players cope with selection and deselection in football*, a report for the Football Association of Ireland and the Professional Footballers' Association (2005), pp. 23–25.
170 Ibid., p. 24.
171 Ibid., p. 81.
172 Michael Brennan, 'Young Irish Players Are Victims of Bullying at English Clubs', *Irish Independent*, 3 Oct. 2011, http://www.independent.ie/irish-news/young-irish-players-are-victims-of-bullying-at-english-soccer-clubs-26777943.html [accessed 15 July 2013].
173 Ibid.
174 Department of Foreign Affairs and Trade, 'Minister Micheal Martin Welcomes the Appointment of Terry Conroy as New Football Welfare Officer in Britain', 28 Nov. 2008, http://www.dfa.ie/home/index.aspx?id=79503 [accessed 15 July 2013].
175 Harding, *Living To Play*, pp. 81–83.
176 *Commission on Emigration*, p. 143.
177 Mary E. Daly, *The Irish State and the Diaspora*, NUI Centennial Lecture 2008 (Dublin: National University of Ireland, 2009), pp. 8–9.
178 'Grassroots: Excellence Programme', http://www.irishfa.com/grassroots/excellence-programme [accessed 12 Oct. 2013].
179 Sam Griffin, 'Three-quarters of Irish Emigrants Homesick – Study', http://www.independent.ie/irish-news/three-quarters-of-irish-emigrants-homesick-study-31045144.html [accessed 24 May 2016].
180 Best, *Blessed: the autobiography*, p. 40; *Shoot!*, 29 Nov. 1969.
181 Jennings, *Pat Jennings: an autobiography*, pp. 15–16.
182 Brady, *So Far So Good*, p. 24.
183 Interview with Richie Sadlier, 23 July 2013.
184 Interview with Paddy Mulligan, 13 Nov. 2013.
185 Ibid.
186 Dunphy, *The Rocky Road*, p. 90.
187 Delaney, *The Irish in Post-war Britain*, p. 25.
188 McParland, *Going for Goal*, p. 17.
189 Giles, *A Football Man*, p. 54.
190 *Irish Independent*, 24 Feb. 1973; Whiteside, *Determined Norman Whiteside*, p. 67.
191 *Soccer Magazine*, no. 3 (1985), p. 18. Players staying there included Whiteside, Dave McCreery, Ashley Grimes, Kevin Moran, Anto Whelan and Paul McGrath.
192 Interview with Seamus Heath, 26 Sept. 2013.
193 Ibid.
194 Interview with Shane Supple, 8 July 2013.
195 Ibid.
196 Interview with Michael McHugh, 29 Oct. 2013.
197 Interview with David Miskelly, 21 Jan. 2014.

198 Interview with Michael Carvill, 8 Oct. 2013.
199 Ibid.
200 Ibid.
201 Interview with Damien Richardson, 13 Aug. 2013.
202 *Commission on Emigration*, p. 137.
203 Ibid., p. 138.
204 Delaney, *The Irish in Post-war Britain*, p. 19.
205 Delaney, *Irish Emigration Since 1921*, p. 13.
206 Brady, *So Far So Good*, pp. 14–15.
207 Hugman, *The PFA Premier and Football League Players' Records*, p. 316.
208 'NIFG: Ray Ferris', http://nifootball.blogspot.ie/2006/11/ray-ferris.html [accessed 23 Jan. 2017].
209 Giles, *A Football Man*, p. 17.
210 *Commission on Emigration*, p. 137 and p. 142.
211 Interview with Brian Mooney, 30 Sept. 2013.
212 Ibid.
213 Interview with Michael Carvill, 8 Oct. 2013.
214 Paul Kimmage, 'Liam Tuohy To Retire', *Irish Independent*, 10 Feb. 2002, http://www.independent.ie/sport/soccer/liam-tuohy-to-retire-26239164.html [accessed 14 Aug. 2013].
215 *Soccer Magazine*, no. 76 (Dec. 1992/Jan. 1993), p. 13.
216 Interview with Mick Meagan, 11 Nov. 2013.
217 Ibid.; *Charles Buchan's Football Monthly*, no. 88 (1958), p. 13.
218 *Charles Buchan's Football Monthly*, no. 70 (1957).
219 Interview with Mick Meagan, 11 Nov. 2013.
220 Delaney, *The Irish in Post-war Britain*, pp. 95–96.
221 Ibid. p. 95.
222 Ibid., p. 29 and pp. 52–53.
223 Daly, *The Irish State and the Diaspora*, p. 7.
224 *Commission on Emigration*, p. 141.
225 MacRaild, *The Irish Diaspora in Britain*, p. 3.
226 Interview with Mick Meagan, 11 Nov. 2013.
227 Daly, *The Irish State and the Diaspora*, p. 13.
228 Interview with Mick Meagan, 11 Nov. 2013.
229 Ibid.
230 Ibid.
231 Taylor, *The Association Game*, p. 427.
232 Ibid.
233 Ibid.
234 Interview with Seamus Kelly, 22 Aug. 2013.
235 Delaney, *The Irish in Post-war Britain*, p. 80.
236 Interview with Alfie Hale, 27 Sept. 2013.
237 Ibid.
238 Ibid.

239 Seán Ryan and Stephen Burke, *The Book of Irish Goalscorers* (Tralee: The Kerryman, 1987), p. 27.
240 Delaney, *The Irish in Post-war Britain*, p. 129.
241 Interview with Alfie Hale, 27 Sept. 2013.
242 Daly, *The Irish State and the Diaspora*, p. 18.
243 Interview with Alfie Hale, 27 Sept. 2013.
244 Ibid.
245 Interview with Paddy Mulligan, 13 Nov. 2013.
246 Ibid.
247 Taylor, *The Association Game*, pp. 216–17.
248 Interview with Alfie Hale, 27 Sept. 2013.
249 Ibid.
250 Ibid.
251 Ibid.; interview with Billy Humphries, 14 Jan. 2014.
252 Interview with Billy Humphries, 14 Jan. 2014.
253 Interview with Alfie Hale, 27 Sept. 2013.
254 Dunphy, *The Rocky Road*, p. 89.
255 Interview with Hubert Barr, 7 Jan. 2014.
256 Stead and Maguire, '"Rite De Passage"', p. 47.
257 Interview with Barry Prenderville, 13 July 2013.
258 Interview with John McClelland, 29 Jan. 2014.
259 Delaney, *The Irish in Post-war Britain*, p. 66.
260 *Irish Post*, 24 March 1979.
261 Ibid., 24 Nov. 1979.
262 Delaney, *The Irish in Post-war Britain*, pp. 127–75.
263 Ibid., p. 206.
264 MacRaild, *The Irish Diaspora in Britain*, p. 5.
265 Alan Bairner, 'Simply the (George) Best: Ulster Protestantism, conflicted identity and "The Belfast Boy(s)"', *The Canadian Journal of Irish Studies*, vol. 32, no. 2 (Fall, 2006), pp. 34–41, at p. 37.
266 Delaney, *The Irish in Post-war Britain*, p. 68.
267 Interview with Damien Richardson, 23 Aug. 2013.
268 Interview with Richie Sadlier, 23 July 2013; interview with Seamus Kelly, 22 Aug. 2013.
269 Interview with Seamus Kelly, 22 Aug. 2013.
270 Interview with Martin Russell, 11 July 2013; interview with Richie Sadlier, 23 July 2013.
271 Interview with Paddy Mulligan, 13 Nov. 2013.
272 Interview with Seamus Heath, 26 Sept. 2013.
273 Interview with Barry Prenderville, 13 July 2013.
274 Interview with Brian Mooney, 30 Sept. 2013; interview with Michael McHugh, 29 Oct. 2013.
275 Interview with Richie Sadlier, 23 July 2013.
276 Interview with Denis Behan, 6 Dec. 2013.
277 Interview with Alan Blayney, 13 Jan. 2014.

278 Interview with Damien Richardson, 13 Aug. 2013.
279 Davies, *The Glory Game*, p. 33.
280 *Charles Buchan's Football Monthly*, no. 58 (June 1956), p. 10.
281 Interview with Barry Prenderville, 13 July 2013.
282 Interview with Richie Sadlier, 23 July 2013.
283 Ibid.
284 Interview with Barry Prenderville, 13 July 2013.
285 Interview with Michael Carvill, 8 Oct. 2013.
286 *Irish Independent*, 9 Aug. 1946.
287 *Shoot!*, 20 March 1971.
288 Interview with Seamus Heath, 26 Sept. 2013.
289 Interview with David Miskelly, 21 Jan. 2014.
290 Interview with Brian Mooney, 30 Sept. 2013.
291 Interview with Martin Russell, 13 July 2013.
292 Interview with Andy Waterworth, 8 Oct. 2013.
293 Interview with Michael Carvill, 8 Oct. 2013.
294 Interview with Denis Behan, 6 Dec. 2013.
295 Interview with Damien Richardson, 13 Aug. 2013.
296 Interview with Richie Sadlier, 23 July 2013.
297 Interview with Mick Meagan, 11 Nov. 2013; interview with Richie Sadlier, 23 July 2013.
298 Interview with Brendan Bradley, 16 Jan. 2014.
299 *Soccer Magazine*, no. 5 (1985), pp. 15–16.
300 Interview with Brian Mooney, 30 Sept. 2013; interview with John McClelland, 29 Jan. 2014.
301 Arthur Hopcraft, *The Football Man: people and passions in soccer* (London: SportsPages, 1968), pp. 87–92.
302 Hannigan, *The Garrison Game*, pp. 79–81.
303 Harding, *Living To Play*, p. 73.

CHAPTER 4. PLAYING EXPERIENCES

1 Interview with Seamus Kelly, 23 Aug. 2013.
2 Mason, *Association Football and English Society*, p. 89.
3 Ibid.
4 Ibid., pp. 108–9.
5 *Football Sports Weekly*, 17 July 1926.
6 Ibid.
7 Mason, *Association Football and English Society*, p. 109.
8 *Football Sports Weekly*, 31 July 1926.
9 Ibid.
10 Dixon and Garnham, 'Drink and the Professional Footballer in 1890s England and Ireland', pp. 375–89, pp. 385–86.
11 Mason, *Association Football and English Society*, p. 178.

12 *Football Sports Weekly*, 17 July 1926.
13 Ibid.
14 Ibid.
15 Ibid., 17 and 31 July 1926.
16 Ibid., 15 Jan. 1927.
17 Ibid., 5 May 1928.
18 Ibid.
19 Ibid.
20 Interview with Damien Richardson, 13 Aug. 2013.
21 *Soccer Magazine*, no. 15 (1986), p. 15.
22 Interview with Seamus Kelly, 22 Aug. 2013; interview with Paddy Mulligan, 13 Nov. 2013.
23 Interview with Seamus Kelly, 22 Aug. 2013.
24 Interview with Mick Meagan, 11 Nov. 2013.
25 Interview with Hubert Barr, 7 Jan. 2014.
26 Ibid.; *Irish Press*, 27 June 1962.
27 Interview with Hubert Barr, 7 Jan. 2014; interview with Billy Humphries, 14 Jan. 2013.
28 Davies, *The Glory Game*, p. 19.
29 Eamon Dunphy, *Only a Game? The diary of a professional footballer* (Middlesex: Penguin, 1976), pp. 15–16.
30 Interview with Brendan Bradley, 16 Jan. 2014.
31 Interview with Damien Richardson, 13 Aug. 2013.
32 Interview with Michael McHugh, 29 Oct. 2013.
33 Interview with Martin Russell, 11 July 2013.
34 Interview with David Miskelly, 21 Jan. 2014.
35 Interview with Shane Supple, 8 July 2013.
36 Interview with Richie Sadlier, 23 July 2013.
37 Interview with Barry Prenderville, 12 July 2013.
38 Interview with Denis Behan, 6 Dec. 2013.
39 Roderick, *The Work of Professional Football*, p. 151.
40 Interview with Martin Russell, 11 July 2013.
41 Interview with Mick Meagan, 11 Nov. 2013.
42 Ibid.
43 Interview with Alfie Hale, 27 Sept. 2013.
44 Interview with Michael McHugh, 29 Oct. 2013.
45 Ibid.
46 Interview with Barry Prenderville, 12 July 2013.
47 Harding, *Living To Play*, p. 82.
48 Interview with David Miskelly, 21 Jan. 2014.
49 Interview with Richie Sadlier, 23 July 2013.
50 Ibid.
51 Interview with Michael Carvill, 8 Oct. 2013.
52 Interview with Andy Waterworth, 8 Oct. 2013.
53 Interview with Mick Meagan, 11 Nov. 2013.

54 Roderick, *The Work of Professional Football*, p. x.
55 Interview with Barry Prenderville, 12 July 2013; interview with Richie Sadlier, 23 July 2013; interview with Michael McHugh, 29 Oct. 2013.
56 Interview with Seamus Kelly, 22 Aug. 2013; David James, 'High-Pressure Game Without a Net When You Hang Up Gloves', http://www.theguardian.com/football/blog/2012/mar/10/david-james-900th-game [accessed 4 Nov. 2013].
57 Paul McVeigh, *The Stupid Footballer Is Dead: insights into the mindset of a professional footballer* (London: Bloomsbury, 2013), p. 7.
58 Ibid., p. 8.
59 Interview with Richie Sadlier, 23 July 2013.
60 Interview with Andy Waterworth, 8 Oct. 2013.
61 Interview with Alan Blayney, 13 Jan. 2014.
62 Interview with David Miskelly, 21 Jan. 2014.
63 Steven Gerrard, *My Story* (London: Penguin, 2015), pp. 219–22.
64 Davies, *The Glory Game*, p. 12.
65 Interview with Denis Behan, 6 Dec. 2013.
66 Interview with David Miskelly, 21 Jan. 2014.
67 Ibid.
68 Interview with Seamus Kelly, 22 Aug. 2013.
69 Interview with Shane Supple, 8 July 2013.
70 Interview with Alfie Hale, 27 Sept. 2013.
71 Interview with Mick Meagan, 11 Nov. 2013.
72 Interview with Michael McHugh, 29 Oct. 2013.
73 Ibid.
74 Interview with Alfie Hale, 27 Sept. 2013.
75 Ibid.
76 Taylor, *The Association Game*, pp. 195–96.
77 Interview with Mick Meagan, 11 Nov. 2013.
78 Taylor, *The Association Game*, p. 195.
79 Interview with Denis Behan, 6 Dec. 2013.
80 Interview with Billy Humphries, 14 Jan. 2014.
81 Interview with Alan Blayney, 13 Jan. 2014.
82 Interview with Mick Meagan, 11 Nov. 2013.
83 Interview with Seamus Kelly, 22 Aug. 2013.
84 Interview with Shane Supple, 8 July 2013.
85 Interview with Denis Behan, 6 Dec. 2013.
86 Interview with David Miskelly, 21 Jan. 2014.
87 Interview with Richie Sadlier, 23 July 2013.
88 Interview with Alfie Hale, 26 Sept. 2013.
89 Interview with Seamus Kelly, 22 Aug. 2013.
90 Interview with Shane Supple, 8 July 2013.
91 Interview with Seamus Heath, 26 Sept. 2013.
92 Ibid.
93 Roderick, *The Work of Professional Football*, p. 4.
94 Interview with Richie Sadlier, 23 July 2013.

95 Roderick, *The Work of Professional Football*, p. 36.
96 Toni Schumacher, *Blowing the Whistle* (London: WH Allen, 1988), pp. 103–12.
97 Interview with Paddy Mulligan, 13 Nov. 2013.
98 Whiteside, *Determined Norman Whiteside*, pp. 71–72.
99 Ibid.
100 Interview with Brian Mooney, 30 Sept. 2013.
101 Roderick, *The Work of Professional Football*, p. 82.
102 Taylor, *The Association Game*, p. 226.
103 Ibid.
104 Roderick, *The Work of Professional Football*, p. viii and pp. 71–74.
105 Interview with Mick Meagan, 11 Nov. 2013.
106 Interview with Alfie Hale, 27 Sept. 2013.
107 Interview with Hubert Barr, 7 Jan. 2014.
108 Interview with Gerry Burrell, 13 Jan. 2014.
109 Interview with Michael McHugh, 29 Oct. 2013.
110 Interview with Denis Behan, 6 Dec. 2013.
111 Ibid.
112 Roderick, *The Work of Professional Football*, p. viii.
113 Ibid., pp. 44–45.
114 Interview with Alan Blayney, 13 Jan. 2014.
115 Interview with Paddy Mulligan, 13 Nov. 2013.
116 Roderick, *The Work of Professional Football*, p. 16.
117 Ibid., p. 23.
118 Interview with Richie Sadlier, 23 July 2013.
119 *Charles Buchan's Football Monthly* (December 1955), pp. 20–21 and p. 31.
120 Interview with Barry Prenderville, 12 July 2013.
121 Interview with Seamus Kelly, 22 Aug. 2013.
122 Interview with Paddy Mulligan, 13 Nov. 2013.
123 MacRaild, *The Irish Diaspora*, p. 161.
124 Ibid., p. 217.
125 Mary J. Hickman, 'The Irish in Britain: racism, incorporation and identity', *Irish Studies Review*, vol. 3, no. 10 (1995), pp. 16–19, at p. 16.
126 Ibid.
127 Taylor, *The Association Game*, pp. 375–83.
128 Interview with Richie Sadlier, 23 July 2013; interview with Damien Richardson, 13 Aug. 2013; interview with Seamus Kelly, 22 Aug. 2013.
129 Interview with Brian Mooney, 30 Sept. 2013.
130 Kelly, 'The Migration of Irish Professional Footballers', p. 13.
131 Interview with Seamus Kelly, 22 Aug. 2013.
132 Interview with Richie Sadlier, 23 July 2013.
133 Ibid.
134 Interview with Seamus Kelly, 22 Aug. 2013.
135 Interview with Alan Blayney, 13 Jan. 2014.
136 Ibid.
137 Interview with Paddy Mulligan, 13 Nov. 2013.

138 Whiteside, *Determined Norman Whiteside*, pp. 55–57; interview with Richie Sadlier, 23 July 2013.
139 Interview with David Miskelly, 21 Jan. 2014.
140 Interview with Damien Richardson, 23 Aug. 2013.
141 John Terry quoted on *Soccer AM*, 30 April 2016.
142 *Soccer Magazine*, no. 34 (1988), p. 24.
143 'Former Stoke City Trainee Claims Club and Ex-England Captain Ignored Abuse', http://www.irishtimes.com/sport/soccer/english-soccer/former-stoke-city-trainee-claims-club-and-ex-england-captain-ignored-abuse-1.1623330 [accessed 15 Dec. 2013]. At the time of writing, a number of those involved in English professional football as underage coaches were being investigated for sexual abuse of young players.
144 Interview with Mick Meagan, 11 Nov. 2013.
145 Interview with Denis Behan, 6 Dec. 2013.
146 Kelly, 'The Migration of Irish Professional Footballers', p. 11.
147 Interview with Paddy Mulligan, 13 Nov. 2013.
148 Interview with Richie Sadlier, 23 July 2013; interview with Damien Richardson, 13 Aug. 2013.
149 Interview with Seamus Kelly, 23 Aug. 2013.
150 Davies, *The Glory Game*, p. 24.
151 Interview with Paddy Mulligan, 13 Nov. 2013.
152 Ibid. And see, for example, *Irish Independent*, 15 March and 3 April 1969 and *Irish Press*, 17 March and 3 April 1969.
153 Roderick, *The Work of Professional Football*, p. 83.
154 Interview with Paddy Mulligan, 13 Nov. 2013.
155 Delaney, *The Irish in Post-war Britain*, p. 13.
156 Coogan, *Wherever Green Is Worn*, p. 141.
157 Delaney, *The Irish in Post-war Britain*, p. 89.
158 Interview with Seamus Heath, 26 Sept. 2013.
159 Interview with Paddy Mulligan, 13 Nov. 2013.
160 Ibid.
161 Interview with Damien Richardson, 13 Aug. 2013.
162 Chris Moore, *United Irishmen: Manchester United's Irish connection* (Edinburgh: Mainstream, 1999), p. 113; Seán Ryan, 'The Irish in Britain: Cassidy's Brace, Then Out', *Irish Independent*, 20 Nov. 1973, p. 18.
163 Davies, *The Glory Game*, pp. 271–72.
164 Interview with John McClelland, 29 Jan. 2014.
165 Interview with Richie Sadlier, 23 July 2013.
166 Interview with David Miskelly, 21 Jan. 2014.
167 Interview with Damien Richardson, 13 Aug. 2013; interview with Brian Mooney, 30 Sept. 2013.
168 Interview with Alan Blayney, 13 Jan. 2014.
169 Interview with Raymond Campbell, 10 Dec. 2015.
170 Daniel Brown, 'Linfield's "Hawk of Peace": pre-ceasefires reconciliation in Irish League football', in Curran and Toms (eds), 'Going Beyond the "Garrison Game"', *Soccer and Society*.

171 Harding, *Living To Play*, p. 174.
172 Roderick, *The Work of Professional Football*, p. 30.
173 Liam Ryan, 'Ken DeMange', *Soccer Magazine*, no. 77 (1993), p. 15.
174 Paul and Eugene Deering, 'The Deering Brothers, Paul and Eugene, Talk to Derry City's New Signing Martin Bayly', *Soccer Magazine*, no. 33 (1988), pp. 22–23.
175 Interview with John McClelland, 29 Jan. 2014.
176 Ibid.
177 Roderick, *The Work of Professional Football*, p. 118.
178 Interview with John McClelland, 29 Jan. 2014.
179 Ibid. And see Lanfranchi and Taylor, *Moving With the Ball*, pp. 213–29 for a discussion of the impact of the Bosman ruling. In 1995 the European Court of Justice ruled that 'restrictions on the use of citizens of other European Union (EU) member states were ruled to be a clear discrimination on the grounds of nationality which contradicted Article 48 of the Treaty of Rome relating to the free movement of workers'. This development emerged as a result of Belgium-born footballer Jean-Marc Bosman's efforts to leave Royal Football Club Liège to join French club US Dunkerque-Littoral.
180 Interview with John McClelland, 29 Jan. 2014.
181 Interview with Denis Behan, 6 Dec. 2013.
182 Interview with Alfie Hale, 27 Sept. 2013.
183 Ibid.
184 Harding, *Living To Play*, p. 174.
185 Interview with Raymond Campbell, 10 Dec. 2013.
186 Roderick, *The Work of Professional Football*, pp. 88–89.
187 Interview with Seamus Heath, 26 Sept. 2013.
188 *Soccer Magazine*, no. 42 (1989), p. 42.
189 Roddy Dell, 'Championship Is Russell's Target', *Soccer Magazine*, no. 85 (1994), p. 26.
190 Interview with Martin Russell, 11 July 2013.
191 Interview with Brian Mooney, 30 Sept. 2013.
192 Interview with Barry Prenderville, 12 July 2013.
193 Interview with Dean Kelly, 13 Jan. 2014.
194 Interview with Raymond Campbell, 10 Dec. 2013.
195 Interview with John McClelland, 29 Jan. 2014.
196 Interview with Michael Carvill, 8 Oct. 2013.
197 Harding, *Living To Play*, p. 177.
198 Ibid. and p. 81.
199 Interview with Andy Waterworth, 8 Oct. 2013.
200 Roderick, *The Work of Professional Football*, p. 144.
201 Ibid., p. 140.
202 *Soccer Magazine*, no. 28 (1986), p. 21 and no. 29 (1987), p. 12.
203 *The Rod Squad (Roddy Collins at Carlisle United)*, episode 4, https://www.youtube.com/watch?v=zbGQwcGhVxE [accessed 21 May 2016].

204 'Never Say Die: the Stephen Hunt story', http://www.rte.ie/radio1/podcast/podcast_radio1specials.xml [accessed 7 Aug. 2013].
205 Interview with Michael McHugh, 29 Oct. 2013.
206 Interview with Martin Russell, 11 July 2013.
207 *Soccer Magazine*, no. 61 (1991), p. 12.
208 Simon Kuper and Stefan Szymanski, *Why England Lose and Other Curious Football Phenomena Explained* (London: HarperSport, 2010), pp. 73–79.
209 See, for example, Jerzy Dudek, *A Big Pole in Our Goal: my autobiography* (Liverpool: Sport Media, 2016), pp. 110–11.
210 Interview with Damien Richardson, 13 Aug. 2013; interview with Alfie Hale, 27 Sept. 2013.
211 Interview with Mick Meagan, 13 Nov. 2013.
212 Ibid.
213 Alan Bairner, 'Irish Sport', in Joe Cleary and Claire Connolly (eds), *The Cambridge Companion to Modern Irish Culture* (Cambridge: Cambridge University Press, 2005), pp. 190–205, at pp. 190–91.
214 Interview with Paddy Mulligan, 13 Nov. 2013.
215 Taylor, *The Association Game*, p. 184.
216 Harry Gregg (with Roger Anderson), *Harry's Game: the autobiography* (Edinburgh: Mainstream, 2002), p. 86.
217 Interview with John McClelland, 29 Jan. 2014.
218 Ibid.
219 Davies, *The Glory Game*, p. 7.
220 Roderick, *The Work of Professional Football*, p. 150.
221 Hickman, 'The Irish in Britain', p. 16.
222 Ryan and Burke, *The Book of Irish Goalscorers*, p. 83.
223 Interview with Billy Humphries, 14 Jan. 2014.

CHAPTER 5. MIGRATION TO SCOTLAND, EUROPE AND NORTH AMERICA

1 Interview with John McClelland, 29 Jan. 2014.
2 Richard B. McCready, 'Revising the Irish in Scotland', in Bielenberg (ed.), *The Irish Diaspora*, pp. 37–50, at p. 39.
3 Emms and Wells, *Scottish League Players' Records. Division One 1890/91 to 1938/39*, p. 126.
4 'NIFG: Peter Boyle', http://nifootball.blogspot.ie/2006/08/peter-boyle.html [accessed 1 Nov. 2016].
5 *Lancashire Evening Post*, 14 Nov. 1896.
6 Emms and Wells, *Scottish League Players' Records*, p. 139.
7 *Ulster Saturday Night*, 21 Sept. 1895.
8 Garnham, *Association Football and Society*, p. 34.
9 Emms and Wells, *Scottish League Players' Records*, p. 181, p. 195, p. 224 and p. 228.

10 Ibid., p. 153.
11 Joyce, *Football League Players' Records*, p. 34; 'NIFG: Sam English', http://nifootball.blogspot.ie/2006/10/sam-english.html [accessed 1 Nov. 2016].
12 Taylor, *The Association Game*, pp. 121–22.
13 'The Scottish Professional Football League', http://spfl.co.uk/spfl [accessed 26 Jan. 2014].
14 Interview with Barry Prenderville, 12 July 2013; Hugman (ed.), *The PFA Footballers' Who's Who, 2010–11*, p. 232.
15 See, for example, 'Field Club Explores Scottish Links', http://www.independent.ie/regionals/sligochampion/news/field-club-explores-scotland-links-27580084.html [accessed 7 May 2016]; Curran, *The Development of Sport in Donegal*, pp. 14–22 and pp. 185–86.
16 *Irish Permanent Presents 'The Packie Bonner Story'* (Dublin: Copperfield Publications Ltd, 1991), p. 16.
17 Interview with Andy Waterworth, 8 Oct. 2013.
18 Interview with Shane Supple, 8 July 2013.
19 Emms and Wells, *Scottish League Players' Records*, p. 74; *Football Sports Weekly*, 30 Oct. 1926.
20 Beal and Emms, *Scottish League Players' Records*, p. 24, p. 40, p. 48 and p. 52. Earlier Buncrana-born football migrants to Scotland include Charlie and Billy O'Hagan.
21 Interview with Gerry Burrell, 13 Jan. 2014.
22 Ibid.
23 'Kirk Broadfoot Given Record 10 Game Ban for James McClean Abuse', http://www.irishtimes.com/sport/soccer/english-soccer/kirk-broadfoot-given-record-10-game-ban-for-james-mcclean-abuse-1.2295992 [accessed 25 July 2015].
24 Whiteside, *Determined Norman Whiteside*, pp. 67–69; Lennon, *Man and Bhoy*, p. 54.
25 Interview with Shane Supple, 8 July 2013; interview with Barry Prenderville, 12 July 2013.
26 Interview with Barry Prenderville, 12 July 2013.
27 Ibid.
28 Ibid.
29 Interview with John McClelland, 29 Jan. 2014.
30 McCready, 'Revising the Irish in Scotland', in Bielenberg (ed.), *The Irish Diaspora*, pp. 37–50, at pp. 40–41.
31 See Joseph Bradley, 'Football in Scotland: a history of political and ethnic identity', *The International Journal of the History of Sport*, vol. 12, no. 1 (1995), pp. 81–98; 'Integration or Assimilation?' Scottish society, football and Irish immigrants', *The International Journal of the History of Sport*, vol. 13, no. 2 (1996), pp. 61–79.
32 Bradley, 'Integration or Assimilation', p. 62.
33 Bradley, 'Football in Scotland', p. 83.
34 Ibid., p. 84.

35 Ibid., p. 85.
36 Ibid., pp. 84–85.
37 Ibid.
38 Ibid., pp. 85–86.
39 Taylor, *The Association Game*, p. 100.
40 Joan McAlpine, 'Celtic and Rangers: across Scotland's sectarian divide', http://www.guardian.co.uk/commentisfree/2011/mar/20/celtic-rangers-football-religion-sectarian [accessed 21 July 2013].
41 Taylor, *The Association Game*, p. 100.
42 'NIFG: John McClelland', http://nifootball.blogspot.ie/2006/12/john-mcclelland.html [accessed 27 April 2016].
43 Interview with John McClelland, 29 Jan. 2014.
44 *Irish Permanent Presents 'The Packie Bonner Story'*, p. 20.
45 Ibid., pp. 29–30.
46 Seán Ryan, *The Boys in Green: the FAI international story* (Edinburgh: Mainstream, 1997), p. 198.
47 Uprichard (with Chris Westcott), *Norman 'Black Jake' Uprichard* (2011), pp. 52–3 and p. 133.
48 Taylor, *The Leaguers*, p. 223; Joyce, *Football League Players' Records, 1888–1939*, p. 77.
49 Taylor, *The Leaguers*, p. 231.
50 Ibid., p. 230.
51 Ibid.
52 Joyce, *Football League Players' Records*, p. 84.
53 *Football Sports Weekly*, 21 Aug. 1926.
54 Taylor, *The Leaguers*, p. 219.
55 *Soccer Magazine*, no. 1 (1984), p. 5.
56 Ibid.
57 Ibid.
58 Gray and Emms, *Scottish League Players' Records*, p. 74; 'The Wild Geese: Liam Buckley', http://irishfootballersineurope.blogspot.ie/2012/08/liam-buckley.html [accessed 2 May 2016].
59 Gray and Emms, *Scottish League Players' Records*, p. 15.
60 Delaney, *Irish Emigration Since 1921*, p. 11.
61 Ibid.
62 David Hassan, 'The Role of Gaelic Games in the Lives of the Irish Diaspora in Europe', *Sport in Society*, vol. 10, no. 3 (2007), pp. 385–401.
63 Ibid., pp. 393–94.
64 Lanfranchi and Taylor, *Moving With the Ball*, p. 68.
65 This refers to the top divisions in France, Germany, Italy and Spain.
66 Lanfranchi and Taylor, *Moving With the Ball*, p. 67.
67 Ibid., pp. 64–67.
68 Ibid.; Ulrich Hesse-Lichtenberger, *Tor! The story of German football* (new edition) (London: WSC Books, 2003), pp. 146–48.
69 Hassan, 'The Role of Gaelic Games', p. 390.

70 Eoin O'Callaghan, 'From St Pat's to the Bundesliga', http://www.irishexaminer.com/sport/soccer/from-st-pats-to-the-bundesliga-291232.html [accessed 26 April 2016].
71 'The Wild Geese: Joe Kendrick', http://irishfootballersineurope.blogspot.ie/2012/09/joe-kendrick.html [accessed 2 May 2016].
72 John Foot, *Calcio: a history of Italian football* (updated edition) (London: Harper Perennial, 2007), p. 437.
73 *Irish Independent*, 29 July 1980.
74 *Sunday Independent*, 17 May 1981.
75 'Liam Brady with Juventus, 1980–1982', https://www.youtube.com/watch?v=nCBP7mgwgJU [accessed 1 May 2016]; 'The Wild Geese: Liam Brady', http://irishfootballersineurope.blogspot.ie/2012/07/liam-brady.html[accessed 1 May 2016].
76 *Sunday Independent*, 17 May 1981.
77 Ibid.
78 Foot, *Calcio*, pp. 460–61.
79 Lanfranchi and Taylor, *Moving With the Ball*, p. 63; Foot, *Calcio*, p. 461; 'NIFG: Joshua "Paddy" Sloan', http://nifootball.blogspot.ie/2007/04/josiah-paddy-sloan.html [accessed 26 April 2016].
80 Foot, *Calcio*, p. 461.
81 Hugman (ed.), *The PFA Premier & Football League Players' Records*, p. 27.
82 'NIFG: Jim Hagan', http://nifootball.blogspot.ie/2007/01/jim-hagan.html [accessed 16 Jan. 2016].
83 Hugman (ed.), *The PFA Premier & Football League Players' Records*, p. 253 and p. 436; Hugman (ed.), *The PFA Footballers' Who's Who, 2008–09*, p. 153 and p. 192.
84 Hassan, 'The Role of Gaelic Games', p. 391.
85 *Soccer Magazine*, no 34 (1988), p. 29; 'The Wild Geese: Frank Stapleton', http://irishfootballersineurope.blogspot.ie/2012/08/frank-stapleton.html [accessed 26 April 2016].
86 *Irish Press*, 22 May 1959.
87 Ryan and Burke, *The Book of Irish Goalscorers*, p. 140.
88 *Soccer Magazine*, no. 30 (1987), p. 18.
89 Interview with Paddy Mulligan, 9 May 2016.
90 Simon Burnton, 'The Forgotten Story of ... Johnny Crossan's Ban from Football', http://www.theguardian.com/sport/blog/2011/nov/02/forgotten-story-john-crossan-ban [accessed 26 April 2016]; *Irish Examiner*, 4 Nov. 1959.
91 *Irish Examiner*, 29 Sept. 1959; *Irish Independent*, 6 Oct. 1959.
92 *Soccer Magazine*, no. 68 (1992), p. 15.
93 *Irish Independent*, 6 Oct. 1959.
94 *Soccer Magazine*, no 34 (1988), p. 29; 'The Wild Geese: Frank Stapleton'.
95 Frank Stapleton, *Frankly Speaking* (Dublin: Blackwater Press, 1991), p. 89.
96 Hugman (ed.), *The PFA Premier and Football League Players' Records, 1946–2005*, p. 147, p. 209 and p. 583.
97 'NIFG: Sammy Morgan', http://nifootball.blogspot.ie/2007/08/sammy-morgan.html [accessed 15 Jan. 2016].

98 'NIFG: Tommy Cassidy', http://nifootball.blogspot.ie/2006/08/tommy-cassidy.html [accessed 15 Jan. 2016].
99 Tony Scholes, 'Steve McAdam Passes Away', http://www.clarets-mad.co.uk/news/tmnw/steve_mcadam_passes_away_182109/index.shtml [accessed 7 May 2016].
100 'NIFG: Sammy McIlroy', http://nifootball.blogspot.co.uk/2006/10/sammy-mcilroy.html [accessed 15 Jan. 2016].
101 'NIFG: Paul Ramsey', http://nifootball.blogspot.ie/2006/12/paul-ramsey.html [accessed 16 Jan. 2016].
102 Interview with Seamus Heath, 26 Sept. 2013.
103 Ibid.
104 'NIFG: Roy Carroll', http://nifootball.blogspot.ie/2006/08/roy-carroll.html [accessed 16 Jan. 2016].
105 'NIFG: Kyle Lafferty', http://nifootball.blogspot.ie/2007/01/kyle-lafferty.html [accessed 16 Jan. 2016].
106 Delaney, *Irish Emigration Since 1921*, pp. 7–8.
107 Ibid., p. 10.
108 Ferriter, *The Transformation of Ireland, 1900–2000*, p. 330.
109 *Commission on Emigration*, pp. 134–35.
110 Ibid.
111 Ibid.
112 Kevin Kenny, *The American Irish: a history* (Harlow: Pearson Education Ltd, 2000), p. 221.
113 George Brown Tindall and David E. Shi, *America: a narrative history*, 6th edition (New York/London: WW Norton & Co. Ltd, 2004), p. 699.
114 Ibid., p. 697.
115 Lanfranchi and Taylor, *Moving With the Ball*, p. 144.
116 Ibid.
117 Ibid., p. 145.
118 *Sport*, 1 Oct. 1921.
119 Ibid.
120 *Irish Examiner*, 2 March 1923.
121 Taylor, *The Leaguers*, p. 202.
122 *Irish Examiner*, 2 March 1923.
123 Ibid.
124 Lanfranchi and Taylor, *Moving With the Ball*, p. 146 and p. 148.
125 Jose, *American Soccer League, 1921–1931*.
126 Lanfranchi and Taylor, *Moving With the Ball*, p. 148.
127 See, for example, *Sport*, 14 Oct. 1922.
128 Joyce, *Football League Players' Records*.
129 Taylor, *The Leaguers*, p. 208.
130 *Sport*, 19 May 1923.
131 Joyce, *Football League Players' Records*; Jose, *American Soccer League*.
132 See Joyce, *Football League Players' Records*.

133 *Sport*, 23 Feb. 1924; '"Tucker" Croft', http://nifootball.blogspot.ie/2006/09/tucker-croft.html [accessed 8 Oct. 2016].
134 *Football Sports Weekly*, 4 Sept. 1926; *Sport*, 18 Aug. 1928.
135 *Football Sports Weekly*, 23 July 1927.
136 Jose, *American Soccer League*, p. 368 and pp. 424–25.
137 Kenny, *The American Irish*, p. 183.
138 Ibid., p. 182.
139 Jose, *American Soccer League, 1921–31*, p. 9 and p. 16.
140 Kenny, *The American Irish*, p. 184.
141 Ibid., p. 185.
142 Ibid., p. 184.
143 *Football Sports Weekly*, 4 June 1927.
144 Ibid., 4 June, 2 and 16 July 1927.
145 Ibid., 23 July and 13 Aug. 1927.
146 Steve Holroyd, 'The ASL's "Philadelphia Celtic": Philly's last chance at success in US soccer's "golden age"', http://www.phillysoccerpage.net/2014/03/14/the-asls-philadelphia-celtic-phillys-last-chance-at-success-in-us-soccers-golden-age [accessed 28 July 2016].
147 Lanfranchi and Taylor, *Moving With the Ball*, p. 147 and p. 149.
148 Holroyd, 'The ASL's "Philadelphia Celtic"'.
149 Ibid.
150 *Evening Herald*, 5 Oct. 1927; Jose, *American Soccer League*, p. 412.
151 *Football Sports Weekly*, 23 Oct. 1926; *Evening Herald*, 5 Aug. 1927; *Irish Independent*, 29 Sept. 1927.
152 *Football Sports Weekly*, 1 Oct. 1927.
153 *Irish Independent*, 29 Sept. 1927; Holroyd, 'The ASL's "Philadelphia Celtic"'.
154 *Evening Herald*, 31 Oct. 1927 and 2 Nov. 1927.
155 *Football Sports Weekly*, 1 Oct. 1927.
156 *Evening Herald*, 15 Oct. 1924.
157 Joyce, *Football League Players' Records, 1888 to 1939*, p. 220; Taylor, *The Leaguers*, p. 229.
158 *Football Sports Weekly*, 4 Sept. and 18 Dec. 1926.
159 *Evening Herald*, 3 July 1930.
160 *Sunday Independent*, 28 July 1928.
161 *Evening Herald*, 15 Oct. 1924; *Sport*, 30 Oct. 1926.
162 'Player Profile: David McMullan', http://www.lfchistory.net/Players/Player/Profile/750 [accessed 19 Aug. 2016].
163 Kenny, *The Irish in America*, p. 141.
164 Taylor, *The Leaguers*, p. 228.
165 Ibid., p. 147.
166 Ibid.; Irish Football Association Papers, Senior Protests and Appeals Committee Minutes, 10 Feb. 1927.
167 *Irish Examiner*, 7 June 1927.
168 Lanfranchi and Taylor, *Moving With the Ball*, p. 147; Irish Football Association Papers, Senior Protests and Appeals Committee Minutes, 20 Dec. 1928.

169 See, for example, Irish Football Association Papers, Senior Protests and Appeals Committee Minutes, 17 March 1927.
170 *Evening Herald*, 12 Nov. 1924.
171 Irish Football Association Papers, Senior Protests and Appeals Committee Minutes, 26 March 1925.
172 Ibid.
173 Ibid.
174 *Football Sports Weekly*, 12 and 19 Sept. 1925.
175 Irish Football Association Papers, Council Minutes, 2 Nov. 1925.
176 Irish Football Association Papers, Senior Protests and Appeals Committee Minutes, 8 Dec. 1925.
177 Ibid., 7 and 21 Oct. 1926.
178 Ibid., 20 Sept. 1928.
179 Ibid., 4 Oct. 1928.
180 Ibid., 18 Oct. and 20 Dec. 1928.
181 Ibid., 7 Aug. 1930.
182 See Kenny, *The American Irish*, pp. 139–40.
183 *Evening Herald*, 12 Nov. 1924; *Football Sports Weekly*, 25 Sept. 1926.
184 Irish Football Association Papers, Senior Protests and Appeals Committee Minutes, 6 Aug. 1931.
185 Ibid., 14 Oct. 1931.
186 Ibid., 6 Aug. 1931.
187 *Irish Independent*, 3 Sept. 1926.
188 Ibid., 18 Aug. 1927.
189 *Football Sports Weekly*, 19 Nov. 1927.
190 Ibid., 25 Feb. 1928; *Evening Herald*, 11 and 25 May 1928; *Irish Times*, 6 Dec. 1955.
191 *Football Sports Weekly*, 21 and 28 Jan. and 14 and 21 April 1928.
192 Ibid., 28 Jan. 1928; Toms, *Soccer in Munster*, pp. 187–88.
193 Lanfranchi and Taylor, *Moving With the Ball*, p. 150.
194 Ibid.
195 *Irish Examiner*, 1 April 1930.
196 Jose, *American Soccer League*, p. 368.
197 Ibid., pp. 402–3; 'NIFG: Bob "Whitey" McDonald', http://nifootball.blogspot.ie/2007/08/bob-whitey-mcdonald.html [accessed 26 Oct. 2016].
198 Taylor, *The Leaguers*, p. 229.
199 Ibid.; *The Northern Whig and Belfast Post*, 30 July 1928.
200 Taylor, *The Leaguers*, p. 229.
201 Goldblatt, *The Ball Is Round*, p. 100.
202 Ibid.
203 'NIFG: Danny Blanchflower', http://nifootball.blogspot.ie/2006/08/danny-blanchflower.html [accessed 23 Jan. 2016]; 'NIFG: Peter McParland', http://nifootball.blogspot.ie/2007/04/peter-mcparland.html [accessed 23 Jan. 2016].
204 Delaney, *Irish Emigration Since 1921*, p. 8.
205 Lanfranchi and Taylor, *Moving With the Ball*, p. 154.
206 *Irish Independent*, 3 Jan. 1967.

207 Lanfranchi and Taylor, *Moving With the Ball*, p. 154.

208 See Mike Cronin, 'The Gaelic Athletic Association's Invasion of America, 1888: travel narratives, microhistory and the Irish-American "other"', *Sport in History*, vol. 27, no. 2 (2007), pp. 190–216; David Toms, 'The *Cork Sportsman*: a provincial sporting newspaper, 1908–1911', *Sport in Society*, vol. 19, no. 1 (2016), pp. 24–37.

209 Kenny, *The American Irish*, p. 226.

210 These players were Fran O'Brien, Pat Byrne, Eddie Byrne, John Giles and Pierce O'Leary.

211 Billy Caskey, Chris McGrath, David McCreery and Victor Moreland were all noted as playing for Tulsa Roughnecks while Tom Armstrong, Hilary Carlyle, Martin Donnelly and Gerry O'Kane all had spells with San Diego clubs.

212 *Irish Press*, 22 March 1967; *Irish Examiner*, 4 May 1967.

213 'Boston Rovers Rosters', http://www.nasljerseys.com/Rosters/Rovers_Rosters.htm [accessed 26 Jan. 2016]; *Irish Press*, 27 May 1967.

214 Interview with Paddy Mulligan, 9 May 2016.

215 *Irish Press*, 12 and 24 May 1967.

216 Ibid., 26 April 1967.

217 Ibid., 22 March, 26 April and 30 May 1967.

218 Interview with Paddy Mulligan, 9 May 2016.

219 Ibid.

220 *Irish Independent*, 3 Jan. 1967.

221 Ibid., 31 Jan. and 23 June 1967.

222 'Cleveland Stokers Rosters', http://www.nasljerseys.com/Rosters/Stokers_Rosters.htm [accessed 26 Jan. 2016]; 'Dallas Tornado Rosters', http://www.nasljerseys.com/Rosters/Tornado_Rosters.htm [accessed 26 Jan. 2016].

223 'Chicago Mustangs Rosters', http://www.nasljerseys.com/Rosters/Mustangs_Rosters.htm [accessed 26 Jan. 2016].

224 Jose, *North American Soccer League Encyclopaedia*, p. 377.

225 *Irish Independent*, 23 June 1967.

226 Interview with Paddy Mulligan, 9 May 2016.

227 Lanfranchi and Taylor, *Moving With the Ball*, p. 154.

228 Ibid.

229 Ibid.

230 Ibid., p. 163.

231 Interview with Paddy Mulligan, 9 May 2016.

232 Ibid.

233 Ibid.

234 Ibid.

235 Ibid.

236 Ibid.

237 Lanfranchi and Taylor, *Moving With the Ball*, p. 155.

238 Ibid., p. 159.

239 Interview with Paddy Mulligan, 9 May 2016.

240 Interview with Alfie Hale, 27 Sept. 2013.

241 Lanfranchi and Taylor, *Moving With the Ball*, p. 155.
242 Ibid., p. 157.
243 'Joe Haverty: skilful Arsenal and Republic of Ireland left-winger known for his trickery and dribbling', http://www.independent.co.uk/news/obituaries/joe-haverty-skilful-arsenal-and-republic-of-ireland-left-winger-known-for-his-trickery-and-dribbling-1650631.html [accessed 23 Jan. 2016].
244 'North American Soccer League Players: Brian Quinn', http://nasljerseys.com/Players/Q/Quinn.Brian.htm [accessed 28 April 2016].
245 Jose, *North American Soccer League Encyclopedia*, p. 25 and p. 32.
246 Interview with Brendan Bradley, 2 June 2016.
247 Ibid., p. 220.
248 Ibid., p. 347.
249 Jose, *North American Soccer League Encyclopedia*, p. 200 and p. 275.
250 Giles, *A Football Man*, p. 303.
251 Lanfranchi and Taylor, *Moving With the Ball*, p. 161.
252 'Resisting Ireland's Soccer Raiders', *Football Handbook: the glory years* (London: Marshall Cavendish Ltd, 1978 and 2006), pp. 124–28, at p. 125.
253 Lanfranchi and Taylor, *Moving With the Ball*, p. 161.
254 *Soccer Magazine*, no. 11 (1985), p. 14.
255 North American Soccer League Players: Brian Quinn', http://nasljerseys.com/Players/Q/Quinn.Brian.htm [accessed 28 April 2016].
256 *Soccer Magazine*, no 18 (1986), p. 18.
257 'Heighway Makes Full-Time Academy Return', http://www.liverpoolfc.com/news/academy/196819-heighway-makes-full-time-academy-return [accessed 28 April 2016].
258 'NIFG: Billy Caskey', http://nifootball.blogspot.ie/2006/08/billy-caskey.html [accessed 16 Jan. 2016]; 'NIFG: Vic Moreland', http://nifootball.blogspot.ie/2007/09/vic-moreland.html [accessed 16 Jan. 2016].
259 Interview with Paddy Mulligan, 9 May 2016.
260 'NIFG: Michael O'Neill', http://nifootball.blogspot.ie/2007/08/michael-oneill.html [accessed 23 Jan. 2016].
261 'NIFG: Steve Morrow', http://nifootball.blogspot.ie/2007/07/steve-morrow.html [accessed 23 Jan. 2016].
262 'NIFG: Pat Sharkey', http://nifootball.blogspot.ie/2007/07/pat-sharkey.html [accessed 6 May 2016]; 'NIFG: Derek Spence', http://nifootball.blogspot.ie/2006/12/derek-spence.html [accessed 6 May 2016]; 'NIFG: Allen McKnight', http://nifootball.blogspot.ie/2007/07/allen-mcknight.html [accessed 6 May 2016]; *Soccer Magazine*, no. 47 (1989), p. 27.
263 *Soccer Magazine*, no. 80 (1993), p. 11.
264 'NIFG: Bobby Braithwaite', http://nifootball.blogspot.ie/2006/08/bobby-braithwaite.html [accessed 6 May 2016]; Eoin Hand, *The Eoin Hand Story* (Dublin: Brophy Books, 1986), p. 13.
265 'NIFG: Jimmy O'Neill', http://nifootball.blogspot.ie/2007/08/jimmy-oneill.html [accessed 6 May 2016]; 'NIFG: George Best', http://nifootball.blogspot.ie/2006/08/george-best.html [accessed 6 May 2016].

266 'NIFG: Terry McCavana', http://nifootball.blogspot.ie/2007/06/terry-mccavana.html [accessed 6 May 2016].
267 *Soccer Magazine*, no. 28 (1987), p. 11.
268 Ibid., no. 35 (1988), p. 22 and no. 46 (1989), p. 5.
269 Delaney, *Irish Emigration Since 1921*, p. 9.
270 Graeme Souness, 'Thirty Years On', *Sunday Times* (Sport), 17 April 2016, pp. 6–7.
271 Hassan, 'The Role of Gaelic Games', p. 393.
272 'BBC Sport: Liam Miller Leaves Hibs for Perth Glory in Australia', http://www.bbc.com/sport/football/13639527 [accessed 7 May 2016].

CHAPTER 6. POST-PLAYING CAREERS

1 Interview with Alfie Hale, 27 Sept. 2013.
2 Garnham, *Association Football and Society*, p. 93.
3 Fitzpatrick, *Irish Emigration, 1801–1921*, pp. 5–6.
4 *Ireland's Saturday Night*, 13 Aug. 1904.
5 'NIFG: Billy Gillespie', http://nifootball.blogspot.ie/2006/12/billy-gillespie.html [accessed 25 June 2016].
6 Mason, *Association Football and English Society*, p. 118.
7 Joyce, *Football League Players' Records*, p. 59.
8 'NIFG: Jimmy Dunne', http://nifootball.blogspot.ie/2006/11/jimmy-dunne.html [accessed 25 June 2016].
9 Mark Simpson, 'Appeal Over Belfast Man. Utd Player John Peden's Grave', http://www.bbc.com/news/uk-northern-ireland-26177699 [accessed 5 Feb. 2016]; 'NIFG: Sid Reid', http://nifootball.blogspot.ie/2007/10/sid-reid.html [accessed 16 June 2016]; Garnham, *Association Football and Society*, p. 93.
10 Fra Coogan, 'Was Mickey Hamill Belfast Celtic's Greatest Player?', http://www.belfastceltic.org/archive/hamill.html [accessed 5 Feb. 2016].
11 'NIFG: Matt "Gunner" Reilly', http://nifootball.blogspot.ie/2008/01/matt-gunner-reilly.html [accessed 16 June 2016].
12 'NIFG: Tom Priestley', http://nifootball.blogspot.ie/2007/10/tom-priestley.html [accessed 16 June 2016]; 'NIFG: Hugh Blair', http://nifootball.blogspot.ie/2006/08/hughie-blair.html [accessed 16 June 2016].
13 Mason, *Association Football and English Society*, p. 119.
14 'NIFG: Lawrie Cumming', http://nifootball.blogspot.ie/2006/09/lawrie-cumming.html [accessed 13 March 2017].
15 *Football Sports Weekly*, 21 Aug. 1926.
16 Ibid., 19 June 1926.
17 Nuala McCann, 'Patrick O'Connell: Barcelona FC saviour they called "Don Patricio"', http://www.bbc.com/news/uk-northern-ireland-29426450 [accessed 13 March 2017]; 'NIFG: Pat "Don Patricio" O'Connell', http://nifootball.blogspot.ie/2008/02/pat-oconnell.html [accessed 13 March 2017].

18 'NIFG: Harry Buckle', http://nifootball.blogspot.ie/2006/08/harry-buckle.html [accessed 16 June 2016].
19 Mason, *Association Football and English Society*, p. 120.
20 Garnham, *Association Football and Society*, p. 94.
21 'NIFG: Archie Goodall', http://nifootball.blogspot.ie/2006/12/archie-goodall.html [accessed 16 June 2016].
22 *Belfast Telegraph*, 2 Feb. 1902.
23 McCann, 'Patrick O'Connell'.
24 Mason, *Association Football and English Society*, p. 121.
25 Harding, *Living To Play*, p. 251.
26 Ibid., pp. 235–36.
27 Taylor, *The Association Game*, p. 231.
28 Ibid., p. 234.
29 Ibid.
30 Harding, *Living To Play*, pp. 240–48.
31 Interview with Alfie Hale, 27 Sept. 2013.
32 Ibid.
33 Taylor, *The Association Game*, pp. 396–97.
34 Miguel Delaney, *From Stuttgart to Saipan: the players' stories* (Dublin: Mentor, 2010), p. 219.
35 Ibid., pp. 164–66.
36 *Irish Press*, 8 Nov. 1967.
37 Tuohy resigned from his Republic of Ireland manager's post in 1973 after only two years due to the low pay and the fact that he was also coaching Shamrock Rovers and working as an ice-cream salesman.
38 Interview with Alfie Hale, 27 Sept. 2013.
39 Ibid.
40 Ryan and Burke, *The Book of Irish Goalscorers*, p. 149.
41 At senior international level, Billy Bingham, Terry Neill, Dave Clements, Danny Blanchflower, Bryan Hamilton, Sammy McIlroy, Nigel Worthington and Michael O'Neill have all managed Northern Ireland. At club level Neil Lennon has enjoyed a successful spell at Celtic while Martin O'Neill became Republic of Ireland manager.
42 Peter Corr, Joe Haverty, Reg Ryan, Mick Martin and David Campbell have all been employed as scouts.
43 Interview with Gerry Burrell, 13 Jan. 2013.
44 John Campbell, Bill Collins, William Dickson, Norman Uprichard, Sammy Chapman, Alan Campbell, Willie McFaul, Eric McManus, Billy Hamilton, Barry Hunter and Keith Rowland were also identified as having worked in this capacity.
45 Ivan Ponting, 'Obituary; Danny Blanchflower', http://www.independent.co.uk/news/people/obituary-danny-blanchflower-1466455.html [accessed 12 Oct. 2013].
46 Eamonn Collins, Shane Supple, Wayne Henderson, Clive Clarke, Dessie Byrne, Graham Barrett, Don Givens, Kevin Moran, Tommy Butler and David Worrell have all worked as agents.

47 Harding, *Living To Play*, p. 251. A few Republic of Ireland-born players, including Theo Foley, Terry Conroy and Ashley Grimes have worked as matchday hosts, while former Northern Ireland players Pat Jennings and John McClelland have also become involved in this. Others connected with club entertainment include Willie Irvine and Sammy Nelson while Norman Whiteside, George Best and Jackie Blanchflower have all worked as after-dinner speakers.

48 Stephen Devine, Gary Fleming, Pat McGibbon, Paul Morgan and Paul Ferris have all become physiotherapists while Norman Whiteside qualified as a chiropodist after being forced to quit the game through injury.

49 Harding, *Living To Play*, p. 251.

50 Conall Murtagh is now employed as a sports scientist at Liverpool FC, while Crusader's Michael Carvill also works part-time as a personal trainer.

51 *Soccer Magazine*, no. 26 (1987), p. 7.

52 Johnny Gavin, Maurice Swan, Alfie Hale, Jackie O'Driscoll, Gerry Ryan, Jackie Blanchflower, Jim Feeney, Sammy McCrory, Norman Uprichard, Johnny Crossan, Jimmy Shiels and Sean O'Neill have all run pubs after finishing their playing careers.

53 Those found to have opened shops include Johnny Crossan (sports shop and trophy business), Jackie Blanchflower (sweetshop and bookmaker), William Hughes (tobacco and newsagent), Sammy Smyth (bookmaker and sports shop owner), David Craig (newsagent), Billy Humphries (newsagent), Ian Lawther (tailor's shop), John Cowan (trophy business), Jackie Vernon and Wilbur Cush (butchers).

54 *Soccer Magazine*, no. 34 (1988), p. 24.

55 Ibid., no. 82 (1993), p. 13.

56 Ibid., no. 24 (1987), p. 13. Prior to joining Nottingham Forest, Keane 'took the odd labouring job when one could be found' before joining the first FÁS football trainee course in 1989.

57 McParland, *Going For Goal*, p. 12; *Soccer Magazine*, no. 15 (1986), p. 15 and no. 36 (1988), p. 15.

58 Interview with Damien Richardson, 23 Aug. 2013.

59 Ibid.

60 *Soccer Magazine*, no. 22 (1986), p. 27.

61 Roderick, *The Work of Professional Football*, p. 172.

62 Interview with Mick Meagan, 11 Nov. 2013.

63 Interview with Damien Richardson, 13 Aug. 2013.

64 Ibid.

65 Interview with Richie Sadlier, 23 July 2013.

66 *Irish Independent*, 4 Feb. 1959.

67 Interview with Gerry Burrell, 13 Jan. 2013.

68 *Irish Independent*, 21 June 1958.

69 Danny Blanchflower, *The Double and Before: the autobiography of Danny Blanchflower* (London: N. Kaye, 1961), pp. 7–12; Neill, *Revelations of a Football Manager*, p. 29.

70 Mark Metcalfe, *Charlie Hurley: the greatest centre half the world has ever seen* (Cheltenham: SportsBooks, 2008), p. 15.
71 Interview with Alfie Hale, 27 Sept. 2013.
72 Interview with Mick Meagan, 11 Nov. 2013.
73 Delaney, *The Irish in Post-war Britain*, p. 32.
74 Ibid., pp. 31–32.
75 Delaney, *Irish Emigration Since 1921*, pp. 15–16.
76 Ibid., p. 19.
77 Ibid., p. 16.
78 CAIN Service, 'Discrimination and Education' from 'Perspectives on Discrimination and Social Work, Northern Ireland', http://cain.ulst.ac.uk/issues/discrimination/gibson1.htm [accessed 27 Feb. 2016].
79 See, for example, David Langan (with Trevor Keane and Alan Conway), *Running Through Walls* (Derby: DB Publishing, 2012), pp. 29–30.
80 Interview with Richie Sadlier, 23 July 2013.
81 Interview with Raymond Campbell, 10 Dec. 2013.
82 Interview with Brian Mooney, 30 Sept. 2013.
83 Roderick, *The Work of Professional Football*, p. 171.
84 Kelly, 'The Migration of Irish Professional Footballers', p. 85; interview with Seamus Heath, 26 Sept. 2013.
85 Davies, *The Glory Game*, p. 70.
86 Bourke, 'The Dream of Being a Professional Soccer Player', p. 416.
87 Roderick, *The Work of Professional Football*, p. 175.
88 Interview with Mick Meagan, 11 Nov. 2013.
89 *Soccer Magazine*, no. 66 (1991), p. 21 and no. 102 (1995), p. 8; Gary Howlett, Richie Sadlier, Barry Prenderville and Keith O'Neill were noted as finishing their secondary school education before migrating to England.
90 Interview with Hubert Barr, 7 Jan. 2014.
91 Ibid.
92 *Soccer Magazine*, no. 16 (1986), p. 24, no. 17 (1986), p. 5 and no. 92 (1994), pp. 10–11; *Irish Press*, 20 Oct. 1976.
93 Tony Reid, 'John O'Neill', *Soccer Magazine*, no. 17 (1986), p. 5; Keane, *Keane: the autobiography*, pp. 11–12.
94 Harding, *Living To Play*, p. 249.
95 Interview with Richie Sadlier, 23 July 2013.
96 Interview with Michael McHugh, 29 Oct. 2013.
97 *The Irish Times*, 5 May 2000.
98 Interview with Raymond Campbell, 10 Dec. 2013.
99 Harding, *Living To Play*, p. 79.
100 Interview with Shane Supple, 8 July 2013.
101 Interview with Michael Carvill, 8 Oct. 2013.
102 Interview with Alan Blayney, 13 Jan. 2014.
103 Interview with Mick Meagan, 11 Nov. 2013.
104 Roderick, *The Work of Professional Football*, p. 16.
105 Ibid., p. 25.

106 'Stephen Hunt: GAA players would find life tough in the Premier League', http://www.independent.ie/sport/soccer/premier-league/stephen-hunt-gaa-players-would-find-life-tough-in-premier-league-30785091.html [accessed 2 July 2015].
107 Interview with David Miskelly, 21 Jan. 2014.
108 Ibid.
109 Interview with Michael Carvill, 8 Oct. 2013.
110 Interview with Barry Prenderville, 12 July 2013.
111 Interview with Damien Richardson, 13 Aug. 2013.
112 'Sunderland's Duncan Watmore Graduates with First-Class Degree from Newcastle University', http://www.theguardian.com/football/2015/dec/10/sunderland-duncan-watmore-graduates-first-class-degree-newcastle [accessed 11 Dec. 2015].
113 Kuper and Szymanski, *Why England Lose*, pp. 22–23.
114 Harding, *Living To Play*, p. 252.
115 John Harding, *Behind the Glory: 100 years of the PFA* (Derby: Breedon Books, 2009), p. 179.
116 'PFA Membership', https://www.thepfa.com/thepfa/aboutpfa/membership [accessed 29 Aug. 2013].
117 Interview with Dean Kelly, 13 Jan. 2014.
118 Interview with Barry Prenderville, 12 July 2013; interview with Seamus Kelly, 22 Aug. 2013; interview with Michael Carvill, 8 Oct. 2013.
119 Interview with Richie Sadlier, 23 July 2013.
120 Interview with Barry Prenderville, 12 July 2013.
121 Interview with Seamus Kelly, 22 Aug. 2013.
122 Interview with Seamus Heath, 26 Sept. 2013.
123 Interview with Mick Meagan, 11 Nov. 2013.
124 'PFA Membership', http://www.thepfa.com/members/membership [accessed 29 Aug. 2013].
125 *Irish Echo*, March 1995, p. 16.
126 'Mutual Casa Del Futbolista', http://www.futbolleyendas.com/#!quienes-somos/cghg [accessed 6 March 2016].
127 Johanne Devlin Trew, 'Reluctant Diasporas of Northern Ireland: migrant narratives of home, conflict, difference', *Journal of Ethnic and Migration Studies*, vol. 36, no. 4 (2010), pp. 541–60, at pp. 541–42.
128 Interview with Hubert Barr, 7 Jan. 2014.
129 Interview with Seamus Heath, 26 Sept. 2013.
130 Interview with Shane Supple, 8 July 2013; interview with Richie Sadlier, 23 July 2013; interview with Martin Russell, 11 July 2013; interview with Barry Prenderville, 12 July 2013; interview with Alfie Hale, 27 Sept. 2013; interview with Brian Mooney, 30 Sept. 2013; interview with Denis Behan, 6 Dec. 2013; interview with Dean Kelly, 13 Jan. 2014; interview with Alan Blayney, 13 Jan. 2014; interview with David Miskelly, 21 Jan. 2014; interview with Michael Carvill, 8 Oct. 2013.
131 Interview with Brendan Bradley, 16 Jan. 2014.

132 Interview with Shane Supple, 8 July 2013; interview with Brian Mooney, 30 Sept. 2013.
133 Interview with Michael McHugh, 29 Oct. 2013.
134 Roderick, *The Work of Professional Football*, p. 173.
135 Interview with Barry Prenderville, 12 July 2013; interview with Brian Mooney, 30 Sept. 2013.
136 'NIFG: Bobby Burke', http://nifootball.blogspot.ie/2008/03/bobby-burke.html [accessed 6 May 2016].
137 'NIFG: Billy Dickson', http://nifootball.blogspot.ie/2006/11/billy-dickson.html [accessed 6 May 2016]. See also Alfie Hale.
138 Dunphy, *The Rocky Road*, p. 231.
139 Delaney, *Irish Emigration Since 1921*, p. 18.
140 Keith Gillespie, *How Not To Be a Football Millionaire: my autobiography* (Liverpool: SportMedia, 2013), p. 278.
141 Interview with Martin Russell, 11 July 2013.
142 *Soccer Magazine*, no. 86 (1994), p. 3.
143 Interview with Alan Blayney, 13 Jan. 2014.
144 'Alan Blayney Wins Ulster Footballer of the Year Award', http://www.bbc.com/sport/0/football/13391481 [accessed 28 Nov. 2015].
145 Interview with Michael Carvill, 8 Oct. 2013.
146 Interview with Billy Humphries, 14 Jan. 2014.
147 Interview with David Miskelly, 21 Jan. 2014.
148 Interview with Brian Mooney, 30 Sept. 2013.
149 Interview with Denis Behan, 6 Dec. 2013.
150 Interview with Raymond Campbell, 10 Dec. 2013.
151 Interview with Seamus Heath, 26 Sept. 2013.
152 Ibid.
153 Interview with Barry Prenderville, 13 July 2013.
154 *Commission on Emigration*, p. 141.
155 Gerard Leavey, Sati Sembhi and Gill Livingstone, 'Older Irish Migrants Living in London: identity, loss and return', *Journal of Ethnic and Migration Studies*, vol. 30, no. 4 (2004), pp. 763–79, at p. 764 and p. 777.
156 Alan Barrett and Irene Mosca, 'Social Isolation, Loneliness and Return Migration: evidence from older Irish adults', *Journal of Ethnic and Migration Studies*, vol. 39, no. 10 (2013), pp. 1659–77, at p. 1661.
157 Delaney, *The Irish in Post-war Britain*, p. 66 and p. 69.
158 Ibid., p. 69.
159 Interview with Seamus Heath, 26 Sept. 2013.
160 Interview with Damien Richardson, 13 Aug. 2013.
161 'NIFG: Frank McCourt', http://nifootball.blogspot.ie/2007/04/frank-mccourt.html [accessed 6 May 2016]; 'NIFG: Eric Ross', http://nifootball.blogspot.ie/2007/09/eric-ross.html [accessed 6 May 2016]; 'NIFG: Dave Clements', http://nifootball.blogspot.ie/2006/08/dave-clements.html [accessed 6 May 2016].

162 Roderick, *The Work of Professional Football*, p. 17.
163 Ibid.
164 Interview with Brendan Bradley, 16 Jan. 2014.
165 Interview with Damien Richardson, 13 Aug. 2013.
166 Interview with Raymond Campbell, 10 Dec. 2013.
167 'Ex-footballer Warren Aspinall Almost Took His Own Life', http://www.bbc.co.uk/sport/0/football/17741055 [accessed 17 Aug. 2013]; 'Dean Windass Discusses His "Shame" at Depression Battle', http://www.bbc.co.uk/sport/0/football/17596050 [accessed 17 Aug. 2013]; 'Football's Suicide Secret', http://www.youtube.com/watch?v=cPyTCpMHico [accessed 17 Aug. 2013].
168 Paul Rowan, 'McAteer Works Himself Back from Brink', *Sunday Times*, 25 Aug. 2013.
169 'Health Service Blamed for Suicide', http://news.bbc.co.uk/2/hi/uk_news/northern_ireland/7469750.stm [accessed 16 Jan. 2016].
170 'PFAI Join Lean on Me Campaign', http://www.pfai.ie/news/286-pfai-join-lean-on-me-campaign [accessed 20 Jan. 2014].
171 Kelly, 'The Migration of Irish Professional Footballers', pp. 17–18.
172 Harding, *Living To Play*, p. 241.
173 Interview with Seamus Kelly, 22 Aug. 2013.
174 O'Brien, 'Highs, Lows and a Brush with Ronaldo', *Sunday Independent* (Sport), 7 April 2013, p. 9.
175 In 2016, he joined Bohemians.
176 Interview with Shane Supple, 8 July 2013.
177 *Ulster Herald*, 27 Sept. 1975.
178 These players were identified as Ciaran Lyng, Mark Ronaldson, Shane Supple, Ciaran Greene, John Connellan and Paul Cahillane. I am grateful to Vincent Butler for supplying me with this information.
179 Interview with Richie Sadlier, 23 July 2013.
180 Ibid.
181 Ibid.
182 Barrett and Mosca, 'Social Isolation, Loneliness and Return Migration', pp. 1674–75.
183 Brown and Potrac, '"You've Not Made the Grade, Son"', p. 155.
184 Ibid.
185 Kuper and Szymanski, *Why England Lose*, p. 135.
186 'St Kevin's Boys FC'. The club website states: 'A one-year YTS and a one-year contract would not in our opinion be a commitment to the player from the club, or indeed a two-year YTS contract'; interview with Richie Sadlier, 23 July 2013.
187 Interview with Richie Sadlier, 23 July 2013.
188 Dunphy, *The Rocky Road*, p. 95.
189 Gillespie, *How Not To Be a Football Millionaire*, p. 262.

CHAPTER 7. THE DECLINE OF IRISH-BORN FOOTBALL MIGRANTS IN TOP-FLIGHT ENGLISH LEAGUE FOOTBALL

1 Interview with Dean Kelly, 13 Jan. 2014.
2 Professional football in Ireland was legalised by the IFA in 1894 but after the Leinster FA, based in the Irish Free State, split from the IFA in 1921, clubs south of the border began to play in the League of Ireland rather than the Irish League. See Taylor, *The Association Game*, p. 64 and pp. 168–69.
3 See for example, 'We're Losing Too Many Talented Young Players to the British System', http://www.the42.ie/niall-quinn-young-irish-footballers-2402585-Oct 2015 [accessed 28 Oct. 2015].
4 Elliott, 'Football's Irish Exodus', p. 159.
5 Lanfranchi andTaylor, *Moving With the Ball*, p. 220.
6 Interview with Alfie Hale, 27 Sept. 2013.
7 *Soccer Magazine*, no. 68 (1992), p. 19.
8 'FIFA Solidarity and Compensation Payments', http://www.fai.ie/football-services-a-education/player-a-club-services/fifa-solidarity-and-compensation-payments.html [accessed 6 Nov. 2011].
9 Hugman (ed.), *The PFA Footballers' Who's Who, 2010–11.*
10 'CIES Football Observatory', http://www.mapping-football-observatory.com/modules/carto/map. php?lg=en [accessed 16 Dec. 2013].
11 McGovern, 'Globalization or Internationalization?', p. 29.
12 Ibid., pp. 29–30.
13 Taylor, *The Association Game*, p. 307.
14 Ibid., p. 308.
15 Ibid., p. 396.
16 Ibid., pp. 396–97.
17 See Gordon Taylor, 'Meltdown: the nationality of Premier League players and the future of English football', in Geoff Walters and Giambattista Rossi (eds), *Labour Market Migration in European Football: key issues and challenges*, conference proceedings from the Feet-Drain Conference hosted by the Birkbeck Sport Business Centre in May 2008, Birkbeck Sport Business Centre Research Paper Series, vol. 2, no. 2 (2009), pp. 51–70; Hugh McIlvanney, 'Foreign Legion Fuels Failure', *Sunday Times* (Sport), 28 April 2013.
18 'CIES Football Observatory Digital Atlas: % Expatriates by Club (2015)', http://www.football-observatory.com/IMG/sites/atlas/en/expatriates.html [accessed 6 May 2016].
19 'CIES Football Observatory Digital Atlas: Debutant Players', http://www.football-observatory.com/IMG/sites/atlas/en/debutant-players.html [accessed 6 May 2016].
20 'CIES Football Observatory Digital Atlas: Club-trained Players', http://www.football-observatory.com/IMG/sites/atlas/en/club-trained.html [accessed 6 May 2016].
21 Kuper and Szymanski, *Why England Lose*, pp. 16–20.

22 Taylor, 'Football, Migration and Globalisation', pp. 1–21, at p. 16.
23 *Irish Post*, 14 May 1983.
24 Interview with Richie Sadlier, 23 July 2013.
25 Interview with Barry Prenderville, 12 July 2013.
26 Interview with Seamus Heath, 26 Sept. 2013.
27 Ibid.
28 Interview with Hubert Barr, 7 Jan. 2014.
29 Interview with Raymond Campbell, 10 Dec. 2013.
30 Interview with Hubert Barr, 7 Jan. 2014.
31 Interview with Alan Blayney, 13 Jan. 2014.
32 Interview with Brendan Bradley, 16 Jan. 2014.
33 Interview with John McClelland, 29 Jan. 2014.
34 Interview with Shane Supple, 8 July 2013.
35 Interview with Billy Humphries, 14 Jan. 2014.
36 Interview with Brian Mooney, 30 Sept. 2013.
37 Roderick, *The Work of Professional Football*, p. 23.
38 'CIES Football Observatory Digital Atlas: Average Stay', http://www.football-observatory.com/IMG/sites/atlas/en/average-stay.html [accessed 5 May 2016].
39 Woolridge, 'A New Breed', p. 533.
40 Delaney, *Irish Emigration Since 1921*, p. 12.
41 Woolridge, 'A New Breed', p. 534.
42 'CIES Football Observatory Digital Atlas: Average Stay'.
43 *Soccer Magazine*, no. 33 (1988), pp. 22–23 and no. 66 (1991), p. 21; interview with Barry Prenderville, 12 July 2013; interview with Brian Mooney, 30 Sept. 2013.
44 *Soccer Magazine*, no. 33 (1988), pp. 22–23 and no. 66 (1991), p. 21.
45 *Irish Independent*, 24 Feb. 1973.
46 Ibid.
47 *Irish Press*, 5 Dec. 1975.
48 Ibid.
49 Ibid., 6 Dec. 1975.
50 Ibid.; interview with Martin Russell, 11 July 2013.
51 Interview with Barry Prenderville, 12 July 2013.
52 Ibid.
53 Interview with Damien Richardson, 13 Aug. 2013.
54 Interview with Hubert Barr, 7 Jan. 2014.
55 Interview with John McClelland, 29 Jan. 2014.
56 Interview with Dean Kelly, 13 Jan. 2014.
57 Interview with Raymond Campbell, 10 Dec. 2013.
58 Ibid.
59 Ibid.
60 Interview with Denis Behan, 6 Dec. 2013.
61 Ibid.
62 Ibid.
63 Ibid.
64 Interview with Damien Richardson, 13 Aug. 2013.

65 Interview with Mick Meagan, 11 Nov. 2013.
66 1995 has been used as a cut-off point here as a number of migrants in the 1996–2005 and 2006–10 periods were found to be still playing in English league football.
67 Interview with Shane Supple, 8 July 2013.
68 Ruaidhri Croke, 'Young Irish Players Need an Elite Football Education, Says Quinn', http://www.irishtimes.com/sport/soccer/young-irish-players-need-an-elite-football-education-says-niall-quinn-1.2306870 [accessed 8 Aug. 2015].
69 Interview with Hubert Barr, 7 Jan. 2014.
70 Interview with Alan Blayney, 13 Jan. 2013.
71 Interview with Denis Behan, 6 Dec. 2013.
72 Richie Sadlier, 'Don't Be Fooled by League's Play-at-Home Promptings', *Sunday Independent* (Sport), 2 June 2013.
73 Ibid.
74 Interview with Richie Sadlier, 23 July 2013.
75 Barretstown Talks Present Roy Keane in Conversation, Olympia Theatre, 25 June 2015.
76 *The Irish Times*, 17 Jan. 1998.
77 Dunphy, *The Rocky Road*, p. 205.
78 *Soccer Magazine*, no. 79 (1993), p. 27.
79 Interview with Martin Russell, 11 July 2013.
80 Interview with Seamus Kelly, 22 Aug. 2013.
81 'FAI FÁS Youth Soccer Courses Registration Open', http://www.fai.ie/football-services-a-education/50-education/103354-fai-fas-youth-soccer-courses-registration-open.html [accessed 25 Jan. 2014]; *Soccer Magazine*, no. 60 (1991), p. 19 and no. 88 (1994), pp. 24–25.
82 Interview with Dean Kelly, 13 Jan. 2014.
83 'Footballers REAP Awards at DCU', https://www.dcu.ie/news/2002/jul/s0207l.shtml [accessed 12 March 2016]; interview with Denis Behan, 6 Dec. 2013.
84 Interview with Raymond Campbell, 10 Dec. 2013.
85 Interview with Michael Carvill, 8 Oct. 2013; interview with Andy Waterworth, 8 Oct. 2013.
86 Interview with Michael Carvill, 8 Oct. 2013.
87 Interview with John McClelland, 29 Jan. 2014.
88 Interview with Andy Waterworth, 8 Oct. 2013.
89 Interview with Denis Behan, 6 Dec. 2013.
90 Interview with Damien Richardson, 13 Aug. 2013.
91 *Commission on Emigration*, p. 136.
92 Lanfranchi and Taylor, *Moving With the Ball*, p. 6.

CONCLUSION

1 For a discussion of the GAA's organisational prowess, see Paul Rouse, *Sport & Ireland: a history* (Oxford: Oxford University Press, 2015), pp. 308–9.

2 Raphael Honigstein, *Das Reboot: how German football reinvented itself and conquered the world* [paperback edition] (London: Yellow Jersey Press, 2016), pp. 107–9.
3 Eamon Dunphy, speaking on *Euro 2016 Qualifier*, RTÉ, 13 June 2015.
4 *FIFA Football* programme, Setanta Ireland, 2 June 2016.
5 See Curran, *The Development of Sport in Donegal*, Chapter 6.
6 I am grateful to Seamus for providing me with this information.
7 Dunphy, *Only a Game?*, pp. 150–53.
8 Interview with Alfie Hale, 27 Sept. 2013.
9 MacRaild, *The Irish Diaspora in Britain*, p. 218.
10 Delaney, *The Irish in Post-war Britain*, p. 5.
11 MacRaild, *The Irish Diaspora in Britain*, p. 218.
12 Davies, *The Glory Game*, p. 7.
13 See Richie Sadlier, 'Rejected Teenagers Must Get Professional Help', http://www.independent.ie/sport/soccer/other-soccer/richie-sadlier-rejected-teenagers-must-get-professional-help-30916117.html [accessed 9 March 2016]; Denis Walsh, 'Parting Is Such Sorrow for Counties' Discarded Players', *Sunday Times* (Sport), 31 Jan. 2016, p. 13.
14 Brown and Potrac, '"You've Not Made the Grade, Son"', p. 155.
15 John Bale, *Sports Geography* (London: E & FN Spon, 1989), p. 2.
16 Kevin Whelan, 'The Geography of Hurling', *History Ireland* (Spring, 1993), pp. 27–31; Cronin, Duncan and Rouse, *The GAA: county by county*.
17 Kenny, *The American Irish: a history*, p. 262.

Bibliography

PRIMARY SOURCES

Archival and Oral Sources

Football League Archives, Preston

Charles Buchan's Football Monthly, 1951–74
Shoot!, 1969–1972

National Library of Ireland

Commission on Emigration and Other Population Problems (Dublin: The Stationery Office, 1955)
Soccer Magazine, 1984–1996
11-a-Side, 1993–94

Newspapers

Anglo-Celt
Ballina Herald
Belfast Telegraph
Connacht Sentinel
Connaught Telegraph
Connacht Tribune
Derry People and Donegal News
Donegal Democrat
Evening Herald
Fermanagh Herald
Football Sports Weekly
Ireland's Saturday Night
Irish Independent
Irish Examiner
Irish Post
Irish Press
Irish Times
Kilkenny People
Lancashire Evening Post
Leinster Express
Limerick Leader
Longford Leader
Mayo News
Meath Chronicle
Munster Express
Northern Whig and Belfast Post
Sligo Champion
Sport
Strabane Chronicle
Sunday Independent
Sunday Times
The Kerryman
Ulster Herald
Westmeath Examiner
Western People

Public Record Office of Northern Ireland

Irish Football Association Papers, D/4196
Irish Football League Papers, D/4511
Northern Ireland Ministry/Department of Education Papers, Ed/13/1/2745
Northern Ireland Ministry/Department of Education Papers, Ed/13/36

University College Dublin

Football Association of Ireland Papers, P/137

Player Interviews

Republic of Ireland-born players

1945–55

Interview with Mick Meagan, 11 Nov. 2013

1956–65

Interview with Alfie Hale, 27 Sept. 2013

1966–75

Interview with Damien Richardson, 13 Aug. 2013
Interview with Paddy Mulligan, 13 Nov. 2013 and 9 May 2016

1976–85

Interview with Martin Russell, 11 July 2013
Interview with Brian Mooney, 30 Sept. 2013

1986–95

Interview with Barry Prenderville, 12 July 2013
Interview with Michael McHugh, 29 Oct. 2013

1996–2005

Interview with Shane Supple, 8 July 2013
Interview with Richie Sadlier, 23 July 2013
Interview with Seamus Kelly, 22 Aug. 2013

2006–10

Interview with Denis Behan, 6 Dec. 2013
Interview with Dean Kelly, 13 Jan. 2014

Northern Ireland-born players

1945–55

Interview with Gerry Burrell, 8 Jan. 2014

1956–65

Interview with Hubert Barr, 7 Jan. 2014
Interview with Billy Humphries, 14 Jan. 2014

1966–75

Interview with Brendan Bradley, 16 Jan. 2014
Interview with John McClelland, 29 Jan. 2014

1976–85

Interview with Seamus Heath, 26 Sept. 2013

1986–95

Interview with Raymond Campbell, 10 Dec. 2013

1996–2005

Interview with Alan Blayney, 13 Jan. 2014
Interview with David Miskelly, 21 Jan. 2014

2006–10

Interview with Michael Carvill, 8 Oct. 2013
Interview with Andy Waterworth, 8 Oct. 2013

SECONDARY SOURCES

Books and Articles

Akenson, D.H., 'Emigration', in S.J. Connolly (ed.), *Oxford Companion to Irish History* (paperback edition) (Oxford: Oxford University Press, 2004), p. 179

Augusteijn, Joost, Fitzpatrick, David, Hart, Peter and Townshend, Charles, 'Anglo-Irish War', in Connolly (ed.), *Oxford Companion to Irish History*, p. 17

Bairner, Alan, 'Irish Sport', in Joe Cleary and Claire Connolly (eds), *The Cambridge Companion to Modern Irish Culture* (Cambridge: Cambridge University Press, 2005), pp. 190–205.

—, 'Simply the (George) Best: Ulster Protestantism, conflicted identity and "The Belfast Boy(s)"', *The Canadian Journal of Irish Studies*, vol. 32, no. 2 (Fall, 2006), pp. 34–41.

Bale, John, 'Sport and National Identity: a geographical view', *The British Journal of Sports History*, vol. 3, no. 1 (1986), pp. 18–41.

—, *Sports Geography* (London: E & FN Spon, 1989)

— and Maguire, Joseph (eds), *The Global Sports Arena: athletic talent migration in an interdependent world* (London: Frank Cass, 1994)

Bardon, Jonathan, *A History of Ulster* (updated edition) (Belfast: Blackstaff Press, 2005)

— and Stephen Conlin, *Belfast: 1000 years* (Belfast: Blackstaff Press, 1985)

Barrett, Alan and Mosca, Irene, 'Social Isolation, Loneliness and Return Migration: evidence from older Irish adults', *Journal of Ethnic and Migration Studies*, vol. 39, no. 10 (2013), pp. 1659–77

Barrett, Norman S. (ed.), *Purnell's New Encyclopedia of Association Football* (Maidenhead, Purnell & Sons Ltd, 1980)

—, *The Daily Telegraph Football Chronicle* (London: Carlton Books Ltd, 1993)

Bartlett, Thomas, *Ireland: a history* (Cambridge: Cambridge University Press, 2010)

Beal, Richard and Emms, Steve, *Scottish League Players' Records: Division One, 1946/47 to 1974/75* (Nottingham: Tony Brown, 2004)

Berthoud, Jerome and Poli, Raffaele, 'L'après-carrière des footballeurs professionnels en Afrique du Sud', *STAPS: Revue internationale des sciences du sport et de l'éducation physique*, no. 94 (2011), pp. 25–38

Best, George, *Best of Both Worlds* (London: Pelham Books, 1968)

— and Wright, Graeme, *Where Do I Go from Here? An autobiography* (London: Queen Anne Press, 1981)

— (with Ross Benson), *The Good, the Bad and the Bubbly: my autobiography* (updated edition) (London: Pocket Books, 1999)

— (with Roy Collins), *Blessed* (London: Ebury Press, 2003)

Blanchflower, Danny, *The Double and Before: the autobiography of Danny Blanchflower* (London: N. Kaye, 1961)

Bonner, Packie, *The Last Line: my autobiography* (London: Ebury Press, 2015)

Bourke, Anne, 'The Road to Fame and Fortune: insights on the career paths of young Irish professional footballers in England', *Journal of Youth Studies*, vol. 5, no. 4 (2002), pp. 375–89

—, 'The Dream of Being a Professional Soccer Player: insights on career development options of young Irish players', *Journal of Sport & Social Issues*, vol. 27, no. 4 (2003), pp. 399–419

Bradley, Joseph, 'Football in Scotland: a history of political and ethnic identity', *International Journal of the History of Sport*, vol. 12, no. 1 (1995), pp. 81–98

—, 'Integration or Assimilation? Scottish society, football and Irish immigrants', *International Journal of the History of Sport*, vol. 13, no. 2 (1996), pp. 61–79

Brady, Liam, *So Far So Good: a decade in football* (London: Stanley Paul, 1980)

Brodie, Malcolm, *The History of Irish Soccer* (Glasgow: Arrell Publications, 1968)

—, *100 Years of Irish Football* (Belfast: Blackstaff Press, 1980)

Brown, Gavin and Potrac, Paul, '"You've Not Made the Grade, Son": de-selection and identity disruption in elite youth level football', *Soccer & Society*, vol. 10, no. 2 (2009), pp. 143–59

Brown Tindall, George and Shi, David E., *America: a narrative history*, 6th edn (New York/London: WW Norton & Co. Ltd, 2004)

Browne, Jared, *Dunphy: a football life* (Dublin: New Island Books, 2012)

Buttner, Paul, *The Official FA Ireland Annual, 1993* (Manchester: World International Publishing, 1992)

Byrne, Peter, *Green Is the Colour: the story of Irish football* (London: Carlton Books, 2012)

Carter, Neil, *The Football Manager: a history* (London: Routledge, 2006)

Clark, Norman, *The Ballymena Boy* (Middlesex: The author, 1997)

Connolly, S.J. (ed.), *Oxford Companion to Irish History* (Oxford: Oxford University Press, 2004)

Coogan, Tim Pat, *Wherever Green Is Worn: the story of the Irish diaspora* (London: Arrow, 2000)

Cronin, Mike, *Sport and Nationalism in Ireland: Gaelic games, soccer and Irish identity since 1884* (Dublin: Four Courts Press, 1999)

Cronin, Mike, Duncan, Mark and Rouse, Paul, *The GAA: county by county* (Cork: The Collins Press, 2011)

Cronin, Mike, 'Playing Away from Home: identity in Northern Ireland and the experience of Derry City Football Club', *National Identities*, vol. 2, no. 1 (2000), pp. 65–79

Cronin, Mike, 'The Gaelic Athletic Association's Invasion of America, 1888: travel narratives, microhistory and the Irish-American "other"', *Sport in History*, vol. 27, no. 2 (2007), pp. 190–216

Curran, Conor, *The Development of Sport in Donegal, 1880–1935* (Cork: Cork University Press, 2015)

—, 'Networking Structures and Competitive Association Football in Ulster, 1880–1914', *Irish Economic and Social History*, vol. 41 (Manchester: Manchester University Press 2014), pp. 74–92

—, 'The Migration of Irish-born footballers to England, 1945–2010', in Jane Clayton (ed.), '150 Years of Association Football', special edition of *Soccer & Society*, vol. 16, nos 2–3 (2015), pp. 360–76

—, 'Post-playing Careers of Irish-born Footballers in England, 1945–2010', *Sport in Society*, vol. 18, no. 10 (2015), pp. 1273–86

—, 'Irish-born Players in England's Football Leagues, 1945–2010: an historical and geographical assessment', in Richard McElligott and David Hassan (eds), 'Sport in Ireland: social and historical perspectives', special edition of *Sport in Society*, vol. 19, no. 1 (2016), pp. 74–94

—, 'The Development of Schoolboy Coaching Structures for Association Football in Ireland, 1945–1995', in Conor Curran and David Toms (eds), 'Going Beyond the "Garrison Game": new perspectives on association football in Irish history', special edition of *Soccer & Society*, DOI:10.1080/14660970.2016.1230340 [accessed 27 Dec. 2016]

—, 'The Social Background of Ireland's Pre-World War I Association Football Clubs, Players and Administrators: the case of south and west Ulster', *International Journal of the History of Sport* (ID: 1304381 DOI:10.1080/09523367.2017.1304381)

Daly, Mary E., *The Irish State and the Diaspora*, NUI Centennial Lecture 2008 (Dublin: National University of Ireland, 2009)

Darby, Paul, Akindes, Gerard and Kirwin, Matthew, 'Football Academies and the Migration of African Football Labor to Europe', *Journal of Sport & Social Issues*, vol. 31, no. 2 (2007), pp. 143–61

Darby, Paul and Hassan, David (eds), *Emigrant Players: sport and the Irish diaspora* (London: Routledge, 2008)

Darby, Paul, *Gaelic Games, Nationalism and the Irish Diaspora in the United States* (Dublin: UCD Press, 2009)

Davies, Hunter, *The Glory Game: the new edition of the British football classic* (Edinburgh: Mainstream, 2001)

Davis, Graham, 'The Irish in Britain, 1815–1939', in Andy Bielenberg (ed.), *The Irish Diaspora* (Harlow: Pearson, 2000), pp.19–36

Delaney, Enda, *Irish Emigration Since 1921* (Dundalk: The Irish Economic and Social History Society, 2002)

—, *The Irish in Post-war Britain* (paperback edition) (Oxford: Oxford University Press, 2013)

— and MacRaild, Donald (eds), *Irish Migration, Networks and Ethnic Identities Since 1750* (London: Routledge, 2007)

Delaney, Miguel, *From Stuttgart to Saipan: the players' stories* (Dublin: Mentor, 2010)

Devlin Trew, Johanne, 'Reluctant Diasporas of Northern Ireland: migrant narratives of home, conflict, difference', *Journal of Ethnic and Migration Studies*, vol. 36, no. 4 (2010), pp. 541–60

Dixon, Pamela and Garnham, Neal, 'Drink and the Professional Footballer in 1890s England and Ireland', *Sport in History*, vol. 25, no. 3, pp. 375–89

Doherty, Peter, *Spotlight on Football* (London: Art and Education Publishers, 1947)

Dougan, Derek, *How Not To Run Football* (Wolverhampton: All Seasons, 1981)

—, *The Sash He Never Wore … Twenty-Five Years On* (Newtonabbey: Lagan Books and All Seasons, 1997)

Dudley Edwards, Ruth, *An Atlas of Irish History*, [3rd edn] (with Bridget Hourican) (London and New York: Routledge, 2005)

Dunphy, Eamon, *Only a Game? The diary of a professional footballer* (Middlesex: Penguin, 1976)

—, *The Rocky Road* (Dublin: Penguin, 2013)

Dudek, Jerzy, *A Big Pole in Our Goal: my autobiography* (Liverpool: Sport Media, 2016)

Elliott, Richard, 'Football's Irish Exodus: examining the factors influencing Irish player migration to English professional leagues', *International Review for the Sociology of Sport*, vol. 49, no. 3 (2014), pp. 1–15

Emms, Steve and Wells, Richard, *Scottish League Players' Records. Division One, 1890/91 to 1938/39* (Nottingham: Tony Brown, 2007)

Fitzpatrick, David, *Irish Emigration, 1801–1921: studies in Irish economic and social history 1* (Dundalk: Dundalgan Press, 1984)

—, 'Militarism in Ireland, 1900–1922', in Thomas Bartlett and Keith Jeffery (eds), *A Military History of Ireland* [paperback edition] (Cambridge: Cambridge University Press, 1997), pp. 379–406

Ferriter, Diarmaid, *The Transformation of Ireland, 1900–2000* (London: Profile Books, 2004)

—, *Ambiguous Republic: Ireland in the 1970s* (London: Profile Books, 2012)

Fleming, N.C., 'Education Since the Late Eighteenth Century', in Kennedy and Ollerenshaw, *Ulster Since 1600*, pp. 211–27

Foot, John, *Calcio: a history of Italian football* [updated edition] (London: Harper Perennial, 2007)

Football Handbook: the glory years (London: Marshall Cavendish Ltd, 1978 and 2006)

Garnham, Neal, *Association Football and Society in Pre-partition Ireland* (Belfast: Ulster Historical Foundation, 2004)

—, 'Ein Spiel in zwei Nationen: fussball in Irland, 1918–1939', in Christian Koller and Fabian Brändle (eds) *Fussball zwischen den Kriegen: Europa 1918–1939* (Münster: Lit Verlag, 2010), pp. 65–86

—, 'Soccer', in Connolly (ed.), *Oxford Companion to Irish History*, pp. 545–46

Gerrard, Steven, *My Autobiography* (London: Transworld Publishers, 2006)

—, *My Story* (London: Penguin, 2015)

Giles, John, *A Football Man: the autobiography* (Dublin: Hachette Books Ireland, 2011)

Gillespie, Keith, *How Not To Be a Football Millionaire: my autobiography* (Liverpool: SportMedia, 2013)

Giulianotti, Richard, *Football: a sociology of the global game* (Cambridge: Polity Press, 1999)

Goldblatt, David, *The Ball Is Round: a global history of football* (paperback edition) (London: Penguin, 2007)

—, *The Game of Our Lives: the making and meaning of English football* (paperback edition) (London: Penguin, 2015)

Gray, Derek and Emms, Steve, *Scottish League Players' Records: Premier Division and Premier League, 1975/76 to 1999/2000* (Nottingham: Tony Brown, 2002)

Gregg, Harry (with Roger Anderson), *Harry's Game: the autobiography* (Edinburgh: Mainstream, 2002)

Hand, Eoin (with Peter O'Neill), *The Eoin Hand Story* (Dublin: Brophy Books, 1986)

Hannigan, Dave, *The Garrison Game: the state of Irish football* (Edinburgh: Mainstream, 1998)

Harding, John, *Behind the Glory: 100 years of the PFA* (Derby: Breedon Books, 2009)

— (with Gordon Taylor), *Living To Play: from soccer slaves to soccerati – a social history of the professionals* (London: Robson Books, 2003)

Harrison, David and Gordos, Steve, *The Doog: the incredible story of Derek Dougan, football's most controversial figure* (Studley: Know the Score Books, 2008)

Hassan, David, McCullough, Shane and Moreland, Elizabeth, 'North or South: Darron Gibson and the issue of player eligibility within Irish soccer', *Soccer & Society*, special issue: 'Why Minorities Play or Don't Play Soccer: a global exploration', vol. 10, no. 6 (2009), pp. 740–53

Hassan, David, 'The Role of Gaelic Games in the Lives of the Irish Diaspora in Europe', *Sport in Society*, vol. 10, no. 3 (2007), pp. 385–401

Hesse-Lichtenberger, Ulrich, *Tor! The story of German football* (new edition) (London: WSC Books, 2003)

Hickman, Mary J., 'The Irish in Britain: racism, incorporation and identity', *Irish Studies Review*, vol. 3, no. 10 (1995), pp. 16–19

Honigstein, Raphael, *Das Reboot: how German football reinvented itself and conquered the world* (paperback edition) (Yellow Jersey Press: London, 2016)

Hopcraft, Arthur, *The Football Man: people and passions in soccer* (London: SportsPages, 1968)

Hunt, Tom, *Sport and Society in Victorian Ireland: the case of Westmeath* (Cork: Cork University Press, 2007)

Irish Permanent Presents The Packie Bonner Story (Dublin: Copperfield Publications Ltd, 1991)

Jennings, Pat, *Pat Jennings: an autobiography – one of the world's greatest goalkeepers* (London: Granada, 1984)

Jones, Luke and Denison, Jim, 'Challenge and Relief: a Foucauldian analysis of retirement from professional association football in the United Kingdom', *International Review for the Sociology of Sport*, DOI:101177/1012690215625348 [accessed 27 Dec. 2016]

Judt, Tony, *Post-war: a history of Europe since 1945*, [2nd edn] (London: Vintage Books, 2010)

Kay, Oliver, *Forever Young: the story of Adrian Doherty – football's lost genius* (London: Quercus, 2016)

Keane, Roy (with Eamon Dunphy), *Keane: the autobiography* (London: Michael Joseph, 2003)

Keane, Paul, *Gods vs Mortals: Irish clubs in Europe … a front row seat at ten of the greatest games* (Kells: Irish Sports Publishing, 2010)

Kelly, Seamus, 'The Migration of Irish Professional Footballers: the good, the bad and the ugly', in Richard Elliott and John Harris (eds), *Football and Migration: perspectives, places, players* (London: Routledge, 2014), pp. 76–92

Kelly, Stephen F., *The Hamlyn Illustrated History of Liverpool, 1892–1998* (London: Hamlyn, 1998)

Kennedy, Liam and Ollerenshaw, Philip (eds), *Ulster Since 1600: politics, economy and society* (Oxford: Oxford University Press, 2013)

Kennedy, Liam and Ollerenshaw, Philip, 'Preface', in Kennedy and Ollerenshaw (eds), *Ulster Since 1600*, pp. vii–viii

Kenny, Kevin, *The American Irish: a history* (Harlow: Pearson Education Ltd, 2000)

Keogh, Dermot, *Twentieth Century Ireland: revolution and state building* (revised edition) (Dublin: Gill & Macmillan, 2005)

Kuper, Simon and Szymanski, Stefan, *Why England Lose and Other Curious Football Phenomena Explained* (London: HarperSport, 2010)

Lanfranchi, Pierre, Eisenberg, Christiane, Mason, Tony and Wahl, Alfred *100 Years of Football: the FIFA centennial book* (London: Weidenfeld & Nicolson, 2004)

Lanfranchi, Pierre and Taylor, Matthew, *Moving With the Ball: the migration of professional footballers* (Oxford: Berg, 2001)

Langan, Dave (with Trevor Keane and Alan Conway), *Running Through Walls* (Derby: DB Publishing, 2012)

Leavey, Gerard, Sembhi, Sati and Livingstone, Gill, 'Older Irish Migrants Living in London: identity, loss and return', *Journal of Ethnic and Migration Studies*, vol. 30, no. 4 (2004), pp. 763–79

Lennon, Neil, *Man and Bhoy* (London: HarperSport, 2006)

MacRaild, Donald M., *The Irish Diaspora in Britain, 1750–1939*, [2nd edn] (London: Palgrave Macmillan, 2011)

MacRaild, Donald M. and Smith, Malcolm, 'Migration and Emigration, 1600–1945', in Kennedy and Ollerenshaw (eds), *Ulster Since 1600*, pp. 140–59

Magee, Jonathan and Sugden, John, '"The World at Their Feet"': professional football and international labor migration', *Journal of Sport and Social Sciences*, vol. 26, no. 4 (2002), pp. 421–37

Mason, Tony, *Association Football and English Society, 1863–1915* (Brighton: Harvester Press, 1980)

McCready, Richard B., 'Revising the Irish in Scotland', in Bielenberg (ed.), *The Irish Diaspora*, pp. 37–50

McGarrigle, Stephen, *Green Gunners: Arsenal's Irish* (Edinburgh: Mainstream, 1991)

McGovern, Patrick, 'The Brawn Drain: English league clubs and Irish footballers 1946–1995', *British Journal of Sociology*, vol. 32, no. 36 (2000), pp. 401–18

—, 'Globalization or Internationalization? Foreign footballers in the English league, 1946–95', *Sociology*, vol. 36, no. 1 (2002), pp. 23–42

McGrath, Paul (with Vincent Hogan), *Back from the Brink* (London: Century, 2006)

McIlvanney, Hugh, 'Foreign Legion Fuels Failure', *Sunday Times* (Sport), 28 April 2013

McMahon, Deirdre, 'Anglo-Irish Treaty', in Connolly (ed.), *Oxford Companion to Irish History*, p. 16

—, 'Irish Free State', in Connolly (ed.), *Oxford Companion to Irish History*, pp. 280–81

—, 'Republic of Ireland', in Connolly (ed.), *Oxford Companion to Irish History*, p. 508

McParland, Peter, *Going for Goal: my life in football by Aston Villa's flying Irishman* (London: Souvenir Press, 1960)

McVeigh, Paul, *The Stupid Footballer Is Dead: insights into the mindset of a professional footballer* (London: Bloomsbury, 2013)

Merriman, John, *A History of Modern Europe: from the Renaissance to the present*, [3rd edn] (New York and London: WW Norton & Co., 2010)

Metcalfe, Alan, 'Football in the Mining Communities of East Northumberland', *International Journal of the History of Sport*, vol. 5, no. 3 (1988), pp. 269–91

Metcalfe, Mark, *Charlie Hurley: the greatest centre half the world has ever seen* (Cheltenham: SportsBooks, 2008)

Moore, Chris, *United Irishmen: Manchester United's Irish connection* (Edinburgh: Mainstream, 1999)

Moore, Cormac, *The Irish Soccer Split* (Cork: Cork University Press, 2015)

Morris, R.J., 'Urban Ulster Since 1600', in Kennedy and Ollerenshaw (eds), *Ulster Since 1600*, pp. 121–39

Neill, Terry, *Revelations of a Football Manager* (London: Sidgwick & Jackson, 1985)

Neville, Gary, 'North of England Falls off Map in Football's Changing Geography', *Irish Independent*, 26 Sept. 2015

O'Callaghan, Liam, *Rugby in Munster: a social and cultural history* (Cork: Cork University Press, 2011)

O'Donoghue, Thomas A., 'The Attempt by the Department of Defence to Introduce the Sokol System of Physical Education into Irish Schools in the 1930s', *Irish Educational Studies*, vol. 5, no. 2 (1985), pp. 329–42

'One-on-One: your questions answered by Shay Given', *Four-Four-Two Magazine*, no. 216 (June 2012), pp. 8–13

Parkinson, Michael, *Best: an intimate biography* (London: Hutchinson, 1975)

Pringle, Andy and Fissler, Neil, *Where Are They Now? Over 2,000 players* (London: Two Heads, 1996)

Power, Brendan, 'The Functions of Association Football in the Boys' Brigade in Ireland, 1888–1914', in Leanne Lane and William Murphy (eds), *Leisure and the Irish in the Nineteenth Century* (Liverpool: Liverpool University Press), pp. 41–58

Redmond, Patrick R. *The Irish and the Making of American Sport, 1880–1935* (Jefferson, NC: McFarland & Company, Inc., 2014)

'Resisting Ireland's Soccer Raiders', in *Football Handbook: the glory years* (London: Marshall Cavendish Ltd, 1978 and 2006)

Roderick, Martin, *The Work of Professional Football: a labour of love?* (London: Routledge, 2006)

—, 'A Very Precarious Profession: uncertainty in the working lives of professional footballers', *Work, Employment and Society*, vol. 20, no. 2 (2006), pp. 245–65

—, 'Domestic Moves: an exploration of intra-national labour mobility in the working lives of professional footballers', *International Review for the Sociology of Sport*, vol. 48, no. 4 (2012), pp. 387–404

—, 'An Unpaid Labour of Love: professional footballers, family life, and the problem of job relocation', *Journal of Sport and Social Issues*, vol. 36, no. 3 (2012), pp. 317–38

Rouse, Paul, *Sport & Ireland: a history* (Oxford: Oxford University Press, 2015)

Rowan, Paul, 'Grealish an Excellent Servant for Ireland', *Sunday Times* (Sport), 28 April 2013

—, 'McAteer Works Himself Back from Brink', *Sunday Times* (Sport), 25 Aug. 2013

Russell, David, *Football and the English: a social history of association football in England* (Preston: Carnegie, 1997)

Ryan, Seán, *The Boys in Green: the FAI international story* (Edinburgh: Mainstream, 1997)

— and Burke, Stephen, *The Book of Irish Goalscorers* (Tralee: The Kerryman, 1987)

Ryle Dwyer, T., 'Guests of the State', in Dermot Keogh and Mervyn O'Driscoll (eds), *Ireland in World War Two: diplomacy and survival* (Cork: Mercier Press, 2004), pp. 107–25

Sadlier, Richie, 'Don't Be Fooled by League's Play-at-Home Promptings' in *Sunday Independent* (Sport), 2 June 2013

Schumacher, Toni, *Blowing the Whistle* (London: WH Allen, 1987)

Sleap, Mike, 'A Survey of Physical Education in Irish Post-primary Schools', *The Irish Journal of Education*, vol. xii, no. 2 (1978), pp. 107–18

Soar, Phil, Tyler, Martin and Widdows, Richard, *The Hamlyn World Encyclopedia of Football*, [4th edn] (London: Hamlyn, 1984)

Souness, Graeme, 'Thirty Years On', *Sunday Times* (Sport), 17 April 2016, pp. 6–7

Stapleton, Frank, *Frankly Speaking* (Dublin: Blackwater Press, 1991)

Stead, David and Maguire, Joseph, '"Rite De Passage" or Passage to Riches? The motivation and objectives of Nordic/Scandinavian players in English league soccer', *Journal of Sport and Social Issues*, vol. 24, no. 1 (2000), pp. 36–60

Sugden, John and Alan Bairner, *Sport, Sectarianism and Society in a Divided Ireland* (paperback edition) (Leicester: Leicester University Press, 1995)

Sullivan, Patrick (ed.), *Patterns of Migration, vol. 1* (Leicester: Leicester University Press, 1992)

Taylor, Gordon, 'Meltdown: the nationality of Premier League players and the future of English football', in Geoff Walters and Giambattista Rossi (eds), 'Labour Market Migration in European Football: key issues and challenges', conference proceedings from the Feet-Drain Conference hosted by the Birkbeck Sport Business Centre in May 2008, Birkbeck Sport Business Centre Research Paper Series, vol. 2, no. 2 (2009), pp. 51–70

Taylor, Matthew, *The Leaguers: the making of professional football in England, 1900–1939* (Liverpool: Liverpool University Press, 2005)

—, *The Association Game: a history of British football* (Harlow: Pearson/Longman, 2008)

—, 'From Source to Subject: sport, history and autobiography', *Journal of Sports History*, vol. 35, no. 3 (2008), pp. 469–91

—, 'Football, Migration and Globalisation: the perspective of history', pp. 1–21, http://www.idrottsforum.org/articles/taylor/taylor070314pdf [accessed 16 April 2016]

The Malcolm Brodie Northern Ireland Soccer Yearbook (Belfast: Ulster Tatler Group, 2014)

Toland, Andrew, 'PRONI's Football Archives', paper given at 'Going Beyond the "Garrison Game": new perspectives on association football in Irish history' Symposium, Public Record Office of Northern Ireland, 17 Feb. 2017

Toms, David, 'Darling of the Gods': Tom Farquharson, Irish footballing migrant', *Soccer & Society*, vol. 16, no. 4 (2015), pp. 508–20

—, *Soccer in Munster: a social history, 1877–1937* (Cork: Cork University Press, 2015)

—, 'The *Cork Sportsman*: a provincial sporting newspaper, 1908–1911', *Sport in Society*, vol. 19, no. 1 (2016), pp. 24–37

Uprichard, Norman (with Chris Westcott), *Norman 'Black Jake' Uprichard* (Stroud: Amberley, 2011)

Vamplew, Wray, 'Successful Workers or Exploited Labour? Golf professionals and professional golfers in Britain, 1888–1914', *Economic History Review*, vol. 61, no. 1 (2008), pp. 54–79

—, 'Close of Play: career termination in English professional sport, 1870–1914', *Canadian Journal of History of Sport and Physical Education*, vol. 15, no. 1 (1984), pp. 64–79

Walsh, Denis, 'Parting Is Such Sorrow for Counties' Discarded Players', *Sunday Times* (Sport), 31 Jan. 2016, p. 13

Whelan, Daire, *Who Stole Our Game? The fall and fall of Irish soccer* (Dublin: Gill & Macmillan, 2006)

Whelan, Kevin, 'The Geography of Hurling', *History Ireland* (Spring, 1993), pp. 27–31

Whelan, Ronnie (with Tommy Conlon), *Walk On: my life in red* (London: Simon & Schuster, 2011)

White, John D.T., *Irish Devils: the official story of Manchester United and the Irish* (London: Simon & Schuster, 2011)

Wilson, Bob, *You've Got To Be Crazy: on goalkeepers and goalkeeping* (London: Weidenfeld & Nicolson, 1989)

Whiteside, Norman, *Determined Norman Whiteside* (London: Headline, 2007)

Reports

Curran, Conor, 'Professionals on the Move: Irish footballers in Britain, 1945–2010, an historical and contemporary assessment', unpublished FIFA Joao Havelange Research Scholarship, final report to FIFA/CIES, January 2014

Kelly, Seamus, 'The Recruitment, Assessment and Development of Professional Soccer Players in the UK and Ireland', unpublished research project (2011)

Woods, Catherine, Buckley, Finian and Kirrane, Melrona, *Career Transitions in Young Footballers: a study of how young players cope with selection and deselection in football*, a report for the Football Association of Ireland and the Professional Footballers' Association (2005)

Directories and Works of Reference

Hayes, Dean, *Football Stars of the '70s: and where are they now?* (Gloucester: Sutton, 2003)

—, *Northern Ireland: international football facts* (Belfast: Appletree, 2007)

—, *The Republic of Ireland International Football Facts* (Cork: The Collins Press, 2008)

Hugman, Barry J. (ed.), *The PFA Premier & Football League Players' Records, 1946–2005* (Harpenden: Queen Anne Press, 2005)

—, *The PFA Footballers' Who's Who, 2005–6* (Harpenden: Queen Anne Press, 2005)

—, *The PFA Footballers' Who's Who, 2006–7* (Edinburgh: Mainstream, 2006)

—, *The PFA Footballers' Who's Who, 2007–8* (Edinburgh: Mainstream, 2007)
—, *The PFA Footballers' Who's Who, 2008–9* (Edinburgh: Mainstream, 2008)
—, *The PFA Footballers' Who's Who, 2009–10* (Edinburgh: Mainstream, 2009)
—, *The PFA Footballers' Who's Who, 2010–11* (Edinburgh: Mainstream, 2010)
Joyce, Michael, *Football League Players' Records, 1888 to 1939*, [3rd edn] (Nottingham: Tony Brown, 2012)
Jose, Colin, *American Soccer League, 1921–1931: the golden years of American soccer* (Lanham, MD: Scarecrow Press, 1998)
Jose, Colin, *North American Soccer League Encyclopedia* (Haworth, NJ: St Johann Press, 2003)

Online Sources

'About the Boys' Brigade in Belfast', http://www.belfastbb.org.uk [accessed 28 April 2016]
'Alan Blayney Wins Ulster Footballer of the Year Award', http://www.bbc.com/sport/0/football/13391481 [accessed 28 Nov. 2015]
'BBC On this Day: 1968 – Manchester United Win the European Cup', http://news.bbc.co.uk/onthisday/hi/dates/stories/may/29/newsid_4464000/4464446stm [accessed 30 March 2016]
'BBC Sport: Liam Miller leaves Hibs for Perth Glory in Australia', http://www.bbc.com/sport/football/13639527 [accessed 7 May 2016]
'Blatter Backs Republic's Stance', http://news.bbc.co.uk/sport2/hi/football/internationals/7917738stm [accessed 19 April 2013]
'Boston Rovers Rosters', http://www.nasljerseys.com/Rosters/Rovers_Rosters.htm [accessed 26 Jan. 2016]
Brennan, Michael, 'Young Irish Players Are Victims of Bullying at English Clubs', http://www.independent.ie/irish-news/young-irish-players-are-victims-of-bullying-at-english-soccer-clubs-26777943html [accessed 15 July 2013]
Brown, Daniel, 'Linfield's "Hawk of Peace": pre-ceasefires reconciliation in Irish League football', in Conor Curran and David Toms (eds), 'Going beyond the "Garrison Game": new perspectives on association football in Irish history', special edition of *Soccer & Society*, DOI:101080/1466097020161230342 [accessed 1 May 2016]
Burnton, Simon, 'The Forgotten Story of … Johnny Crossan's Ban from Football', http://www.theguardian.com/sport/blog/2011/nov/02/forgotten-story-john-crossan-ban [accessed 26 April 2016]
'CAIN Service: Discrimination and Education', from 'Perspectives on Discrimination and Social Work in Northern Ireland', http://cain.ulst.ac.uk/issues/discrimination/gibson1htm [accessed 27 Feb. 2016]
Census 2006, Principal Demographic Results (Dublin: The Stationery Office, 2007), p. 13, http://www.cso.ie/en/media/csoie/census/documents/Amended,Final,Principal,Demographic,Results,2006pdf [accessed 18 May 2014]
'Chicago Mustangs Rosters', http://www.nasljerseys.com/Rosters/Mustangs_Rosters.htm [accessed 26 Jan. 2016]

'CIES Football Observatory', http://www.mapping-football-observatory.com/modules/carto/map.php?lg=en [accessed 16 Dec. 2013]

'CIES Football Observatory Digital Atlas: Average Stay', http://www.football-observatory.com/IMG/sites/atlas/en/average-stay.html [accessed 5 May 2016]

'CIES Football Observatory Digital Atlas: % Expatriates by Club (2015)', http://www.football-observatory.com/IMG/sites/atlas/en/expatriates.html [accessed 6 May 2016]

'CIES Football Observatory Digital Atlas: Club-trained Players', http://www.football-observatory.com/IMG/sites/atlas/en/club-trained.html [accessed 6 May 2016]

'CIES Football Observatory Digital Atlas: Debutant Players', http://www.football-observatory.com/IMG/sites/atlas/en/debutant-players.html [accessed 6 May 2016]

'Clare Schoolboys/Girls Soccer League', http://www.cssleague.ie [accessed 14 Oct. 2013]

'Cleveland Stokers Rosters', http://www.nasljerseys.com/Rosters/Stokers_Rosters.htm [accessed 26 Jan. 2016]

'Coca-Cola', http://www.fifa.com/about-fifa/marketing/sponsorship/partners/coca-cola.html [accessed 24 March 2016]

Coogan, Fra, 'Was Mickey Hamill Belfast Celtic's Greatest Player?', http://www.belfastceltic.org/archive/hamill.html [accessed 5 Feb. 2016]

Croke, Ruaidhri, 'Young Irish Players Need an Elite Football Education, Says Quinn', http://www.irishtimes.com/sport/soccer/young-irish-players-need-an-elite-football-education-says-niall-quinn-12306870 [accessed 8 Aug. 2015]

'Dallas Tornado Rosters', http://www.nasljerseys.com/Rosters/Tornado_Rosters.htm [accessed 26 Jan. 2016]

'Dean Windass Discusses His "Shame" at Depression Battle', http://www.bbc.co.uk/sport/0/football/17596050 [accessed 17 Aug. 2013]

Department of Foreign Affairs and Trade: 'Minister Micheál Martin welcomes the appointment of Terry Conroy as New Football Welfare Officer in Britain', 28 Nov. 2008, http://www.dfa.ie/home/index.aspx?id=79503 [accessed 15 July 2013]

'Discrimination and Education', http://cain.ulst.ac.uk/issues/discrimination/gibson1htm [accessed 10 March 2016]

'Doherty, Paddy', http://www.hoganstand.com/Down/ArticleForm.aspx?ID=8758 [accessed 30 Jan. 2017]

Doyle, Garry 'Irish Demise at Arsenal Shows Ireland Are in Danger of Being Left Behind', http://irishpost.co.uk/irish-demise-at-arsenal-shows-ireland-is-in-danger-of-being-left-behind/ [accessed 6 May 2016]

'Emerging Talent', http://www.fai.ie/domestic/take-part-programmes/emerging-talent [accessed 6 Aug. 2015]

'Enrolment Fees', http://www.irishfa.com/kit/model/11/player-development-programme [accessed 12 Oct. 2013]

'Eoin Hand Welcomes New Regulations for Scouts and Trials', http://www.fai.ie/football-services-a-education/player-a-club-services/100500-eoin-hand-welcomes-new-regulations-for-scouts-and-trials.html [accessed 5 May 2013]

Eoin O'Callaghan, 'From St Pat's to the Bundesliga', http://www.irishexaminer.com/sport/soccer/from-st-pats-to-the-bundesliga-291232html [accessed 26 April 2016]

'Ex-footballer Warren Aspinall Almost Took His Own Life', http://www.bbc.co.uk/sport/0/football/17741055 [accessed 17 Aug. 2013]

'FAI FÁS Youth Soccer Courses Registration Open', http://www.fai.ie/football-services-a-education/50-education/103354-fai-fas-youth-soccer-courses-registration-open.html [accessed 25 Jan. 2014]

'FAI Schools: About Us', http://www.fais.ie/about-us [accessed 20 Oct. 2013]

Feeney, Tom, 'Dunne, James (Jimmy)', *Dictionary of Irish Biography*, http://dib.cambridge.org/viewReadPage.do;jsessionid=B1CB0DC3C71B72FC8A9FEEAA054A68DB?articleId=a2857 [accessed 24 March 2017]

'Field Club Explores Scottish links', http://www.independent.ie/regionals/sligo-champion/news/field-club-explores-scotland-links-27580084html [accessed 7 May 2016]

'FIFA Solidarity and Compensation Payments', http://www.fai.ie/football-services-a-education/player-a-club-services/fifa-solidarity-and-compensation-payments.html [accessed 6 Nov. 2011]

'Footballers REAP Awards at DCU', https://www.dcu.ie/news/2002/jul/s0207l.shtml [accessed 12 March 2016]

'Football Results 2015–16', http://www.methody.org/School-Activities/Sport-Games.aspx [accessed 3 May 2016]

'Football's Secret Suicide', http://www.youtube.com/watch?v=cPyTCpMHico [accessed 17 Aug. 2013]

'Former Stoke City Trainee Claims Club and Ex-England Captain Ignored Abuse', http://www.irishtimes.com/sport/soccer/english-soccer/former-stoke-city-trainee-claims-club-and-ex-england-captain-ignored-abuse-11623330 [accessed 15 Dec. 2013]

Glanville, Brian, 'Noel Cantwell', http://www.theguardian.com/news/2005/sep/09/guardianobituaries.football [accessed 30 March 2016]

—, 'Sir Walter Winterbottom', http://www.theguardian.com/news/2002/feb/18/guardianobituaries.football1 [accessed 23 Sept. 2015]

'Grassroots: Excellence Programme', http://www.irishfa.com/grassroots/excellence-programme [accessed 12 Oct. 2013]

'Grassroots', http://www.irishfa.com/grassroots/primary-school-coaching-programme/ [accessed 3 Dec. 2015]

Griffin, Sam, 'Three-quarters of Irish Emigrants Homesick – Study', http://www.independent.ie/irish-news/three-quarters-of-irish-emigrants-homesick-study-31045144html [accessed 24 May 2016]

'Health Service Blamed for Suicide', http://news.bbc.co.uk/2/hi/uk_news/northern_ireland/7469750stm [accessed 16 Jan. 2016]

'Heighway Makes Full-Time Academy Return', http://www.liverpoolfc.com/news/academy/196819-heighway-makes-full-time-academy-return [accessed 28 April 2016]

'History of NIBFA', http://www.nibfa.org/?tabindex=5&tabid=913 [accessed 12 Oct. 2013]

'History of the Milk Cup', http://www.nimilkcup.org/index.php?option =com_k2&view=item&layout=item&id=27&Itemid=90 [accessed 12 Oct. 2013]

'History of the Roscommon and District League', http://www.sportsmanager.ie/uploaded/8525/history_from_beginning_up_to_2006pd [accessed 11 Sept. 2013]

Holroyd, Steve, 'The ASL's "Philadelphia Celtic": Philly's last chance at success in US soccer's "golden age"', http://www.phillysoccerpage.net/2014/03/14/the-asls-philadelphia-celtic-phillys-last-chance-at-success-in-us-soccers-golden-age [accessed 28 July 2016]

'Home Farm FC Host Under 16 Tournament this Weekend', http://www.fai.ie/domestic-a-grassroots/17-district-leagues/103629-home-farm-fc-hosts-u16-tournament-this-weekend.html [accessed 25 Oct. 2013]

http://nifootball.blogspot.ie

http://www.soccerbase.com/

'Hughes Insurance Foyle Cup: About', http://www.foylecup.com/About.aspx [accessed 12 Oct. 2013]

Hunt, Stephen, 'GAA Players Would Find Life Tough in the Premier League', http://www.independent.ie/sport/soccer/premier-league/stephen-hunt-gaa-players-would-find-life-tough-in-premier-league-30785091html [accessed 2 July 2015]

'IFA Launches Youth Football Strategy', http://irishfa.com/news/item/10103/ifa-launches-youth-football-strategy [accessed 3 Dec. 2015]

James, David, 'High-Pressure Game Without a Net When You Hang Up Gloves', http://www.theguardian.com/football/blog/2012/mar/10/david-james-900th-game [accessed 4 Nov. 2013]

'Joe Haverty: skilful Arsenal and Republic of Ireland left-winger known for his trickery and dribbling', http://www.independent.co.uk/news/obituaries/joe-haverty-skilful-arsenal-and-republic-of-ireland-left-winger-known-for-his-trickery-and-dribbling-1650631html [accessed 23 Jan. 2016]

'Kildare and District Football League', http://www.kdfl.ie/about.htm [accessed 11 Sept. 2013]

'Kilkenny GAA Roll of Honour', http://www.kilkennygaa.ie/page/Roll%20of%20honour [accessed 7 March 2016]

Kimmage, Paul, 'Liam Tuohy to Retire', http://www.independent.ie/sport/soccer/liam-tuohy-to-retire-26239164html [accessed 14 Aug. 2013]

'Kirk Broadfoot Given Record 10 Game Ban for James McClean Abuse', http://www.irishtimes.com/sport/soccer/english-soccer/kirk-broadfoot-given-record-10-game-ban-for-james-mcclean-abuse-12295992 [accessed 25 July 2015]

'Leitrim Genealogy Centre', http://www.leitrimroots.com [accessed 27 Dec. 2013]

'Liam Brady with Juventus, 1980–1982', https://www.youtube.com/watch?v=nCBP7mgwgJU [accessed 1 May 2016]

'Linfield Academy Trip to Murray Park', http://www.linfieldfc.com/academynews.asp?id=13953 [accessed 25 July 2015]

'Lisburn Youth Football Club – About Us', http://www.lisburnyouth.co.uk/about-us/ [accessed 22 Jan. 2013]

'Meath and District League: providing a structured system for clubs in Meath', http://www.yellowtom.ie/155446 [accessed 25 Oct. 2013]

'Membership: all former professional footballers ARE X-Pro members', http://www.xpro.org/content/1/2/membership.html [accessed 29 Aug. 2013]

'Men's League History', http://inform.fai.ie/League/Clubs/portals/MAFL/mayo-mensleaguehistory.aspx?ClubID=1283 [accessed 12 Sept. 2013]

McAlpine, Joan, 'Celtic and Rangers: across Scotland's sectarian divide', http://www.guardian.co.uk/commentisfree/2011/mar/20/celtic-rangers-football-religion-sectarian [accessed 21 July 2013]

McAnallen, Dónal, 'The GAA and the Great War', paper given at 'Sport and the Great War' Conference, PRONI, 5 Nov. 2016, https://www.youtube.com/watch?v=mk4d9Tr2eto [accessed 12 March 2017]

McCann, Nuala, 'Patrick O'Connell: Barcelona FC saviour they called "Don Patricio"', http://www.bbc.com/news/uk-northern-ireland-29426450 [accessed 13 March 2017]

'Midlands Schoolboys/ Girls League', http://www.msleague.ie [accessed 14 Oct. 2013]

'Mutual Casa Del Futbolista', http://www.futbolleyendas.com/#!quienes-somos/cghg [accessed 6 March 2016]

'Never Say Die: the Stephen Hunt story', http://www.rte.ie/radio1/podcast/podcast_radio1specials.xml [accessed 7 Aug. 2013]

'New Perspectives on Association Football in Irish History', https://www.youtube.com/watch?v=sETL8PU08CY [accessed 5 April 2017]

'NIFG: Allen McKnight', http://nifootball.blogspot.ie/2007/07/allen-mcknight.html [accessed 6 May 2016]

'NIFG: Archie Goodall', http://nifootball.blogspot.ie/2006/12/archie-goodall.html [accessed 16 June 2016]

'NIFG: Billy Caskey', http://nifootball.blogspot.ie/2006/08/billy-caskey.html [accessed 16 Jan. 2016]

'NIFG: Billy Gillespie', http://nifootball.blogspot.ie/2006/12/billy-gillespie.html [accessed 25 June 2016]

'NIFG: Bob "Whitey" McDonald', http://nifootball.blogspot.ie/2007/08/bob-whitey-mcdonald.html [accessed 26 Oct. 2016]

'NIFG: Bobby Braithwaite', http://nifootball.blogspot.ie/2006/08/bobby-braithwaite.html [accessed 6 May 2016]

'NIFG: Bobby Burke', http://nifootball.blogspot.ie/2008/03/bobby-burke.html [accessed 6 May 2016]

'NIFG: Danny Blanchflower', http://nifootball.blogspot.ie/2006/08/danny-blanchflower.html [accessed 30 March 2016]

'NIFG: Dave Clements', http://nifootball.blogspot.ie/2006/08/dave-clements.html [accessed 6 May 2016]

'NIFG: Derek Spence', http://nifootball.blogspot.ie/2006/12/derek-spence.html [accessed 6 May 2016]

'NIFG: Eric Ross', http://nifootball.blogspot.ie/2007/09/eric-ross.html [accessed 6 May 2016]
'NIFG: Frank McCourt', http://nifootball.blogspot.ie/2007/04/frank-mccourt.html [accessed 6 May 2016]
'NIFG: From School to Full', http://nifootball.blogspot.ie/2007/01/from-schoolboy-to-full.html [accessed 24 May 2016]
'NIFG: George Best', http://nifootball.blogspot.ie/2006/08/george-best.html [accessed 6 May 2016]
'NIFG: Gerry McElhinney', http://nifootball.blogspot.ie/2007/01/gerry-mcelhinney.html [accessed 12 April 2015]
'NIFG: Harry Buckle', http://nifootball.blogspot.ie/2006/08/harry-buckle.html [accessed 16 June 2016]
'NIFG: Hugh Blair', http://nifootball.blogspot.ie/2006/08/hughie-blair.html [accessed 16 June 2016]
'NIFG: Jimmy Dunne', http://nifootball.blogspot.ie/2006/11/jimmy-dunne.html [accessed 25 June 2016]
'NIFG: Jim Hagan', http://nifootball.blogspot.ie/2007/01/jim-hagan.html [accessed 16 Jan. 2016]
'NIFG: Jimmy O'Neill', http://nifootball.blogspot.ie/2007/08/jimmy-oneill.html [accessed 6 May 2016]
'NIFG: John McClelland', http://nifootball.blogspot.ie/2006/12/john-mcclelland.html [accessed 27 April 2016]
'NIFG: Joshua "Paddy" Sloan', http://nifootball.blogspot.ie/2007/04/josiah-paddy-sloan.html [accessed 26 April 2016]
'NIFG: Kyle Lafferty', http://nifootball.blogspot.ie/2007/01/kyle-lafferty.html [accessed 16 Jan. 2016]
'NIFG: Lawrie Cumming', http://nifootball.blogspot.ie/2006/09/lawrie-cumming.html [accessed 13 March 2017]
'NIFG: Matt "Gunner" Reilly', http://nifootball.blogspot.ie/2008/01/matt-gunner-reilly.html [accessed 16 June 2016]
'NIFG: Michael O'Neill', http://nifootball.blogspot.ie/2007/08/michael-oneill.html [accessed 23 Jan. 2016]
'NIFG: Norman Whiteside', http://nifootball.blogspot.ie/2006/11/norman-whiteside.html [accessed 30 March 2016]
'NIFG: Pat "Don Patricio" O'Connell', http://nifootball.blogspot.ie/2008/02/pat-oconnell.html [accessed 13 March 2017]
'NIFG: Pat Sharkey', http://nifootball.blogspot.ie/2007/07/pat-sharkey.html [accessed 6 May 2016]
'NIFG: Paul Ramsey', http://nifootball.blogspot.ie/2006/12/paul-ramsey.html [accessed 16 Jan. 2016]
'NIFG: Roy Carroll', http://nifootball.blogspot.ie/2006/08/roy-carroll.html [accessed 16 Jan. 2016]
'NIFG: Sam English', http://nifootball.blogspot.ie/2006/10/sam-english.html [accessed 1 Nov. 2016]

'NIFG: Sammy McIlroy', http://nifootball.blogspot.co.uk/2006/10/sammy-mcilroy.html [accessed 15 Jan. 2016]

'NIFG: Sammy Morgan', http://nifootball.blogspot.ie/2007/08/sammy-morgan.html [accessed 15 Jan. 2016]

'NIFG: Sid Reid', http://nifootball.blogspot.ie/2007/10/sid-reid.html [accessed 16 June 2016]

'NIFG: Steve Morrow', http://nifootball.blogspot.ie/2007/07/steve-morrow.html [accessed 23 Jan. 2016]

'NIFG: Terry McCavana', http://nifootball.blogspot.ie/2007/06/terry-mccavana.html [accessed 6 May 2016]

'NIFG: Tom Priestley', http://nifootball.blogspot.ie/2007/10/tom-priestley.html [accessed 16 June 2016]

'NIFG: Tommy Cassidy', http://nifootball.blogspot.ie/2006/08/tommy-cassidy.html [accessed 15 Jan. 2016]

'NIFG: Vic Moreland', http://nifootball.blogspot.ie/2007/09/vic-moreland.html [accessed 16 Jan. 2016]

'NI Schools FA', http://www.irishfa.com/grassroots/ni-schools-fa [accessed 12 Oct. 2013]

'NIFL Premiership', http://en.wikipedia.org/wiki/NIFL_Premiership [accessed 7 Aug. 2013]

'North American Soccer League Players: Brian Quinn', http://nasljerseys.com/Players/Q/Quinn.Brian.htm [accessed 28 April 2016]

'Northern Ireland's Footballing Greats', http://nifootball.blogspot.ie/

O'Brien, John, 'Highs, Lows and a Brush with Ronaldo', *Sunday Independent* (Sport), http://www.independent.ie/sport/soccer/highs-lows-and-a-brush-with-ronaldo-29179241.html

O'Callaghan, Eoin, 'From St Pat's to the Bundesliga', http://www.irishexaminer.com/sport/soccer/from-st-pats-to-the-bundesliga-291232html [accessed 26 April 2016]

Ó Maonaigh, Aaron, 'Who Were the Shoneens? Irish militant nationalists and association football, 1913–1923', in Conor Curran and David Toms (eds), 'Going Beyond the "Garrison Game": new perspectives on association football in Irish history', *Soccer & Society*, DOI:101080/1466097020161230339

'PFAI Join Lean on Me Campaign', http://www.pfai.ie/news/286-pfai-join-lean-on-me-campaign [accessed 20 Jan. 2014]

'Player Profile: David McMullan', http://www.lfchistory.net/Players/Player/Profile/750 [accessed 19 Aug. 2016]

'Players Whose Country of Origin is Irlande', http://mapping-football-observatory.com/modules/carto/map.php?&lg=en [accessed 28 Feb. 2013]

Ponting, Ivan, 'Obituary; Danny Blanchflower', http://www.independent.co.uk/news/people/obituary-danny-blanchflower-1466455html [accessed 12 Oct. 2013]

'Post-war English and Scottish Football League A–Z Players Database', http://www.neilbrown.newcastlefans.com [accessed 26 Jan. 2014]

'PFA Membership', http://www.thepfa.com/members/membership [accessed 29 Aug. 2013]

'RBAI Football Champions', http://www.rbai.org.uk/index.php?option=com_content&view=category&layout=blog&id=89&Itemid=372 [accessed 3 May 2016]

'Republic of Ireland into Top 30 in World Rankings', http://www.rte.ie/sport/soccer/2016/0204/765315-ireland-up-to-top-30-in-world-rankings [accessed 25 March 2016]

Sadlier, Richie, 'I Never Dreamt about Telling Anyone in the Dressing Room', http://www.thescore.ie/richard-sadlier-i-never-dreamt-about-telling-anyone-in-the-dressing-room-290992-Nov2011 [accessed 17 Aug. 2013]

—, 'Rejected Teenagers Must Get Professional Help', http://www.independent.ie/sport/soccer/other-soccer/richie-sadlier-rejected-teenagers-must-get-professional-help-30916117html [accessed 9 March 2016]

Scholes, Tony, 'Steve McAdam Passes Away', http://www.clarets-mad.co.uk/news/tmnw/steve_mcadam_passes_away_182109/index.shtml [accessed 7 May 2016]

'Schoolboys Football Association of Ireland', http://www.sfai.ie [accessed 14 Oct. 2013]

Simpson, Mark, 'Appeal over Belfast Man. Utd Player John Peden's Grave', http://www.bbc.com/news/uk-northern-ireland-26177699 [accessed 5 Feb. 2016]

'Small-sided Games Strategy 2013–14', http://www.irishfa.com/fs/doc/Irish_FA_Small-Sided_Games_Strategy_120613pdf [accessed 3 Dec. 2015]

'Soccer Clubs Leagues in Leitrim', http://www.leitrimcoco.ie/eng/Services_A-Z/Community_and_Enterprise/Community-Soccer-Programme/Soccer-Clubs-Leagues-in-Leitrim.html [accessed 11 Sept. 2013]

'Soccer at NUIM: a few words from soccer facilitator Barry Prenderville', http://admissions.nuim.ie/news/Soccer.shtml [accessed 6 July 2013]

'Sport and Games', http://www.methody.org/School-Activities/Sport-Games.aspx [accessed 3 May 2016]

'Sunderland's Duncan Watmore Graduates with First-class Degree from Newcastle University', http://www.theguardian.com/football/2015/dec/10/sunderland-duncan-watmore-graduates-first-class-degree-newcastle [accessed 11 Dec. 2015]

'Super Cup NI 2016 – Entries Close Feb 2nd', http://supercupni.com/latest-news/details-for-supercupni-2016-formerly-the-milk-cup-have-been-released.html [accessed 4 June 2016]

Sutton, Malcolm, 'An Index of Deaths from the Conflict in Ireland: geographical location of the deaths', http://cain.ulst.ac.uk/sutton/tables/Location.html [accessed 16 April 2016]

'The Irish FA: spectator behaviour', http://www.irishfa.com/the-ifa/sporting-laws1 [accessed 30 March 2016]

'The Official Website of the Danske Bank Premiership', http://premiership.nifootballleague.com [accessed 29 Sept. 2013]

The Rod Squad (Roddy Collins at Carlisle United), episode 4, 2003 https://www.youtube.com/watch?v=zbGQwcGhVxE [accessed 21 May 2016]

'The Scottish Professional Football League', http://spfl.co.uk/spfl [accessed 26 Jan. 2014]

'The Wild Geese: Frank Stapleton', http://irishfootballersineurope.blogspot.ie/2012/08/frank-stapleton.html [accessed 26 April 2016]

'The Wild Geese: Joe Kendrick', http://irishfootballersineurope.blogspot.ie/2012/09/joe-kendrick.html [accessed 2 May 2016]

'The Wild Geese: Liam Brady', http://irishfootballersineurope.blogspot.ie/2012/07/liam-brady.html [accessed 1 May 2016]

'"Tucker" Croft', http://nifootball.blogspot.ie/2006/09/tucker-croft.html [accessed 8 Oct. 2016]

'Waterford United: club information', http://www.waterford-united.ie/club-info [accessed 12 April 2015]

'We're Losing Too Many Talented Young Players to the British System', http://www.the42.ie/niall-quinn-young-irish-footballers-2402585-Oct2015 [accessed 28 Oct. 2015]

'Where Are They Now? John Coady', http://www.independent.ie/sport/soccer/league-of-ireland/where-are-they-now-26843008html [accessed 5 July 2013]

'1975 British Home Championship: Northern Ireland football project', http://home.online.no/~smogols/ifcp/archive/northernirelandarchive/britishhome-championship/bhc1975htm [accessed 16 Oct. 2015]

'2013 St Kevin's Boys Club – Academy Cup, Results, Photos', http://www.skbfc.com/2013-tournament-the-best-yet [accessed 25 Oct. 2013]

Unpublished Theses

Mellor, Gavin, 'Professional Football and Its Supporters in Lancashire Circa 1946–1985', unpublished PhD thesis, University of Lancashire, 2003

Peake, Robin, 'The Migrant, the Match Fixer and the Manager: Patrick O'Connell – a typical professional footballer of his time?', unpublished master's of research thesis, University of Ulster, 2010

Tynan, Mark, 'Association Football and Society in Ireland During the Inter-war Period, 1918–39', unpublished PhD thesis, National University of Ireland, Maynooth, 2013

Index

Note: illustrations are indicated by page numbers in **bold**.